"One of the most important books ever on the social construction of the notion that there is a 'white' race." —*Tikkun*

"A scholarly, non-polemical masterpiece of broad historical synthesis, combining political, scientific, economic, and cultural history. *The History of White People* is also a fine visual record, full of diverse and interesting images, blurred charts of a perverted science, morbid reminders of a sorry day for man." —Paul Devlin, *San Francisco Chronicle*

"Nell Irvin Painter stunningly chronicles the logic of ocular proof that has rendered complexion a form of evidence inextricably linked to historically convenient notions of race. . . . Painter provides a fascinating and important contribution to the intellectual project proscribed by Roland Barthes when he expressed his resentment 'at seeing History and Nature confused at every turn.' " —Alan Nadel, *Philadelphia Inquirer*

"In this wide-ranging and passionate book, Nell Painter makes the story of American history into something new. Her array of writers, artists, and politicians, some familiar and some surprising, struggle mightily to create a concept many Americans of all backgrounds now take for granted: 'white people.' " —Edward Ayers, author of *In the Presence of Mine Enemies*

"Impressive. . . . [Painter] tackles a provocative subject with easeful authority, proceeding with admirable restraint and letting flawed scholarship and thinking speak for itself." —Jabari Asim, *Book Forum*

"A brilliant meditation on the invention of the idea of 'whiteness.' Deeply researched and elegantly written, Painter's presentation will

certainly spark conversation and controversy—as it should. Painter's high-octane intelligence makes her perfectly suited to the task."
—Annette Gordon-Reed, Pulitzer Prize–winning author of *The Hemingses of Monticello*

"Presenting vivid psychological portraits of Emerson and dozens of other figures variously famous and obscure, and carefully mapping the links between them, Painter's narrative succeeds as an engaging and sophisticated intellectual history, as well as an eloquent reminder of the fluidity (and perhaps futility) of racial categories." —Brendan Driscoll, *Booklist*, starred review

"Painter has given us an attractively linear account of how the numbers of white Americans grew in distinct 'enlargements,' . . . the construction of a gifted historian, giving shape to a shapeless process by which white Americans maintained their national identity while encompassing a continuous flood of strangers."
—Edmund S. Morgan and Marie Morgan, *New York Review of Books*

"Deeply researched, intelligent, and wonderfully commonsensical, this is a groundbreaking book, and if we're ever going to get to that so-called 'post-racial' society, a necessary book. It locates race where it actually exists, inside our heads, and shows us how recently it came to reside there." —Russell Banks, author of *The Sweet Hereafter* and *Affliction*

"This is an important addition to the nascent academic field of whiteness studies, which examines the social construction of whiteness with particular attention to the American experience. It should be read by all historians and anyone with an interest in cultural studies."
—April Younglove, *Library Journal*

"An insightful—and clearly developed—history . . . [that] will bust your preconceptions and make clear that, when it comes to race, we see only what we've been taught to see." —Kel Munger, *Sacramento News and Review*

"An amazing race-bending narrative. With grace and energy, Painter offers an eye-opening examination of slavery, the creation of whiteness, and the way in which racial categories have been both false and destructive. This is storytelling at its best."

—Ellen Goodman, syndicated columnist,
Washington Post Writers Group

"Not since Stephen Jay Gould's *The Mismeasure of Man* has there been such a synoptically provocative appreciation of the myths by which a now demographically challenged people sustained themselves and restrained others." —David Levering Lewis, professor of history, New York University Abu Dhabi, and Pulitzer Prize–winning author of *W. E. B. Du Bois, 1868–1919: Biography of a Race*

"By opening up and turning over how we think about race in America, Nell Painter tells an important and utterly fascinating story."

—Lani Guinier, Bennett Boskey Professor, Harvard Law School

"For the variable, changing, and often capricious definition of whiteness, Painter offers a kaleidoscopic lens." —*Publishers Weekly*

"*The History of White People* is a brave, groundbreaking, beautifully written study on how the U.S. psyche was built upon the canard of Anglo-Saxon superiority. No word or sentence is out of place. Every page is essential reading for all Americans."

—Douglas Brinkley, professor of history, Rice University

"This brilliant, profound book is most timely—as we proceed on our world journey toward human rights and dignity for all."

—Blanche Wiesen Cook, author of *Eleanor Roosevelt*

"A monumental feat of scholarship and a wonderfully readable story of America's own peculiar preoccupation with race and color."

—Diane McWhorter, author of *Carry Me Home*

THE HISTORY OF WHITE PEOPLE

NELL IRVIN PAINTER

W. W. NORTON & COMPANY

NEW YORK   LONDON

For information about permission to reproduce selections from this book,
write to Permissions, W. W. Norton & Company, Inc.,
500 Fifth Avenue, New York, NY 10110

For information about special discounts for bulk purchases, please contact
W. W. Norton Special Sales at specialsales@wwnorton.com or 800-233-4830

Manufacturing by Worzalla
Book design by Helene Berinsky
Production manager: Devon Zahn

Library of Congress Cataloging-in-Publication Data

Painter, Nell Irvin.
The history of White people / Nell Irvin Painter.
p. cm.
Includes bibliographical references and index.
ISBN 978-0-393-04934-3 (hardcover)
1. Whites—Race identity—United States.
2. Whites—United States—History.
3. United States—Race relations. I. Title.
E184.A1P29 2010
305.800973—dc22
2009034515

ISBN 978-0-393-33974-1 pbk.

W. W. Norton & Company, Inc.
500 Fifth Avenue, New York, N.Y. 10110
www.wwnorton.com

W. W. Norton & Company Ltd.
15 Carlisle Street, London W1D 3BS

To Edwin Barber and the Princeton University Library,
the absolute indispensables.

CONTENTS

INTRODUCTION

I might have entitled this book *Constructions of White Americans from Antiquity to the Present,* because it explores a concept that lies within a history of events. I have chosen this strategy because race is an idea, not a fact, and its questions demand answers from the conceptual rather than the factual realm. American history offers up a large bounty of commentary on what it means to be nonwhite, moving easily between alternations in the meaning of race as color, from "colored" to "Negro" to "Afro-American" to "black" to "African American," always associating the idea of blackness with slavery.* But little attention has been paid to history's equally confused and flexible discourses on the white races and the old, old slave trade from eastern Europe.

I use "white races" in the plural, because for most of the past centuries—when race really came down to matters of law—educated Americans firmly believed in the existence of more than one European race. It is possible, and important, to investigate that other side of history without trivializing the history we already know so well.

Let me state categorically that while this is not history in white versus black, I do not by any means underestimate or ignore the over-

---

* We usually assume definitions of race as color to be straightforward, as though "black" Americans were always dark-skinned. But the long American history of racial adjudication—of deciding who counted legally as black and white—belies any strong equivalence between race as color and actual color of skin.

whelming importance of black race in America. I am familiar with the truly gigantic literature that explains the meaning, importance, and honest-to-god reality of the existence of race when it means black. In comparison with this preoccupation, statutory and biological definitions of white race remain notoriously vague—the leavings of what is not black.[1] But this vagueness does not indicate lack of interest—quite to the contrary, for another vast historical literature, much less known today, explains the meaning, importance, and honest-to-god reality of the existence of white races.

It may seem odd to begin a book on Americans in antiquity, a period long before Europeans discovered the Western Hemisphere and thousands of years before the invention of the concept of race. But given the prevalence of the notion that race is permanent, many believe it possible to trace something recognizable as the white race back more than two thousand years. In addition, not a few Westerners have attempted to racialize antiquity, making ancient history into white race history and classics into a lily-white field complete with pictures of blond ancient Greeks. Transforming the ancients into Anglo-Saxon ancestors made classics unwelcoming to African American classicists.[2]* The blond-ancient-Greek narrative may no longer be taught in schools, but it lives on as a myth to be confronted in these pages. Before launching the trip back to ancient times, however, it may be useful to make a few remarks about the role of science or "science" of race.

I resist the temptation to place the word "science"—even theories and assertions of the most spurious, pernicious, or ridiculous kind—in quotation marks, for the task of deciding what is sound science and what is cultural fantasy would quickly become all-consuming. Better to note the qualifications of yesterday's scientists than to brand as mere "science" their thought that has not stood the test of time. I give scholars of repute in their day pride of place in my pages—no matter that some of their thinking has fallen by the wayside.

---

* William Sanders Scarborough (1852–1926) was a founder of the American Philological Association, which asked him not to attend meetings after 1909.

•

TODAY WE think of race as a matter of biology, but a second thought
reminds us that the meanings of race quickly spill out of merely
physical categories. Even in so circumscribed a place as one book, the
meanings of white race reach into concepts of labor, gender, and class
and images of personal beauty that seldom appear in analyses of race.
Work plays a central part in race talk, because the people who do the
work are likely to be figured as inherently deserving the toil and poverty of laboring status. It is still assumed, wrongly, that slavery anywhere in the world must rest on a foundation of racial difference. Time
and again, the better classes have concluded that those people deserve
their lot; it must be something within them that puts them at the bottom. In modern times, we recognize this kind of reasoning as it relates
to black race, but in other times the same logic was applied to people
who were white, especially when they were impoverished immigrants
seeking work.

Those at the very bottom were slaves. Slavery has helped construct
concepts of white race in two contradictory ways. First, American tradition equates whiteness with freedom while consigning blackness to
slavery. The history of unfree white people slumbers in popular forget-
fulness, though white slavery (like black slavery) moved people around
and mixed up human genes on a massive scale.* The important demographic role of the various slave trades is all too often overlooked as a
historical force. In the second place, the term "Caucasian" as a designation for white people originates in concepts of beauty related to the
white slave trade from eastern Europe, and whiteness remains embedded in visions of beauty found in art history and popular culture.

Today most Americans envision whiteness as racially indivisible,
though ethnically divided; this is the scheme anthropologists laid out
in the mid-twentieth century. By this reckoning, there were only three
real races ("Mongoloid," "Negroid," and Caucasoid") but countless eth-

---

*Although Arthur de Gobineau's racial reasoning in *Essay on the Inequality of the Races* was
wrongheaded in the extreme, he did grasp one fact of human history: economic development leads
to demographic mixing, as the demand for labor draws in people from afar.

nicities. Today, however, biologists and geneticists (not to mention literary critics) no longer believe in the physical existence of races—though they recognize the continuing power of racism (the belief that races exist, and that some are better than others). It took some two centuries to reach this conclusion, after countless racial schemes had spun out countless different numbers of races, even of white races, and attempts at classification produced frustration.

Although science today denies race any standing as objective truth, and the U.S. census faces taxonomic meltdown, many Americans cling to race as the unschooled cling to superstition. So long as racial discrimination remains a fact of life and statistics can be arranged to support racial difference, the American belief in races will endure. But confronted with the actually existing American population—its distribution of wealth, power, and beauty—the notion of American whiteness will continue to evolve, as it has since the creation of the American Republic.

THE
HISTORY
OF
WHITE
PEOPLE

1

GREEKS AND SCYTHIANS

Were there "white" people in antiquity? Certainly some assume so, as though categories we use today could be read backwards over the millennia. People with light skin certainly existed well before our own times. But did anyone think they were "white" or that their character related to their color? No, for neither the idea of race nor the idea of "white" people had been invented, and people's skin color did not carry useful meaning. What mattered was where they lived; were their lands damp or dry; were they virile or prone to impotence, hard or soft; could they be seduced by the luxuries of civilized society or were they warriors through and through? What were their habits of life? Rather than as "white" people, northern Europeans were known by vague tribal names: Scythians and Celts, then Gauls and Germani.

But if one asks, say, who are the Scythians? the question sets us off down a slippery slope, for, over time and especially in earliest times, any search for the ancestors of white Americans perforce leads back to non-literate peoples who left no documents describing themselves.[1] Thus, we must sift through the intellectual history Americans claim as Westerners, keeping in mind that long before science dictated the terms of human difference as "race," long before racial scientists began to measure heads and concoct racial theory, ancient Greeks and Romans had their own means of describing the peoples of their world as they knew it more than two millennia ago. And inevitably, the earliest accounts of our story are told from on high, by rulers dominant at a particular time. Power affixes the markers of history.

Furthermore, any attempt to trace biological ancestry quickly turns into legend, for human beings have multiplied so rapidly: by 1,000 or more times in some two hundred years, and by more than 32,000 times in three hundred years. Evolutionary biologists now reckon that the six to seven billion people now living share the same small number of ancestors living two or three thousand years ago. These circumstances make nonsense of anybody's pretensions to find a pure racial ancestry. Nor are notions of Western cultural purity any less spurious. Without a doubt, the sophisticated Egyptian, Phoenician, Minoan, and Persian societies deeply influenced the classical culture of ancient Greece, which some still imagine as the West's pure and unique source. That story is still to come, for the obsession with purity—racial and cultural—arose many centuries after the demise of the ancients. Suffice it to say that our search for the history of white people must begin in the misty mixture of myth and reality that comprises ancient Greek literature.

Early on, most Greek notions about peoples living along their northeastern border, especially that vaguely known place called the Caucasus, were mythological.[2] Known to Westerners since prehistoric times, the Caucasus is a geographically and ethnically complex area lying between the Black and Caspian Seas and flanked north and south by two ranges of the Caucasus Mountains. The northern Caucasus range forms a natural border with Russia; the southern, lesser Caucasus physically separates the area from Turkey and Iran. The Republic of Georgia lies between the disputed region of the Caucasus, Turkey, Armenia, Iran, and Azerbaijan. (See figure 1.1, Black Sea Region.)

According to Greek mythology, Jason and his Argonauts sought the Golden Fleece in the (Caucasus) land of Colchis (near the present-day Georgian city of Poti) obtaining it from King Aeetes, thanks to the magical powers of the king's daughter, the princess Medea. In Homer's

Fig. 1.1. The Black Sea Region today.

Odyssey, Circe, the sister of King Aeetes, transforms half of Odysseus's men into animals and seduces Odysseus. Later on, Hesiod and Aeschylus take up the tale of Prometheus, son of a Titan, punished for having stolen the secret of fire from Zeus, who chains Prometheus to a mountain in the Caucasus and sends an eagle to peck at his liver every day for thirty thousand years.[3] One can see that to the Greeks, almost anything goes on in the Caucasus. Furthermore, Greek mythology accords women of the Caucasus extraordinary powers, whether the magical of Medea and Circe, or the warlike of the Amazons, variously located in a number of places, including the Caucasus. Even today, these myths reverberate.[4]

Underlying the idea that all people originated between the Black and the Caspian Seas is the text of Genesis 8:1, which has Noah's ark coming to rest "on the mountains of Ararat" after the flood. In the thirteenth century Marco Polo located Mount Ararat in Armenia, just south of

Georgia in eastern Turkey, at the juncture of Armenia, Iraq, and Iran in the country of the Kurds. At any rate, Mount Ararat, at 5,185 meters, or some 17,000 feet high, is Turkey's highest mountain and is still believed by many to mark the site of postdiluvian human history in western Asia. Nor have recent events lessened its importance.

Twentieth- and twenty-first-century wars contest access to oil (South Ossetia, Azerbaijan, Grozny, Maykop, and the Caspian Sea, especially Baku, hold rich old deposits); earlier trade brought slaves, wine, fruit, and other agricultural produce from the valleys along the Black Sea, and a variety of natural resources (e.g., manganese, coal, copper, molybdenum, and tungsten). Current iconography of the Caucasus shows bombed-out cities and oil rigs of Chechnya or bearded nationalists called "terrorists" by the Russians. Occasional photographs of Caucasians show gnarled old people as proof of the life-prolonging powers of yogurt. There was a time when the people of the Caucasus were thought the most beautiful in the world. But documentary images making this case—in pictures, not just words—have proven illusive.

By contrast, vague and savage notions had lodged in the Greek mind concerning Scythians and Celts, who lived in what is now considered Europe. Voicing broad ethnic generalities, Greeks had words—*Skythai* (Scythian) and *Keltoi* (Celt)—to designate far distant barbarians. *Scythian*, for instance, simply meant little known, northeastern, illiterate, Stone Age peoples, and *Celt* denoted hidden people, painted people, strange people, and barbarians to the west. We cannot know what those people called themselves, for the Greek names stuck. Nor can we know how many of those situated in northern, western, and eastern Europe, two or three thousand years ago or earlier, became the biological ancestors of nineteenth-century German, English, and Irish people and twentieth-century Italians, Jews, and Slavs.[5] We know from Greek descriptions of their habits that, whether chiefs or slaves, all had light-colored skin.

For a sense of this vagueness, recall the naming skills of fifteenth-century Europeans as they looked west in the Americas. Their backs to the Atlantic Ocean, Europeans described sparsely settled people they had never seen before as "Indians." Such precision regarding faraway, unlettered peoples has been commonplace throughout the ages. Those at a distance became the Other and, easily conquered, the lesser. But not in antiquity because of race. Ancient Greeks did not think in terms of race (later translators would put that word in their mouths); instead, Greeks thought of place. *Africa* meant Egypt and Libya. *Asia* meant Persia as far to the east as India. *Europe* meant Greece and neighboring lands as far west as Sicily. Western Turkey belonged to Europe because Greeks lived there. Indeed, most of the Greek known world lay to the east and south of what would become recognizable later as *Europe*.

Mostly, Greek scholars focused on climate to explain human difference. Humors arising from each climate's relative humidity or aridness explained a people's temperament. Where the seasons do not change, people were labeled placid. Where seasons shift dramatically, their dispositions were said to display "wildness, unsociability and spirit. For frequent shocks to the mind impart wildness, destroying tameness and gentleness." Those words come from Hippocrates' *Airs, Waters, and Places*.[6]*

DISTANCE WAS all, for travel went at the speed of foot and hoof. Scythians roamed from Georgia in the Caucasus and the lands around the Euxine (Black) Sea to the steppes of Ukraine and on east to Siberia. Interestingly, the word "Ukraine" stems from Polish and Russian language roots meaning "edge of the world."[7] Russians and Ukrainians who now claim ancient Scythians as glorious ancestors look to Yalta in the Crimea as their ancestral home. Some Russian ancestors surely would have lived there, but the region's tumultuous history renders any single origin an invented tradition. Black Sea ancestors were Scythians, yes, but must also have included invaders and migrants of Tartar, Russian, Polish, Turkish, Iranian, and Chinese origin—at the very least.

Nowadays, the notion of Celtic ancestry is widely appealing. Thinking wishfully, self-proclaimed Celts like to root themselves in French

---

*Although Hippocrates of Kos (ca. 460–ca. 380 BCE) became a legendary practitioner of medicine, his works come from a variety of hands, not just his. The island of Kos lies in the southeastern Aegean Sea near the historic city of Halicarnassus, Turkey.

Brittany, the islands of the English Channel, Wales, Scotland, and Ireland, easily separating themselves from Germans, Anglo-Saxons, and Franks. The Greeks, for their part, could not go so far. Across two and a half millennia and lacking good intelligence, they first situated the barbarian Celts in various places from the Danube to the Iberian Peninsula, only later widening Celtic ethnography as Greek scholars learned from long-distance traders, travelers, and one another.

Historians of antiquity credit the traveler and geographer Hecataeus of Miletus (ca. 550–ca. 490 BCE) as the first Greek to map the whereabouts of Celts and Scythians.* We know little about him except that he traveled to Egypt and recognized the extent and power of the Persian empire. But he must have been more widely traveled, for he locates the trading center Massilia (modern French Marseilles) in the land of the Ligurians, near the land of the Celts, and he mentions a Celtic settlement in what is now the southeastern Austrian state of Styria.[8†] Hecataeus also sees much else: the Black Sea sits near the middle of the map, just to the right of "Thrace," with the Sea of Azov sticking up above it. His Danube, Dnieper, and Don Rivers—correctly—empty into the Black Sea from the left, the center, and the Sea of Azov, and the Caspian Sea lies at the far upper right at the edge of the world. Lastly, Hecataeus takes a leap, placing the Scythians between the Danube and the Dnieper Rivers and the Celts in the west, left of what we call the Italian peninsula.[9] A half century later, Herodotus ridiculed Hecataeus's map as vague and untrustworthy, and so it is. But the Greeks were reaching out and learning more.

BORN SEVENTY years after Hecataeus, Herodotus of Halicarnassus (ca. 480–ca. 427 BCE) had an advantage, and he seized it, gaining acclaim as the West's first systematic historian, indeed as the father of history, a title given him by the great Roman orator Cicero. So lasting was Herodotus's reputation that his likeness, real or imagined, was carved in stone

---

* Hecataeus's works include *Periegesis* (*Description of the Earth*) in two volumes: Europe and Asia. *Periegesis* survives as 330 very short fragments. In addition, Hecataeus wrote *Genealogies* (also called *Histories* or "researches"), a biographical dictionary of Greek heroes.
† Graz is the capital of Styria (in German, Steiermark), famous for wine and a relatively dolce vita.

in Greece a century or so after his death and copied later in Rome.[10]* Born and raised in what is now western Turkey, he traveled widely, took good notes, and produced the first unified world history, encompassing Egypt ("Africa"), western Asia ("Asia"), as well as Greece ("Europe"). Where earlier scholars had repeated hearsay, Herodotus seems actually to have visited Egypt, Babylonia, the Balkans, and the Black Sea region. He also most likely reported on Scythians as an eyewitness.[11]

Herodotus's *History*, written in 440 BCE, chronicles a succession of great wars fought between Persians and Greeks during the period 499–479 BCE. More important for our purposes, *The History* also describes barbarians surrounding the Greek known world. Quite naturally, Herodotus puts Greece in the middle of everything and sings its praises. Even so, by modifying Hecataeus's map of fifty years earlier, he did improve upon it greatly. Of course, Herodotus's world is still flat—that notion would stand for another thousand years. But he displayed it wider, including the entire Mediterranean Sea, the Celts in the Iberian Peninsula, and the Scythians north of the Black Sea. He also grants the Amazons an appearance, east of the other Scythians and north of the Caucasus.

Living in the eastern Mediterranean, Herodotus knew far more about eastern Scythians than about western Celts, who lived too far away for him to have good information. Much of book 4 of *The History* describes the various Scythian tribes and their territory. Although concentrating on the settled "Royal" Scythians around the lower Danube, Dnister, and Dnieper Rivers—all emptied into the Black Sea and the Sea of Azov—Herodotus's descriptions reach out to nomadic peoples far east of the Ural Mountains and around the Caspian Sea. Looking east from Athens, Herodotus held an advantage denied earlier historians, for by the time he wrote in the mid-fifth century, the Greek empire extended to the Black Sea, and some Scythian groups were in regular commercial contact with Greeks and Persians. Other various tribes, lumped into the Scythian mélange for convenience, were merely designated as wild.

---

* The portrait of Herodotus accompanying the *Encyclopædia Britannica Online* article comes from a Roman cult sculpture copied from a Greek original from the first half of the fourth century BCE.

Sharing a common view of Scythians as preeminent warriors, Herodotus was agog at what he described as their savage and drug-riddled life in what is now southern Ukraine, not to mention their circumcised penises.[12]* Herodotus knew, perhaps as an eyewitness—historians remain divided on this point—that Scythians smoked marijuana and substituted drug use for bathing: "The Scythians, as I said, take some of this hemp-seed, and, creeping under the felt coverings, throw it upon the red-hot stones; immediately it smokes, and gives out such a vapour as no Grecian vapour-bath can exceed; the Scyths, delighted, shout for joy, and this vapour serves them instead of a water-bath; for they never by any chance wash their bodies with water."[13]

Herodotous's Scythians also drink the blood of the first man they kill in battle, then cut off their victims' heads for delivery to their king or chief for payment: "The Scyth is proud of these scalps," Herodotus reports, "and hangs them from his bridle-rein; the greater the number of such napkins that a man can show, the more highly is he esteemed among them. Many make themselves cloaks, like the sheepskin [garments] of our peasants, by sewing a quantity of these scalps together." Bodies of the vanquished serve a further use as showy quivers for arrows made of the skin of a right arm: "Now the skin of a man is thick and glossy, and would in whiteness surpass almost all other hides. Some even flay the entire body of their enemy, and stretching it upon a frame carry it about with them wherever they ride." The skulls of their very worst enemies served as drinking cups, lined, if the Scythian could afford it, with gold.[14]

As for the Amazons, Herodotus found them fascinating as well. After marrying and settling down, "[t]he women of the Sauromatae have

---

* Herodotus's description of the Colchians in what is now Georgia on the Black Sea is in 2.104–5. He concluded from their dark skin, curly hair, and circumcised penises that Colchians descended from Egyptian armies. Needless to say, this observation has set off a lively controversy between Afrocentrics, who take this remark as corroboration of the spread of Egyptian, i.e., African power, and skeptics, who take Herodotus's comment on Colchians as cause to doubt his reliability as a historian.

Michael Novak, in *The Rise of the Unmeltable Ethnics*, quotes a harrowing scene from Jerzy Kosinski's *The Painted Bird* (1965) in which a similar warrior (identified variously as Kalmuck, Tartar, or Russian) on horseback savagely rapes a captive maiden. We shall encounter Kalmucks again soon.

continued from that day to the present to observe their ancient customs, frequently hunting on horseback with their husbands, sometimes even unaccompanied; in war taking the field; and wearing the very same dress as the men." *The History* also describes man-women as skilled soothsayers called "Enarees."[15]

HIPPOCRATES, ANCIENT Greece's greatest physician and the father of Western medicine, from the Greek island of Kos (off the coast of Herodotus's Halicarnassus, in western Turkey), also wrote widely and with great confidence on many other matters at the peak of Greek imperial power in the third and fourth centuries BCE. His *De aëre, aquis et locis* (*Airs, Waters, and Places*), a universal encyclopedia from 400 BCE, includes the barbarian ways of Scythians, Asians, and Greeks and, true to his medical interests, their practices of sexuality and reproduction.

For Hippocrates, topology and water determine body type, leading to differences between peoples of bracing, high terrain and those in low-lying meadows. Lowlanders he posited as broad, fleshy, and black haired: "they themselves are dark rather than fair, less subject to phlegm than to bile. Similar bravery and endurance are not by nature part of their character, but the imposition of law can produce them artificially." People living where the water stands stagnant "must show protruding bellies and enlarged spleens." Where the living is easy, as in the fertile lowlands, men pay the price in manhood: "the inhabitants are fleshy, ill-articulated, moist, lazy, and generally cowardly in character. Slackness and sleekness can be observed in them, and so far as the arts are concerned they are thick-witted, and neither subtle nor sharp." Generalizing further about the two types he assumes live in the high country, Hippocrates believed that those in a level, windy place will be "large of stature" and "like to one another; but their minds will be rather unmanly and gentle." By contrast, those confined to places where the soil is thin and dry and the seasons change dramatically "will be hard in physique and well-braced, fair rather than dark, stubborn and independent in character and temper. For where the changes of the seasons are most frequent and most sharply contrasted, there you will find the greatest diversity in physique, in character, and in constitution."[16]

Getting to the nub of the matter, Hippocrates' mountainous, rugged Greece clearly shaped his concepts of its European penumbra. A land "blasted by the winter and scorched by the sun," produced handsome men: "hardy, slender, with well-shaped joints, well-braced, and shaggy." The fierce Greek/European temperament would seem to explain Greek imperial domination as well as manly Greek/European beauty: for "where the land is bare, waterless, rough, oppressed by winter's storms and burnt by the sun, there you will see men who are hard, lean, well-articulated, well-braced, and hairy; such natures will be found energetic, vigilant, stubborn and independent in character and in temper, wild rather than tame, of more than average sharpness and intelligence in the arts, and in war of more than average courage."[17]

Such applause for European hardness would reappear over time, depending on the exposure of scholars to armies (mercenary and voluntary) and the relative prestige of militarism, especially in the nineteenth and twentieth centuries, when Americans widely envied the military might of European colonial powers.

Though Hippocrates places various Scythian tribes in a number of different regions and assigns to them an array of body types, he oddly concludes that they all look more or less alike. Some live along the Ukrainian Sea of Azov, the mild northern bay of the Black Sea (also known in antiquity as Palus Maeotis, on the border region between Hippocrates' Europe and Asia).* Others inhabit a cold, humid region and drink water from snow and ice, which Hippocrates believed had an effect on skin color: "The Scythians are a ruddy race because of the cold, not through any fierceness of the sun's heat. It is the cold that burns their white skin and turns it ruddy."[18]

Some Scythians farm, Hippocrates' encyclopedia declares; others were nomads; yet others called Sauromatae, the Amazons of the Palus Maeotis/Sea of Azov region, seem constantly to be at war. Before young

---

* Sevastopol and Yalta, the most famous names of the mild Crimean wine region of southern Russia and eastern Ukraine, now designate health resorts.

girls reached puberty, Amazon mothers cauterized their right breasts, arresting the breast's development and immensely strengthening the right shoulder and arm. Thus did young Amazon women become warriors; raised to throw javelins from horseback and to fight like men—as long as they remained virgins. Their potency demanded abstinence, of course, which lasted until each Amazon had killed three enemies, whereupon the Amazon performed certain ritual sacrifices before engaging in sex with men. Once married, however, Amazons settled down peaceably, returning to war only during times of dire crisis. This lack of a breast seems not to have interfered with Amazon sexuality.[19]

In fact, throughout *Airs, Waters, and Places* one is never far from sex. Hippocrates ties some Scythians' low rate of reproduction to climate, culture, and the bodies of men and women, including the many eunuchs said to be living among them who obviously did not father children. Furthermore, Scythian women, often fat, are said to have damp bellies that tended to close out semen and nullify conception, a serious problem since a rampant effeminacy among Scythian men curtailed the production of semen anyway.* Moistness and softness, "the greatest checks on venery," meant that Scythian men "have no great desire for intercourse." Horseback riding creates further obstacles to fertility. Scythian men remedied the lameness caused by horseback riding through a dubious cure: cutting the vein behind each ear and bleeding until they passed out; then "[a]fterwards they get up, some cured and some not. Now, in my opinion, by this treatment the seed is destroyed. For by the side of the ear are veins, to cut which causes impotence, and I believe that these are the veins which they cut. After this treatment, when the Scythians approach a woman but cannot have intercourse, at first they take no notice and think no more about it." After several failures at sex, they conclude they have sinned against the gods and become transvestites, even though ashamed of comporting themselves like women.[20]

Turning to the east, Hippocrates rates the milder Asian (i.e., Per-

---

*Hippocrates adds that female servants from other, unnamed peoples were active and slender. Unlike the Scythian women, they easily became pregnant.

sian and Babylonian) climate more highly than that of Europe (around Greece). Living in perpetual springtime, the civilized men of Asia were "well nourished, of very fine physique and very tall, differing from one another but little either in physique or stature." Nature and culture do produce weaknesses, however. The lack of well-defined seasons made Asians "feeble." Climatic sameness, puzzlingly, retards fetus development, too, no matter what the season of fertilization.[21] More to the point, monarchy made men into cowards: "For men's souls are enslaved, and refuse to run risks readily and recklessly to increase the power of somebody else." Hippocrates says earlier, "All their worthy, brave deeds merely serve to aggrandize and raise up their lords, while the harvest they themselves reap is danger and death."[22]

Not surprisingly, conditions improved closer to home. Unlike Asians, Hippocrates says, the Europeans/Greeks have no kings to tell them what to do. (In fact, he conveniently ignores a complication—that while his Greeks did live in more or less democratic city-states, warlords ruled the surrounding barbarians, many also European.) In any case, Hippocrates sings the praises of European political institutions that encourage individualism: for "independent people, taking risks on their own behalf and not on behalf of others, are willing and eager to go into danger, for they themselves enjoy the prize of victory. So institutions contribute a great deal to the formation of courageousness."[23] Over succeeding millennia, this contrast between king-ridden Asia and enterprising, individualist Europe hardened into a trope, even amid redefinitions of Europe and even though many Europeans remained under the thumb of kings while others violently overthrew them.

MISSING IN this analysis is any ambivalence regarding slavery. Although Herodotus mentions slaves repeatedly, he always does so in an offhand, matter-of-fact manner, as merely a system within the common hierarchies of antiquity—in Greece, throughout the Greek empire, and among barbarians across the known world. At least as early as the seventh century BCE, nomadic, loosely organized societies around the Black Sea region established an efficient trade network furnishing slaves to the wealthy of Greek society. Regions long fabled in myth, such as Thrace (now southern Bulgaria, northeastern Greece, and northwestern Turkey, homeland of the Roman slave Spartacus) and Colchis (now Georgia), in particular, seem to have supplied the bulk of them. Impoverished parents and kidnapping pirates delivered slaves to the market, and famine and warfare regularly increased the supply of people offered up for sale.[24]

Could oligarchic Greece have thrived without slavery? Could the philosophers and citizens attending to their businesses and that of the state ever have arisen without such a lower class doing the work? Plato owned fifty slaves, and households with ten or more bondspeople were common. Going about town or on long military campaigns, Athenian gentlemen always took along a slave or two. Quite likely, slaves outnumbered free people in the fifth and fourth centuries BCE, probably numbering 80,000 to 100,000 in Athens alone. Multitudes of enslaved women worked primarily at household tasks, providing services that could be sexual, medical, and domestic, while male slaves, skilled and unskilled, labored in the fields, on board ships, and in industrial workshops. Athens used an enslaved Scythian police force numbering between 300 and 1,000, for Scythians were known as skilled archers.[25]

The slave trade worked like this: as noted, the Black Sea line of supply began with barbarian chiefs whose endless warfare steadily drove refugees onto the market, where chiefs sold them to Greek slave traders for luxury goods like wine and clothing. Not that war was a prerequisite— thousands of children also entered the market, having been sold by their parents for salt or other necessities. Two cities, Byzantium (later Constantinople and then modern Istanbul) and Ephesus, Asia Minor's most important Greek city, dominated the market in slaves.[26] (Ephesus is probably best known today as the home of the Ephesians of the Bible, whose Christian church was one of seven in Asia to which Saint Paul addressed his letters.)

No shame attended this brutal business. A Greek Macedonian proudly listed his occupation as slave trader on his funeral stele and had engraved on it the image of eight slaves chained together by their necks.

To be sure, some practices did offend Greek morals. Herodotus mentions a slave trader who was punished for castrating freeborn boys and selling them as eunuchs. But even so, ancient Greeks are rightly known for their appreciation of good-looking boys, and when ancient sources speak of the beauty of slaves, they mean boys, not women and girls.

A ruling class quite easily judges the lower orders to be innately servile. More than a century before Aristotle discoursed on the naturalness of slavery and the inherently slavish nature of the enslaved in *Politics* (books 1, 3–7) and *Nicomachean Ethics* (book 7), Herodotus scolds the Thracians for so readily selling their children for export. Not that matters of slavery were always so simple.

HERODOTUS RELATES an anecdote demonstrating the two sides of slave life: a chance for upward mobility and a circumscribed possibility for success. In roughly 512 BCE the Scythian army undertook a war against the Persian king Darius that continued for twenty-eight years. And the Scythians won. But twenty-eight years of absence had wrought changes at home. As Herodotus explains, "For the Scythian women, when they saw that time went on, and their husbands did not come back, had intermarried with their slaves." On the warriors' return, children of the slaves and the Scythian women put up stiff resistance so long as the warriors fought with spears and bows. But the warriors succeeded once they capitalized on the essentially servile nature of the half-slave children. "Take my advice," one Scythian warrior told his army, "lay spear and bow aside, and let each man fetch his horse-whip, and go boldly up to them. So long as they see us with arms in our hands, they imagine themselves our equals in birth and bravery; but let them behold us with no other weapon but the whip, and they will feel that they are our slaves, and flee before us." Herodotus tells us that this tactic worked: the slaves' progeny "forgot to fight, and immediately ran away."[27] A mere sight of the whip had returned the children of slaves to their innate, slavish character, an early example of the close association of status and temperament.

Whatever the truth of that self-serving story, power relations clearly ruled the day, and the powerful would have their due. According to Herodotus, once again, every fifth year the Colchians and peoples around them traditionally paid a tribute to Persia of one hundred boys and one hundred girls. Already well established in Herodotus's time, this levy's origins could not be traced.[28]* And it must have continued long past the days of Herodotus, for more than three hundred years later, the Greek historian Polybius (ca. 203–120 BCE) notes the Black Sea origin of life's everyday necessities: "cattle and slaves."[29]† Indeed, this slave trade from the Black Sea region (of people later considered white) continued for more than two thousand years, ending only with Ottoman modernization at the turn of the twentieth century.‡ Such was the lot of masses of Europeans in ancient Greece.

---

* Herodotus also mentions a tribute of five boys along with ivory that the Ethiopians owed Persia every third year.
† Polybius's ideas about governmental checks and balances inspired drafters of the Constitution of the United States.
‡ The white slave trade in laborers and sex trade workers from eastern Europe, the Balkans, and Ukraine, now into western Europe and the United States, reappeared in the 1990s after the fall of the Soviet Union deprived these regions of overweening state power and its police protection.

ROMANS, CELTS, GAULS,
AND GERMANI

What we can see depends heavily on what our culture has trained us to look for. As imperial power shifted west from Greece to Rome, so did the dominant culture's view of barbarians. Greek savants continued to investigate the world out of fairly pure intellectual curiosity, while from around the time of the birth of Christ, Roman generals concentrated on practical knowledge for their own purposes of warfare and conquest. Roman armies reached the Atlantic Ocean and the English Channel between the first centuries BCE and CE, encountering for the first time western barbarians on their own turf. Moving north and west, Romans began to separate—to name and to define—Gauls and Germani from among the western peoples the Greeks formerly had vaguely lumped together as Celts. Not that any names or any of these distant peoples emerged with complete clarity: what made a Gaul a Gaul, a Celt a Celt, and a German a German long remained ambiguous.

The Germani first came into Roman view in the 70s or 60s BCE, as Roman scholarship was beginning to replace the Greek and when the most learned man of his time, the Greco-Roman Stoic philosopher Posidonius of Rhodes (ca. 135–51 BCE) bestowed that name on all the northwestern barbaric tribes beyond Roman control.[1] Even within the Roman homeland, the Spartacus slave revolt of 73–71 BCE in the region of Naples, Italy, revealed the popular recognition of northern slave identities. Spartacus himself hailed from the traditional source of ancient slaves: Slavic Thrace (now in neighboring regions of Bulgaria, Greece, and Turkey). But Romans further discerned relatively new slave identities: among the two hundred or so insurrectionary slaves, Romans recognized gangs they termed either Gauls or Germans. Over time the most learned Greco-Romans further sorted out Celts from Gauls and both from Germani with increasing clarity.

Both Diodorus Siculus, a Greek historian from Sicily, controversial for his loose way with facts and quotations from other authors and for plodding repetition, writing in the 50s to the 40s BCE, and the more authoritative Dionysius of Halicarnassus, writing in about 20 BCE, classed the Germani as a branch of the Celts. The greatly influential Greek scholar Strabo, writing during the reign of the great emperor Augustus (27 BCE–14 CE), went further. Strabo saw the Gauls as a kind of double-distilled Germani. Surveying all the peoples known to the Greeks and Romans, his seventeen-volume *Geographica* (7 BCE–23 CE) repeats a description that by his time had become commonplace: "The whole race which is now called both 'Gallic' and 'Galatic' is war-mad, and both high-spirited and quick for battle, although otherwise simple and not ill-mannered. . . . As for their might, it arises partly from their large physique and partly from their numbers. . . . [T]hey are all fighters by nature." To Strabo, the Rhine River hardly constituted a barrier, as "their migrations easily take place, for they move in droves, army and all, or rather they make off, households and all, whenever they are cast out by others stronger than themselves."[2] The wealthy, well-educated Strabo (also from western modern Turkey) thus lumps the Gallic and German peoples together according to physique and culture. He judges their differences merely as a matter of historical contingency rather than as inherent dissimilarity.

Clearly, to the Romans, civilization, not blood, set the two peoples apart. Roman conquest was busily taming the formerly warlike Gauls west to east, while the Germans, still unconquered, maintained their own wild, barbarian ways, remaining a truer kind of Celt than the Gauls. Strabo appeals to etymology to reinforce his reasoning. Romans, he says, named the wild tribes "Germani," because the word means "genuine" in Latin. The Germani, therefore, were "genuine" Gauls.[3] What the Germani still were—big, blond, wild, simple, and warlike—the Gauls had once been. In the West's first close look northwest, imperial Rome's greatest general stresses the fading but still warlike character of the Gauls.

JULIUS CAESAR (ca. 100–44 BCE) was the first to depict the West's original noble savages in his eyewitness account called *De bellum gallico* (*On the Gallic War*) of 54 BCE, a book that lent some clarity to this chaotic nomenclature.[4] On his way to vast imperial power, Caesar spent nine years in the wilds beyond the Roman province we call Provence. Roman Gaul then encompassed modern-day France, the southern Netherlands, Belgium, most of Switzerland, and Germany west of the Rhine. Even so, Gaul, though huge, played a mere supporting role in Caesar's larger ambition of regenerating and reforming the Roman empire as a whole. The Romans had already swallowed up a Greek empire that stretched east toward the Black Sea, and they now were dominant in areas south and west around the Mediterranean in today's Morocco, Algeria, Tunisia, and Libya. Gaul, therefore, belonged to a vast imperial realm.

This is not to say the Gallic war meant nothing. Frontier campaigns like the ones in Gaul funded Caesar's political machinations back in Rome, as the spoils of conquest—booty and slaves—flowed steadily south, paying off allies, securing shaky loyalties, and inserting northern Europeans into Italian society. Caesar's defeat of the Belgae in 57 BCE, for instance, garnered 53,000 people, all of whom he sold at a swoop. On defeating the Veneti of Brittany, Caesar executed the leading men and sold the rest—man, woman, and child—into slavery.[5] As he replenished his coffers in Gaul and added northerners to the population mix of Italy, Caesar came to know the northern tribes as both their conqueror and their military commander. In time, the Roman army inevitably employed masses of northerners as mercenary soldiers, and their aptitude for war appears prominently in Roman descriptions of inherent ethnic traits.

An able and complex man, Caesar both made history and wrote ethnography. As an anthropologist with imperialist goals, he begins to disaggregate from up close the tribes whom Americans would later regard as white ancestors, famously beginning by dividing the whole of Gaul "into three parts, one of which the Belgae inhabit, the Aquitani another, and the third a people who in their own language are called 'Celts,' but in ours, 'Gauls.' "[6]* Already the distinction between Celts and Gauls had come to depend on how the Romans talked about them, and increasingly the terms stood for the barbarian traits. Caesar's term *Germani* came to label only those beyond Roman control. The Belgae—barbarians within Roman Gaul—introduce a little more complexity, however, for they had originally been Germani. Thus, and somewhat messily, the term *Germani* prevailed as a name for the tribes living to the north of the Roman empire from around the first century BCE and six centuries onward. For Roman purposes, politics and warfare defined ethnic identities.

Caesar's classic *Gallic War* remains true to its title, in both its stress on war and its respect for the considerable military prowess of the Gauls, to which he repeats a defining chorus: "There was slaughter everywhere." "Massive slaughter ensued. . . ." "Massive slaughter followed."[7] It seems the defeat of such valiant barbarian warriors demanded massive slaughter, for the Gauls put up a very good fight, if not a shrewd one: "The Gauls are impulsive and sudden in their decision-making," Caesar notes. Indeed, the big, tough Gauls indulged in some foolish overconfidence when initially encountering the smaller, shorter Romans. "For the main part," Caesar says, "Gauls are very tall, and hold our slighter build in contempt." Size counted for only so much on the frontier, however, and Gallic bulk went down to defeat before Roman tactical skill.[8]

Book 7, the last and longest chapter of *The Gallic War*, chronicles the great revolt of Caesar's most formidable Gallic opponent, Vercingetorix (d. 46 BCE).† Although Caesar ultimately defeated Vercingetorix in 52

---

* Romans also divided Gaul in two other ways: between *Gallia Togata*, or the domesticated, Toga-Wearing Gaul, and the more barbaric *Gallia Comata*, or Hairy Gaul.

† An aristocrat from the central Auvergne, Vercingetorix was from near today's city of Clermont-Ferrand, where his equestrian statue now stands in the central square. In my copy of *The Gallic*

BCE, he credits him with waging an epic struggle for the liberty of his tribe: "the whole of Gaul was united in the desire of restoring liberty and their former reputation for warfare."[9] Such heroic tales have a long life, and in the figure of Vercingetorix, book 7 gave nineteenth- and twentieth-century French nationalists their ancestral warrior-hero, the great Gaul of *nos ancêtres les Gaulois* ("our ancestors the Gauls," a phrase dating back to the sixteenth century).* Not only is there the famous French cigarette Gaulois, but also, and more tellingly, the *Astérix* French comic books have depicted the adventures of the fictional, fun-loving Gallic warrior Astérix for more than half a century.† Since their debut in France in 1959, *Astérix* comic books have been translated into a hundred languages. Their hero inspired creation of the amusement Parc Astérix just outside Paris, which opened in 1989, and gave a name to the first French satellite, launched in 1965: Astérix-1.

It might be said that the story of Vercingetorix and his Gaulois reverberates through history, but not solely in France. Caesar's *Gallic War* also foreshadows and parallels chapters in the history of the United States, in which U.S. Americans play Caesar's imperial role. Readers of American history can draw parallels between Caesar's war of conquest and the Indian wars of North America, with Gauls cast as Indians and Vercingetorix as the Seneca chief Pontiac, the Apache chief Geronimo, or the Lakota (Sioux) chief Sitting Bull at Wounded Knee: all valiant, but all defeated.‡ More to the point in the present undertaking, however, Caesar's *Gallic War* introduces the tribes of the ancient Germans and Britons.

War, each of the first six books encompasses between fourteen and thirty-one pages; book 7, on Vercingetorix and the great revolt, is fifty-two pages long.

* François de Belleforest used the phrase in 1579 while describing Hugh Capet's recapture of power from the Frankish aristocracy.

†The main characters in the *Astérix* comic books all have names built around puns playing on the common French "que" suffix's similarity to Gallic names ending in "rix." Thus "Astérix" comes from the idea of star in the French *astérisque* (asterisk); "Obélix" from *obélisque* (obelisk); "Idéfix" from *idée fixe* (fixed idea or obsession); "Assurancetourix" from *assurance tous risques* (comprehensive insurance), *Cétautomatix* from *c'est automatique* (it's automatic); and *Ordralfabétix* from *ordre alphabétique* (alphabetical order).

‡The theme of poetic, valiant defeat appears in nineteenth-century hymns to the Celts, for instance in Matthew Arnold's *On the Study of Celtic Literature* (1867).

•

ON THE whole, Caesar's paragraphs on the Germani are spare, providing only brief and patronizing accounts of barbarians to the north of Roman Gaul. For instance, he denotes the largest of the German tribes, the Suebi Germans living east of the Rhine, only as "ignorant and uncivilized" and mentions just one German character by name, the blowhard Suebi chieftain Ariovistus, who presumes himself the equal of a Roman general, proclaiming "his own excellence" in a loud and long performance. Caesar demeans this pretentious fellow, whose own Germanic language the imperialists cannot understand and who thus is forced to speak to Romans in the Gallic language.[10] Since no other German appears individually, the balance of Caesar's account of the Germani is anthropological.

Sounding not a little like earlier Greek judgments of, say, the Scythians, Caesar heaps scorn mixed with grudging respect on the Suebi's undisciplined manner of living. They farm just a little, feeding themselves mainly on milk and meat: "Their diet, daily exercise, and the freedom from restraint that they enjoy—for from childhood they do not know what compulsion or discipline is, and do nothing against their inclination—combine to make them strong and tall as giants. They inure themselves, in spite of the very cold climate in which they live, to wear no clothing but skins—and these so scanty that a large part of the body is uncovered—and to bathe in the rivers." Interestingly, Caesar says the Suebi consider the use of saddles to be shamefully effeminate.

Furthermore, Caesar echoes Strabo's view of the process that has distinguished Gauls from Germani, drawing a larger lesson from history: "There was a time when the Gauls were more courageous than the Germans and took offensive military action against them," he notes, but *pax romana* has fostered settlement and prosperity. Settlement and prosperity, in turn, did their own work, luring the Gauls from "poverty, privation, and hardship," transforming warriors into mere consumers, docile and militarily impotent.

According to Caesar, this process of civilizing and softening proceeds by degrees. Conquest has already more or less wrecked Gallic bravery. The land of the Gauls lies subdued, so that only the Belgae, living remote from centers of Roman culture, can still claim relative manliness: "the Belgae are the bravest, for they are furthest away from the civilization and culture of the Province. Merchants very rarely travel to them or import such goods as make men's courage weak and womanish. They live, moreover, in close proximity to the Germans who inhabit the land across the Rhine, and they are continually at war with them." The Suebi Germans, swearing not to fall into that trap, forbade the import of wine from the South, thinking that "it makes men soft and incapable of enduring hard toil."[11] Here lies one of Caesar's central themes, setting up a tension between barbarism and civilization that reverberated for two thousand years.

Of course, Caesar did not speak in terms of race, a discourse invented many centuries later. But in the nineteenth century, when race talk ruled, his descriptions of the Germani served theorists searching for immutable Teutonic traits. Looking backward, they magnified the differences Caesar traced between Gauls and Germans, as though they were racial rather than cultural, permanent rather than in flux. Unless we take their word for it, we must turn to Caesar for ourselves.

Speaking always as an imperialist focused on military conquest, Caesar highlights German traits related to war. The sparsely settled Germani, he notes, fiercely ravaged their borderlands, driving away all who drew near, German-speaking or not. And, then, in a step dear to later racial theorists, Caesar apparently linked German sexual ethics, morality, and war. German men, he said, show an admirable sexual restraint; though they live alongside women who bathe in the rivers beside them and wear scanty hides and skins, sex remains off limits until the men reach twenty. Chastity relates to war, for the Germani were said to believe that abstinence makes men taller and braver, evidently channeling sexual frustration into healthy violence: "acts of robbery which take place outside the borders of each state: in fact, Germani claim that these take place to train their young men and reduce their laziness."[12]

Others of Caesar's comments fit poorly into the lore of Teutonists. Consider the central role of women in war. As soothsayers, Caesar notes, women decide when to wage war, and once an enemy is engaged, women and children accompany their warriors into the field to bolster their bravery.[13] Latter-day Teutonists made war a strictly characteristically masculine affair.

CAESAR'S WAS also the first direct Roman report regarding the people of Britain. He obviously knew more about Germani than about Britons, but this lack of knowledge hardly prevented him from describing and judging those peoples across the Channel. He had visited only the coast of southeast Kent and the mouth of the Thames. Even so, he writes confidently of the interior. Britons there, he says, live by hunting and gathering and claim to be original inhabitants. They eat meat and milk, dress in skins, and dye their bodies blue with woad, which makes them "appear more frightening in battle. They have long hair and shave their bodies, all except for the head and upper lip." And then there is, again, sex. In contrast to the Germans' abstinence, in Britain "groups of ten or twelve men share their wives in common, particularly between brothers or father and sons. Any offspring are held to be the children of him to whom the maiden was brought first."[14] All along, Britons contrast poorly with Belgic immigrants from the west bank of the Rhine who had supplanted the natives on England's southern coast and gone on to live quite civilized lives, farming peacefully like the Gauls only a day's sail away on the mainland.

CAESAR'S *GALLIC WAR* endures as the pioneering—and primary—description of ancient Gauls and Germani. Its information, as we have seen, ranges widely, and it inspired those who followed through the centuries. Well into the 1800s, *The Gallic War* was cited as the source of what then seemed immutable truth: the notion of the river Rhine as a dividing line between permanently dissimilar peoples. Regrettably, this notion distorts Caesar's views, transforming what he saw as manifestations of conquest and commerce into inherent racial difference. During Caesar's own time, the Rhine was not yet thought to separate peoples according to essential differences.

•

GAIUS PLINIUS SECUNDUS, Pliny the Elder (23–79 CE), wrote a century after Caesar, completing his *Natural History* in 77 CE. Two years later he died the death of a scientist—while witnessing the eruption of Mount Vesuvius near Naples that buried Pompeii and Herculaneum. The *Natural History* contains thirty-seven "books" of varying length—book 7, "Man," for instance, is only thirty pages long in current book publication. Aiming to sum up all existing knowledge and explain the nature of all things, Pliny drew heavily upon both Greek and Roman authorities. In book 7, Pliny praises Julius Caesar as "the most outstanding person in respect of his mental vigour."[15] To this accumulated knowledge Pliny added the fruit of his own military experience in Germany from 46 CE. The result is an extravagant, entertaining, and comprehensive work of 600-plus pages all told in English translation.

Like most ancient and medieval scholars, Pliny divides the earth into three parts—Europe, Asia, and Africa—and begins, as might be expected, with Europe. His Roman Europe, the "nurse of the people who have conquered all nations, and by far the most beautiful region of the earth," occupies at least half the world. Again as might be expected, he deems his native Italy the best place in the universe, "ruler and second mother of the world" and "the most beautiful of all lands, endowed with all that wins Nature's crown." Without a doubt, the gods themselves had chosen Italy to unite and civilize the world, to "become the sole parent of all races throughout the world."[16]

Pliny's book 7, focusing on humankind generally, includes Scythians and the now better-known Germani. They are cannibals all. The Transalpine tribes of Germany, for example, are depicted as a brutal bunch, practicing "human sacrifice, which is not far short of eating human flesh," while out to the east, "some Scythian tribes—indeed a large percentage of them—feed on human bodies." Picking up on his forebears Hippocrates and Herodotus, Pliny locates the Scythian cannibals ten days' journey north of the river Borysthenes (the Dnieper). Among other uncivilized habits, they drink out of human skulls and use scalps "with the hair attached as napkins [protective material] to cover their chests." Moving ever farther east and south, thirteen days' travel beyond the Dnieper, the Sauromatae or Amazons still live, eating only every two days. Next to them can be found the Arimaspi, "a people noted for having one eye in the middle of their forehead." There are also "certain people" born in Albania with keen-sighted, grayish-green eyes; "bald from childhood, they see more at night than during the day."[17]

Indeed, Pliny's catalog of humankind includes an amazing number of freakish peoples. In addition to the one-eyed folk, it describes others who grow a foot so big they pull it over their heads for shade from the sun. Still others come into the world with heads like those of dogs. So strong were Pliny's fantastic notions that over a thousand years later, medieval English texts show these monstrous peoples as illustrating several varieties of mankind. (See figures 2.1–4, Monstrous people: Cyclops, Dog-Head, Sciopod, and Panotii.)

The thrilling notion that monstrous peoples existed out there in the wide, wide world survived well into Enlightenment science. Carolus Linnaeus, the eighteenth-century father of taxonomy, invented a revolutionary system that laid a durable groundwork for the naming and classifying of plants and animals. Yet even this scientific pioneer included a category of monstrous people in his classic work *Systema naturae*, and monsters remained part of the accepted scientific view of humanity until Johann Friedrich Blumenbach disproved their existence in his Ph.D. dissertation of 1775. It says a great deal about the intellectual inertia of medieval Western society that the notions to be found in Pliny's *Natural History* held on for fifteen hundred years. Eventually, of course, Pliny's encyclopedia faded into obscurity, as Europeans began to learn more of the world. Meanwhile, a work contemporaneous to Pliny's passed muster as scientific truth among white race theorists well into our times.

EARLY IN his illustrious writing career, the Roman historian Cornelius Tacitus (56–after 117 CE) wrote a short book entitled *De origine et situ Germanorum*, known commonly as *Germania* (98 CE).* A member

---

* Tacitus's text occasionally served German nationalism beginning in the fifteenth century, but it really gained currency during the nineteenth-century decades of German unification and twentieth-century Pan-Germanism. Notions of German racial purity continue to turn up nowadays on white

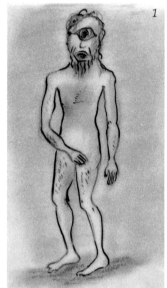

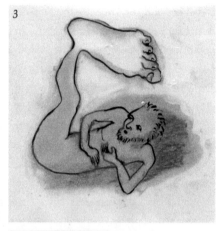

Figs. 2.1–4. Monstrous people: Cyclops, Dog-Head, Sciopod, drawn by Nell Painter from Thomas de Cantimpré; Panotii, drawn by Nell Painter, after the Cotton Tiberius MS of the British Library.

of the Roman elite from either northern Italy or southeastern France, Tacitus was an accomplished orator and author. His major works, *The Histories* and *The Annals*, tell the story of the Roman empire, and his minor works consist of *Germania*, a biography of his father-in-law,

nationalist websites, such as that of the Aryan Nations: "It's not a matter of White Supremacy it's about Racial Purity!"

Agricola, and a book on rhetoric entitled *Dialogus*. With the end of antiquity, Tacitus's more important works lost currency, but within the history of white people, his reputation rests on *Germania*, more precisely on a myopic interpretation of *Germania*'s pronouncements on German endogamy.

Like Caesar, whose work he echoes, Tacitus draws a line between tamer Gauls west of the Rhine and wild Germani to the east. Recognizing the importance of migration and conquest, Tacitus agrees with Caesar that the term *Germania* is of recent coinage. Tacitus explains—in phrases now quite confusing—that "since those who first crossed over the Rhine and drove out the Gauls (and now are called the Tungri) were at that time called Germani. Thus the name of a tribe, and not of a people, gradually became dominant, with the result that they were all called Germani, at first by the conquered from the name of the conquerors because of fear, and then, once the name had been devised, also by the Germani themselves."[18] Distinguishing in some mysterious fashion between tribes and peoples, Tacitus is saying here that a tribe called Germani migrated into the territory of people whom the Romans once called Gauls but now call Tungri and conquered them. All of them came to be known as Germani. This garbled explanation may not illuminate what happened, but it does show how migration, conquest, and historical change influence the outlines of an ethnic category.

For Tacitus, as for "the divine Caesar," warfare is uppermost in the mind, as barbarian warriors continued to serve widely in armies of the Roman empire. Tacitus also remembers the Gauls of former times as powerful enemies, but now, firmly conquered, they are settled and civilized. Habituated to Roman delicacies like wine, the Gauls have lost their bellicose masculinity and tipped toward effeminacy. Meanwhile, those noble savages, the Germani, largely retain their barbaric vigor by dint of warlike standoffishness, even as cupidity has been drawing them toward the allures of civilization: "They take particular pleasure in the gifts of neighbouring tribes, sent not only by individuals but also by whole communities: choice horses, splendid weapons, ornamental discs and torques; we have now taught them to take money also."[19]

German men constantly bear arms, for warfare represents their coming of age and their citizenship. Whenever they grow sluggish from sustained peace and leisure, privileged young men pick fights. It is through fighting, not trade or politics, that they accumulate prestige and support a large body of free and enslaved retainers. "To drink away the day and night disgraces no one. Brawls are frequent, as is normal among the intoxicated, and seldom end in mere abuse, but more often in slaughter and bloodshed." Here Tacitus spies weakness and a foolproof means of vanquishing German warlords: "[if] one indulges their drunkenness by supplying as much as they long for, they will as soon succumb to vices as to arms."[20]

Even so, conquest of the Germani is not a likely prospect according to Tacitus, who etches the Roman empire's political boundaries more deeply than Caesar and highlights the uniqueness of the Germani off on the empire's far eastern side. Moreover, *Germania* downplays many differences within German tribes and instead pronounces the liberty and warfare characteristic of all small-scale societies as inherently Germanic traits.[21] Thus the failure of the Romans to subdue the Germani flows not from Roman shortcomings but from a particularly German virility. Perhaps their avoidance of the vices of civilization, or their sexual abstinence and its attendant potency, protects them from conquest. These qualities as they appear in *Germania*—warfare, masculinity, and barbarism—lie at the base of modern ethnogender stereotyping.

Looking backward, we may find it puzzling that both Tacitus and Caesar critique the effects of Roman civilization. After all, the vast Roman empire lasted some five hundred years and laid the linguistic, legal, architectural, and political foundations of the Western world. How could eminent citizens of this great empire squeeze out admiration for the dirty, bellicose, and funny-looking barbarians to the north? The answer lies in notions of masculinity circulating among a nobility based on military conquest. According to this ideology, peace brings weakness; peace saps virility. The wildness of the Germani recalls a young manhood lost to the Roman empire.

Long a critic of imperial Rome's luxury and decadence, Tacitus found in the rough Germani a freedom-loving people embodying the older, better values of Augustinian times. Their homeland may be ugly and its climate cruel, but its simple folk possess a certain charm born of freedom, frequently manifested as anarchy and fighting, and the chastity that Caesar also noted.[22] To Tacitus, rude German simplicity trumps Roman decadence: "In every home they grow up, naked and filthy, into those long limbs and large bodies that amaze us so. Each child suckles at his own mother's breasts, not handed over to slave girls and nurses. . . . Love comes late to the young men, and their virility is not drained thereby. Nor are maidens hurried along."[23]

INTERESTINGLY—AND FOR hardly the last time in history—citified men seem fated to admire tough, virile barbarians. Caesar headed a train of civilized male observers—with Tacitus among the most famous— contrasting the hard with the soft, the strong and the weak, the peaceful and the warlike, all to the detriment of the civilized, dismissed as effeminate. As we see, the seeds of this stereotype—a contrast between civilized French and barbarian Germans—lie in the work of ancient writers, themselves uneasy about the manhood costs of peacetime.

Later commentators cite Tacitus to prove their claims of German manliness and racial purity. Tacitus, of course, did not speak of *race* in the modern sense, for that meaning had not been invented. But he did write, "For myself, I agree with the views of those who think that the inhabitants of Germania have not been tainted by any intermarriage with other tribes, but have existed as a distinct and pure people, resembling only themselves. Consequently, they also all have the same physical appearance . . . fierce blue eyes, tawny hair, bodies that are big but strong only in attack."[24]

And why are the Germani pure? Not out of any furious ethnic pride, but because they live in a place no one else wants, for "who would abandon Asia or Africa or Italy and seek out Germania, with its unlovely landscape and harsh climate, dreary to inhabit and behold, if it were not one's native land?"[25] With the passage of time, Tacitus's rhetorical question—and its answer—fell away, leaving only the notion of rugged German standoffishness.

•

IN TRUTH, it simply is not possible to tie those whom the Romans called Germani to modern Germans securely. Humanity moves around so much that no clear lines of descent trace back over two millennia. Even the efficient Romans lacked solid knowledge of frontiers beyond their own Gallic provinces.

Caesar notes the ways of migration: Germans who moved into Gaul soon became Belgae, and migrants from Belgium now settled across the Channel belong to the British population.[26] Their migrations were part of a much wider phenomenon that marked the first millennium BCE and thereafter. Nomadic and seminomadic tribes, moving east to west under pressure from the Huns, left today's Turkistan, crossing overland from Asia through Ukraine. In the far west, peoples piled up along the Rhine border of the Roman empire, driving a process so fluid that the tribes fought over territory within themselves and with one another, all the while merging and mingling biologically.

We may think of pre-unification (i.e., pre-1870) "Germans" as a single linguistic group, but in the time of Caesar and Tacitus, speakers of Germanic languages lived well into what is now Poland and, perhaps, beyond. Roman observers did not mention language as a characteristic of the Germani, focusing rather on cultural patterns and physical appearance. Between language, body, and lifestyle, already the identity of the Germani is rife with incongruities.

Such confusions eventually plunged Caesar's term *Germani* into disuse until the rise of religious and political Pan-German sentiment.[27] By the time German-speakers embraced a common name in the eleventh century, that name had morphed into *Deutsch*. In fact, "German" does not appear in English until the sixteenth century, replacing the French cognate, *Alemain*.[28] Nor has time brought clarity. On the eastern side of what is now the Federal Republic of Germany, controversies still rage over the Germanic or Slavic identity of Wends, Vandals, and various neighboring Germans and Slavs in the eastern German region known as Saxony.[29]

One lesson here is that wars and imperial fortunes render political boundaries notoriously prone to dispute; furthermore, cultural boundaries are even harder to pin down. When we speak of "Germany" before the late nineteenth century, we can only mean a cultural idea and a linguistic grouping. But we know now that neither culture (e.g., marriage or burial habits) nor language provides a reliable index to biological descent. Naming does not help either, for we can comfortably reel off a roll call that includes Brandon Riveras, Matthew Feinsteins, and Tamika Washingtons—names that reflect both history and present cultural preference rather than genealogy. White race chauvinists are loath to admit that brown-skinned people speak the English language fluently.

In terms of naming, the Native American Indian parallel with the ancient Germani once again has bearing. The untamed Germans outside the Roman empire called themselves by an abundance of local names: Marsians, Gambrians, Vandalians, Tungrians, Araviscans, Osians, Treverians, Nervians, Batavians, Vangiones, Tribocians, Nemetes, Ubians, Mattiacians, Cattans, Usipians, Tencterians, Bructerians, Chamavians, Angrivarians, Bructerians, Dulgibinians, Chasuarians, Frisians, Chaucians, Fosians, Cheruscans, Cimbrians, and Suevians (divided into several communities all bearing distinct names: Langobards, Reudignians, Aviones, Angles, Varinians, Eudoses, Suardones Nuithones, Hermondurians, Nariscans, Marcomanians, Quadians. Marsignians, Gothinians, Osians, Burians, Arians, Helvicones, Manimians, Elysians, Naharvalians, Lygians, Gothones, Rugians, Lemovians, and Suiones). The list comes from Tacitus in 98 CE.

German-speakers who entered Roman society, however, often as mercenary soldiers, adopted Roman usage and called themselves Germani, just as Native Americans within the United States have found reason to evoke a unifying identity as Indians. Beyond Roman reach, the various German-speaking tribes east of the Rhine considered themselves distinct one from another, sharing no sense of common identity or common interest until several centuries after the collapse of the empire.*

---

* The German tribes continued to move, war, merge, even disappear, and to split up politically, until unification under Prussia in 1870. As we know from twentieth-century history, even unification did not stabilize German boundaries. German defeat after the First World War reduced territory acquired at the expense of France and Poland in the nineteenth century. After defeat in 1945, Germany was partitioned and, in 1949, became two separate states, one in the east (the German Democratic Republic) and one in the west (the Federal Republic of Germany). After the fall of the Democratic Republic, Germany reunified in 1990.

As the Roman empire crumbles, our narrative of people who would later be called "white" moves north. During the so-called Dark Ages between mid-fifth century CE and the fourteenth-century Renaissance, seafaring raiders appeared, perturbing northern societies in a ceaseless quest for plunder. Although much history of these chaotic times has not survived, a key name—Saxon—appears for the first time. It does not denote the people of England, but foreigners: raiders from continental Europe—Scandinavians, Angles, and Jutes, whoever could reach for plunder in Roman Britain. Even the great progenitor of what was later called "Saxon England," King Alfred (849–99), called his people *englisc* and himself the king of the *Angelcynn*.[30] Interestingly enough, Irish attacking Britain from the west were called Scotti.[31] Insecurity forced the peoples of northern Europe to hunker down, pouring the wealth to be had into cities to the south and east.

WHILE WARLORDS fought in the west, medieval cities and kingdoms at the edges of Christendom glittered in far-flung, cosmopolitan empires. Trade made the difference, trade in people as well as spices, silk, cotton, dyestuffs, medicines, salt, and, increasingly, sugar. First the seafaring merchants of Pisa, Genoa, and, most gloriously, Venice controlled the Asian trade. After the Ottoman conquest of Constantinople in 1453, Venice began to decline. Iberian kingdoms in the far west fattened on trade with Africa and the newly discovered Americas. In Italy and Iberia, wealth and peoples from immense trading networks met and fornicated within polyglot, multicolored, and religiously diverse populations.

Here was a rich and glorious world built on subjugation. Hundreds of thousands in the Italian and Iberian empires were, in fact, not free, but were objects of an ever-flourishing trade. During Roman and medieval times this traffic in workers had flowed one way, from various peripheries toward the metropoles. The Greco-Roman historian Diodorus Siculus offers a clue. When the Celts discovered they could buy Italian wine even without money—for they had no money—they flooded the market with slaves. A good Celtic bargain exchanged a slave for one amphora of wine holding about seven gallons.[32] The various slave trades brought thousands of northern barbarians—Celts, Gauls, Germani—into the centers of wealth and power, altering those gene pools as surely as did the older flow from the Black Sea. Up in their impoverished, cold, and remote land, ancient Germans saw no such influx from afar. Compared with wealthy centers to the south, German tribal territory remained relatively contained, while the Roman world and its successors blended the descendants of many a hapless barbarian.

This millennium of Venetian and Iberian hegemony barely appears in American white race history as it jelled over the past two hundred years. Rather, race-chauvinist history depends on Tacitus's ancient Germani and medieval German heroes called Saxons. The race narrative ignores early European slavery and the mixing it entailed, leading today's readers to find the idea of *white* slavery far-fetched. But in the land we now call Europe, most slaves were white, and that fact was unremarkable.

3

WHITE SLAVERY

A notion of freedom lies at the core of the American idea of whiteness. Accordingly, the concept of slavery—at any time, in any society—calls up racial difference, carving a permanent chasm of race between the free and the enslaved. Any good library embodies this logic by housing a literature of African slavery stretching tens of linear feet. This bibliography seems infinite compared with the literature of white slavery, for the American conventions of slavery have blanketed the topic. Slavery in the Roman empire may be recalled primarily through film and historical fiction, but the Vikings of the Dark Ages are hardly remembered as the preeminent slavers they actually were. If we are to understand the peopling of Europe with its great mixing of folk, we must take Vikings—those great movers of people—into account.

Vikings raided northern Europe and Russia hundreds of times in the fifth to the eleventh century, plundering as they went and scooping up human chattel by the thousands. To sell the enslaved, a system of permanent markets evolved around settlements like Novgorod (where Vikings warehoused and distributed the people they captured or purchased along the rivers Don, Volga, and Dnieper) and in Bristol and Dublin (where they gathered hapless westerners from Germany through the Iberian Peninsula). It is said that Dublin was Europe's largest slave market during the eleventh century. The Viking slave trades, eastern and western, carried northern European slaves to neighboring localities or into wealthy Mediterranean lands.[1]* These slave businesses changed the face of Europe.

History's most famous British slave of the early medieval period is Patrick, born Succat, Ireland's patron saint, who provides a cogent example. Patrick's father was a local official and Christian deacon somewhere near the west coast of Roman Britain or perhaps Gaul in about 373 or about 389 or about 456.[2] Although much of his life remains mysterious, his saint's name, Patrick, from "patrician," emerges conspicuously. Identifying Patrick as no ordinary slave matters hugely, for fourth-century Europeans harbored unflattering stereotypes of those lowest in society. (These stereotypes reappeared centuries later and an ocean away as "Sambo.") Anglo-Saxon and Old Norse literature depicts the *wealh* (a Welsh person, a slave) as drunken and sexually aggressive, and the notion that the Welsh and Celts generally were dark—had hair and skin darkened by exposure to the sun—circulated as the typical coloring of slaves.[†] In the Old Norse Icelandic poem *Rigsthula, thralls* (slaves) appear as dirty, sun-tanned people with ugly, quarrelsome, lazy, gossipy, and smarmy children.[3] The heroic figure of Saint Patrick had to be lifted out of this squalid mass, even though his enslavement was perfectly routine.

At any rate, like tens of thousands of his contemporaries living within reach of slave raiders, fifteen- or sixteen-year-old Patrick fell victim to Viking raiders, who carried him far from home. After serving six years as a shepherd and farm laborer, probably in today's County Antrim, Ireland, he escaped, an event he credited to divine intervention. Certainly the escape inspired Patrick's permanent vocation, a mission to convert the heathen Irish to Christianity that lasted some thirty years. The year of his death—461, 490, or 493—remains as uncertain as the year of his birth. Legend, however, declares precisely the day of his death, widely

---

*The Finlandic *Laxdaela* saga tells the story of the Irish princess Melkorla, one of the legions of Irish captured in Viking raids. After purchase in a Norwegian slave market, Melkorla was transported as a slave back to Ireland.

†Late nineteenth-century anthropology continued to associate dark color with the Irish, as in the anthropologist John Beddoe's "Index of Nigrescence," discussed in chapter 15 of this book.

celebrated on March 17. Another five centuries passed before the British Isles quieted down.

In Anglo-Saxon Britain as elsewhere, slaves were valuable property, worth each about eight oxen; in Ireland a female slave represented a unit of currency, like a dollar or a euro.[4] Moreover, slavery in Anglo-Saxon Britain applied not merely to the captives themselves, for slave status could also be inherited, as had been the case among the Thracians of antiquity. We cannot know how many of the British poor sold themselves and their children into bondage, but the number must have been significant, for attempts at reform were made repeatedly. Kings Alfred the Great and Canute (1014–35) tried, with uncertain success, to restrict slavery, especially with regard to daughters. Nonetheless, about one-tenth of the eleventh-century British population is estimated to have been enslaved, a proportion rising to one-fifth in the West Country.[5] So embedded were slaves in the economy of the British Isles that the Catholic Church, quite a wealthy institution, owned vast numbers of them.[6]

The Norman conquest of 1066 and subsequent unification did reduce British exposure to slave raiding by local warlords and Vikings. Relative peace, however, did not end hereditary bondage, for serfdom largely replaced slavery, leaving 40 to 50 percent of the rural population in hereditary servitude, some two million people in England at any one time.[7] The British case belonged to a much wider pattern.

The medieval slave trade exempted no one, as Viking, Italian, and Ottoman merchants moved their captives across long distances for sale. Wealthy Italy was well supplied with slaves, many from Asia. Lumped together as "Tartars," they might be of Russian, Circassian (Caucasian), Greek, Moorish, or Ethiopian descent. Viking slavers in league with Jewish and Syrian merchants from Asia Minor also shipped some of these Tartar slaves westward from Russia, and others from Poland and Germany for sale in Gaul and Italy. At the same time, Arab merchants sold North African slaves in the Iberian Peninsula.

Eunuchs were also a facet of the business. Centers of castration—

"manufacturers" of eunuchs—existed in the town of Verdun (now in northern France) and on the island of Sicily. Most of the Mediterranean region (except Greece) eagerly employed altered young men, so while the market for eunuchs shrank, it disappeared only around 1900. Farther east, Venice, a cosmopolitan commercial crossroads, controlled the market for all eastern commodities, including slaves, until the middle of the fifteenth century. Genoa and Venice between them regulated the slave trade, and Venice levied a head tax on every slave sold in the Venetian market. Between 1414 and 1423, at least ten thousand slaves were sold in Venice.[8]*

These systems held well in place until the sixteenth century, when rising prices and a loss of wealth among the Italian city-states virtually removed them from the slave trade. By then the Ottoman conquest of the Black Sea had closed sources to Italian merchants and deprived many Venetians of their livelihood. As the price of slaves increased and slaves became luxury goods, the Italian trade shifted away from able-bodied workers toward good-looking youth, especially adolescent girls. Women with a more European appearance seemed more attractive and fetched higher prices than strong young Tartars. The rare girl considered beautiful rated a higher *prezzo d'affezione*. In 1459, for instance, a Venetian slave agent bought his Medici pope a Circassian woman seventeen or eighteen years old, "not too delicate in face, but of good appearance."[9] Obviously a welcome purchase, this union of servitude and beauty would endure in the European imagination, often associated with the Ottoman harem. In Britain, to the contrary, the idea of freedom became more attractive than the image of slavery.

SLAVERY FIGURES prominently in the notion of English identity, even in the British national anthem, which vigorously proclaims, "Britons never shall be slaves." Psychologists often label so emphatic a pro-

---

*The Italian slave market demanded strong, very young women and girls, along with a few very young men. Slaves came through two central markets dating back to antiquity, at Tana, on the Sea of Azov at the mouth of the Don River, and at Caffa, on the Crimean shore of the Black Sea, both Genoese trading colonies. These two Black Sea markets gathered a varied crowd of traders and slaves alike.

nouncement a "deception clue," a hint of something concealed. In this case, the label fits, for, as we saw, Englishmen and women *have* been enslaved. The hero of Daniel Defoe's best-selling 1719 novel *Robinson Crusoe*, it may be recalled, was not only a slave trader but also a slave for two years in Morocco before his island shipwreck.[10] Crusoe's story brings together the older story of white slaves with the newer Africa-to-Americas slave trade.

In a chapter of *Robinson Crusoe* called "Slavery and Escape," we find Crusoe on his way to the West African coast when pirates from Salé, Morocco, capture and enslave everyone on his ship.* Crusoe subsequently serves the pirate captain as a slave in Salé for two years before escaping in the company of a young slave boy, "us slaves," as Crusoe calls them. Their route of escape takes them into the shipping lanes from Africa to Brazil and on to salvation by a Portuguese slaver.[11]

Crusoe's mixed experiences—of both white and black slavery and of enslavement from both sides—were not so unusual at the time. As late as the mid-seventeenth century, some three thousand Britons per year endured involuntary servitude in North Africa, even as the trade from Africa to the Western Hemisphere was gathering momentum and Crusoe was doing his part to profit from it.† It will not be lost on the reader that over more than a millennium, the vast story of Western slavery was primarily a white story. Geography, not race, ruled, and potential white slaves, like vulnerable aliens anywhere, were nearby for the taking.[12]

And then sugar made its way into the Mediterranean and on to Europe. The history begins with New Guineans' domestication of sugar long before the Common Era and continues with its spread through Southeast Asia, China, India, and Persia. The seventh-century Muslim conquest of the Middle East took sugar into the Mediterranean, inspiring the commonplace "sugar follows the Koran," as Muslims planted sugar in Syria, Palestine, Egypt, Rhodes, Malta, Crete, and Cyprus.[13]

---

* Salé, famous as a capital of piracy, lies on the Atlantic coast next to the Moroccan capital of Rabat.
† Overall about 1.25 million northern Christians became enslaved in the southern and eastern Mediterranean between the sixteenth and the eighteenth century.

In the course of their crusades in the eastern Mediterranean, northern Europeans encountered this addictive substance and liked it very much. Thus began another story.

Sugar came into medieval western Europe around the year 1000 in a linkage of sugar and colonialism.[14] In a pattern familiar to Americans later on, Venice processed and sold the sugar that Italian, Greek, Bulgarian, Turkish, and Tartar farm laborers (free, slave, and sharecropper) produced primarily in the Venetian colonies of Crete and Cyprus, where cane grew well. After the Black Death of the mid-1300s created a labor shortage, Christian crusader kingdoms of the eastern Mediterranean resorted increasingly to enslavement. With increased enslavement of people from the Balkans near the crusader kingdoms of the eastern Adriatic—the European slave coast—the word "Slav" turned into the word "slave." Faceless masses of slaves from Greece, Bulgaria, Turkey, and the Black Sea region grew sugar for western tables until the Turkish conquest disrupted the chain of supply.[15]

The fifteenth-century Ottoman occupation of the eastern Mediterranean—of Constantinople, the Balkans, and the sugar islands of Crete and Cyprus—cut those areas off from the West and shut down preexisting trade routes into northern Europe.[16] The closure affected trade in sugar, spices, and slaves and, as we shall see presently with the travel narrative of Jean Chardin, in luxuries of all types. Its role as commercial gateway to the east ending, Venice gradually faded from northern view, except as a romantic tourist destination and art market. Though this rich, powerful empire does not figure in American race theory, its multicultural image survives in Shakespeare's *Othello* and *The Merchant of Venice*.

THE MARKET for sugar demanded other sources and other slaves, prompting the westernmost Europeans to seize the initiative. We still recognize Prince Henry the Navigator (1394–1460) as the vanguard, even though he is not well named, since he himself never went long-distance seafaring. Instead, he sent Portuguese sailors into the Atlantic and down the coast of West Africa, planting sugar on islands like Madeira and São Tomé and finding, in the process, Atlantic currents running from Africa to the land they discovered and named Brazil. Fairly soon the Americas, especially the Caribbean islands, proved so productive that sugar making became synonymous with America—and with African slaves. These new plantations with their African workforce have largely obscured the memory of the older, European history of sugar, with its Mediterranean and Balkan workforce, leaving a large conceptual gap. Yet the Gate of the Sugar Workers still marks the old city walls of Syracuse in Sicily and, clearly, western Europe's critical nexus of sugar and slavery.[17] A similar nexus involving tobacco made Europeans, not Africans, the first unfree laborers in British America.

THIS SHIFT to the west did not, however, signal an end to white slavery, for Britain was still in play. With its rapidly increasing population, religious and royal wars, Irish ethnic cleansing, and fear of rising crime, Britain excelled among the European imperial powers in shipping its people into bondage in distant lands. An original inspiration had flowed from small-scale shipments of Portuguese children to its Asian colonies before the Dutch supplanted the Portuguese as the world's premier long-range shippers.[18] Vagrant minors, kidnapped persons, convicts, and indentured servants from the British Isles might labor under differing names in law and for longer or shorter terms in the Americas, but the harshness of their lives dictated that they be, in the words of Daniel Defoe, "more properly called slaves."* First in

---

*The titles of Defoe's two 1722 novels dealing with Britons transported to Virginia reveal their plots: The FORTUNES AND MISFORTUNES of the Famous Moll Flanders, &c. Who was Born in NEWGATE, and during a Life of continu'd Variety for Threescore Years, besides her Childhood, was Twelve Year a Whore, five times a Wife (whereof once to her own Brother) Twelve Year a Thief Eight Year a Transported Felon in Virginia, at last grew Rich, liv'd Honest, and died a Penitent. Written from her own MEMORANDUMS and The History of the most remarkable life, and extraordinary adventures of the truly Honourable Colonel Jacque, vulgarly called Colonel Jack, who was born a gentleman, put apprentice to a pickpocket, flourished six and twenty years a thief, and was then kidnapped to Virginia; came back a merchant; was five times married to four whores; went into the wars; behaved bravely; got preferment; was made colonel of a regiment; returned again to England; followed the fortunes of the Chevalier de St. George; was taken at the Preston rebellion; received his pardon from the late King; is now at the head of his regiment, in the service of the Czarina, fighting against the Turks, completing a life of wonders, and resolves to die a general.

Barbados, then in Jamaica, then in North America, notably in Virginia, Maryland, and Pennsylvania, bound Britons, Scots, and Irish furnished a crucial workforce in the Americas in the seventeenth and eighteenth centuries. In 1618 the City of London and the Virginia Company forged an agreement to transport vagrant children. London would pay £5 per head to the company for shipment on the *Duty*, hence the children's sobriquet *"Duty* boys." Supposedly bound for apprenticeship, these homeless children—a quarter of them girls—were then sold into field labor for twenty pounds of tobacco each.[19]

A first shipment of 100 homeless children landed in Virginia around Easter in 1619, some four months before the arrival of "20 and odd Negroes" became the symbolic ancestry of African Americans. And so it went, with Africans and Britons, both ostensibly indentured servants, living under complete control of their masters, subject to sale as chattel at any time. The Virginia Company, ever entrepreneurial, also transported poor women on "bridal boats," selling them in Virginia and Maryland for 120 pounds of tobacco. At this point in the seventeenth century, Britons, male and female, outnumbered Africans in American tobacco fields; even by the middle of the century, when Virginia's population of settlers numbered about 11,000, only some 300 were African. Any of them—African, British, Scottish, or Irish—were lucky to outlive their terms of service. Of the 300 children shipped from Britain between 1619 and 1622, only 12 were still alive in 1624.[20]

Most of those forcibly transported ended up in the Chesapeake area, but Massachusetts harbored its share of the unfree. One-fifth of the early New England Puritans were indentured servants, including eight who died while crossing on the *Mayflower* in 1620. John Winthrop, governor of Massachusetts, philosophized in 1630 that "God Almighty in His most holy and wise providence hath so disposed of the condition of mankind as in all times some must be rich, some poor; some high and eminent in power and dignity; others mean and in subjection." Puritans "mean and in subjection," like all the other unfortunates of any race, could be and were sold into bondage in Virginia.[21] Oliver Cromwell's government had begun sending people abroad as indentured servants as a means of putting down an Irish Catholic insurrection, sending some 12,000 political prisoners to Barbados between 1648 and 1655, where voluntary indentured servants had been going since 1627.[22] Field laborer was the role of a white underclass in seventeenth-century North America.

It was a handsome business, this transport of the unwilling. And it endured. Faced with an overflowing prison population, Parliament passed the Transportation Act in 1718, allowing for the removal of convicts to the North American colonies. Tens of thousands were corralled under the act, convicts seen as scarcely human, already known as "crackers," and routinely labeled "scum and dregs."[23] Benjamin Franklin, an eloquent spokesman for the colonists' loathing, proposed that in return for the convicts, Americans send the mother country a like number of rattlesnakes. Between the beginnings of the trade and its ending during the American Revolution, some 50,000 convicts were forcibly transported to British North America.[24] Shortly after American independence, Britain, in need of another outlet, began shipping its convicts—some 160,000 before 1868, when the practice ceased—to Australia, continuing the process for another ninety years.

In sum, before an eighteenth-century boom in the African slave trade, between one-half and two-thirds of all early white immigrants to the British colonies in the Western Hemisphere came as unfree laborers, some 300,000 to 400,000 people.[25]* The eighteenth century created the now familiar equation that converts race to black and black to slave.

---

* Present-day white nationalists resenting the burden of black slavery in terms of white guilt and black demands for redress seek to remind Americans of the history of white slavery. *They Were White and They Were Slaves*, by Michael A. Hoffman II, for instance, begins with the protest, "Today, not a tear is shed for the sufferings of millions of our own enslaved forefathers. 200 years of White slavery in America have been almost completely obliterated from the collective memory of the American People." Drawing on historical scholarship, Hoffman nonetheless blames "professorcrats" and "the corporate media" for hiding information about enslaved whites from the public.

4

WHITE SLAVERY
AS BEAUTY IDEAL

As the eighteenth-century science of race developed in Europe, influential scholars referred to two kinds of slavery in their anthropological works. Nearly always those associated with brute labor—Africans and Tartars primarily—emerged as ugly, while the luxury slaves, those valued for sex and gendered as female—the Circassians, Georgians, and Caucasians of the Black Sea region—came to figure as epitomes of human beauty. By the nineteenth century, "odalisques," or white slave women, often appear young, naked, beautiful, and sexually available throughout European and American art. (The odalisque still plays her role as the nude in art history, though her part in the scientific history of white race has largely been forgotten.)

Needless to say, this early scholarship was ethnographically imprecise, pairing as it did Africans with Tartars (increasingly termed Kalmucks) on the ugly side. But, clearly, figuring some as ugly and some as beautiful seemed much more important than ethnographical consistency. The relationship between slavery and racial classification brings the beauty ideal squarely into the history of whiteness.

Note the earliest known human classification scheme, "Nouvelle division de la terre par les différentes espèces ou races qui l'habitent" ("A New Division of the Earth and the Different Species or Races Living There)," originally published anonymously in April 1684 in *Journal des*

Sçavans, the journal of the Académie Royale des Sciences in Paris. The author turned out to be François Bernier (1625–88), a French traveler and personal physician to the last important Mughal (Persian) emperor of India. Bernier put forward an idiosyncratic taxonomy, one keying on four geographical divisions. It was really no odder than the thousands of other racial schemes to follow.

As usual in Western literature, Bernier's four races give pride of place to Europe and extend over a vast area, including North Africa and Asia as far away as Thailand and Indonesia. (For some reason, "a part of Muscovy," i.e., the area around Moscow, is excluded.) More oddly, American Indians belong to Bernier's first, mostly European species. In the second species are people in sub-Saharan Africa, and in the third are those in Muscovy, part of southeast Asia, China, and the vast lands between China and Russia, including Tartars, all around the Fertile Crescent, and into the Levant. Georgians, Muscovites, Tartars, Usbeks, and Turcomans all belong to the third species. Alone in the fourth species are the Lapps. (Race theoreticians stumbled continually over what to do with the Lapps.)

Why such a weird configuration? At least part of Bernier's answer seems to lie in physical appearance. In skin color, the third people (Asians) are "truly white, but they have broad shoulders, a flat face, a small squab nose, little pig's-eyes long and deep set, and three hairs of a beard." The Lapps are "little stunted creatures with thick legs, large shoulders, short neck, and a face elongated immensely; very ugly and partaking much of the bear."

Veering off toward sexual desire, Bernier dedicates more than half his paper to the relative beauty of women, employing phrases that became commonplace and ideas fated for oblivion. Showing a certain relativism, Bernier admits that each people will have its hierarchy of beautiful and ugly women, but, he insists, some peoples really are better looking than others: "You have heard so much said [already of] the beauty of the Greeks," he says, and "all the Levantines and all the travelers" agree that "the handsomest women of the world are to be found . . . [among the] immense quantity of slaves who come to them from Mingrelia, Georgia, and Circassia." Nothing beyond the commonplace so far. But Bernier continues, speaking, he says, only for himself: "I have never seen anything more beautiful" than the naked black slave girls for sale at Moka, in the Indian Ocean off the coast of East Africa.[1]

While Bernier's paper appeared in a prestigious journal and laid a lot of groundwork, its brevity soon consigned it to history's footnotes. A longer travel account by Jean Chardin appearing five years later gained much wider circulation. Its depiction of the beautiful white slave echoes through the ages.

JEAN-BAPTISTE CHARDIN (1643–1713)—also known as Sir John Chardin—a French Protestant (Huguenot) whose family were jewelers to the court of Louis XIV, traveled routinely to Persia and India in the 1670s and 1680s seeking rare baubles for the French royal household.[*] His two-volume account *Journal du Voyage du Chevalier Chardin en Perse & aux Indes Orientales, par la Mer Noire & par la Colchide* (*The Travels of Sir John Chardin into Persia and the East Indies, 1673–1677*) (1689) describes a trip that deviated from his usual route. Preventing his going via Venice through Constantinople to Asia Minor, local disputes rerouted Chardin north of Constantinople through the wilds of the Caucasus (today's Chechnya) and Georgia. In the seventeenth century, this was untamed country, according to Chardin the lands of "people without Religion, & without Police." A scientist at heart, he took meticulous notes while racked by constant fear.[2] Chardin loathed this chaotic Black Sea region, where brigands controlled the highways, often threatening his goods, his freedom, and his life. As he says of the Circassians,[†] "it is impossible for them to glimpse an opportunity for thievery without taking advantage of it." They eat with their hands, go to the bathroom right next to where they eat, and then continue eating without washing.[3] Chardin is totally disgusted.

---

[*] This Jean Chardin is not to be confused with the French still-life and genre painter Jean-Baptiste-Siméon Chardin (1699–1779). The painter Chardin influenced nineteenth- and twentieth-century impressionist painters such as Vincent Van Gogh, Paul Cézanne, Henri Matisse, and the cubist Georges Braque.

[†] Chardin uses the Turkish form, *Cherkes*, of Circassian.

The habits of the Mingrelians (Caucasian people on the northeast coast of the Black Sea) are vile. They "and their neighbors are huge drunkards, worse than the Germans and all the northern Europeans when it comes to drink." Not only do Mingrelians consider assassination, murder, and incest as admirable traits, they steal each other's wives without compunction. The women are not much better; they wear too much makeup, and their bodily stench overcomes whatever amorous intention their appearance might have inspired. "These people are complete savages," Chardin rails. "They used to be Christians, but now they have no Religion at all. They live in wooden cabins and go around practically naked. . . . The only people who go there are slave traders."[4]

The hugely profitable slave trade powered the Black Sea economy. Turks made the money, but Mingrelians supplied the goods. Chardin deplores Mingrelians' unbelievable "inhumanity—their cruelty toward their compatriots and even people of their own blood. . . . They sell their wives and children, kidnap the children of their neighbors, and do the same thing. They even sell their own children, their wives, and their mothers." Chardin was appalled to find "these miserable creatures were not beaten down; they seemed not to feel the tragedy of their condition. . . . Knowing their value as slaves, women are erotically adept and entirely shameless when it comes to the language of love."[5]

And a precise value it is, too. The cargo of Chardin's Black Sea vessel sold according to an erotic price scale. Pretty girls aged thirteen to eighteen went for twenty crowns,* plainer girls for less. Women went for twelve crowns, children for three or four. Men aged twenty-five to forty sold for fifteen crowns, those older for only eight or ten. A Greek merchant whose room was near Chardin's bought a woman and her baby at the breast for twelve crowns.

The woman was twenty-five years old, with a smooth, even, lily-white complexion and admirably beautiful features. I have never before seen

---

* Chardin gives the prices in *ecus* (crowns) worth about £3 silver each. Thus pretty young girls and livestock cost about the same per head.

such beautifully rounded breasts. That beautiful woman inspired overall sensations of desire and compassion.[6]

This particular scene was destined for greatness, but Chardin found other lovely faces and figures among the people of the Caucasus mountains and, especially, in Georgia.

The blood of *Georgia* is the most beautiful in the Orient, & I would have to say in the world, for I've never noticed an ugly face of either sex in this country, and some are downright Angelic. Nature has endowed most of the women with graces not to be seen in any other place. I have to say it is impossible to look at them without falling in love with them. No more charming faces and no more lovely figures than those of the *Georgians* could serve to inspire painters. They are tall, graceful, slender, and poised, and even though they don't wear many clothes, you never see bulges. The only thing that spoils them is that they wear makeup, and the prettier they are, the more makeup they wear, for they think of makeup as a kind of ornament.[7]

The enduring legend of beautiful white slave women—Circassians, Georgians, Caucasians—dates from Chardin's seventeenth century. (See figure 4.1, "Young Georgian Girl," and figure 4.2, "Ossetian Girl.") However a twentieth-century photo of Georgians shows them as fairly ordinary looking people. (See figure 4.3, Georgians in Tbilisi.)[8]

In fairly short order, Chardin's unflattering descriptions of squalid and smelly Caucasians would fade from race theory, but his image of the powerless, young, disrobed female slave on the Black Sea acquired eugenical power.[9] So well received was the work as a whole that *The Travels of Sir John Chardin into Persia and the East Indies, 1673–1677* gained its author membership in the newly founded Royal Society of London.[10]*

---

* The great European scholarly societies were a product of the seventeenth century, with the Royal Society of London founded in 1660; the most prestigious of all, the Parisian Académie Royale des Sciences, founded in 1666; and the Berlin Akademie der Wissenschaften founded in 1700. However,

Fig. 4.1. "Young Georgian Girl," 1881.

Fig. 4.2. "Ossetian Girl," 1883.

Within fifty years, Chardin's erotic figure had invaded Western art, whose preferred term, "odalisque," derives from the Turkish *odalk*, meaning "harem room." Georgian, Circassian, and Caucasian were interchangeable names for the figure. Each term refers to young white slave women, and each carries with it the aura of physical attractiveness, submission, and sexual availability—in a word, femininity.[11] She cannot be free, for her captive status and harem location lie at the core of her identity.[12]

Along with a number of others, the philosopher Immanuel Kant (1724–1804) picked up this theme. Living in northeastern Germany, now part of Poland, Kant put forward his own ideas of race in *Beobachtungen über das Gefühl des Schönen und Erhabenen* (*Observations on the Feeling of the Beautiful and Sublime*, 1763). Here Kant actually attacks the idea that standards

women were not admitted to these gatekeepers of knowledge until the mid-twentieth century: to the Royal Society in 1945, the Berlin Academie der Wissenschaften in 1949, and the Académie des Sciences in 1979. Women were long the subjects of scientific knowledge, but not acknowledged as creators of knowledge.

of human beauty may differ by culture. Beauty ideals are universal, he maintains, for "the sort of beauty we have called the *pretty figure* is judged by all men very much alike." Cueing on Chardin, Kant agrees that "Circassian and Georgian maidens have always been considered extremely pretty by all Europeans who travel through their lands," as well as by Turks, Arabs, and Persians. He even picks up Chardin's statement that Persians beautify their offspring through connection with slave women and deplores

Fig. 4.3. Georgians reading in the "Square of the Heroes of the Soviet Union in Tbilisi," in Corliss Lamont, The Peoples of the Soviet Union (1946).

the fact that great fortunes could arise from a "wicked commerce in such beautiful creatures" sold to "self-indulgent rich men."[13] Only one ambivalence appears in Kant's analysis: the progeny of such unethical unions often turned out to be beautiful, and clearly, Kant concludes, Turks, Arabs, and Persians (Kant lumps them together in ugliness) could use a lot of genetic help.

Next to weigh in was one of Kant's younger East Prussian colleagues, the philosopher Johann Gottfried von Herder (1744–1803), who remains almost as influential. Although remembered for questioning the idea of an unchanging, universal human nature, Herder's *Ideen zur Philosophie der Geschichte der Menschheit* (*Ideas for the Philosophy of History of Humanity*, 1784–91) carries on by connecting servitude, beauty, and the Black Sea / Caspian Sea region, "this centre of beautiful forms." Like Kant's treatise, Herder's text—when translated into English—echoes Chardin, but changing Chardin's Persians into Turks, and spelling with a lower-case *T*: "The *turks*, originally a hideous race, improved their appearance, and rendered themselves more agreeable, when handsomer nations became servants to them."[14] In taking note of slavery's alteration of a host society's personal appearances, Chardin mentions a demographic role that upper-class Europeans and Americans seldom recognized at home.

By EARLY in the nineteenth century, these iconic notions of beauty and its whereabouts had moved steadily westward, across France and over the English Channel into British literature. In *Travels in Various Countries of Europe, Asia and Africa* (1810), the prolific scholar-traveler Edward Daniel Clarke (1769–1822) considers the notion of Circassian beauty an established truth. The contrast between handsome Circassians and ugly Tartars appears prominently in Clarke's narrative: "Beauty of features and of form, for which the *Circassians* have so long been celebrated, is certainly prevalent among them. Their noses are aquiline, their eye-brows arched and regular, their mouths small, their teeth remarkably white, and their ears not so large nor so prominent as those of *Tahtars* [*sic*]; although, from wearing the head shaven, they appear to disadvantage, according to our *European* notions of beauty." And once again, Circassian beauty resides in the enslaved: "Their women are the most beautiful perhaps in the world; of enchanting perfection of features, and very delicate complexions. The females that we saw were all of them the accidental captives of war, who had been carried off together with their families; they were, however, remarkably handsome."[15]

Also in play were military rivalries that broke out around the Black Sea region, pitting the Russian and Ottoman empires against each other first during Greece's war for independence in the 1820s and then during the Crimean War in the 1850s.* Both hostilities brought white slavery increased attention in the West, especially once word spread that Turkish slave dealers were flooding the market with Circassian women slaves before the Russians cut off the supply. Even Americans followed the Crimean War closely, picking up European culture's enthrallment with the beautiful Circassian slave girl. This was only natural, given the American slave system, with its fascination for beautiful, light-skinned female

---

* The Crimea is the Ukrainian peninsula between the Sea of Azov and the Black Sea.

slaves and growing sectional tensions, as exemplified in the figure
of Eliza in Harriet Beecher Stowe's
best-selling *Uncle Tom's Cabin*
(1851–52).[16]*

The New York impresario P. T.
Barnum, never one to ignore a
commercial opportunity, took note
of this purported glut of white
slaves, and in 1864, as the Civil
War raged, directed his European
agent to find "a beautiful Circassian girl" or girls to exhibit in
Barnum's New York Museum on
Broadway as "the purest example
of the white race." In the American
context, a notion of racial purity

Fig. 4.4. Winslow Homer, "Circassian
Girl," 1883–1910. Ink on paper drawing,
5¾ x 8¾ in.

had clearly gotten mixed up with physical beauty. Barnum cared a lot less
about ethnicity than about how his girls looked, advising his agent that
they must be "pretty and will pass for Circassian slaves."

Barnum's "Circassian slave girls" all had white skin and very frizzy
hair, giving them the appearance of light-skinned Negroes. This combination reconciled conflicting American notions of beauty (that is, whiteness) and slavery (that is, Negro). In light of this figure's departure from
straight-haired European conceptions of Circassian slave girls, it was
probably for the better that Barnum never imported the real thing. In
truth, few in the United States knew what a Circassian beauty would
actually look like. But by the late 1890s Barnum's formulation had jelled
sufficiently for Americans that the idly doodling artist Winslow Homer

---

*William Short, so good a young friend that Thomas Jefferson called him his "adoptive son," wrote
Jefferson that amalgamation would ultimately resolve American race problems, for many mixed-
race women were very beautiful. Sally Hemings—Jefferson's enslaved, long-term consort—her
mother, and her daughter with Jefferson were all reputed to be very beautiful. Jefferson never
replied to Short's letter.

captured her essences of white skin and Negro hair. (See figure 4.4, Homer, "Circassian Girl.")[17]

The durable notion of Circassian beauty invaded even the classic eleventh edition (1910–11) of the *Encyclopædia Britannica*, which fulsomely praised Circassians as the loveliest of the lovely: "In the patriarchal simplicity of their manners, the mental qualities with which they were endowed, the beauty of form and regularity of feature by which they were distinguished, they surpassed most of the other tribes of the Caucasus."[18]

AN INTRIGUING disjunction dogs this literary metaphor—few images existed of actual people, whether in photographs, in paintings, or in the works of anthropologists. Such a deficit left nineteenth-century artists of the odalisque dependent on four sources: the eighteenth-century tradition of erotic art, all those sexually titillating scenes invented for aristocratic patrons; Napoleon's time in Egypt from 1798 to 1801, which yielded a bounty of plundered objects and triggered a harvest of scholarly books; the early nineteenth-century French conquest of Algeria, which opened a window onto the Ottomans; and the Italian career of one of France's greatest painters.[19]

Jean-Auguste-Dominique Ingres (1780–1867), a wildly successful French painter when the French dominated Western fine art, began his career in Italy, a country rife with Eastern influences. His odalisques, epitomes of *luxe et volupté*, lounge languidly amid the splendor of the Turkish harem. They look like the girl next door, always so white-skinned that they could be taken for French. The result was a sort of soft pornography, a naked young woman fair game for fine art voyeurs. Witness *Grande Odalisque* (1814), an early Ingres work painted in Rome, which established his reputation. (See figure 4.5, Ingres, *Grande Odalisque*.) Typical of the Orientalist genre, *Grande Odalisque* depicts an indolent, sumptuously undressed, white-skinned young woman with western European features. Her long, long back to the viewer, she looks over an ivory shoulder with a come-hither glance.

Grande Odalisque portrays the subject by herself, surrounded by

Fig. 4.5. Jean-Auguste-Dominique Ingres, Grande Odalisque, *1819.
Oil on canvas, 91 x 162 cm.*

heavy oriental drapery, but many other works feature a spacious harem full of beautiful young white women. Even when "odalisque" does not figure in the title, characteristic scenery and personnel designate the scene as the Ottoman harem and the naked white woman as a slave. Now and then black characters appear as eunuchs or sister slaves. *Le Bain Turc* (1863), painted when Ingres was eighty-three years old, displays a riot of voluptuous white nudes and one black one lounging about the bath and enjoying a languid musical pastime. (See figure 4.6, Ingres, *Le Bain Turc.*)

American art was not far behind. The country's most popular piece of nineteenth-century sculpture was *The Greek Slave* (1846) by Hiram Powers (1805–73). Larger than life and sculpted from white marble, it depicts a young white

*Fig. 4.6. Jean-Auguste-Dominique Ingres,
Le Bain Turc, 1862. Oil on wood,
110 x 110 cm. diam. 108 cm.*

Fig. 4.7. Hiram Powers, The Greek Slave, *modeled 1841–43, carved 1846. Marble, 66 x 19 x 17 in.*

woman wearing only chains across her wrists and thigh. (See figure 4.7, Powers, *The Greek Slave.*) Granted, Powers's title makes the young woman Greek not Georgian/Circassian/Caucasian, and a cross within the drapery makes her Christian rather than Muslim. But even so, *The Greek Slave* demonstrates Orientalist whiteness in its material, the white Italian marble so critical to notions of Greek beauty. When this monumental piece toured the United States in 1847–48, young men unused to viewing a naked female all but swooned before it. To be sure, *The Greek Slave* was no ordinary naked woman; Powers deemed his sculpture historical, the image of a Greek maiden captured by Turkish soldiers during the Greek war for independence. Only a few abolitionists drew connections between Powers's white slave and the white-skinned slaves of the American South, where no measure of beauty or whiteness or youth sufficed to deliver a person of African ancestry from bondage.[20]

Back in France, the odalisque retained her allure. The popular and prolific painter Jean-Léon Gérôme (1824–1904) occupied the visual art summit as a teacher at the Académie des Beaux Arts in Paris and frequent contributor to the Académie's influential annual salon. His *Slave Market* (ca. 1867) replaces the usual harem with another characteristic Orientalist location. Standing before us is a beautiful white slave girl stripped for examination by buyers. (See figure 4.8, Jean-Léon Gérôme, *Slave Market.*) Once again, a black figure (here an official in the market) reinforces the painting's exotic and erotic character.[21] Not until well into the twentieth century did the genre lose

Fig. 4.8. Jean-Léon Gérôme, Slave Market, *1866.*
Oil on canvas, 33¼ x 25 in.

its attraction, as colonial populations began pressing for independence following the First World War. Oblivious to anticolonialist rumblings, Henri Matisse (1869–1954) painted a score of odalisques in the 1920s, some of the last nonironic odalisques in art history. (See figure 4.9, Henri Matisse, *Odalisque with Red Culottes*.)[22]

Where culture goes, there goes critical theory. Thus, in the late twentieth century, a new field of cultural studies called Orientalism began to explore Western fascination with the exotic East and the feminization of Muslim peoples. Although this new Orientalism squared off against the voyeurism and stereotypes of nineteenth-century Western Orientalism, it remained in the thrall of Gérôme's overpowering white slave iconography. Book jackets on two classic texts—the field's foundational work, Edward Said's *Orientalism* (1978), and Anne McClintock's *Imperial Leather* (1995)—both feature details from paintings by Gérôme:

Fig. 4.9. Henri Matisse, Odalisque with Red Culottes. *Painted in Nice, 1921.*
Oil on canvas, 26⅜ x 33⅛ in.

Said's jacket does depart from the usual female odalisque to show a
naked slave boy. (See figure 4.10, *Orientalism* jacket.) McClintock's
stays with a detail from one of Gérôme's harem bath scenes. (See figure
4.11, *Imperial Leather* jacket.) Here we see more white female naked-
ness, black figures, and interior settings, all hallmarks of the odalisque.
Yet, despite the white slave iconography of their covers, the content of
neither book dwells on white slavery. Late twentieth-century American
scholars seemed unable to escape Gérôme or confront slavery that was
not quintessentially black.[23]

Today's Orientalism no longer caters to Europeans and Americans
who might gaze lustily at naked white women. Scholars have rediscov-
ered commentary from Ottomans quite able to speak for themselves,
such as Zeyneb Hamm's *A Turkish Woman's European Impressions*,
whose letters subject the West to scrutiny, and Melek Hamm's *Abdul
Hamid's Daughter*, the harem as seen from inside, both published in
1913.[24] Furthermore, in 2005 an international coalition of individuals
and organizations set up a "Circassian World" website to strengthen

Fig. 4.10. Jacket of Edward W. Said, Orientalism *(1978), showing a detail of Jean-Léon Gérôme,* The Snake Charmer, *early 1860s. Oil on canvas, 84 x 122 cm.*

Fig. 4.11. Jacket of Anne McClintock, Imperial Leather *(1995), featuring detail of Jean-Léon Gérôme,* The Great Bath at Bursa, *1885. Oil on canvas, 27.6 x 39.6 in.*

Circassian "national" identity and teach about its past. The website includes photographs of Circassians, otherwise still hard to find.[25]

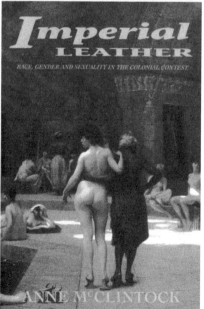

NOWADAYS, BOTH the reality of harem white slavery and the figure of the odalisque have largely disappeared, gone the way of that slavery itself.* Just as the Norman conquest of England's small

---

* That slavery still exists in the present day is chronicled in works such as Kevin Bales's *Disposable People: New Slavery in the Global Economy* (1999), *Understanding Global Slavery* (2005), and *Ending Slavery: How We Free Today's Slaves* (2007). The odalisque has not disappeared entirely, however, as twenty-first century artists use Orientalist iconography ironically. In 2005 the American artist Ellen Gallagher created one example, in which she arranges herself as one of Matisse's odalisques from the 1920s and places Sigmund Freud in front of her with a sketchpad.

kingdoms dampened slavery there, so European and Turkish imperial power closed down long-range slaving out of the Black Sea region. In the west, an abolitionist movement ended the Atlantic slave trade by the mid-nineteenth century. In the east around the same time, Russia abolished slavery and severely curtailed the eastern European and Caucasian slave trade. As this slavery faded, so did its iconography, but ideals of white beauty endured. They had become firmly embedded in the science of race.

5

THE WHITE BEAUTY IDEAL
AS SCIENCE

Historians reckon Johann Joachim Winckelmann (1717–68) to be the father of art history, a fitting tribute to his importance to the field. And while Winckelmann did not contribute directly to theories of race, he does play a large role in this story by passing along assumptions on the ideal form and color of human beauty that inspired much eighteenth- and nineteenth-century racial theorizing. The hard, pure, white aesthetic that Winckelmann popularized rested on the authority of the Renaissance, making the issue of whiteness versus color more than simply a question of taste. (See figure 5.1, Anton Raphael Mengs's Johann Joachim Winckelmann.)

Born a poor cobbler's son in Prussia, Winckelmann began his career as a librarian in Dresden, the capital of Saxony in eastern Germany. Converting to Catholicism in order to study ancient art in Rome, he lived with and worked for Alessandro Cardinal Albani, a politically powerful aristocrat and renowned collector of ancient art. At that time the study of art history was centered in Rome, for access to the glories of Egypt and Greece was severely constricted by Ottoman imperial control. Travel was perilous. Moreover, Italy was a sunny, welcoming place, and a great deal of fun, all of which appealed to eighteenth-century German scholars.

Geschichte der Kunst des Altertums (History of the Art of Antiquity,

Fig. 5.1. Johann Joachim Winckelmann,
by Anton Raphael Mengs, shortly after
1755. Oil on canvas, 25 x 19⅜ in.

1764–67), Winckelmann's towering, two-volume work, quickly became the international gold standard in the history of ancient art. This book, both a chronology and a canon of ancient art loaded with Winckelmann's knowledge, also seeks to correlate differences of style with history and archaeology. Such ambition laid the basis for scientific art historical investigation and lasted far longer than the details of his dating.

Winckelmann's main thesis held that Greek art, the finest of all time, grew out of the freedom of its culture. Going further, Winckelmann advanced the notion that modern Westerners should embrace the Greek way of life and freedom, to achieve Greek excellence in art and, presumably, all of culture. Not only did he establish a chronology and a canon of ancient art; he also championed an ideology of ancient Greek beauty based on his own gay male aesthetic.[1] At the heart of this work were beautiful boys, themselves central to making ancient Greeks into timeless, universal paragons of beauty.

The fetishization of ancient Greek beauty is not of Winckelmann's invention. But as the icon of cultural criticism, he quite easily deepened it. For instance, Winckelmann declared the *Apollo Belvedere*, already the most famous statue in Europe, *the* embodiment of perfect human beauty. (See figure 5.2, *Apollo Belvedere*.)

Like many of his contemporaries, Winckelmann had to balance his Eurocentrism against a certain cultural relativity.[2] He admits that various peoples display different body types, thus causing tastes to vary. Clearly, human beings find people like themselves beautiful. Even so, trapped in his German-Italian aesthetic, he pronounces Chinese eyes "an offense against beauty" and Kalmucks' flat noses "an irregularity" equal to deformity.[3] In the final analysis, however, relativity loses out as he adopts the Kantian notion of a single ideal figure for all humanity— "the Greek profile is the first character of great beauty in the formation of the visage." White skin, he adds, makes bodily appearance more beautiful. Throughout the Western world, these rules soon became as carved in stone as the statues that inspired them.

Winckelmann's appreciation of whiteness initially sprang from his distance from Greece. In Rome, he had near at hand a great many Roman copies of ancient Greek sculpture translated into an Italian sculptural medium. Unaware that the Greek originals were often dark in color, he did not know—or glossed over the knowledge—that the Greeks routinely painted their sculpture. He saw only Roman versions of beautiful young men carved of hard Italian marble that shone a gleaming white. Thus, Winckelmann elevated Rome's white marble copies of Greek statuary into emblems of beauty and created a new white aesthetic. It would apply not only to works from antiquity, not only to Greek art, but to all of art and all of humanity.*

For Winckelmann and his followers, color in sculpture came to mean barbarism, for they assumed that the lofty ancient Greeks were too sophisticated to color their art. The equation of color with primi-

Fig. 5.2. Apollo Belvedere (detail). Roman marble copy of Greek bronze original.

---

* In 1873, Walter Pater maintained that Winckelmann's admiration of the bodies depicted in ancient Greek statuary "was not merely intellectual. . . . Winckelmann's romantic, fervent friendships with young men [brought] him into contact with the pride of the human form." Winckelmann disdained art depicting women, for he considered the "supreme beauty" of Greek art "rather male than female."

tivism meant that experts often suppressed and removed color when they found it in the Greeks. Even now, the discovery of ancient Greek polychromy can still make news, for the allure of Winckelmann's hard, white, young bodies lives on.[4]*

Long after Winckelmann, students and museums all over the world copied classical art for purposes of education. Copying Greek art perforce employed a more common medium—white plaster—which, following Winckelmann, they purposefully left unpainted. Thus Winckelmann's white aesthetic marched on, trampling the fact that smooth white Italian marble was neither the original medium nor the original color of ancient Greek statuary.[5]†

We owe this knowledge to a Scot, Thomas Bruce, the Earl of Elgin, British ambassador extraordinary and minister plenipotentiary to the Ottoman court at Constantinople. Bruce's admiration of Winckelmann's Greeks extended to decorating his new house in Fife, Scotland, with Greek art in order, he said, to elevate the standard of British art. On his way to Constantinople in 1799, he stopped at Athens, then a neglected Ottoman backwater, intending to draw and to take away a few smaller sculptures. But Bruce's desire soon grew into lust for larger pieces, and he started removing sculpture from the Parthenon, Greece's symbol of Athenian democracy.

When local Turkish authorities balked, Bruce appealed to central Ottoman authorities far away in Constantinople. Swayed by his argument that the Parthenon was already prey to vandals, the Ottoman court finally allowed him to pry off and ship huge pieces of the Parthenon's architectural sculpture—metopes, friezes, and pedimental figures—between 1802 and 1806. The cost ultimately exceeded Bruce's pocketbook, forcing him to sell the sculpture to the British government

---

* The white marble ideal seduced just about everybody, especially race-minded experts such as the most prominent academic painter in England, Sir Frederick Leighton. In 1880 Leighton painted his self-portrait with uncolored Parthenon statuary in the background, presumably according to the plaster casts in his studio. Even Winckelmann probably realized his ancient Greeks may have painted and gilded sculpture, but he kept that suspicion to himself.

† White plaster casts of ancient Greek statuary still figured as examples of the best in art in New York City in the 1920s and 1930s. Artists like Arshile Gorky and George McNeil worked from Greek casts in the Metropolitan Museum of Art, and such plaster casts served as decoration in a coffeehouse catering to artists.

in 1816 for exhibit in the British Museum, where it remains, despite
Greek campaigns for its return.

The Parthenon marbles Elgin took to Britain do consist of marble,
but a darkly pitted Greek marble rather than the smooth, snowy white
variety more common in Italy. Here lay an aesthetic problem: whiteness versus color. The alarming history of European marble "cleaning"
includes a chapter on this statuary describing a drive to make ancient
Greek art white that nearly destroyed the art itself. In the 1930s workers in the British Museum were directed to remove the dark patina with
metal tools on the mistaken assumption that their proper color should
be white. Such a "cleaning" seriously damaged the Parthenon marbles,
prompting an inquiry by the museum's standing committee that halted
the work.[6] Clearly, Winckelmann's obsession with whiteness had a large
and lingering downside.

WINCKELMANN WAS murdered in Trieste in 1768 under questionable
circumstances on his way back to Dresden from Rome. His most recent
biographer contends that the murder occurred in the course of a robbery that Winckelmann was resisting, but other authorities suspect
that Winckelmann, an older gay man with a taste for adventure, ran
afoul of rough trade.[7]

When Winckelmann died, Johann Wolfgang von Goethe (1749–
1832), Germany's towering intellectual and the quintessence of German romanticism, was twenty-one years old. Before Goethe, German
aristocrats had studied the ancient Greek language as one facet of a
classical education. But Greek culture overall lacked mythic status, and
after centuries of Ottoman rule, modern Greeks were considered little
more than Turks. Sharing Winckelmann's love of ancient Greek beauty,
Goethe eventually added to it an adoration of Greek intellectual superiority in what an English scholar termed the "Tyranny of Greece over
Germany."[8]* Goethe's dear friend Friedrich von Schiller (1759–1805)

---

* Goethe compared Winckelmann to Christopher Columbus and concluded, "One *learns* nothing
when one reads him, but one *becomes* something." Winckelmann's birthday (9 December) has
been celebrated as a holiday in Berlin since 1828 and in Rome since 1829. Inspired by Goethe, the
English intellectual Walter Pater included an essay on Winckelmann in *The Renaissance* (1867).

wrote several poems on Greek themes, notably *Die Götter Griechen-landes* (*The Gods of the Greeks*, 1788), and Goethe published *Winck-elmann und sein Jahrhundert* (*Winckelmann and His Century*, 1805). Over time, Goethe's prestige made ancient Greek intellectual superiority so dominant that German intellectuals began to claim ancient Greek bodies and culture as their true ancestors.

Goethe first encountered Winckelmann's work as a student in Leipzig in the mid-1760s. During his 1786–88 visit to Italy, Goethe employed Winckelmann's letters and books as guides, just as Ralph Waldo Emerson would rely on Goethe's *Italienische Reise* (*Italian Travels*, 1817) half a century later. Also like Winckelmann, Goethe never actually went to Greece; in the same way, Emerson adored Goethe and the Saxons without ever setting foot on German soil.

In his own work, Goethe repeatedly addressed Greek themes, such as those in *Iphigenia in Tauris* (1787) and in the unfinished *Achilleis*, abandoned in 1800. *Faust* (1808, 1832), his masterpiece, includes an implausible section featuring Helen of Troy, herself an embodiment of perfect human beauty. In *Faust*'s second part, Helen takes refuge from an angry Menelaus in Germany. There she meets Faust, who seduces her, and they have a son, Euphorion, an allegorical Lord Byron. The most famous of the English Romantics and a martyr to the Greek war for independence, Byron synthesized Nordic and Greek ideals. Like Lord Byron, Euphorion must die. Helen follows Euphorion back to the under-world, and Faust returns to Germany.* Here we see in Goethe how the mythologies of Germany and ancient Greece tightly intertwine and how, through Goethe, Winckelmann's aesthetic dominated nineteenth-century German thought.

IN THIS Grecomanic epidemic the anthropologists of Europe played a big role. Anthropological charts proliferated during the eighteenth century, many featuring images of whiteness borrowed from fine art. Two of the

---

Faust and the Helen episode of act 3 caused Goethe great difficulty and took him more than a quarter of a century to write. Its achievement signaled Goethe's realization that Winckelmann was wrong: Germans could not re-create the beauties of ancient Greece, no matter how fine their poetry. Goethe did not invent the Helen episode in the Faust myth. He was reworking older Germanic themes and Marlowe's *Dr. Faustus*.

best-known illustrators—Petrus Camper (1722–89) of the Netherlands and Johann Kaspar Lavater (1741–1801) of Switzerland—intended their elaborately illustrated books for artists as well as for natural scientists. Camper's solid academic background in anatomy and art at the University of Leiden made him a formidable figure in both worlds. Over time he taught at the Universities of Franeker, Amsterdam, and Groningen and traveled widely to demonstrate the theoretical soundness of his facial angle, an angle between two lines drawn on a face. One line ran vertically from the forehead to the teeth; the other line went horizontally across the face through the opening of each ear. The result was a quantification of the relationship between the projection of the forehead, mouth, and chin, a relationship that was visual rather than functional.* The popularity of so simple and beautifully illustrated a method of human classification took Camper quite a long way. Welcomed in England, he was made a fellow of the Royal Society.

Camper's most famous chart (likely drawn in the 1770s but not published until 1792, after his death) delivers sharply conflicting messages in a deeply confusing manner.† (See figure 5.3, Petrus Camper's chart of contrasted faces.) Apparently comparing faces and skulls as viewed straight on with lines drawn through several points on each skull and face, the chart is intended to depict the "facial angles" of an orangutan (chimpanzee), at top left, a Negro, a Kalmuck, over to a European, and *Apollo Belvedere*, in that order. One source of confusion lies in the use of frontal views to illustrate measurements reckoned in the profile. The facial angles shown are 58 degrees for the orangutan/chimpanzee, whose mouth projects beyond his forehead; 70 degrees for both the Negro and the Kalmuck, whose faces are more vertical; 80 degrees for the European; and 100 degrees for the Greek god. Camper's order introduces a further, crucial ambiguity.

As an advocate of human equality, Camper held all along that this chart demonstrates the near parity of the human races. The numbers asso-

---

*Nineteenth- and twentieth-century racial scientists later termed the characteristic Camper measured "prognatism" and linked it to skin color and racial worth.
†On the PetrusCamper.com website of Camper's biographer Miriam Claude Meijer, this is the only image associated with Camper's work.

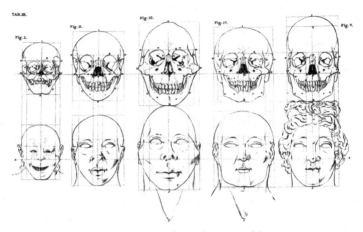

Fig. 5.3. Petrus Camper's chart of contrasted faces, 1770s.

ciated with the chart—58, 70, 80, and 100—do, in fact, reveal Negro and Kalmuck facial angles closer to the European than to the orangutan/chimpanzee and less separate from the European than the European is from the Greek god. This, Camper maintained, was his message, whose fundamental meaning lay in his numbers. He insisted on the unity of mankind, even going so far as to suggest that Adam and Eve might well have been black, because no one skin color was superior to the others. Brotherhood, however, was not the meaning the chart conveyed to others.

A far different message emerges from Camper's chart's visual layout, one that completely undercut his egalitarian beliefs. Circulating at the height of the Atlantic slave trade in the late eighteenth century, his image places the Negro next to the orangutan/chimpanzee and the European next to the *Apollo Belvedere*. Position, not relative numbers, came across most clearly. The apparent pairing in this visual architecture soon embodied anthropological truth among laymen.

European scholars, meanwhile, were asking harder questions.* In France and Germany, Camper faced mounting criticism, and in the long

---

* In 1779 Camper presented his ideas to skeptical learned men in Göttingen, including the young Johann Friedrich Blumenbach. Over the years, Blumenbach grew ever more doubtful of the validity of Camper's system, rejecting it as too simple to provide scientific data. Lavater outlived Camper and also came to harbor reservations regarding the usefulness of the facial angle.

run his paltry record of publication hindered his scholarly reputation. While he produced hundreds of papers and drawings, he published no one dominant book, and the "facial angle" lost credibility in academic science. By the mid-nineteenth century, methodical measurers of skulls had denounced Camper's simplistic reliance on a single head measurement. But even as Camper lost scholarly standing in continental Europe, scientific racists in Britain and the United States such as Robert Knox, J. C. Nott, and G. R. Gliddon went on reproducing his images as irrefutable proof of a white supremacy that Camper himself had never embraced. Johann Kaspar Lavater of Switzerland traveled a somewhat parallel trajectory.

As a Protestant clergyman and poet in Zurich, Lavater firmly believed that God had decreed one's outer appearance, especially the face, to reflect one's inner state. His illustrated books *Von der Physiognomik* (*On Physiognomy*, 1772) and *Physiognomische Fragmente, zur Beförderung der Menschenkenntis und Menschenliebe* (*Essays on Physiognomy Designed to Promote the Knowledge and Love of Mankind*, 1775–78) were immediately translated and widely circulated. Familiar among scholars and laymen alike, these works lavishly demonstrate the supposed correlation between personal beauty and human virtue, between outer looks and inner soul—an attractive and simpleminded notion.

Lavater amplified Winckelmann's views on the ancient Greeks, dedicating sections of his masterwork, *On Physiognomy*, to "the Ideal Beauty of the Ancients." He also repeated the commonplace that modern Greeks differed fundamentally from the ancients: "The Grecian race was then [in antiquity] more beautiful than we are; they were better than us—and the present generation [of Greeks] is vilely degraded!"[9] Although Lavater, like Camper, saw Greek beauty as typically European, he disagreed with Camper over the ideal facial angle, and this was an important feature in their minds. The forehead of Lavater's Apollo sloped backwards rather than rising vertically. Of course, none of these (to us) trivial disagreements undermined the central concept of white beauty's embodiment in the same Greek god.

Opinions swept back and forth across Europe on these racial matters. At first Lavater (like Camper) impressed practically everyone, including the young Goethe, with his vivid illustrations, and his books became best sellers. But Goethe and other supporters soon fell away as Lavater faced critics led by Blumenbach's friend, the Göttingen intellectual Georg Christoph Lichtenberg (1742–99), known then for his witty epigrams (none understandable in English and now remembered mainly in Germany). Lichtenberg had excellent reasons for mistrust. According to Lavater's theories, he—being humpbacked and uncommonly ugly in the popular view—would thereby lack inner worth: there was nothing Grecian about Lichtenberg. Camper, too, viewed Lavater's work skeptically, even though the two men shared the same conceptual weaknesses.

Scholars also ultimately rejected Lavater's views as too simplistic, yet his conceits—that the skull and face, in particular, reveal racial worth and that the head deserves careful measurement—lingered on among natural scientists.[10] Lavater, for his part, went much further, publishing books filled with portraits of the illustrious and the lowly in order to document what he deemed the close relationship between head shape and character. Both Camper and Lavater correlated outer appearance with inner worth through the instinct of "physiognomonical sensation," and both used images of Greek gods to stand for the ideal white person; others they took from people off the street. Their theories and images, a huge extension of the association of whiteness with beauty, soon reverberated through the work of authors writing in English, as Camper's and Lavater's images moved across the English Channel through the learned lectures and publications of John Hunter and Charles White.[11]

DR. JOHN HUNTER (1728–93), an overbearing, arrogant, unpolished Scot, had served as a surgeon in the British army during the Seven Years'/French and Indian War in North America. Returning to London in 1763, and now possessed of much practical knowledge, he gained high patronage positions (surgeon extraordinary to the king, surgeon general of the army, inspector of army hospitals) through advantageous political connections in prosperous Hanoverian London. By the mid-1780s Hunter also enjoyed the recognition conferred by membership in several learned societies.*

Scholarly communication between Europe and England flourished. Hunter knew Camper's work and, like Camper, had analyzed a series of human and animal skulls to illustrate gradations of the vertical profile, an exercise rather similar to Camper's work on the facial angle. Hunter compared various human skulls (*the* European, *the* Asian, *the* American, *the* African) to the skulls of an ape, a dog, and an alligator. And although he specifically denied any hierarchical intent, Hunter's imagery inspired the obstetrician Charles White (1728–1813) to think about race as physical appearance.

Like Hunter, White had made his reputation as an innovative surgeon. Specializing in obstetrics, he was known as a "man midwife" and initially practiced alongside his physician father.† As eighteenth-century industrial Manchester grew in wealth and power, White's social and intellectual reputation soared. Long interested in natural history, he increased his study of the links between various kinds of humans and animals in the 1790s. One of White's illustrated 1795 lectures to the Literary and Philosophical Society of Manchester (of which he was a founding member) appeared in print in 1799 as *An Account of the Regular Gradation in Man, and in Different Animals and Vegetables; and from the Former to the Latter.*‡ (See figure 5.4, Charles White's chart.)

Following Camper, White arranges his human heads (skulls and

---

* Not least was the London Royal Society, over which the wealthy naturalist Sir Joseph Banks, baronet, presided. Hunter so cherished his membership in the Royal Society that he named his only surviving son John Banks Hunter. After Hunter's death, in 1793, Banks refused the gift of Hunter's painstakingly collected 13,682 dried and wet animal specimens, not considering it to be "an object of importance to the general study of natural history." After being shifted from place to place in London following Hunter's death, two-thirds of the collection disappeared in the Nazi bombing of London in 1941. Like many others interested in presenting humanity hierarchically, Hunter was a conservative who "would rather have seen his museum on fire than show it to a democrat."

† White advocated natural childbirth; his *Treatise on the Management of Pregnant and Lying-in Women*, published in 1773, was translated into French and German and appeared in an American edition as well. White had studied medicine in London with John Hunter's brother William, to whom he dedicated the treatise.

‡ A well-respected medical doctor in his own right, White also published notes from John Hunter's lectures in anatomy, as well as treatises on gynecology and obstetrics.

faces in profile) hierarchally, left to right, and names them by race, status, and geography. The "Negro," whose mouth juts far out in front of the rest of his face, sits next to the ape. On the other side of the Negro are, in ascending order, the "American Savage," the "Asiatic," and three "Europeans," one the model of a "Roman" painter. At the far right, next to the "Roman" painter's model sits the "Grecian Antique," whose nose and forehead hang far over his mouth. White's text crucially departs from Camper's, however, by questioning the descent of all people from a single Adam-and-Eve pair. Occasionally employing the word "specie" rather than "race," White surmises that different colored humans grew from separate acts of divine creation. This view, soon known as polygenesis, traced humanity to more than the one origin of Genesis. Polygenesis went on to flourish in the mid-nineteenth century among racists of the American school of anthropology. While the publication of *The Origin of Species* in 1859 much reduced the allure of creationism of all kinds, Darwinism did not kill off polygenetic thinking entirely.

White correlated economic development with physical attractiveness, joining the lengthening lineage of those who considered the leisured white European not only the most advanced segment of humanity but also "the most beautiful of the human race." To close his *Account of the Regular Gradation in Man*, White poses a series of rhetorical questions focused on two persistent themes of racial discourse: intelligence and beauty.

White asks, "Where shall we find, unless in the European, that nobly arched head, containing such a quantity of brain . . . ?" The mention of brain leads to a physiognomy of intelligence that recalls Camper's facial angle; White continues, "Where the perpendicular face, the prominent nose, and round projecting chin?" He ends with a soft-porn love note to white feminine beauty that incorporates the fondness for the blush found in many a hymn to whiteness. White and Thomas Jefferson shared with many others this enthusiasm for the virtuous pallor of privileged women.* White asks, "In what other quarter of the globe

---

* In Query XIV in *Notes on the State of Virginia*, written in the early 1780s, Jefferson asks rhetorically, "Is not the foundation of greater or less share of beauty in the two races [of importance]? Are not

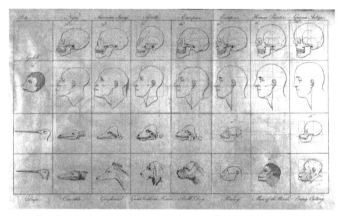

Fig. 5.4. *Charles White's human chart, 1799, in Charles White,*
An Account of the Regular Gradation in Man, and in Different Animals
and Vegetables; and from the Former to the Latter *(1799).*

shall we find the blush that overspreads the soft features of the beautiful
women of Europe, that emblem of modesty, of delicate feelings, and of
sense? Where that nice expression of the amiable and softer passions in
the countenance; and that general elegance of features and complexion?
Where, except on the bosom of the European woman, two such plump
and snowy white hemispheres, tipt with vermillion?"[12]

IN GUSHING prose or in drier scientific utterance, beauty early rivaled
measurement as a salient racial trait. While scholars seldom approached
White's exuberance of language, others of much greater influence got
the science of race barreling along, with beauty steadily rising as a
meaningful scientific category.

---

the fine mixtures of red and white, the expressions of every passion by greater or less suffusions
of colour in the one preferable to that eternal monotony which reigns in the countenances, that
immovable veil of black which covers all the emotions of the other race?"

6

JOHANN FRIEDRICH BLUMENBACH NAMES WHITE PEOPLE "CAUCASIAN"

A reader might sensibly wonder why the social sciences, the criminal justice system, and, indeed, much of the English-speaking world label white people "Caucasian." Why should this category have sprung from a troublesome, mountainous, borderland just north of Turkey, from peoples perpetually at war with Russia in the present-day regions of Chechnya, Stavropol Kray, Dagestan, Ingushetia, North Ossetia, South Ossetia, and Georgia? The long story begins in Göttingen, Lower Saxony, in 1795, and the better-known part of it belongs to Johann Friedrich Blumenbach. (See figure 6.1, Johann Friedrich Blumenbach.)

Blumenbach (1752–1840) was born into a well-connected, academic family in the east central German region of Thuringia. Recognized as a prodigy by age sixteen in 1768, he delivered a flattering address to an influential audience on the occasion of the local duke's birthday, thereby opening the way to further recognition. Seven years later, his 1775 Göttingen doctoral dissertation, *De generis humani varietate nativa* (*On the Natural Variety of Mankind*), only fifteen pages long in revision, was the fruit of a year's study with an older professor who owned an extraordinarily large and disordered natural history collection. *De generis humani* went into several editions and made Blumenbach both a medical doctor and an instant star in the German academic

Fig. 6.1. Johann Friedrich Blumenbach in 1825, Katalog, Commercivm Epistolicvm J. F. Blvmenbachii. *Niedersächsische Staats-und Universitätsbibliothek, Göttingen, Germany.*

firmament.* Now in his mid-twenties, he quickly joined the faculty of the Georg-August University at Göttingen, the most prestigious center of modern education for young German nobles. Much sought after as an intellectual mentor, Blumenbach taught a bevy of aristocrats and other privileged men, including three English princes, the crown prince of Bavaria, and the scholarly, aristocratic brothers Wilhelm and Alexander von Humboldt.[1]

The university in Lower Saxony (whose capital was Hanover) offered not only the most up-to-date scholarship but also an opening to the educated, English-speaking world, for Hanoverians ruled Britain in the eighteenth century. Thus Göttingen's situation accounts for a good part of the rapid spread of Blumenbach's ideas.†

Maintaining the status of a world-renowned scholar demanded more than profound thinking on important topics such as the place of humankind in nature. It also required influential contacts, honors, the backing of strong institutions, and something to show off—for instance, a collection of skulls or a royal garden. In the two generations preceding Blumenbach, the greatest European naturalists had tended royal

---

*The great Linnaeus, the inventor of the Western system of taxonomy, shot high even faster. After one week he received his Ph.D. for a thirteen-page dissertation from the Dutch University of Harderwijk, which one historian of science designated as a "mail-order" institution. This seems unduly harsh. Nevertheless, the University of Harderwijk was known for selling degrees.
†Blumenbach's prime years in the last quarter of the eighteenth century coincided with his university's apogee.

gardens—Carolus Linnaeus in Uppsala, Sweden, and Georges-Louis Leclerc, Comte de Buffon, in Paris, France, offer two prominent examples. In a sense, Blumenbach's garden was his collection of human skulls. And he knew how to cultivate his learned connections.

Scholarly networking explains Blumenbach's dedication of the third edition of *On the Natural Variety of Mankind* to the immensely rich and powerful English wool merchant naturalist Sir Joseph Banks (1740–1820), someone he hardly knew. Blumenbach thanks Banks fulsomely for skulls and other precious scientific items and for his hospitality in London in 1792. As president of the Royal Society, Banks ruled the natural history establishment of the day, dominating worldwide scientific exploration.[2] Blumenbach's dedication to Banks was intended to cement this tie between a humble researcher in Göttingen (still a provincial town compared with London and Paris) and a sovereign in Europe's scientific kingdom. For Blumenbach, corresponding with Banks not only bolstered his standing as a scientist with international connections; it also eased the way for requests to Banks for exotic skulls and other specimens Banks controlled.

Among Banks's many sponsorships was his support of the collection of the unique plant and animal specimens gathered during Captain James Cook's second voyage (1772–75) to the bay in newly discovered Australia that Cook named Botany. Blumenbach coveted these rare specimens for his collection, but without success. In 1783 he initiated a correspondence (in French) with Banks, sending him information on German plants. Blumenbach soon joined the legions of pilgrims to Banks's home and his vast scientific collection. In a 1787 letter back to Blumenbach, Banks explains the impossibility of sending Blumenbach a skull from the South Sea, because Petrus Camper in the Netherlands has an earlier claim.[3] But Blumenbach was not easily deterred. By dint of persistent correspondence in French and then in English, he finally wangled a South Seas skull out of Banks, who sharply reminded Blumenbach of the difficulty of wresting body parts from native peoples. At any rate, continuing to flatter the most powerful figure in late eighteenth-century natural history, Blumenbach proclaimed the South

Seas skull as representative of a new variety—the Malay—and placed it between the beautiful Caucasian and the ugly Mongolian. Thus Blumenbach's 1795 dedication to Banks both cemented a western European alliance and made an offering to a god of science. By the end of his life Blumenbach owned Europe's greatest collection—he called it his "Golgotha"—245 whole skulls and fragments and two mummies.[4]*

Blumenbach was no firebrand. He worked along strictly scientific lines of the time, advancing the burgeoning science of human taxonomy in two important aspects. First, he eliminated the popular and long-standing classification of monsters (including diseased people) as separate human varieties, a category that had appeared even in the otherwise solid work of Linnaeus.† Second, he used what he and his peers saw as a complete and scientific means of classification: in addition to the now commonly accepted index of skin color, he factored in a series of other bodily measurements, notably of skulls.

Unlike Petrus Camper, Blumenbach measured skulls in a number of ways, inaugurating a mania for ever more elaborate measurement. Placing scores of human skulls from around the world in a line and measuring the height of the foreheads, the size and angle of the jawbone, the angle of the teeth, the eye sockets, the nasal bones, and also Camper's facial angle, Blumenbach came up with what he called the *norma verticalis*.[5] (See figure 6.2, Blumenbach's *norma verticalis*.) Adding skin color to the *norma verticalis*, he classified the single species of human beings into four and then five "varieties." As we shall see, such meticulous measurement endowed the "Caucasian" variety with an unimpeachable scientific pedigree.

The first edition of *On the Natural Variety of Mankind* (1775) has many strengths. For one thing, it corrects a serious misconception about differences between various peoples. Climate, Blumenbach

---

* Germany's National Socialist regime took such anthropological collecting of skeletons and skulls to a perverted, murderous extreme.
† Less gently than Blumenbach, Buffon criticized Linnaeus for confusing monsters with races. Linnaeus also associated geography with temperament, a linkage that became commonplace in the nineteenth and twentieth centuries.

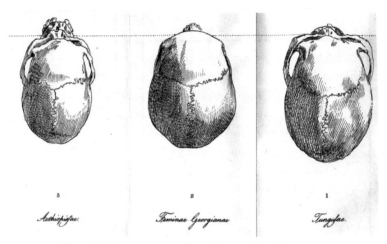

3   2   1

Aethiopisae.   *Feminae Georgianae*   *Tungusae.*

Fig. 6.2. Blumenbach's norma verticalis: *Ethiopian, female Georgian, Asian,*
The Anthropological Treatises of Johann Friedrich Blumenbach,
trans. Thomas Bendyshe, 1865.

says—reasonably but in contradiction to others—produces differences
in skin color, so that dark-colored people live in hot places and light-
colored people live in cold places, a fact noted in antiquity but subsequently acknowledged only intermittently in the scholarly literature.
He reminds readers that all individual human bodies contain lighter and
darker places. The genitals, for instance, of light-colored people may be
dark, and outdoor work darkens even people with light skin. Poor people
who work outside become darker, and European skin becomes lighter in
winter: "our own experience teaches us every year, when in spring very
elegant and delicate women show a most brilliant whiteness of skin,
contracted by the indoor life of winter." If those women are careless and
go into the summer sun and air, they lose "that vernal beauty before the
arrival of the next autumn, and become sensibly browner."[6]

Blumenbach also cautions against drawing conclusions about whole
peoples on the basis of only a small sample, a warning unfortunately
not heeded, as the world of anthropology invariably continued to speak
of human "types" embodied in the image of one single person. Take as
an example the aforementioned Kalmucks of the northeastern Caucasus

and western Asian regions, says Blumenbach. Well aware of the stereotype of Kalmucks as epitomes of ugliness, he warns us quite properly
that one traveler's drawing of an ugly Kalmuck's skull cannot sustain
conclusions about the group as a whole.

Blumenbach imagines that another traveler might describe Kalmuck
men as beautiful, even as symmetrical, and conclude that their young
women "would find admirers in cultivated Europe."[7] Blumenbach's allusion to young women's sexual attractiveness to European men evokes
a gauge common among European travelers and scholars as far back
as François Bernier in the seventeenth century. The French naturalist
Buffon, for instance, pronounced Kalmucks the ugliest of peoples, the
women as ugly as the men, but Circassians and Georgians the beautiful
wives of eastern sultans.[8]

As we are seeing, Kalmucks remained salient exemplars of home-
liness well into the nineteenth century. However, photographs from
William Z. Ripley's 1899 *Races of Europe* and Corliss Lamont's *Peoples of the Soviet Union* of 1946 show two rather ordinary Kalmucks
and a handsome one. (See figure 6.3, Ripley's Kalmucks, and figure 6.4,
Lamont's Kalmyk Sailor.) Thus assumptions about the beautiful or the
ugly pertained more to ideas than to actual physical appearance. As we
have also seen regarding Circassians, Caucasians, and Georgians, the
notion of their surpassing beauty became codified more by repetition
than by any circulation of actual images of real people.

Like other race theorists, Blumenbach walked a tightrope between
contradictions. On the one hand, he held fast to the prominent role that
culture and climate play in determining outward appearance. Even so, he
believed that certain groups maintain their distinctive physical and cultural characteristics over successive generations. Among the people of
Europe, say, the Swiss retain their open countenance; the Turks remain
manly and serious; the people of the far north keep their simple and
guileless look; and, despite long residence among Gentiles, "the Jewish
race presents the most notorious and least deceptive [example], which
can easily be recognized everywhere by their eyes alone, which breathe
of the East."[9] This last statement, delivered as scientific fact, turns up

155.   Cephalic Index 86.   KALMUCKS.   Cephalic Index 79.   156.

Fig. 6.3. "Mongol Types," Kalmucks, in William Z. Ripley,
The Races of Europe (1899).

Fig. 6.4. "A Kalmyk Sailor," in Corliss
Lamont, The Peoples of the Soviet Union
(1946).

throughout racial science, death-
less as the worship of the beautiful
Caucasian/Circassian/Georgian.

ALL OF this classification appears
in Blumenbach's first edition.
Revising *On the Natural Variety
of Mankind* in 1781, he adds the
newly discovered Malays, thereby
introducing a fivefold categoriza-
tion. Note, however, that Europeans are not yet labeled Caucasian.
Blumenbach explains that five groups, termed "varieties," are "more
consonant to nature" than the four Linnaeus had enumerated and
that Blumenbach had originally accepted.* In 1781 Blumenbach also

---

*To explain his addition of the new group "Malay," Blumenbach cites the account of Johann
Reinhold Forster (1729–98) of Captain James Cook's second voyage to the South Pacific (1772–75),
on which Forster and his son Georg (1754–94) headed a team of naturalists. Of English background,

returns to the problem of the Lapps, finally admitting them as Europeans of Finnish origin, "white in colour, and if compared with the rest, beautiful in form."[10] As Europeans continued to discover ever more human communities, increasing numbers of peoples and their geographical boundaries aggravated the chaos of classification. Blumenbach revised once again.

In his third edition, published on 11 April 1795, Blumenbach does not increase the number of human varieties. But he gamely notes the existence of twelve competing schemes of human taxonomy and invites the reader to "choose which of them he likes best." Three experts, including his Göttingen colleague Christoph Meiners, designate two varieties (Meiners's were "handsome" and "ugly"); one posits three; six designate four; one, Buffon, speaks of six varieties (Lapp or polar, Tatar, South Asian, European, Ethiopian, and American); and one designates seven.[11] Such anarchy had dogged human taxonomy from the beginning, for scholars could never agree on how many varieties of people existed, where the boundaries between them lay, and which physical traits counted in separating them. Nor have two hundred and more years of racial inquiry diminished confusion on this issue. Blumenbach's idea of five varieties gained acceptance, but it was his introduction of aesthetic judgments into classification in 1795 that gave us the term "Caucasian."[12]

BY 1795, twenty years had passed since the first publication of *On the Natural Variety of Mankind*. In the interim, skin color, not heretofore the crucial factor for Blumenbach, had risen to play a large role. He now sees it necessary to rank skin color hierarchically, beginning, not surprisingly, with white. Believing it to be the oldest variety of man, he puts it in "the first place." His reckoning includes a large dose of

both Forsters lived and worked in Germany. They published accounts of the voyage: Georg Forster, *A Voyage round the World, in His Britannic Majesty's Sloop, Resolution, Commanded by Capt. James Cook, during the Years 1772, 3, 4, and 5* (1777); and Johann Reinhold Forster, *Observations Made during a Voyage round the World, on Physical Geography, Natural History, and Ethic Philosophy* (1778). Johann Reinhold Forster was accepted into the Royal Society in 1771, Georg Forster in 1777, sponsored by Sir James Banks.

aesthetic reasoning, led by the blush.* "1. The white colour holds the first place, such as is that of most European peoples. The redness of the cheeks in this variety is almost peculiar to it: at all events it is but seldom to be seen in the rest." After white comes "*the yellow, olive-tinge.*" Then, third, "*copper colour* (Fr. *bronzé*)"; fourth is "*Tawny* (Fr. *basané*)"; last, "the *tawny-black,* up to almost a pitchy blackness (*jet-black*)."[13] Like the first and second editions, this third edition of *On the Natural Variety of Mankind* keeps on ascribing differences of skin color to climate and individual experience in non-Europeans as well as Europeans.

Blumenbach seems once again to be arguing with himself, disregarding his own equitable explanation of individual difference and yet describing *the* "racial face" of each of his five human varieties. He dwells longest and lovingly on the Caucasian, from whom Lapps, having in 1781 been allowed a place, are once again excluded:

> *Caucasian variety.* Colour white, cheeks rosy; hair brown or chestnut-colored; head subglobular; face oval, straight, its parts moderately defined, forehead smooth, nose narrow, slightly hooked, mouth small. The primary teeth placed perpendicularly to each jaw; the lips (especially the lower one) moderately open, the chin full and rounded. In general, that kind of appearance which according to our opinion of symmetry, we consider most handsome and becoming. To this first variety belong the inhabitants of Europe (except the Lapps and the remaining descendants of the Finns) and those of Eastern Asia, as far as the river Obi, the Caspian Sea and the Ganges; and lastly, those of Northern Africa.[14]

Like many other anthropologists, Blumenbach labels North Africans "Caucasian." No problem there, at least not for the moment. But by placing the Caucasian variety's eastern boundaries farther to the east than the Ural Mountains and as far south as the Ganges, Blumenbach

---

* The most accessible discussion of Blumenbach and his fivefold racial classification lies in Stephen Jay Gould, *The Mismeasure of Man*, rev. ed. (New York: W. W. Norton, 1996), esp. 401–12. However, as Thomas Junker points out, Gould's visual representation of Blumenbach's "racial geometry" conveys a misleading impression. See Junker, "Blumenbach's Racial Geometry," *Isis* 89, no. 3 (1998): 498–501.

enlarges Caucasian territory beyond the limits then becoming accepted as European.* Russia, always a problem, was sometimes placed within, sometimes outside Europe.

By bringing India into the Caucasian fold, Blumenbach was doubtless thinking linguistically. In 1786, the linguist Sir William Jones had traced similarities in various European and Asian languages to the archaic language of Sanskrit. Blumenbach's colleague and friend Georg Forster had translated Jones's version of an ancient Sanskrit classic drama into German in 1791. Others soon transformed a linguistic category, the Indo-European, or Aryan, into a race, giving rise to the idea of a biologically determined Indo-European people. By the mid-nineteenth century, scrupulous scholars had rejected any biological basis to the Indo-European/Aryan language group, but that hardly mattered. The judgment of sound scholarship did not suffice to kill off the notion of an Indo-European/Aryan race, with Germans and Greeks within and Semites outside. For determined racists, especially in the twentieth century, racial identity and language always had to coincide, and appearance would always figure in concepts of race. Race begat beauty, and even scientists succumbed to desire.

WITH THE concept of human beauty as a scientifically certified racial trait, we come to a crucial turning point in the history of white people. Now linking "Caucasian" firmly to beauty, Blumenbach remained divided of mind. Holding first place in his classification was always the scientific measurement of skulls. But second within human variety came a concern for physical beauty, going well beyond the beauty of skulls and giving birth to a powerful word in race thinking: "*Caucasian variety*. I have taken the name of this variety from Mount Caucasus, both because its neighborhood, and especially its southern slope, produces the most beautiful race of men, I mean the Georgian." A long footnote follows, quoting the seventeenth-century traveler Jean Chardin as only one of a "cloud of eye-witnesses" praising the beauty

---

* Blumenbach places Caucasians as far east as the river Ob'. One of Russia's greatest rivers, the Ob' flows north out of central Asia, passing Novosibirsk, Russia's third most populous city, and empties into the Kara Sea.

of Georgian women. Blumenbach's quote leaves out Chardin's disapproval of Georgians' heavy use of makeup, their sensuality, and the many bad habits Chardin had deplored. Now Chardin intones to Blumenbach the gospel of Georgian beauty:

> The blood of Georgia is the best of the East, and perhaps in the world. I have not observed a single ugly face in that country, in either sex; but I have seen angelical ones. Nature has there lavished upon the women beauties which are not to be seen elsewhere. I consider it to be impossible to look at them without loving them. It would be impossible to point to more charming visages, or better figures, than those of the Georgians.[15]

Beauty's charms reached into science, but what of science's bedrock, the measurement of skulls?

Now Blumenbach squirms. By turns he embraces Enlightenment science—the measurements of his skulls—then lets go to reach for romanticism's subjective passion for beauty. Yes, skull measurements count, but when it comes down to it, bodily beauty counts for more, but no, no, not conclusively. Even while extolling Caucasian beauty, he adopts a third line of reasoning meant to puncture European racial chauvinism. Consider the toads, says Blumenbach: "If a toad could speak and were asked which was the loveliest creature upon god's earth, it would say simpering, that modesty forbad it to give a real opinion on that point."[16] As in the first edition of *On the Natural Variety of Mankind*, Blumenbach qualifies his estimation of European beauty as rife with European narcissism.

Even so, he uses the word "beautiful" five times on one page in describing the bony foundation of his favorite typology, a Georgian woman's skull. It is "my beautiful typical head of a young Georgian female [which] always of itself attracts every eye, however little observant.* (See figure 6.5, Blumenbach's "Beautiful Skull.")

---

* Here, as would other so-called authorities in race thinking, Blumenbach falls back on the authority of untutored observers to reinforce his scientific truths.

THE STORY of Blumenbach's skull belongs within a long and sorry history of Caucasian vulnerability to eighteenth-century Russian imperialism. Blumenbach's benefactor Georg Thomas (Egor Fedotvich), Baron von Asch (1729–1807), is little known today. Born in St. Petersburg of German parents, Asch had secured his medical degree from the University of Göttingen in 1750 and then joined the Russian army's medical service in the imperial forces of Catherine the Great. A military man and a leader of Russia's learned societies in St. Petersburg and Moscow, Asch traveled around the expanding Russian empire both in his official capacity and as a patron of science. Regarding the latter, he collected skulls, manuscripts, and various other trophies from throughout Russia and its hinterlands in the 1780s and 1790s, specimens he showered on Blumenbach and the research collections of his Göttingen alma mater.*

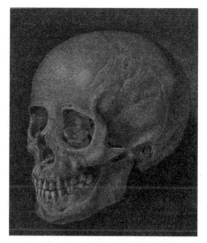

Fig. 6.5. Blumenbach's "Beautiful Skull of a Female Georgian."

In 1793, shortly after Catherine had won her second Caucasian war against the Ottomans, Asch sent Blumenbach a pristine female skull, explaining its provenance in a cover letter.[17] The skull came from a Georgian woman the Russian forces had taken captive, precisely the kind of situation figuring in so many descriptions of beautiful Caucasian and Circassian women: as an archetype, she is a pitiful captive lovely in her

---

*Asch had begun his medical studies in Tübingen and then finished them in Göttingen in 1750, with the famous Albrecht von Haller, before Blumenbach's time. Asch was born in the same year as Blumenbach's brother-in-law, the classicist Christian Gottlob Heyne (1729–1812), who was responsible for the Göttingen University library. The Asch-Heyne correspondence, begun in 1771, holds over 120 letters from Asch to Heyne, many accompanying Asch's generous gifts to the Göttingen University library. In Göttingen, Asch is known as one of the library's foremost patrons, for in addition to sending Blumenbach numerous skulls, he also enriched the university library's collection with gifts of Slavic and Persian books.

subjection. Actually, the perfect appearance of the teeth support a suspicion that the owner was a very young person, indeed, more adolescent than woman. In this case, the story continued to its tragic end when the woman or girl was brought back to Moscow. Although Asch sheds little light on her life in Russia, he does tell us that she died from venereal disease. An anatomy professor in Moscow had performed an autopsy before forwarding the skull to Asch in St. Petersburg. Ironically, perhaps, the woman whose skull gave white people a name had been a sex slave in Moscow, like thousands of her compatriots in Russia and the Ottoman empire.

Blumenbach labeled his prize skull "beautiful" and "female Georgian," going on to call the human variety it inspired "Caucasian," a mysterious slippage he did not explain. Why not call it "Georgian," we may ask, since the skull came from Georgia? The answer may lie in North America, where the newly formed United States already included a state called Georgia and, presumably, people called Georgians.* At any rate, during Blumenbach's time, the notion of "Caucasian" achieved wide circulation.

BLUMENBACH'S IDEA of Caucasian was as much mythical as geographical. On the one hand, he means the 170,000 square miles of land separating the Black Sea and the Caspian Sea, comprising the embattled Muslim Chechnya as well as Christian Georgia and being home to some fifty ethnic groups. Today anthropologists parse these ethnicities into three main categories: Caucasian, Indo-European, and Altaic. Among the Altaic peoples are the Kalmyk/Kalmuck, whom Western tradition deemed ugly. Right beside them live the Circassians and Georgians, those beautiful white slave people of legend, both in the category of Caucasian peoples. Note that in 1899 William Z. Ripley pictured Caucasians in his authoritative *Races of Europe*. (See figure 6.6, Ripley's "Caucasus Mountains.")

---

* In the twentieth century, the most famous of the people from the Georgia of Russian fame was Iosif Vissarionovich Dzhugashvili (1879–1953), better known as Joseph Stalin ("Man of Steel"), whose relentless use of power largely overshadowed considerations of his looks.

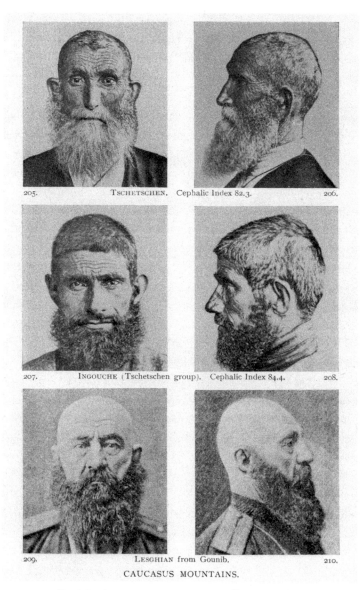

Fig. 6.6. "Caucasus Mountains," in William Z. Ripley,
The Races of Europe (1899).

WHITENESS NOW takes its place in racial classification, reorienting the science of human taxonomy from Linnaeus's geographical regions to Blumenbach's emphasis on skin color as beauty. Once Blumenbach had established Caucasian as a human variety, the term floated far from its geographical origin. Actual Caucasians—the people living in the Caucasus region, cheek by jowl with Turks and Semites of the eastern Mediterranean—lost their symbolic standing as ur-Europeans. Real Caucasians never reached the apex of the white racial hierarchy; indeed, many Russians call them *chernyi* ("black") on account of their supposed wild troublesomeness.[18] Somehow specificity faded while the idea of a supremely beautiful "Caucasian" variety lived on, eventually becoming the scientific term of choice for white people. When scholars nowadays use "Caucasian" as racial terminology, they are harking back to the illustrious Blumenbach. But the term has a more complex genealogy, too, one connecting it to the larger history of race, beauty, and reactionary politics.

That part of the story brings in Blumenbach's cranky Göttingen colleague Christoph Meiners (1747–1810). (See figure 6.7, Christoph Meiners.) For lack of documentation, we cannot know the exact degree of the personal interaction between Blumenbach and Meiners.[19] Clearly, however, Meiners, with his preoccupation with human beauty and his counterrevolutionary politics, shadows the background of German racial theory.

Both Blumenbach and Meiners studied and then taught at the University of Göttingen, where Meiners assumed a professorship in 1776, about the same time as Blumenbach.* The eminence of the egalitarian-minded Blumenbach lives on, and when Blumenbach died at eighty-eight, in 1840, his membership in seventy-eight learned societies attested to his eminence in the masculine realm of letters.[20†] Led by the

---

* Meiners's life is not nearly as well documented as Blumenbach's. The fullest recent sources for information in his regard are found in the work of Dougherty, Zantop, Britta Rupp-Eisenreich, and Carhart, mentioned in this chapter's endnotes.
† Organizations like the Royal Societies of London and St. Petersburg and Göttingen's own Royal Scientific Society brought together "scholars and moneybags" from across the Western world.

illustrious Humboldts, Blumenbach's students had supervised
the celebration of his jubilee—the
fiftieth anniversary of his doctorate—in 1825. The politically retrograde Meiners has largely been
forgotten.

During the 1790s Blumen-
bach, already the more distinguished colleague, seems to have
taken note of Meiners's volumi-
nous, if obscure, publications.[21] To
be sure, Meiners's name appears
only once in the 1795 edition of
Varieties of Humankind, but Blu-

Fig. 6.7. *Christoph Meiners.*

menbach's emphases—notably beauty (and the evocation of an ancient
Greek ideal), the repeated mention of Tacitus and the "ancient Germans'" racial purity, and even the name "Caucasian"—betray the pull
of his contrary colleague.

Both Meiners and Blumenbach focused on the same towering
subject—humankind's divisions—but otherwise their views diverged
over methodology, politics, and conclusions, converging only on the
naming of varieties and, increasingly, the importance of personal appearance. Blumenbach, as we know, accorded pride of place to skull measurement, whereas Meiners relied on travel literature, with its inevitable
ethnocentrism. Another difference: Meiners wrote hastily and at great
length, distorting the meaning of scholars he cited and filling his pages
with wildly contradictory claims. Blumenbach and more rigorous colleagues, though themselves no paragons of consistency, objected to such
sloppiness, criticizing Meiners's reactionary intellectual one-sidedness.
Meiners made no bones about it—inferior peoples' inferiority justified,
even required, their enslavement and the use of despotism for their control.[22] Beauty and ugliness, he said, led naturally to different fates. Blumenbach did not agree.

Meiners initially posited a counterintuitive binary racial scheme whose strange two-way racial classification appears in *Grundriß der Geschichte der Menschheit* (*Foundations of the History of Mankind*), published in 1785:

1. Tartar-Caucasian, divided into Celtic and Slavic, and
2. Mongolian.

The Tartar-Caucasian was first and foremost the beautiful race. The Mongolian was the ugly race, "weak in body and spirit, bad, and lacking in virtue," as characterized by the Kalmucks. Meiners classifies Jews as Mongolian (i.e., Asian) along with Armenians, Arabs, and Persians, all of whom Blumenbach defined as Caucasian. Meiners makes his ugly Mongolian race dark-skinned. And he joined most of his German contemporaries in locating the ideal of human beauty in ancient Greece, but, he adds immodestly, the Germans rival the Greeks in beauty and bodily strength.[23]

Göttingen's scholarly community muttered a good deal about Meiners's lack of rigor and cranky conclusions, but mostly the criticism remained buried in private and rather academic letters. In any case, Meiners's fringy popularity was widespread, and his work circulated extensively. *Grundriß der Geschichte der Menschheit* went through three editions and was translated into several languages.* His circle included French counterrevolutionaries who later fed the intellectual history of twentieth-century National Socialism.

Blumenbach may well have borrowed the name "Caucasian" from Meiners. But even if that borrowing took place, Blumenbach reached for higher authority in publication. He cited the illustrious Jean Chardin, not his neighbor's cantankerous book. Though Meiners lacked the status of a member of the Royal Society, he did convince a certain circle of his own acolytes.

In the early 1790s, Meiners began to move racial discourse in Göt-

---

* The popular Berlin writer August Lafontaine (1758–1831) published a four-volume satiric novel making fun of Meiners and his ugly dark and beautiful blond people in 1795–96.

tingen beyond comparisons between Europeans and non-Europeans and to concentrate on an intra-European hierarchy of lightness and beauty, with ancient Germans on top.[24] In a series of articles vaunting the superiority of Germans among Europeans, Meiners describes non-German Europeans' color as "dirty white" and compares it unfavorably with the "whitest, most blooming and most delicate skin" of the Germans. The early Germans he describes as "taller, slimmer, stronger, and with more beautiful bodies than all the remaining peoples of the earth." Meiners maintains, following Tacitus, that Germans possess the prized quality of racial purity. By the late eighteenth century, Meiners was making claims for stereotypical Nordic/Teutonic attributes that some in the academic world would echo for another hundred years.[25] That was radical enough, but he did not stop there.

As his thought continued to evolve, Meiners teased out distinctions not only between different kinds of Europeans but also between different kinds of Germans: Germans of the north and Germans of the south. Northerners, such as the Protestants of Dresden, Weimar, Berlin, Hanover, and Göttingen were in; southerners—the Catholics of Vienna—were out.

This may seem a strained dichotomy, but, in fact, it was not new. At this time the idea of southern Germany meant Vienna, the sophisticated, nineteen-hundred-year-old capital of the Holy Roman Empire. That empire, self-proclaimed heir of the Roman empire of antiquity, sprawled across Europe from the Low Countries to the Czech, Slovak, and Hungarian lands bordering the Ottoman empire. It might have been on its next-to-last legs, but Vienna, created as a barrier against the Germani tribes, still occupied at least a rhetorical space between peoples within and those outside civilization. Thus differences between southern and northern Germans in the late eighteenth century could be thought to resemble Caesar's and Tacitus's civilized Gauls within the Roman empire and wild Germans—those northerners outside. Envy also played its part. A wealthy imperial capital, Vienna had long boasted a high culture beyond the means of Germans of the north.

Such envy coupled easily with contempt. It was only a small step for north Germans to feminize the Viennese, to turn them into soft Gauls and trumpet the enduring masculinity of untamed northerners. This anticivilization strategy gendered north and south, Gaul and German, a Gaul/French, German/German metaphor that held a promising future as an anthropological strategy. It also contained a political dimension. Like most advocates of racial hierarchy, Meiners resented the French for their revolution, which had led to unfortunate leveling tendencies in the German lands and, critically, to Jewish emancipation.

It is not surprising, therefore, that Meiners later became the Nazis' favorite intellectual ancestor, for he knew his Tacitus and built castles upon it. In phrases characteristic of nineteenth-century Teutomania, Meiners describes Germans' possession of the "whitest, most blooming and most delicate skin," the "tallest and most beautiful" men not only in Europe, but in the entire world, and a "purity of blood" that made them the physical, moral, and intellectual superiors of everyone. The ancient Germans were "strong like oak-trees," but their descendants, though still better than everyone else, had degenerated through indulgence in civilization's luxuries. Rigorous practice of the martial arts would restore Germans to their former virility and beauty. [26]

Some in Europe lapped up this super-racist theory, as Meiners attracted a coterie of French counterrevolutionaries in the late 1790s, including Jean-Joseph Virey, whose *Histoire naturelle du genre humain* (1800) divided humanity into "beautiful whites" and "ugly browns or blacks," and Charles de Villers.[27] A correspondent with Madame Germaine de Staël and an expert on Kant, Villers settled in Göttingen and studied with Meiners. With his influence on de Staël, German racial theory moved west. It consisted of a bundle of notions predicated on contrasts between European and African, but also between European and Asian, northerner and southerner, lighter and darker, and Germans and French.

GERMAINE DE STAËL'S
GERMAN LESSONS

In the world of influence and the transmission of ideas, it is good to be rich, and Anne-Louise-Germaine Necker de Staël (1766–1817) was one the richest—materially and intellectually.[1] (See figure 7.1, Madame de Staël.) Without question a giant of her age, de Staël wrote novels featuring beautiful, smart, and independent protagonists who star as foremothers for women writers to come. Reaching across time and space, her work has inspired women writers as various as George Sand, George Eliot, Harriet Beecher Stowe, and Willa Cather. De Staël also furnished a template for the American transcendentalist Margaret Fuller, the brainiest in her company of elevated spirits.[2] All of that was yet to come, but in her own time de Staël also built the crucial conveyor belt between German thinkers of all kinds and a vast audience of lay readers in France, Britain, and the United States who lacked direct access to writing in German. She publicized the genius of Goethe, the naturalist religion of transcendentalism, and the way of categorizing Europeans as members of several different races. Her book *De l'Allemagne* (*On Germany*, 1810–13), in particular, forms the vital link between German and non-German intellectuals.

Possessing "a European spirit in a French soul," Germaine Necker displayed a passionate intellectual curiosity early on.[3] Her mother, Suzanne Curchod Necker (1737–94), nurtured Germaine's intelligence,

Fig. 7.1 Germaine de Staël as Corinne, by Elisabeth Vigée-Lebrun, French painter of the aristocracy, ca. 1807. Oil on canvas, 140 x 118 cm.

exposing her to the best minds (Denis Diderot, Jean D'Alembert, Claude Helvétius, and other luminaries frequenting Madame Necker's salon) and encouraging her even as a child to write novels and poetry. Such nurturing came naturally to the phenomenally wealthy Necker family. Jacques Necker, a Protestant banker originally from Geneva, had made a fortune in the financial world and gone on to serve as controller general of finances for Louis XVI. When Germaine at age twenty married an aristocratic Swedish diplomat, her husband received a dowry of £80,000, the equivalent of more than US$1.5 million in the early twenty-first century.[4]*

Although her husband soon squandered the dowry, Madame de Staël still continued to enjoy ample wealth and a large retinue throughout

---

* De Staël's mother was famous as the love of the author Edward Gibbon and the host of a noted Parisian salon. The equivalence between £80,000 in 1786 and US$1.5 million today can only be approximate, given the difference in currency and the passage of so much time.

her life. She lived in her own château, traveled in comfort, and met other aristocrats on an equal footing. (She and her fellow exiles ran short of money while in England in 1792 only because the revolutionary government froze her French accounts.) Towering German intellectuals served her pedagogic needs. She learned German from Wilhelm von Humboldt, the Berlin aristocrat responsible for Prussia's educational system and the founding of the University of Berlin and brother of the noted traveling scholar Alexander von Humboldt.* She also employed August Wilhelm Schlegel, a poet and critic known as an originator of German romanticism, as her son's tutor.

Because she was a woman, descriptions of de Staël always mention her appearance. More charitable observers balance their evaluation of her looks with an appreciation of her brilliance. One 1802 visitor noted, "The man who should murmur against her lack of beauty would fall at her feet dazzled by her intellect. She was born an intellectual conqueror."[5] The English avatar of romanticism, Lord Byron, thought she towered over all other women, concluding, "She ought to have been a man." Like most of the men she encountered, Byron found her "overwhelming—an avalanche."[6] Her first American biographer, the American feminist abolitionist author Lydia Maria Child, began her 1832 study of de Staël as follows: "In a gallery of celebrated women, the first place unquestionably belongs to Anne Marie Louise Germaine Necker, Baroness de Staël Holstein."

But brilliance could not outweigh the nearly universal impulse to make unattractiveness—she was a fairly ordinary-looking, slightly plump matron—Madame de Staël's main characteristic. Maria Child chose to note only her "finely formed hands and arms," which Child described as "of a most transparent whiteness."[7] In linking transparency to whiteness, Child employs a trope of white beauty whose illogic has not diminished

---

* Early in the nineteenth century Wilhelm von Humboldt set German education on the classics, thereby furthering German Grecomania. Founded in 1810, the University of Berlin became known as Humboldt University when Germany and Berlin were partitioned between Western and Soviet spheres after the Second World War. In 1948 scholars from Humboldt founded the Free University in West Berlin. Since German reunification in the 1990s the two universities in Berlin have lived in increasingly uneasy coexistence.

its longevity. Transparent skin—skin with a minimum of melanin—is not white. Instead, it reveals the subcutaneous body as a mottled pink, blue, and gray. This is the "blue" of blue bloods.* On the other hand, the appearance of whiteness, of light skin color, requires some melanin to mask the darker blood vessels and flesh underneath. Thus, the metaphor of "transparent whiteness" may signify an idea of perfect whiteness in language, but it has little to do with actual physical appearance.

DE STAËL matured during an age of literal revolution. The French Revolution, starting in 1789, with its Enlightenment ideals of human equality and brotherhood, reinforced trends already underway. On one side, it undercut arguments supporting slavery and inequality, fostering emancipation even in places beyond the reach of French power. On another side, however, French revolutionary ideology annoyed conservative believers in natural human hierarchy. De Staël rather tended toward the liberal side, but her lofty social status also attracted trouble.

In fact, de Staël fell quickly on two wrong sides of turbulent French politics. The too radical and too bloody revolution trampled her preference for a constitutional monarchy, which she loudly proclaimed. Her opposition to tyranny, her defense of unlimited freedom of speech, and her outspokenness as a woman made her persona non grata first in Paris and then in all of France. At least she had places to go: fleeing Paris in 1792, she crossed over to England and then doubled back to her family's château at Coppet, Switzerland. Her parents, originally from the Lake Geneva region, had purchased the Coppet château on the lake before the revolution.

Returning to Paris in 1794, after the Reign of Terror, she leaped into politics, promoting Napoleon Bonaparte's coup in September 1799 (or 18 Fructidor, according to the French revolutionary calendar) and

---

* "Blue blood" is a nineteenth-century expression in English intended to differentiate people of the leisure class—i.e., people who do no work outside and whose veins therefore show through untanned skin—from workers whose outdoor labor darkens their skin sufficiently to mask the veins. It came into English from the Spanish *sangre azul*, denoting people of noble Visigothic rather than Jewish or Moorish descent.

maneuvering her former lover, the agile aristocratic diplomat Charles-Maurice de Talleyrand into his post as minister of foreign affairs. But politics did not occupy de Staël totally. Her literary career took off commercially with two novels, *Delphine* (1802) and *Corinne* (1807). Both feature the aforementioned brilliant, free-spirited, autobiographical heroines who soar intellectually and emotionally but must eventually fall victim to their limitations as women. *Delphine* and *Corinne* were widely translated and widely read, but *Corinne* became so famous that the very name still symbolizes a smart, independent-minded woman. This was not a figure likely to please Napoleon, whose relationship with de Staël quickly soured.

In a conflict of the "Emperor of Matter vs. the Empress of Mind," Napoleon disapproved of Madame de Staël for almost two decades, from their first meeting in 1797 until his ultimate downfall in 1815.* Toward the end of his life Napoleon reread her *Corinne*, reminding him what he thought of her: "I detest that woman."[8] Ostensibly it was her outspoken opposition to his policies and her Anglophilia that motivated his persecution, but he also simply could not stand a woman who was so loud.

And de Staël did talk incessantly, about politics and anything else. A friend called her a "talking machine." To the men who heeded her views, her femininity seemed less essential than her intelligence. Although three children survived her, she failed to embody one of Napoleon's fundamental womanly ideals: fecund motherhood. In 1803 he forced her to put 150 miles between herself and Paris. So she went to Weimar, in the Saxon center of German romanticism starring the poets Johann Wolfgang von Goethe and Friedrich von Schiller, and on to Berlin, where she associated with the brothers Schlegel and Johann Gottlieb Fichte, inventors of early German romanticism, with its nature-centered themes of transcendentalism.

De Staël had already written a study of European literature, *De la littérature considérée dans ses rapports avec les institutions sociales* (lit-

---

* The phrase comes from Charles Sainte-Beuve (1804–69), a prominent mid-nineteenth-century French literary critic and member of the Académie Française.

erally "On Literature Considered according to Its Relationship to Social Institutions," usually translated simply as *On Literature*, 1800). This work examines the literatures of Italy, France, and Germany; because Germany was only just becoming visible as a source of interesting literature, German intellectuals appreciated notice from a representative of French letters, even an exile. Even a woman. The success of *On Literature* and the warmth of its reception in Germany inspired three German research trips, in 1803, 1804, and 1807, in preparation for de Staël's greatest work of nonfiction, *De l'Allemagne* (*On Germany*).

   During most of Napoleon's reign de Staël remained exiled outside her beloved Paris, her book on Germany unpublished. Napoleon had seen to that, ordering the destruction not only of the entire 5,000-copy print run of *On Germany* but also of its plates and manuscript. Fortunately de Staël somehow managed to salvage the plates and manuscript for later publication. Such a severe blow to her writing raised fundamental questions: Should she admit defeat, give up on life in Europe, and start afresh in the New World? She and her seventeen-year-old son, Albert, secured passports and prepared to immigrate to the United States.

   IN 1810 de Staël wrote to President Thomas Jefferson, saying she and her son planned to make a life in the United States. The president and de Staël were not strangers. Decades earlier he had frequented her Paris salon. In a warm return letter Jefferson assured her that her military-aged son would find a good welcome in the United States. About Madame de Staël herself, however, he said nothing, a silence that spoke volumes about the current state of American society. Jefferson knew de Staël could never have survived a long stay in such a crude land. Charles-Maurice de Talleyrand, one of de Staël's closest friends, had spent much of 1795 in the United States as a young man, and the experience had driven him to a singular conclusion: "If I stay here another year I'll die."[9] Certainly, no American city of the early nineteenth century could give de Staël the brio she enjoyed in Paris. Furthermore, by 1810 not only was de Staël no longer young—at forty-four years old—but she was also addicted to opium, and fragile in health. She obviously needed her brilliant retinue as much as her European setting.

De Staël actually owned land in upper New York State on the shores of Lake Ontario, purchased in 1800. An important factor in this purchase had been one of New York's founding fathers, Gouverneur Morris (1752–1816), whom de Staël's family had met in the early 1790s when Morris represented the United States in France. Ever the booster, he urged the rich Neckers to invest in American land. After de Staël and her father did so, Morris advised them on the management of their holdings.

Boosterism notwithstanding, Morris joined the chorus advising de Staël to stay put. During his years in Paris, Morris had experienced the gulf between American and French levels of sophistication. In the Necker/de Staël salon at Coppet, the "Estates General of European Thought," Morris felt like a provincial bumpkin: "I feel very stupid in this group," and "I am not sufficiently brilliant for this consultation," he wrote in a letter back home. Hardly a dull American, Morris at home belonged to the highest reaches of American society. He had attended King's College (now Columbia University) and studied with New York's most prominent lawyer. No mean wordsmith, Morris wrote the phrase "We the People of the United States, in order to form a more perfect union." Among Americans, Morris could never be a bumpkin. But even upon its highest summit, American society lacked the brilliance of de Staël's French milieu. Morris described her salon as "a kind of Temple of Apollo." Utterly lacking counterparts in the United States, she would wilt and die, for Americans "are ignorant of the charms of good French society."[10]

Over to the east, Alexander Pushkin, Russia's leading poet, drew parallel conclusions. He had seen how the cream of Russian society bored de Staël to death when she visited there as a refugee from Napoleon's France in 1812. Moscow's best and brightest had tried to entertain her, but Pushkin realized they were simply not good enough: "How empty our high society must have looked to such a woman! . . . not a thought, not a remarkable word during these three long hours: frozen faces, a stiff attitude. How she was bored!"[11] Over time, Americans and Russians would often find themselves equated as members of young and promising, but crude, societies.

In any event, Madame de Staël did not immigrate to the United States. In fact, she never even visited or wrote a book about the United States and its people.* She continued to hold strong opinions regarding American society, however, and viewed slavery as the country's weak spot. In *Considérations sur la Révolution française* (1813–16) she glimpsed the possibility of American future greatness, but with a major caveat: "There is one nation that will one day be truly great: that is the Americans. Only one stain obscures the perfect reflection that brightens that country: it is the slavery that still exists in the South."[12] Unlike many others, she could not separate the institution of slavery from the meaning of the United States as a society.

MEANWHILE, THOUGH Napoleon foiled the intended French publication of *De l'Allemagne* in 1810, it did appear in London in 1813. In the early nineteenth century the rest of the Western world was waking up to the value and power of German scholarship, but knowledge of it remained shadowy in France, Britain, and the United States because very few non-German intellectuals read German. Some means was needed to internationalize German thought and views. De Staël's accessible introduction to German thinking filled that need.

De l'Allemagne/On Germany took the British intelligentsia by storm. France, the rest of Europe, and a number of cosmopolitan Americans began singing its praises. The reason is not hard to see. First, many of de Staël's readers largely shared her unrepublican inclinations and thus her conservative picture of German thought. Importantly, her chapters on German mysticism and enthusiasm ("God in us") introduced Americans to what became known as transcendentalism. But for

---

* De Staël met her last partner in love, Albert-Jean-Michel Rocca (1788–1817), a Swiss hussar, in the winter of 1810–11, when she was forty-four and he twenty-two. They had a child in 1812 and married in 1816.

our purposes, her discussion of race, which appears at the beginning of
On Germany, is paramount.

VARIOUS ANALYSTS had, through the years, posited a varying number
of European races. De Staël chooses three—Latin, German, and Slav—
tracing differences between them to climate, government, language,
and history. In her view, Roman dominance (political and religious)
had shaped the Latins—Italians, French, and Iberians—and endowed
them with earthy interests and pleasures. Being proud, she explains,
the Germanic or Teutonic races—Germans, Swiss, English, Swedes,
Danes, and Dutch—had long successfully resisted Roman conquest
and Christianization. In the process, Germans had grown more adept
at abstract thought than Latins and more deeply marked by medieval
chivalry. Regarding the Slavic race—led by Poles and Russians—de
Staël has little to say, for she considers Slavs too new and unformed
a race to have struck a balance between their European and Asiatic
components.[13]

Much of de Staël's racial commentary in *De l'Allemagne* flows
directly from one of her prime advisers on German thought, a little
remembered bicultural counterrevolutionary from the French-German
boundary region of Lorraine who thought the French ought to take lessons from the Germans.[14] After a career in the French military, Charles-
François-Dominique Villers (1765–1815) had begun studying at the
University of Göttingen at the late age of thirty-one in 1796. Between
1797 and 1800 he was a prime contributor to the Hamburg *Spectateur
du Nord, journal politique, littéraire et moral,* in which he published
some sixty articles.[15] These articles cover much of what de Staël relates
in *On Germany.*

Villers had first come to de Staël's attention as an essential guide to
the notoriously difficult philosophy of Immanuel Kant. In addition to
several short pieces on Kant, Villers published *La Philosophie de Kant,
ou Principes fondamentaux de la philosophie transcendantale* in 1801,
and he began corresponding with de Staël in 1802 after reading her *De*

la literature, with its survey of the literature of Germany.* Thereafter, Villers guided de Staël through German thought; in return, *On Germany* includes a note praising him as one always at the forefront of all "noble and generous" views: "he seems called, by the grace of his spirit and the profundity of his studies, to represent France in Germany and Germany in France."[16]

As a member of the reactionary, race-obsessed Göttingen circle of Christoph Meiners, Charles Villers felt certain that race determined culture. In an 1809 essay on German history and literature, he divides Europe between two opposite "peoples," one Gallic, the other Germanic. To Villers, Gallic literature encompasses the empire of reality, while the literature of Germanic peoples encompasses the empire of ideas. According to Villers, "our little Europe" includes two neighboring peoples whose "genius and character [fall] at the two extremities of the intellectual line which it is given to man to traverse. These are the French and the Germans . . . [who] offer in their general ideas and the views which they take of life such contradictions and such total opposition, that it appears as if all means of understanding one another were impracticable, and all efforts to do so superfluous."[17] Four years later, de Staël repeats this supposed contradiction in *On Germany.*[18]

De Staël also reiterates Villers's definition of romanticism, but in better French; she preferred to speak of *enthousiasme.* Villers had so thoroughly Germanicized himself that he expresses his contempt for the French language by speaking of "*la* Romantique," a suspiciously German turn of phrase. The French *romantisme* is a masculine noun; the German *Romantik* is feminine. She and Villers saw that German romanticism has grown out of a native national literature based on medieval chivalry and Christianity—never mind the definition of Germans as people who had resisted the Romans and their Christian religion. This she contrasts with Greek and French classicism.[19]

---

* De Staël and Villers got along famously at first in agreement on mysticism as well as philosophy. She welcomed mystics at Coppet, and at twenty-two he had published a novel, *Le Magnétiseur amoureux* (1787), whose basic theme was mesmerism. Even though relations between them cooled, she came to his defense in 1815 after he had been dismissed from his professorship at Göttingen.

The theme of French/German opposition resonated throughout the nineteenth and twentieth centuries, in belles lettres, anthropology, war, and peace. Until the turn of the nineteenth century, the genealogy of European genius and the source of its power had run directly back through the French Enlightenment and the Italian Renaissance to Greco-Roman antiquity. Villers, de Staël, and their followers took another path. In their view it was medieval northern European paganism that fueled the fire of nineteenth-century greatness.* Paradoxically, perhaps, enthusiasm for the Dark Ages and its pagan barbarians increased as northern Europe grew richer and more powerful.

For the most part, Charles de Villers's influence on *On Germany* remains in the background, much like his colleague Christoph Meiners's near-invisibility in the anthropological work and Caucasian theories of Johann Friedrich Blumenbach. By contrast, another rising leader of German letters stands at the forefront of *On Germany*'s text.

NORTHERN GERMAN genius needed an iconic figure to make the Meiners-Villers-de Staël race theory work, and it found one in the person of Johann Wolfgang von Goethe. *On Germany* contains a chapter on Goethe's intellect, additional chapters on his principal writings, and excerpts from his work. De Staël concludes, "Goethe alone can represent the whole of German literature," for he "possesses all by himself the principal traits of German genius."[20] Goethe, as we have seen, was closely associated with the town of Weimar in eastern Germany, and the German cultural renaissance was centered in Saxony. For the purposes of the present book, we need to keep in mind the existence of three different Saxonys. One Saxony, important for Europeans, would remain anchored in this eastern German province bordering Poland, with Dresden and Leipzig prominent as central Europe's richest cultural and mercantile cities. Another, western Lower Saxony produced the Hanoverian kings of England and the University at Göttingen.

---

* With roots in Renaissance Italy, the *querelle des anciens et des modernes* divided scholars in France and Britain in 1690s. The Ancients advocated the respect of models from antiquity; the Moderns preferred to take their cue from their own century (in France, the century of Louis XIV).

The third Saxony, the mythical homeland of the medieval Saxons of England, lay on the western side of the Germans lands, off between Denmark and the Netherlands on the North Sea. This third, obscure Saxony towered in importance only in the minds of British and American Anglo-Saxonists.

De Staël had admired Goethe's work since the publication of *The Sorrows of Young Werther* (1774), praising its "sublime combination of thoughts and feelings, enthusiasm and philosophy." In return, Goethe had reviewed *Delphine* positively.[21] Yet their personal relationship did not run smoothly when de Staël came to Weimar in 1807 to work on her German book. Goethe avoided her as long as possible. When she finally caught up with him, he found her hard to take, despite respecting her as a celebrated French intellectual at a time when the French led the world intellectually. She talked too much; she clung too fiercely to her own convictions (she let it be known that Goethe spoke most brilliantly only after finishing off a bottle of champagne); she did not, in short, defer to him sufficiently.[22] In the end, however, *On Germany* pretty well satisfied Goethe as a means of increasing German national self-esteem after its Napoleonic manhandling in 1806–07 and perpetual intellectual subservience to the French—and, doubtless, as a very nice puff piece for himself.

De Staël's admiration of Goethe as the quintessence of German genius contained serious contradictions. On the one hand, she conveyed his Winckelmann-inspired fascination with ancient Greece into the nineteenth century. On the other, however, she accepted Villers's depiction of romanticism as quintessentially German, stemming from medieval Christianity. *On Germany* promotes romanticism (briefly) and depicts classicism (at length) without ever solving the long-standing ancient-medieval contradiction.* Greeks and Germans frequently appear together in *De l'Allemagne*, as though modern Germans descended from ancient Greeks. They stayed together in the nineteenth century, as *On Germany* soared in influence.

---

* Recognizing the great good *On Germany* could do toward fostering a German identity, Goethe dismissed her contrast between classicism and romanticism as unimportant.

The cosmopolitan American abolitionist author Maria Child reckoned that de Staël did "more than any other mortal to give foreigners a respect for German literature, and German character."[23] And, indeed, de Staël did. London's first edition of 1813 sold out in three days. French and German editions appeared in 1814. Positively and internationally reviewed in 1814, *On Germany* inspired at least five pamphlets within a year and remained the most traveled route into German thought—the bible of the romantics—well into the 1830s.[24]

DE STAËL not only introduced German thinking to Westerners who did not read German; she clearly located German genius in northern, not southern, Germany. She found energy and imagination in the north, whereas Vienna, the cultural capital of Germany, seemed stuck in a monotonous, Frenchified past. In this way de Staël replaced Vienna with Saxon Weimar, Dresden, and other northern German intellectual centers where the identification between Germans and ancient Greeks flourished. She made German genius Saxon.

It was by virtue of such influences that, by the nineteenth century, virtually all Western belletrists echoed de Staël's and Villers's location of worthiness in the north and frivolity in the south. German theory thus inspired writers in English, and English thinkers, in turn, passed along to Americans German theories of racial meaning. With German assumptions at its base, Anglo-American thought thoroughly incorporated notions of personal beauty as an index of inner worth and of ancient Greeks as perfect beauty's singular representation.

And that was important because, while lofty themes of ancient Greek beauty and German theories of race originated worlds away from the muddy facts of American life, by the late eighteenth and early nineteenth centuries, Western intellectuals were recognizing the United States as an important white outpost. Race theory there fell on fertile ground, for the emergence of class as a dimension of race thought was already underway across the Atlantic.

EARLY AMERICAN
WHITE PEOPLE OBSERVED

North America's unique jumble of peoples appealed to Western intellectuals as a test case for humanity. Who are the Americans? What are they like? Might the United States, so far across the western sea, reveal mankind's future? Or at least Europeans' future? Some observers saw Americans as white and egalitarian; others perceived a multiracial assortment of oppressors and oppressed. Meanwhile, the government of this new republic went about its own mundane business, answering its own questions by counting its people according to its own devices.

In article 1, sections 2 and 9, of the Constitution, the United States created a novel way of apportioning representation and direct taxation: a national census every ten years. The first U.S. census, taken in 1790, recognized six categories within the population: (1) the head of each household, (2) free white males over sixteen, (3) free white males under sixteen, (4) free white females, (5) all other free persons by sex and color, and (6) slaves.[1] U.S. marshals conducted this first census, recording results on whatever scraps of paper lay at hand. The effort required eighteen months and counted 3.9 million people, incidentally a number George Washington called too low. The first undercount.

Three terms parsed the only race mentioned—white—and two categories demarcated slave and free legal statuses. (See figure 8.1, U.S. cen-

[3]

SCHEDULE of the whole Number of Persons within the several Districts of the United States, taken according to "An Act providing for the Enumeration of the Inhabitants of the United States;" passed March the 1st, 1790.

DISTRICTS.	Free white Males of sixteen years and upwards, including heads of families.	Free white Males under sixteen years.	Free white Females, including heads of families.	All other free persons.	Slaves.	Total.
*Vermont	22,435	22,328	40,505	255	16	85,539
New-Hampshire	36,086	34,851	70,160	630	158	141,885
Maine	24,384	24,748	46,870	538	NONE	96,540
Massachusetts	95,453	87,289	190,582	5,463	NONE	378,787
Rhode-Island	16,019	15,799	32,652	3,407	948	68,825
Connecticut	60,523	54,403	117,448	2,808	2,764	237,946
New-York	83,700	78,122	152,320	4,654	21,324	340,120
New-Jersey	45,251	41,416	83,287	2,762	11,423	184,139
Pennsylvania	110,788	106,948	206,363	6,537	3,737	434,373
Delaware	11,783	12,143	22,384	3,899	8,887	59,094
Maryland	55,915	51,339	101,395	8,043	103,036	319,728
Virginia	110,936	116,135	215,046	12,866	292,627	747,610
Kentucky	15,154	17,057	28,922	114	12,430	73,677
North-Carolina	69,988	77,506	140,710	4,975	100,572	393,751
South-Carolina						
Georgia	13,103	14,044	25,739	398	29,264	82,548

	Free white Males of sixteen years and upwards, including heads of families.	Free Males under sixteen years.	Free white Females, including heads of families.	All other free Persons.	Slaves.	Total.
					257,180	
S. Western Territory	6,271	10,277	15,365	361	3,417	35,691
N. Do.					540,603	3,580,353

Truly stated from the original Returns deposited in the Office of the Secretary of State.

TH: JEFFERSON.

October 24, 1791.

*This return was not signed by the marshal, but was enclosed in and referred to in a letter written and signed by him.

Fig. 8.1. "Schedule of the whole Number of Persons within the several Districts of the United States . . ." (1790).

sus, 1790.) Unfree white persons, of whom there were many in the new union, seem to have fallen through the cracks in 1790, though the fourfold mention of the qualifier "free" by inference recognizes the nonfree white status of those in servitude. Had all whites been free and whiteness meant freedom, as is often assumed today, no need would have existed to add "free" to "white." The 1800 census fixed this problem through an enumeration of "all other persons, except Indians not taxed."* For these early censuses, "free" formed a meaningful classification not identical with "white."

Census categories kept changing every ten years, as governmental needs changed and taxonomical categories shifted, including taxonomies of race. Throughout American census history, non-Europeans and part-Europeans have been counted as part of the American population, usually lumped as "nonwhite," but occasionally disaggregated into black and mulatto, as in the censuses of 1850 and 1860.

Counting free white males by age sprang from a need to identify men eligible for militia service, the only armed service of the time. To calculate each state's congressional representation, Congress counted all the free persons (women, too, although they did not have the vote) and three-fifths of "others," that is, indentured laborers and slaves. Later on, realities behind the census's careful separation of bondage and race changed, calling for new categories. As politics freed all white people and ideology whitened the face of freedom, "free white males" seemed a useless redundancy.[†]

DURING THE early nineteenth century, when "free white males" was losing its usefulness because fewer and fewer whites were not free, another phrase was coming into use, one with a much longer life: "universal suffrage." The United States was the first nation to drastically lower economic barriers to voting. Between 1790 and the mid-1850s the ideology of democracy gained wide acceptance, so that active citizenship was opened to virtually all adult white men, including most immigrant settlers. Mere adult white maleness thus replaced eighteenth-century requirements of a stake in society (property ownership, tax paying) and

---

*Indians appeared in the census of 1800, and colored people gained their own category in 1820; thereafter, the races broke down into white, black, and mulatto in 1850. Chinese people appeared in 1870.

†The census of 1840 asked for the number of "free white males and females" and "free colored males and females." By 1850 the question addressed simply "each free person in a household." The three-fifths clause remains in article 1, section 2, paragraph 3 of the U.S. Constitution, however, in which people bound to a term of servitude—presumably white—are counted as whole persons.

political independence (one's own steady income) before a man could vote. With the vote came inclusion in public life, so that the antebellum period associated with the rise of the Jacksonian common man witnessed the first major extension of the meaning of what it meant to be American.[2]

All women, people ineligible to become citizens (Native American Indians and Asians), the enslaved, and free people of African descent outside New England continued to be excluded, as well as paupers, felons, and transients such as canal workers and sailors. (Even today, children, noncitizens, and most convicted felons cannot vote. People who cannot meet residency requirements and do not register prior to voting are also disenfranchised.) In this situation, "universal suffrage" meant adult white male suffrage, though from time to time the definition of "white" came into question. Were men with one black and one white parent or three white and one black grandparent "white"? Did "white" mean only Anglo-Saxons, or all men considered Caucasian, including those classed as Celts?*

The abolition of economic barriers to voting by white men made the United States, in the then common parlance, "a white man's country," a polity defined by race and limited to white men. Once prerequisites for active citizenship came down to maleness and whiteness, poor men could be welcomed into the definition of American, as long as they could be defined as white—the first enlargement of American whiteness.

WE CAN date the pairing of "American" with descendants of Europeans to the quickly translated, widely read, and endlessly quoted *Letters from an American Farmer* of 1782, by the French soldier-diplomat-author Michel-Guillaume-Jean de Crèvecoeur (1735–1813). Crèvecoeur inaugurated a hardy tradition, that of contrasting class-riven Europe, the land of opulent aristocrats and destitute peasants, with the egalitarian United States, home of mobility and democracy.

---

* Rhode Island delayed ratification of the Fifteenth Amendment to the Constitution until 1870, because legislators feared it might enfranchise members of the Celtic race. Black men had been able to vote there since 1840.

Crèvecoeur's road to fame meandered far and wide. After immigrating to Canada and fighting on the French side during the Seven Years'/ French and Indian War of 1754–63, he moved to New York and changed his name to J. Hector St. John. The gratifying picture of Americans in *Letters from an American Farmer* and Crèvecoeur's subsequent success as a French diplomat in the United States raised him high, earning election to the exclusive American Philosophical Society, plus many a local honor. The Vermont legislature so revered Crèvecoeur that it named a town St. Johnsbury after him; it became the largest city in Vermont's impoverished and deeply conservative northeast region.

Crèvecoeur's letter 3 asks, "What then is the American, this new man?"—and answers,

> He is either an European or the descendant of an European, hence that strange mixture of blood, which you will find in no other country. I could point out to you a family whose grandfather was an Englishman, whose wife was Dutch, whose son married a French woman, and whose present four sons have now four wives of different nations. He is an American who, leaving behind him all his ancient prejudices and manners, receives new ones from the new mode of life he has embraced, the new government he obeys, and the new rank he holds. . . . Here individuals of all nations are melted into a new race whose labors and posterity will one day cause great changes in the world. . . . From involuntary idleness, service dependence, penury, and useless labor [in Europe], he has passed to toils of a very different nature, rewarded by ample subsistence.—This is an American.[3]

In addition to a willingness to innovate and to think new thoughts, heterogeneous—but purely European—ancestry characterizes the American.

This "new man" escapes old Europe's oppression, embraces new opportunity, and glories in freedom of thought and economic mobility. Now a classic description of *the* American, Crèvecoeur's paragraph constantly reappears as an objective eyewitness account of American identity. But letter 3 is only one part of the story. When other classes, races, sexes, and the South entered Crèvecoeur's picture, all sorts of revisions became necessary. For instance, poor and untamed white people, particularly southerners, continued to occupy a separate category well below *the* American. While *the* American and the poor white might both be judged white according to American law, poor white poverty and apparent wildness kept him at a remove from the charmed circle. Such complexity ensured that the *who* question could not be answered clearly. But European and American observers never stopped pursuing it.

Crèvecoeur conceded the existence of other Americans—other white Americans—who do "not afford a very pleasing spectacle." He offers a hope that the march of American progress would soon displace or civilize these drunken idlers; meanwhile, white families living beyond the reach of law and order "exhibit the most hideous parts of our society." Crèvecoeur cannot decide whether untamed frontier families represent a temporary stage or a degeneration beyond redemption: "once hunters, farewell to the plow." Indians appear positively respectable beside mongrelized, half-savage, slothful, and drunken white hunting families.

Concerning slavery, ugly scenes in Charleston, South Carolina, break Crèvecoeur's heart, but his pessimism arises most from the shock of his hosts' callousness. The rich slaveholders entertaining Crèvecoeur are the "gayest" people in America—but gay at the cost of their humanity: "They neither see, hear, nor feel the woes" of their slaves or the blood-curdling violence of their social arrangements. Crèvecoeur can only marvel at such insouciance. In their situation, he says,

> never could I rest in peace; my sleep would be perpetually disturbed by a retrospect of the frauds committed in Africa in order to entrap them, frauds surpassing in enormity everything which a common mind can possibly conceive. . . . Can it be possible that the force of custom should ever make me deaf to all these reflections, and as insensible to the injustice of that [slave] trade, and to [slaves'] miseries, as the rich inhabitants of this town seem to be?[4]

Face-to-face with the realities of southern slavery, Crèvecoeur becomes the first to predict slave insurrection as an inevitable consequence of "inveterate resentment" and a "wish of perpetual revenge." This is a European thinking in terms of rampant poverty and obscene wealth and seeing the enslaved as the poor, not simply as a race of people. Thus Crèvecoeur's America is split as much by class as by race, a society in contrast with the sunny, democratic image of his more popular pronouncement.

WRITING A few years after Crèvecoeur, Thomas Jefferson (1743–1826) missed the class dimension that so alarmed Crèvecoeur. Born and raised in Virginia, Jefferson never questioned that American society was structured according to race, not class; to him, the poor people who served, including most prominently his slaves, belonged to a naturally servile race. By taking note of black people, he did not concede them status as Americans, who are "our people."

Like many other intellectuals, Jefferson held that slavery harms whites more than blacks. "Query XVIII: Manners," in *Notes on the State of Virginia* (1787), reflects upon the "unhappy" influence of slavery on the slave-owning class, scarcely mentioning the suffering of the enslaved. Rather it dwells on the price paid by the South's white slave owners. Slave-owning children mimic their parents' abuse of the people they own, coarsening their character and, thereby, their society. The white child, "thus nursed and educated, and daily exercised in tyranny," Jefferson warns, "cannot but be stamped by it with odious peculiarities. The man must be a prodigy who can retain his manner and morals undepraved by such circumstances."[5]

In apportioning the injuries of slavery, Jefferson and Crèvecoeur mostly agreed. But their theories of American ancestry conflict, for the eloquent Jefferson rejected any idea of a mongrel American, even though he fathered seven of them with Sally Hemings, a woman he owned. He also rejected Crèvecoeur's "Dutch" man—probably meaning a *deutsch* man, or German—as essential to the American family tree. Jefferson's family tree was of sturdy oak, the Saxons of England.

Throughout his life Thomas Jefferson believed in the Saxon myth, a story of American descent from Saxons by way of England. He had conceived a fascination with it as a student at William and Mary College in 1762 and never wavered in it. Over fifty years of book collecting—his personal library formed the basis of the Library of Congress—Jefferson came to own the country's largest collection of Anglo-Saxon and Old English documents.[6]

As a founding father, Jefferson theorized Americans' right to independence on the basis of Saxon ancestry. Laying out that claim in July of 1774, he makes English people "our ancestors," and the creators of the Magna Carta "our Saxon ancestors." Though the Magna Carta dates from 1215 and the Norman conquest from 1066, Jefferson maintains that the system of rights of "our ancestors" was already in place when "Norman lawyers" connived to saddle the Saxons with unfair burdens.[7] He continued to associate Saxons with the liberal Whigs and Normans with the conservative Tories, as though liberal and reactionary parties had existed from time immemorial, almost as a matter of blood.[8] For Jefferson, English-style Saxon liberty was not a trait to be found in Germans.

Jefferson's Saxon genealogy ignored a number of inconvenient facts. The oppressive English king George III was actually a Saxon and also the duke of Brunswick-Lüneburg as well as elector of Hanover in Lower Saxony. Furthermore, George III's father and grandfather, Hanoverian kings of England before him, had been born in Germany and spoke German as a first language. It hardly mattered. To Jefferson, whatever genius for liberty Dark Age Saxons had bequeathed the English somehow thrived on English soil but died in Germany.*

In the Philadelphia Continental Congress of 1776, Jefferson went so far as to propose embedding his heroic Saxon ancestors in the great seal of the United States. Images of "Hengist and Horsa, the Saxon

---

*The tangled history of the two Saxon regions in Germany would have put Jefferson off, had he sought to trace the relationship between Hengist and Horsa—who, according to Bede (ca. 730) were Jutes—and the English and Americans of his own time. Until German unification under the Prussians, provincial borders changed with the marriages, wars, and alliances of practically every new generation of rulers.

chiefs from whom we claim the honor of being descended," would aptly commemorate the new nation's political principles, government, and physical descent.[9]* This proposition did not win approval, but Jefferson soldiered on. In 1798 he wrote *Essay on the Anglo-Saxon Language*, which equates language with biological descent, a confusion then common among philologists. In this essay Jefferson runs together Old English and Middle English, creating a long era of Anglo-Saxon greatness stretching from the sixth century to the thirteenth.

With its emphasis on blood purity, this smacks of race talk. Not only had Jefferson's Saxons remained racially pure during the Roman occupation (there was "little familiar mixture with the native Britons"), but, amazingly, their language had stayed pristine two centuries after the Norman conquest: Anglo Saxon "was the language of all England, properly so called, from the Saxon possession of that country in the sixth century to the time of Henry III in the thirteenth, and was spoken pure and unmixed with any other."[10] Therefore Anglo-Saxon/Old English deserved study as the basis of American thought.

One of Jefferson's last great achievements, his founding of the University of Virginia in 1818, institutionalized his interest in Anglo-Saxon as the language of American culture, law, and politics. On opening in 1825, it was the only college in the United States to offer instruction in Anglo-Saxon, and Anglo-Saxon was the only course it offered on the English language. *Beowulf*, naturally, became a staple of instruction. Ironically, the teacher hailed from Leipzig, in eastern German Saxony. An intensely unpopular disciplinarian, Georg Blaettermann also taught French, German, Spanish, Italian, Danish, Swedish, Dutch, and Portuguese. After surviving years of student riots and protests, Blaettermann was fired in 1840 for horsewhipping his wife in public.[11]

---

*Hengist ("Stallion") and Horsa ("Horse"), legendary founders of Saxon England, were said to have come from Jutland (now part of Denmark). According to Bede in his *Ecclesiastical History*, King Vortigern invited them from Jutland to England in 449 to help repulse attacks by the Picts and Scots. Vortigern gave them the Isle of Thanet in gratitude. The *Anglo-Saxon Chronicle* makes Hengist and Horsa joint kings of Kent.

•

JEFFERSON'S ENTHUSIASM for teaching Anglo-Saxon stayed confined to southern colleges until the 1840s, and his *Essay on the Anglo-Saxon Language*, a rambling 5,400 words composed mostly in 1798, did not appear in print until 1851.* Clearly, slavery and the characteristics of black people were stirring more passion than any American claim to Anglo-Saxon ancestry. By contrast, Jefferson's *Notes on the State of Virginia* (1784) immediately enjoyed a wide and impassioned readership. This eloquent, though very self-centered, summary of American (not just Virginian) identity, impugns the physical appearance of African Americans and makes them out to be natural slaves. Not that this insult toward an oppressed people inspired only approval. One of a multitude of critics resided at the most Virginian of northern colleges: the College of New Jersey.

HANDSOME, ELEGANT Samuel Stanhope Smith (1751–1819) became president of the College of New Jersey (later Princeton College) at forty-three, its first alumnus president. (See figure 8.2, Samuel Stanhope Smith.) Both of Smith's parents had strong Princeton connections: his mother's father had been a founding trustee, and Smith's father, a Presbyterian minister and schoolmaster, also served as a trustee. Smith graduated from Princeton with honors in 1769. As a tutor and postgraduate student with John Witherspoon, an eminent scholar from Scotland, Smith imbibed the "Common Sense" ideals of Scottish realism.

Following an established Princeton trajectory, Smith went south to Virginia as a missionary and became rector and then president of the academy in Prince Edward County that became Hampden-Sydney College. His future secure, he married John Witherspoon's daughter and bought a plantation, evidently intending to remain among his appreciative Virginia hosts. However, a Princeton professorship in moral phi-

---

* Randolph-Macon College and the University of Alabama offered Anglo-Saxon before any northern college. Amherst (1841) and Harvard (1849) Colleges were the earliest non-southern institutions to teach Anglo-Saxon.

Fig. 8.2. Samuel Stanhope Smith as president of Princeton College.

losophy lured Smith back to New Jersey.

Ensconced once again in Princeton, Smith collected the young nation's honors: Yale made him doctor of divinity in 1783, and in 1785 the American Philosophical Society took him into its membership. After Thomas Jefferson proposed a measure advocating widespread primary education in Virginia in 1788, he and Smith exchanged letters in its support. The measure did not pass, and the politics of the two men subsequently diverged. By 1801 Smith had turned politically conservative enough to deplore Jefferson's presidential candidacy as likely to cause "turbulance [*sic*] & anarchy."[12]

By then Smith had succeeded his mentor Witherspoon as president of Princeton, and had turned into an intellectual maverick, downgrading the college's classics and Presbyterianism in favor of science, thereby antagonizing its trustees.[13] As Smith grew older and Princeton students more rowdy, he expelled three-quarters of the student body for rioting in 1807. When the Presbyterian Church established a theological seminary right inside the college's Nassau Hall, Smith grasped just where his lack of orthodoxy was leading. In 1812 he was forced to resign the presidency, and he died seven years later.[14] All that lay ahead in 1787, when he addressed the American Philosophical Society on differences in skin color, and his star was still ascendant.

SMITH'S ADDRESS looked back to the polygenetic essay of a Scottish philosopher named Henry Home, Lord Kames, entitled *Discourse on the Original Diversity of Mankind* (1776). One of Kames's main points was a rejection of biblical doctrine that traces the unity of humanity through descent back to a single originating couple. Smith disagreed with Kames. Every people did belong to the same species, and differences sprang from circumstance: "I believe that the greater part of the varieties in the appearance of the human species," Smith declares, "may justly be denominated habits of the body." Where people live, not their ultimate ancestors, explains variations in human skin color: "In tracing the origin of the fair German, the dark coloured Frenchman, and the swarthy Spaniard, and Sicilian, it has been proved that they are all derived from the same primitive stock."[15] All mankind descended from Adam and Eve, subsequently diverging though adaptation.

Smith's defense of biblical truth met so warm a reception that the lecture appeared immediately in print. Mary Wollstonecraft, the feminist pioneer, favorably reviewed Smith's *Essay* in the London *Analytical Review*, welcoming his insistence on the unity of mankind. Smith's distinguished physician-historian brother-in-law, David Ramsay, a Pennsylvanian living in South Carolina, pitched in. Ramsay seconded Smith's views on skin color, lauded his criticism of Thomas Jefferson's antiblack slurs, and agreed with Smith about the dominance of climate in shaping human culture. Writing directly to Jefferson, Ramsay noted that "the state of society" also plays a crucial part. In complete agreement with Crèvecoeur and Smith, Ramsay added, "Our back country people are as much savage as the Cherokees."[16]* Jefferson seems not to have replied to Ramsay. But encouraged by support, Smith continued tinkering with his *Essay*.

One influence was Blumenbach's 1795 edition of *De generis humani*

---

* Reviewing Smith's work, Mary Wollstonecraft wrote, "We cannot dismiss this article without expressing the pleasure the perusal has afforded us; it is certainly a very interesting subject; whatever tends to make *visible* the wisdom of the Supreme Being in the world we inhabit, is of the utmost importance to our happiness; the gratification of curiosity, when excited by trivial objects, is undoubtedly pleasant; but in this instance it is a fresh support to virtue."

David Ramsay told Jefferson he admired his "generous indignation at slavery; but think you have depressed the negroes too low. I believe all mankind to be originally the same and only diversified by accidental circumstances. I flatter myself that in a few centuries the negroes will lose their black color. I think now they are less black in Jersey than in Carolina, their [lips] less thick, their noses less flat." A graduate of Princeton from Lancaster, Pennsylvania, Ramsey (1749–1815) married one of John Witherspoon's daughters in 1783 in Philadelphia and bought a small plantation in South Carolina in 1792 before moving to Charleston in 1811.

varietate nativa, which Smith read in its original Latin and incorporated into an enlarged 1810 edition of his lecture, *An Essay on the Causes of the Variety of Complexion and Figure in the Human Species*.[17] Here Smith assumes that civilization, not barbarism, was humanity's original condition; uncivilized people would have regressed on account of their harsh living conditions. Different climates, for instance, create differences in human skin color—not a new explanation. Beauty is not all that important, in any case, Smith goes on to say, citing the physical attractiveness of even some black people: "In Princeton, and its vicinity I daily see persons of the African race whose limbs are as handsomely formed as those of the inferior and laboring classes, either of Europeans, or Anglo-Americans."

A bit—but only a bit—of a cultural relativist, Smith recognizes more emphatically than Blumenbach or Camper the cultural specificity of beauty ideals: "Each nation differs from others as much in its ideas of beauty as in personal appearance. A Laplander prefers the flat, round faces of his dark skinned country women to the fairest beauties of England."[18] Meanwhile, as we have seen, anthropologists of the time were debating whether Lapps in the north of Sweden and Finland might count as Europeans at all. Linnaeus, the great taxonomist, for instance, said no; Blumenbach, Germany's leading racial classifier, wavering, said yes. Eventually the question faded into insignificance as anthropology's terms of analysis moved away from questionable attempts to rank order of physical beauty.

We should note that Smith was no multiculturalist. His Americans, like Crèvecoeur's, descend only from Europeans. While acknowledging the presence of Native Americans and Africans on American soil and occasionally comparing the height of Osage Indians to that of the ancient Germans, Smith had no intention of widening the category of *American*.

Thomas Jefferson and Samuel Stanhope Smith had both prospered in a Virginia of many mixed-race people, some right in Jefferson's own family. We do not know the makeup of Smith's household in Virginia, but we do know that the two men figured the notion of purity differ-

ently. Jefferson somehow kept the rainbow people of Monticello beyond
the reach of his race theory, allowing him to conceive of a platonic "pure
and unmixed" Saxon ideal. For Smith there could be no such European
thing, "in consequence of the eternal migrations and conquests which
have mingled and confounded its inhabitants with the natives of other
regions" in a continuing process of perpetual change.[19] Smith and Jefferson found words for purity and mixture in Europe, even among
Europeans in the New World. But the African-Indian-European mixing occurring right under their noses in eighteenth-century Virginia
overwhelmed their rhetorical abilities. The leaders of American society
could not face that fact squarely. For them mixing produced a unique
new man, this American, but mixing only among Europeans.

So if climate is paramount, what of the American climate, with its
extremes of heat and cold and its stagnant waters? Not much good
comes of it, Smith feels, for it imparts to Americans "a certain paleness
of countenance, and softness of feature . . . in general, the American
complexion does not exhibit so clear a red and white as the British, or
the German. And there is a tinge of sallowness [paleness, sickliness, yel-
lowness] spread over it." Elevation and proximity to the sea also affect
skin color. Hence the white people of New Jersey have darker skins than
white people in hilly Pennsylvania. White skin darkens farther south.
White southerners, especially the poor, living in a hot climate and at
lower elevations, are visibly darker than northerners. Americans living
in different climates look different, but, all in all, Americans look pretty
much the same.[20]

To justify his tortured climatic theories, Smith has to practice a sort
of wild conflation of climate to skin color to savagery. Even when all
their ancestors were European, Smith finds that lower-class southerners
look very much like Indians and live in a "state of absolute savagism."
This idea, that living among Indians made white Americans resemble
them in skin color, enjoyed wide currency in the eighteenth and early
nineteenth centuries. Crèvecoeur exclaimed that "thousands of Europeans are Indians," and others in colonial America testified to the tendency
in Europeans living with Indians to come to resemble them in color as

well as in dress. Moreover, such a life rendered their bodies so "thin and meagre" that their bones showed through their skin. Had poor southerners been discovered in some distant land, Smith surmises, polygenesists would display them as proof of multiple human origins.[21] Echoing Crèvecoeur, Smith calls uncivilized poor southerners—"without any mixture of Indian blood"—a potential drag on American society.

So much for the bottom of the American barrel. But Smith also demeans elite southern whites like Thomas Jefferson and his self-satisfied, privileged class. In *Notes on the State of Virginia* Jefferson had scorned the poetry of the Boston slave Phillis Wheatley as proof that *the* Negro could never demonstrate genius. Smith's retort vindicates black people and insults southern whites: Jefferson was just plain wrong to deride the abilities of a race living so wretchedly, first in Africa, then in American slavery. "Genius," Smith says, "requires freedom" and the educational and psychological conditions permitting creative thought. Not stopping there, Smith goes after the intellectual abilities of Jefferson's own class, asking, "Mr. Jefferson, or any other man who is acquainted with American planters, how many of those masters could have written poems equal to those of Phillis Whately [*sic*]?"[22] In all of this we can see that for a hundred more years, identity of *the* American would contain a contradiction: Americans look and act pretty much the same, but southerners are different—and inferior.

As LONG as observers thought only of European peoples as Americans, the country's rosy egalitarian image glowed nicely. Always present, however, though little known, was a counterargument that calculated Americanness by experience rather than skin color. Though black authors often generalized about the character of white people, most of their commentary came in the form of asides embedded in work focused on people of African descent. David Walker and Hosea Easton represented their views, addressing their fellow Americans as critics of white supremacy.[23]

In 1829 David Walker (1785–1830), a thoughtful and politically engaged African American living in Boston, published an eighty-page tract with a jaw-breaking title: *David Walker's Appeal: in four articles, together with a preamble, to the coloured citizens of the world, but in particular, and very expressly, to those of the United States of America.** Born free in Wilmington, North Carolina, Walker had moved to Boston around 1825 and made his living as a dealer in used clothing. Among his many activities, he wrote for and distributed the nation's first black newspaper, *Freedom's Journal,* and frequently delivered public addresses at black Bostonians' celebrations—of Haitian independence, for instance, or a visit to Boston by an African prince recently emancipated from southern slavery. A Mason and Methodist (but a critic of black religiosity), Walker was well known and well respected as an activist among Boston's black people, who numbered about one thousand, and within the antislavery community that surrounded William Lloyd Garrison. Garrison reviewed *Walker's Appeal* positively in an early number of the *Liberator,* soon to become the nation's most influential abolitionist periodical.

Walker's Appeal spread a wide net, excoriating "whites" and, indeed, "Christian America" for its inhumanity and hypocrisy. Over the long sweep of immutable racial history, Walker traces two essences. On one side lies black history, beginning with ancient Egyptians ("Africans or coloured people, such as we are") and encompassing "our brethren the Haytians." On the other lie white people, cradled in bloody, deceitful ancient Greece. Racial traits within these opposites never change:

> The whites have always been an unjust, jealous, unmerciful, avaricious and blood-thirsty set of beings, always seeking after power and authority.—We view them all over the confederacy of Greece, where they were first known to be anything, (in consequence of education) we see them there, cutting each other's throats—trying to subject each other to wretchedness and misery—to effect which, they used all kinds of deceitful, unfair, and unmerciful means. We view them next in Rome, where the spirit of tyranny and deceit raged still higher. We view them in Gaul, Spain, and Britain.—In *fine,* we view them all over Europe,

---

* The first edition of *David Walker's Appeal to the Coloured Citizens of the World* appeared in late 1829; three more editions followed in the spring of 1830. Though differences between the editions are minor, Walker sharpened his scornful indictment of white American hypocrisy.

together with what were scattered about in Asia and Africa, as heathens, and we see them acting more like devils than accountable men.*

Murder, Walker concludes, remains the central feature of whiteness, though a sliver of hope for their future might reside in the American heritage of freedom—he ends by quoting the Declaration of Independence, which he exempts from white Americans' wickedness. The English, for instance, had surmounted their history, turned their backs on slaving, and offered black people the hand of friendship. Once the English stopped oppressing the Irish, Walker opines, their regeneration would be complete.[24]

At bottom, *David Walker's Appeal* speaks to "white Christians," blaming, ridiculing, and threatening them with destruction in retribution for their mistreatment of blacks. Given white people's moral and behavioral weaknesses, he wonders, coyly, just which is the inferior race: "I, therefore, in the name and fear of the Lord and God of Heaven and of earth, divested of prejudice either on the side of my colour or that of the whites, advance my suspicion of them whether they are as *good by nature* as we are or not."[25] This is not to say that Walker was ready to boast about the slaves: as for black people, "we, (coloured people of these United States of America) are the *most wretched, degraded* and *abject* set of beings that *ever lived* since the world began." He aimed pointed criticism at free northern blacks: "some of them can write a good hand, but who, notwithstanding their neat writing, may be almost as ignorant, in comparison, as a horse." Walker discerns "a mean, servile spirit" among the people he calls "my colour." Only when black people organize and throw off the oppressor's yoke will they "arise from this death-like apathy" and "be men!"[26]

Walker's Appeal testifies to its author's immersion in the classics of

---

* After the Civil War, one of Emerson's African American contemporaries in letters, William Wells Brown (1814–84), in *The Rising Son; or, The Antecedents and Achievements of the Colored Race* (1874), described early northern Europeans in terms reminiscent of those of both Herodotus and David Walker: "See them in the gloomy forests of Germany, sacrificing to their grim and gory idols; drinking the warm blood of their prisoners, quaffing libations from human skulls; infesting the shores of the Baltic for plunder and robbery; bringing home the reeking scalps of enemies as an offering to their king."

American and European culture as well as to his familiarity with current politics affecting the Irish, Jews, and Greeks. He strongly indicts white American hypocrisy as exhibited by the Declaration of Independence and the work of Thomas Jefferson. Jefferson had died in 1826, but Walker, like Samuel Stanhope Smith, felt that the insults from an American of Jefferson's stature demanded a response. How could Jefferson, a man of enormous learning and "excellent natural parts," stoop to judge "a set of men in chains." Jefferson may have believed that black people wanted to be white, but in this he is "dreadfully deceived—we wish to be just as it pleased our Creator to have made us."[27]

An effective promoter, Walker spread his *Appeal* widely, even, via black and white sailors, into the slaveholding South, where it made its author well known and much hated. The incendiary pamphlet, addressed directly to African Americans, so alarmed Virginia's upper classes that discussion of it took place in a closed-door session of the General Assembly. In New Bern and Wilmington, North Carolina, any black readers associated with *Walker's Appeal* paid with their lives.[28]

In 1830, at only forty-five years of age, Walker died of tuberculosis. That scourge of the nineteenth-century urban poor had, only days before, taken his daughter. A few months earlier, he had issued what became, by default, the final edition of *Walker's Appeal*. Now, Boston's Maria Stewart, the first American woman to publicly address "promiscuous" audiences (i.e., audiences including women as well as men), eulogized Walker as "most noble, fearless, and undaunted." In the revolutionary year of 1848, the Reverend Henry Highland Garnet lauded Walker as a tireless fighter for freedom. Walker's activism, Garnet concludes, "made his memory sacred." Walker's memory remained vivid among abolitionists well into the mid-nineteenth century, only to fade after the Civil War. But meanwhile, he had struck a strong blow against the notion that whiteness, throughout history, deserved to be judged positively.[29]

THE REVEREND Hosea Easton (1799–1837) of Hartford, Connecticut, had been born into an activist family with a quintessentially American mixed background, but of a sort Crèvecoeur had not been able to see. Easton's mother was of at least partial African ancestry, and his father, James, a veteran of the Revolutionary War, had descended from Wampanoag and Narragansett Indians. After the war James Easton had prospered as an iron manufacturer in North Bridgewater (now Brockton, Massachusetts). With his complicated lineage, Hosea identified himself as "colored," effectively suppressing the Indian ancestry, probably in the interest of achieving undisputed citizenship.*

Color lines were hardening in the first quarter of the nineteenth century in Massachusetts, with the result that the Easton family found itself rejected from the public sphere. After a long, spirited, dispiriting, and losing protest against enforcement of racial segregation in their local school and church, James Easton opened a school for colored youth in the mid-1810s.

Becoming a minister and following in his father's activist footsteps, Hosea Easton attended the first meeting of the National Convention of Free People of Color in Philadelphia in 1831, when he was thirty-two. Times were harsh for people of color, and a mob of angry white supremacists attacked Easton's parishioners and burned down his church in Hartford in 1836. Not one to back off, Easton issued his response the following year in the form of *A Treatise on the Intellectual Character and Civil and Political Condition of the Colored People of the U. States; and the Prejudice Exercised towards Them: with a Sermon on the Duty of the Church to Them.*[30]

Citing ancient and current history, Easton's *Treatise* echoes *David Walker's Appeal* by comparing the history of Africa—starting with Ham and ancient Egypt—to Europe's from its roots in ancient Greece. A stout Afrocentrist, Easton maintains that black and brown ancient Egyptians taught the Greeks everything of value. Conversely, he considers European history one long saga of bloodletting, a particular irony since nineteenth-century Europeans and white Americans loudly proclaimed themselves superior in civilization:

---

* Benjamin Roberts, leader of the struggle against segregation in Boston schools, was Hosea Easton's nephew and James Easton's grandson. Paul Cuffee, the prosperous Afro-Indian seafaring merchant from New Bedford, married Mary Easton, one of James Easton's daughters

It is not a little remarkable, that in the nineteenth century a remnant of this same barbarous people should boast of their national superiority of intellect, and of wisdom and religion; who, in the seventeenth century, crossed the Atlantic and practised the same crime their barbarous ancestry had done in the fourth, fifth and sixth centuries: bringing with them the same boasted spirit of enterprise; and not unlike their fathers, staining their route with blood, as they have rolled along, as a cloud of locusts, toward the West. The late unholy war with the Indians, and the wicked crusade against the peace of Mexico, are striking illustrations of the nobleness of this race of people, and the powers of their mind.

Five and a half pages of grisly wrongs perpetrated by Europeans through the ages close, "Any one who has the least conception of true greatness, on comparing the two races by means of what history we have, must decide in favor of the descendants of Ham. The Egyptians alone have done more to cultivate such improvements as comports to the happiness of mankind, than all the descendants of Japhet put together."

What white supremacists praise as the products of energy and enterprise, Easton describes as booty obtained

> by the dint of war, and the destruction of the vanquished, since the founding of London, A. D. 49. Their whole career presents a motley mixture of barbarism and civilization, of fraud and philanthropy, of patriotism and avarice, of religion and bloodshed. . . . And instead of their advanced state in science being attributable to a superior development of intellectual faculties, . . . it is solely owing to . . . their innate thirst for blood and plunder.[31]

In a slight concession, Easton connects civilization to white people, but only as an outcome of violence rather than of innate intelligence. White people are not smarter; they are meaner.

Despite their pungency, neither *Walker's Appeal* nor Easton's *Treatise*

on the Intellectual Character ever truly penetrated the public consciousness at home or in Europe during the nineteenth century. The visibility
of *Walker's Appeal* grew in the late twentieth and early twenty-first
centuries, but never approached the reputation of the champion of foreign analysts.

DEMOCRACY IN AMERICA must hold a record as the most quoted French
text in the United States. The Princeton University Library holds
thirty-one English editions of the originally two-volume work, published to great acclaim in 1835 and 1840. The reason for such popularity is not far to seek. Alexis de Tocqueville (1805–59) not only approved
of the United States; he possessed a lineage Americans prized in their
visiting friends. (See figure 8.3, Alexis de Tocqueville.)

Tocqueville's conventionally Catholic, conventionally conservative
aristocratic family lived in Normandy. As a young man, he rose in the
legal service of King Charles X, prospering in Versailles until the king's
abdication in the wake of the 1830 July Revolution. Such upheaval at
the top of French management threatened Tocqueville's future. So much
so, it seemed a good moment for Tocqueville and a dear friend, Gustave
de Beaumont, another aristocratic lawyer of progressive turn of mind,
to take a sabbatical from France in the United States, ostensibly to study
prison reform. In fact, Beaumont and Tocqueville did publish a report
on prisons, in 1833.[32] But it was Tocqueville's subsequent study on the
United States, *Démocratie en Amérique* (*Democracy in America*, 1835),
which made him famous.

Democracy in America is seldom cited as part of any tradition of
racial thought, for Tocqueville ascribes American behavior to the whole
of American society rather than to any racial trait. Society grows out
of laws, governance, and economic opportunity. Finding an exceptional
society in the United States, Tocqueville locates the source of this excep-
tionalism in American democracy. While American religion plays a role
in American life, democracy trumps it, setting the tone in spheres both
private and public. "Equality" provides the keyword.

On its first page, *Democracy in America* mentions "the equality

Fig. 8.3. Alexis de Tocqueville.

of social conditions" three times, and many of the following 800-plus pages elaborate that basic point. The opening statements and the hundreds more pages label the United States a country populated by white people directly descended from the English. The phrase "the English race" appears repeatedly in headings and in the body of the text. In the conclusion to volume 1, Tocqueville glimpses "the whole future of the English race in the New World." Chapter 3 of volume 2 bears the title "Why the Americans Show More Aptitude and Taste for General Ideas Than Their Forefathers, the English."[33]*

---

* Speaking of "our German ancestors," the views of Tacitus, and "Germanic institutions," in France, Tocqueville echoes the views of his protégé Gobineau. This idea of two disparate French races is usually ascribed to the class-minded, extreme hereditarian historian Henri de Boulainvilliers (1658–1722). Born in Normandy (and, therefore, by some accounts a descendant of the Vikings), Boulainvilliers was "an aristocrat of the most pronounced type" according to the 1911 *Encyclopædia Britannica*. He saw the aristocracy as the descendants of Franks from Germany and the peasants the descendants of mongrel Gauls and Romans.

The American of *Democracy in America* is primarily a northerner, usually a New Englander of British, Puritan descent. If he lacks brilliance and bores his guests, it is because he concentrates on making money. But *the* American's heart is in the right place, right enough, at any rate, for him to be about building a country of certain future greatness. Tocqueville does not make slavery a crucial theme of analysis, for his *the* American is a citizen of Massachusetts, a quintessential free state. Therefore he nestles his discussion of slavery in the chapter on race—admittedly a topic he prefers to leave to his friend Beaumont—and thereby minimizes one of the core issues in American politics and culture.

Only after 370 pages (in the Penguin Classic edition) does Tocqueville concede any racial heterogeneity to the United States, and with heterogeneity comes much unpleasantness. The following 100 pages, entitled "A Few Remarks on the Present-day State and the Probable Future of the Three Races Which Live in the Territory of the United States," contrast sharply with the rest of volume 1. On the Lower Mississippi River, Tocqueville and Beaumont encounter Indians on the Trail of Tears, "these forced migrations" whose "fearful evils . . . are impossible to imagine. . . . I have witnessed evils," Tocqueville admits a couple of paragraphs later, "I would find it impossible to relate."* Regarding the plight of Indians in the United States, words practically fail Tocqueville.

As for black people, they seem less fated for extinction than Native Americans, but their situation is nevertheless dire: black people, enslaved or free, "only constitute an unhappy remnant, a poor little wandering tribe, lost in the midst of an immense nation which owns all the land." Such an assessment seems strange, if not ridiculous, to the twenty-first-century ear, since "this poor little wandering tribe" comprised more than two million people, more than 18 percent of the total population.

Tocqueville very clearly realizes that slavery damages southern white people as well as the southern economy. Because of slavery,

---

* Early on, Tocqueville quickly mentions the pernicious influence of slavery in the United States: idleness, ignorance, pride, poverty, and indulgence, the weaknesses of white southerners, then moves on to the Americans he sees as typical Americans: New Englanders.

southern white people's customs and character compare poorly with those of other Americans. Echoing Crèvecoeur and Jefferson, Tocqueville complains, "From birth, the southern American is invested with a kind of domestic dictatorship . . . and the first habit he learns is that of effortless domination . . . [which turns] the southern American into a haughty, hasty, irascible, violent man, passionate in his desires and irritated by obstacles. But he is easily discouraged if he fails to succeed at his first attempt." While impatience robs southerners of the determination necessary to succeed, energy constitutes *the* American's great talent: *he* goes about taming the wilderness and wrenching riches from the land. Not the southerner. "The southerner loves grandeur, luxury, reputation, excitement, pleasure, and, above all, idleness; nothing constrains him to work hard for his livelihood and, as he has no work which he has to do, he sleeps his time away, not even attempting anything useful."[34]

The severity of discrimination against African Americans alarms Tocqueville, prompting his prediction of an inevitable war of the races that will entail "great misfortunes": "If America ever experiences great revolutions, they will be instigated by the presence of blacks on American soil; that is to say, it will not be the equality of social conditions but rather their inequality which will give rise to them."[35]

While the danger of "revolution" presses imminently in the South, the North enjoys no exemption. The specter of race war "constantly haunts the imaginations of [all] Americans like a nightmare," but Tocqueville leaves his fears with that.[36] Pursuing this line of thought would distort his egalitarian image of the United States. In truth, Tocqueville does not know what to do with the problem of slavery or how to integrate the South into his depiction of the United States. Revolutions do not arise on a level playing field, and he needs a level playing field to justify his sunny, democratic analysis. He solves his conundrum by cutting the South, slavery, and black people out of his theory, admitting, in a footnote in volume 2 that only Americans living in the free states conform to his image of a democratic, egalitarian society.[37]

The Ohio River offers a convenient dividing line. In Ohio, *the* American, driven to succeed, achieves through ingenuity. South of the Ohio River in slaveholding Kentucky, the southerner disdains labor: "living in a relaxed idleness, he has the tastes of idle men; money has lost a part of its value in his eyes; he is less interested in wealth than excitement and pleasure. . . . Slavery, therefore, not merely prevents the whites from making money but even diverts them from any desire to do so." Northerners own the ships that ply the nation's rivers and seas, the factories that produce untold wealth, the railroads that deliver produce to market, and canals that link the continent's great natural waterways.[38] Only the North possesses these symbols of America.

This long and tortured chapter seldom figures in the broadcast image of Tocqueville's United States. Little read and less often heeded, it has even been omitted from abridged editions. Whether or not literally cleansed of anything pertaining to race war and the general American nastiness surrounding questions of race, Tocqueville's *America* does not face all its racial facts.[39]* As he finally walks away from the topic of multiracial America, Tocqueville excuses the brevity of his own discussion by sending readers along to the novel of his friend Beaumont.

GUSTAVE DE BEAUMONT (1802–66), Tocqueville's fellow lawyer, roommate in Versailles in the 1820s, traveling companion, lifelong friend, biographer, and literary executor, accompanied him in travels across the United States and Ireland in 1835. (See figure 8.4, Gustave de Beaumont.) Beaumont, not so theory driven, took more interest than Tocqueville in slavery and the conventions of racial identity. His sociological novel, *Marie, ou L'esclavage aux États-Unis, tableau de moeurs américaines* (*Marie, or Slavery in the United States, a Picture of American Manners*) in fact made slavery an integral, rather than

* Margaret Kohn notes that many scholars either remain silent on Tocqueville's commentary regarding slavery and race or criticize him for evasion. Tocqueville's own strategies corroborate the latter charge. The first and more famous volume of *Democracy in America* leads off with equality and relegates the discussion of three American races to the end of the book. Tocqueville admits that slavery and southern society belie his generalizations about the United States in footnotes and asides, though in his text he faults the South for sluggishness and laziness. He refers his readers to Beaumont's work rather than integrating the multiracial theme into his analysis. Thomas Bender's fond introduction to *Democracy in America* concedes Tocqueville's avoidance of the fact of internal conflict in the United States and agrees with others who see Tocqueville as a prominent source for consensus thinkers such as Marvin Meyers and Louis Hartz.

an incidental, facet of American society. *Marie* appeared in two volumes in 1835, the same year as the first volume of Tocqueville's *Democracy in America*. Both books won the Prix Montyon of the Académie Française, and both authors were elected members of the Académie des Sciences Morales et Politiques, but only Tocqueville was eventually inducted into the far more prestigious Académie Française, after an assiduous campaign for acceptance.

Fig. 8.4. *Gustave de Beaumont, 1848.*

In his novel, Beaumont's protagonists are Ludovic, a French immigrant to the United States, and his beloved American, Marie, the daughter of parents who both look white: a Bostonian father and a mother who grew up in New Orleans. According to American mores, Beaumont says, the father really is white; the mother is not. Marie's Louisianan mother, whose great-grandmother was a mulatto, transmits to Marie the invisible taint of black blood. Although Marie's imperceptible mixed ancestry does not dissuade her French suitor Ludovic, Americans' one-drop rule makes her black even in the so-called free North. Marie's drop of blackness marks her marriage to the Frenchman as miscegenation, an infraction sufficient to inspire a riot in New York City.* The marriage cannot proceed. Ludovic and Marie seek peace in the wilds of Michigan. But before they can settle down, Marie dies. Ludovic remains an exile in the wilderness.

Despite his novel's grim message, Beaumont evinces a sly sense of humor. In the foreword to *Marie*, he relates an anecdote illustrating Americans' preposterous racial rules. Although the theater was actually in New Orleans, Beaumont relates the incident as though taking place in Philadelphia:

---

*Beaumont does not use the word "miscegenation," coined only in 1864.

The first time I attended a theater in the United States [in October 1831], I was surprised at the careful distinction made between the white spectators and the audience whose faces were black. In the first balcony were whites; in the second, mulattoes; in the third, Negroes. An American, beside whom I was sitting, informed me that the dignity of white blood demanded these classifications. However, my eyes being drawn to the balcony where sat the mulattoes, I perceived a young woman of dazzling beauty, whose complexion, of perfect whiteness, proclaimed the purest European blood. Entering into all the prejudices of my neighbor, I asked him how a woman of English origin could be so lacking in shame as to seat herself among the Africans.

"That woman," he replied, "is colored."

"What? Colored? She is whiter than a lily!"

"She is colored," he repeated coldly; "local tradition has established her ancestry, and everyone knows that she had a mulatto among her forebears."

He pronounced these words without further explanation, as one who states a fact which needs only be voiced to be understood.

At the same moment I made out in the balcony for whites a face which was very dark. I asked for an explanation of this new phenomenon; the American answered:

"The lady who has attracted your attention is white."

"What? White! She is the same color as the mulattoes."

"She is white," he replied; "local tradition affirms that the blood which flows in her veins is Spanish."

Following the anecdote, Beaumont explains the deadly meaning of race prejudice in the United States. Echoing Crèvecoeur and Jefferson, he concludes that white supremacy in America corrupts white people by schooling them in "domination and tyranny," while blasting Negro fate and engendering in them violent hatreds and resentments bound to provoke bloody crisis.[40]

Although as much an aristocrat as Tocqueville, Beaumont deeply disagrees with his friend over the nature of U.S. society. Tocqueville, it seems, can only see a virtuous democracy where Beaumont focuses on barriers as impassable as Europe's. White Americans, Beaumont concludes, belong to a hereditary aristocracy by dint of a mythology driven by the notion of tainted blood and a belief in invisible ancestry. This fact alone suffices to destroy the possibility of a true democracy. David Walker's indictment of hypocrisy reappears.

Beaumont's mouthpiece Ludovic instructs a young traveler from France who is drawn to the United States by "the laws and customs of this country; they are liberal and generous. Every man's rights are protected here." Not so, advises Ludovic, who having lived with a family of color, knows that such impressions are mere "illusions" and "chimeras."[41]

THESE TWO seminal books—very much two sides of the same coin—experienced contrasting fates in translation. *Democracy in America* was translated into English immediately upon publication in 1835, but *Marie* had to wait 123 years, until 1958, for its first English translation. An accessible paperback in English did not appear anywhere for 164 years, when published in 1999 by the Johns Hopkins University Press. One fact, a title change, says much about the elevation of Tocqueville at the expense of Beaumont: in 1938 George Wilson Pierson published *Tocqueville and Beaumont in America,* a scholarly analysis based on their notebooks and letters. When Johns Hopkins University Press republished Pierson's book in 1996, its contents unaltered, Beaumont had disappeared from the title, now simply *Tocqueville in America.* Thus quietly but definitely, Beaumont and his troubled, multiracial United States ceded place to Tocqueville's egalitarian, democratic, white male America.

Walker, Easton, and Beaumont, each in his own way, cast a wary eye on the myth of American democracy. Concurrently, another story was playing in the history of American whiteness.

THE FIRST ALIEN WAVE

Two centuries ago, Americans had already fallen into a number of thought patterns familiar to us. In a society largely based on African slavery and founded in the era that invented the very idea of race, race as color has always played a prominent role. It has shaped the determination not only of race but also of citizenship, beauty, virtue, and the like. The idea of blackness, if not the actual color of skin, continues to play a leading role in American race thinking.

Today's Americans, bred in the ideology of skin color as racial difference, find it difficult to recognize the historical coexistence of potent American hatreds against people accepted as white, Irish Catholics. But anti-Catholicism has a long and often bloody national history, one that expressed itself in racial language and a violence that we nowadays attach most readily to race-as-color bigotry, when, in fact, religious hatred arrived in Western culture much earlier, lasted much longer, and killed more people. If we fail to connect the dots between class and religion, we lose whole layers of historical meaning. Hatred of black people did not preclude hatred of other white people—those considered different and inferior—and flare-ups of deadly violence against stigmatized whites.

By 1850, a prideful Saxon-American juggernaut was elevating Protestant Americans above Catholics of all classes and provenance. Obviously Irish Catholics were white, and, especially in the South, white enough to hold themselves above black and Chinese people in the name of whiteness. As Celts, however, the poor Irish could also be judged racially different enough to be oppressed, ugly enough to be compared to apes, and poor enough to be paired with black people.

Before about 1820, most Irish immigrants had been Protestants from the north of Ireland, fairly easily incorporated into American society as simply "Irish." On the other hand, Irish Catholic immigration, while moderate before 1830, had now and then drawn Federalists and then Whigs toward nativist rhetoric, prompting the Protestant Irish to term themselves "Scotch Irish," as distinguished from Catholics.[1] And after 1830, as hardship in Ireland pushed the poor to America in growing numbers, opposition to them and their religion grew. To understand this antagonism we need some historical background.

ANTI-CATHOLIC LEGISLATION had long existed in the British colonies, inherited from the anti-Catholic struggles of England, led most notably by Henry VIII in the mid-sixteenth century and Oliver Cromwell during the mid-seventeenth-century English Civil War against Charles I. Various American colonial statutes forbidding, for example, the practice of the Roman Catholic religion, endured long past their rigorous enforcement. Until 1821 New York denied citizenship to Catholics unless they renounced allegiance to the pope in all matters, political or religious. In Massachusetts, all persons, Catholic and Protestant alike, were taxed to support state-sponsored Protestant churches until 1833. New Jersey's constitution contained anti-Catholic provisions until 1844.[2]

When Ireland's potato famine came to a crisis in the 1830s and 1840s, it turned the starving Irish into a sort of perverse tourist attraction. Intellectuals of all sorts, including Alexis de Tocqueville, Gustave de Beaumont, and Thomas Carlyle, sailed to Ireland to see for themselves whether such gut-wrenching reports could possibly be true. After their visit to the United States, Beaumont and Tocqueville toured Ireland and recorded their impressions. Tocqueville's notes remained in manuscript until the mid-twentieth century, but Beaumont published his study as

L'Irlande sociale, politique et religieuse (*Ireland: Social, Political and Religious*) in 1839.[3]

Before his time in Ireland, Beaumont had figured that parallels between American people of color and the Irish poor would make good sense. Thinking he had seen unmatched degradation in the United States—he considered Indians and Negroes "the very extreme of human wretchedness"—he was astonished to see in Ireland the worst of both American worlds: the impoverished Irish lacked the freedom of the Indian as well as the slave's relative security. Consequently, "Irish misery [formed] a type by itself of which neither the model nor the imitation can be found anywhere else." At bottom, Ireland lacked other countries' varied histories, in which poor and rich played a part. For Beaumont, as for many others unable to see beyond the famine, Ireland had only a single essence: "the history of the poor is the history of Ireland."[4]

Beaumont located the roots of the curse of Ireland in its history of pernicious British policy. Since occupying Ireland in the seventeenth century, Protestant English settlers had dispossessed the Catholic natives, depriving them of ownership or even unfettered use of the land, reducing them to abject poverty. Irish natives lived on potatoes, and when the potato blight destroyed this staple food, more than a million died of starvation. Twice that number emigrated, many to the United States. In the grimmest irony, while Irish people starved, Ireland was exporting food from settler-owned farms. Beaumont investigated this colonial history and drew his own conclusions. Blaming politics rather than the Irish themselves, he contradicted the prevailing assumption that inherent racial defects caused Irish wretchedness.

According to nineteenth-century popular wisdom and anthropological science, the Irish were Celts, a particular race separate from and inferior to the Anglo-Saxon English. Beaumont's enlightened views would ultimately prevail, but at the time they found few supporters among the Western world's theorists. Thomas Carlyle (1795–1881), the most influential essayist in Victorian England, held the racial-deficiency view, having fled Ireland's scenes of destitution in disgust after brief visits in 1846 and 1849. In one cranky article he called Ireland "a human dog kennel."[5]

From his perch in London, Carlyle saw the Irish as a people bred to be dominated and lacking historical agency. He took it for granted that Saxons and Teutons had always monopolized the energy necessary for creative action. Celts and Negroes, in contrast, lacked the vision as well as the spunk needed to add value to the world. Pushing the analogy further, Carlyle played on the antislavery question "Am I not a man and a brother?" But whereas the abolitionist query stresses the brotherhood of man, Carlyle refashioned the question to denigrate the oppressed. In his essay "The Present Time," the first of several splenetic *Latter Day Pamphlets* (1850), he asks, "Am I not a horse, and half-brother?" then juxtaposes "Black Jamaica" and "White Connemara" as "our Black West Indies and our White Ireland."[6] The "sluttishly starving" Irish remind him of shiftless emancipated Negroes in the West Indies: "a *Black Ireland*; 'free,' indeed, but an Ireland, and Black!"[7]

Carlyle was hardly singular in turning the Irish into animals. A younger British Teutonist, the Oxford professor Charles Kingsley, termed the poor Irish "white chimpanzees." Robert Knox in Scotland considered intermarriage between Saxons and Celts as much contrary to natural law as unions between Saxons and Hottentots.[8]

By the mid-1840s, as two million desperate Irish immigrants poured into the northern port cities of the United States, a backlash had developed. The Native American Party had appeared in New York City in 1835, and a number of anti-Catholic journals and organizations followed in New York and New England. Samuel F. B. Morse, father of the American telegraph, and Lyman Beecher, Yale-educated Presbyterian minister and father of the novelist Harriet Beecher Stowe and the Reverend Henry Ward Beecher, published slashing denunciations of Catholicism. Morse's work carried windy titles: *Foreign Conspiracy against the Liberties of the United States* and *Imminent Dangers to the Free Institutions of the United States through Foreign Immigration and the Present State of the Naturalization Laws, by an American.* In it Morse evokes "the great truth, clearly and unanswerably proved," that the Catholic monarchies of Europe, especially Austria and its allies the Jesuits, were sending "shiploads of Roman Catholic emigrants, and for the sole purpose of converting us to the religion of Popery."[9] Beecher's *Plea for the West* accused Europeans of trying to subvert the Protestant virtues of American democracy, also by flooding the country with Catholics. In Beecher's view it was tragic that poor Catholics could vote and hold office just like white men. In New York City and many another northeastern city, bourgeois voices joined those of Morse and Beecher in deploring "the very scum and dregs of Human nature" and the "low Irishmen" who decided election outcomes.[10]

In 1834, Beecher was heading the Lane Seminary in Cincinnati, a city housing a large number of Germans. From time to time, however, he returned to Boston, where he had lived during the 1820s. On one such occasion he preached three violently anti-Catholic sermons in a single day, and within twenty-four hours a mob had burned down the Ursuline convent school in neighboring Charlestown, setting off a wave of church burnings throughout New England and the Midwest.[11] More obscenity was yet to come.

AFTER SERIAL publication in 1835, the sensational, pornographic *Awful Disclosures of Maria Monk: The Hidden Secrets of a Nun's Life in a Convent Exposed* appeared in book form in 1836 and went on to sell some 300,000 copies by 1860. Second only to *Uncle Tom's Cabin, Awful Disclosures of Maria Monk* became antebellum America's most popular book.[12]

A Canadian born in 1816, Monk begins her exposé by explaining, "One of my great duties [as a nun] was to obey the priests in all things; and this I soon learnt, to my utter astonishment and horror, was to live in the practice of criminal intercourse with them."[13] Monk vividly describes priests' rape of nuns, the murder of the offspring, and the beating to death of recalcitrant nuns. Monk's story traced just one example of a favorite plot—the escaped nun's tale—a more or less graphic depiction of a former Protestant girl seduced by a priest. Such books pictured the Catholic Church as inherently sexually immoral. Not only were Catholics not Protestant; they drank liquor, partied on the Sabbath, and had near-constant sex—especially in their convents and churches.[14]

Although investigation quickly disproved Monk's allegations, the book excited nativists as much as later abolitionist descriptions of sex between masters and slaves. Failing to capitalize on her literary fame, Monk disappeared into the urban underworld and died in 1839 a poor, obscure, and abandoned single mother.[15]

While Monk's ignominious end passed unnoticed, anti-Catholic hatred surged. Between 1830 and 1860, some 270 books, 25 newspapers, 13 magazines, and a slew of ephemeral publications carried on.[16] This plethora of anti-Catholic newspapers included New York City's *The Protestant*, the *Protestant Vindicator* (which had published *Awful Disclosures of Maria Monk* in serial form), and the *Downfall of Babylon*.

IN TRUTH, the era's sociopolitical context had created much anxiety. The Western world was being buffeted by an extraordinary set of crises in the mid-1840s. In France, Germany, Italy, and central Europe, political unrest spurred by widespread unemployment and poverty culminated in revolution in 1848. Such uprisings crystallized the thinking of writers eager to interpret class conflict as race war. In France, Arthur de Gobineau wrote his *Essay on the Inequality of Races*, published in the mid-1850s. Robert Knox in London published his mean-spirited lectures on race in 1850 as *Races of Men: A Fragment*. The revolutionary year of 1848 also generated unrest among educated women and workers: the first conference for women's rights took place in Seneca Falls, New York. In Great Britain, Chartists advocating workers' rights and universal male suffrage presented their third (and last) People's Charter to the House of Commons.* As Chartism was dying and revolutionary sentiment strengthened throughout Europe, the Irish situation grew ever more desperate.

---

* Chartists had submitted the first People's Charter petition to the House of Commons in 1839, an action that Thomas Carlyle, moving away from his earlier sympathy with working people, answered with an influential pamphlet, "Chartism," that expressed doubt that the needed reforms would ever be enacted. The second People's Charter, bearing three million signatures, was submitted in 1842. Subsequent confrontation with police had led to twenty-four deaths. The House of Commons rejected all three petitions. By the 1840s Carlyle was expressing downright contempt for democracy.

Ireland attracted the most attention in English-speaking lands, but continental Europe, where background conditions were similar, was sending distressed immigrants to the United States from German-speaking lands. Central Europeans were fleeing reactionary politics and the poverty caused not only by industrialization's displacement of hand workers but also by failed harvests of wheat, wine, and potatoes. Such an upsurge of hard-pressed immigrants alarmed the U.S. government. For the first time, it answered the need to tabulate just how many desperate people were entering the country.

The U.S. census of 1850 was the first to collect statistics on immigrants. In a total population of 23,191,876, some 2,244,600 were deemed immigrants; among them, 379,093 from Great Britain, 583,774 from Germany, and a whopping 961,719 from Ireland. In the years of hardship in western Europe, especially 1845–55, 1,343,423 came from Ireland and 1,011,066 from the German-speaking lands.[17]

The Germans were a heterogeneous group in terms of wealth, politics, and religion. Settling largely in the Midwest in the "German Triangle" of Milwaukee, Cincinnati, and St. Louis, they stirred relatively little controversy, compared with the outcry against the Irish.[18] For one thing, German Americans had been blending into Protestant white American life since before the Revolution, and many had climbed to the top of the nation's economic ladder. Johann Jakob Astor, for instance, born near Heidelberg in 1763 and immigrating to the United States in 1784, was the richest man in the United States at his death in 1848. In the nineteenth century the Radical Republican Carl Schurz and the railroad magnate Henry Villard also presented a certifiably loyal image of middle- and upper-class German Americans.* Schurz had joined hundreds of other Germans turning to the United States after the failed revolutions of 1848. A taint of radicalism might

---

* Carl Schurz (1829–1906), a Union Army general during the Civil War and U.S. secretary of the interior, was the first German American to serve in the U.S. Senate. Henry Villard (1835–1900), born Ferdinand Heinrich Gustav Hilgard, married Helen Garrison, the daughter of the abolitionist William Lloyd Garrison. Their son Oswald Garrison Villard became a leading liberal journalist (publisher of the *Nation*) in the early twentieth century.

dog them locally, but only sporadically did German radicalism raise the alarm on a national scale. The Catholic Irish were something else entirely.

SOME FIFTY thousand Irish lived in Boston by 1855, making the city one-third foreign born, the "Dublin of America." There they found low-paying work in manufacturing, railroad and canal construction, and domestic service. Before long, Irishmen had gained a sorry reputation for mindless bloc voting on the Democratic (southern-based and proslavery) ticket, and also for drunkenness, brawling, laziness, pauperism, and crime. All these defects attached to the figure of "the Paddy."

When Ralph Waldo Emerson, the leading American intellectual before the Civil War, casually referred to poor Irishmen as "Paddies," he drew upon stereotypes of improvidence and ignorance as old as Sir Richard Steele's 1714 description of "Poor Paddy," who "swears his whole Week's Gains away."[19] As a young minister in the late 1820s, Emerson posited a multitude of inferior peoples that included Irish Catholics. Cataloging the traits of backward races, he set stagnation atop the list, as though stagnation ran in the blood of human beings. Over the years Emerson's cast of incompetent races would rotate indiscriminately around the globe, but two peoples nearly always figured: the African and the Irish. In a very early musing, Emerson actually expels the Irish from the Caucasian race:

> I think it cannot be maintained by any candid person that the African race have ever occupied or do promise ever to occupy any very high place in the human family. Their present condition is the strongest proof that they cannot. The Irish cannot; the American Indian cannot; the Chinese cannot. Before the energy of the Caucasian race all the other races have quailed and ser done obeisance.

That was in 1829. Nothing had changed by 1852, when Emerson wrote,

The worst of charity, is, that the lives you are asked to preserve are not worth preserving. The calamity is the masses. I do not wish any mass at all, but honest men only, faculitied men only, lovely & sweet & accomplished ~~m~~women only; and no shovel-handed Irish, & no Five-Points, or Saint Gileses, or drunken crew, or mob or stockingers, or 2 millions of paupers receiving relief, miserable factory population, or lazzaroni, at all.[20]

Here we have the heart of Emerson's view of the poor, typified by the Irish.

After the failure of the Hungarian revolution in 1848 and Lajos Kossuth's triumphant tour as a hero in exile, Emerson found a way to view the Hungarian situation through an Irish lens: "The paddy period lasts long. Hungary, it seems, must take the yoke again, & Austria, & Italy, & Prussia, & France. Only the English race can be trusted with freedom."[21] Emerson pontificated against Central Europeans as well as the Irish: "*Races.* Our idea, certainly, of Poles & Hungarians is little better than of horses recently humanized."[22]

Emerson would probably not have been surprised that Polish jokes abounded in the late twentieth century. Certainly during his time Paddy jokes amused the better classes, having been recycled from eighteenth-century English "jester" books. This one about the two sailors, one a dumb Irishman, lived for more than a century:

Two sailors, one Irish the other English, agreed reciprocally to take care of each other, in case of either being wounded in an action then about to commence. It was not long before the Englishman's leg was shot off by a cannon-ball; and on his calling Paddy to carry him to the doctor, according to their agreement, the other very readily complied; but he had scarcely got his wounded companion on his back, when a second ball struck off the poor fellow's head. Paddy, who, through the noise and disturbance, had not perceived his friend's last misfortune, continued to make the best of his way to the surgeon, an officer observing him with a headless trunk upon his shoulders, asked him where he was going? "To the doctor," says Paddy. "The doctor!" Says the officer, "why you blockhead, the man has lost his head." On hearing this he flung the body from his shoulders, and looking at it very attentively, "by my soul, says he, he told me it was his leg."[23]*

Cartoons played an important role in reinforcing the Paddy stereotype. Frequently apelike, always poor, ugly, drunken, violent, superstitious, but charmingly rascally, Paddy and his ugly, ignorant, dirty, fecund, long-suffering Bridget differed fundamentally from visual depictions of sober, civilized Anglo-Saxons. (See figure 9.1, "Contrasted Faces.") Most Paddy phrases—such as "Paddy Doyle" for a jail cell, "in a Paddy" for being in a

Fig. 747.—FLORENCE NIGHTINGALE. Fig. 748.—BRIDGET McBRUISER.

Fig. 9.1. "Contrasted Faces," Florence Nightingale and Bridget McBruiser, in Samuel R. Wells, New Physiognomy, or Signs of Character, Manifested through Temperament and External Forms, and Especially in "The Human Face Divine" (1871).

---

* Today the Web offers a profusion of updated Paddy jokes, such as this one featuring the American golfer Tiger Woods:

Taking a wee break from the golf circuit, Tiger Woods drives his new BMW into an Irish gas station. An attendant greets him in typical Irish manner, unaware who the golf pro is, "Top o' the morning to ya."

As Tiger gets out of the car, two tees fall out of his pocket. "So what are those things, my son?" asks the attendant.

"They're called tees," replied Tiger.

"And what would ya be using 'em for, now?" inquired the Irishman.

"Well, they're for resting my balls on when I drive," replies Tiger.

"Aw, Jaysus, Mary an' Joseph!" exclaimed the Irish attendant. "Those fellas working for BMW think of everything!"

Fig. 9.2. Thomas Nast, "The Ignorant Vote—Honors Are Easy," Harper's Weekly, 1876.

rage, "Paddyland" for Ireland, and "Paddy" for white person—have lost currency in today's vernacular; only "paddy wagon" endures to link Irishmen to the American criminal class.

AMERICAN VISUAL culture testifies to a widespread fondness for likening *the* Irishman to *the* Negro. No one supplied better fodder for this parallel than Thomas Nast, the German-born editorial cartoonist for *Harper's Weekly*. In 1876, for instance, Nast pictured stereotypical southern freedmen and northern Irishmen as equally unsuited for the vote during Reconstruction after the American Civil War. (See figure 9.2, Nast, "The Ignorant Vote.")

This cartoon does two things at once: It draws upon anti-Irish imagery current in Britain and the United States, and depicts both figures in American racial terms. Bumpkin clothing and bare feet mark the figure labeled "black" as a poor rural southerner, while the face, expression, and lumpy frock coat of the "white" figure are stereotypically Irish. It is important here to recognize that the Irish figure is not only problematical but also, and most importantly, labeled white. Nast drew for a Republican journal identified with the struggle against slavery. However, figures on the other side of the slavery issue could just as easily draw the black-Irish parallel. James Henry Hammond, nullifier congressman, U.S. senator, and governor of South Carolina, denounced the British reduction of the Irish to an "absolute & unmitigated slavery."[24] And George Fitzhugh in *Cannibals All! or Slaves without Masters* (1855) intended his Irish comparisons to prove that enslaved workers fared better than the free.[25] Fitzhugh hardly meant to recommend freedom to either poor community.

Abolitionists saw the other side of the coin, frequently championing kindred needs for emancipation. In the 1840s, Garrisonians made Irish Catholic emancipation an integral part of their campaign for universal reform. Visiting the United States, Daniel O'Connell (1775–1847), the first Catholic since the Reformation to sit in the British House of Commons, the leading Irish champion of Catholic emancipation, and an indefatigable campaigner for Irish independence, saw the needs of starving Irish and enslaved blacks as analogous. The American abolitionists Wendell Phillips and Frederick Douglass adopted the same rhetorical ploy. In a visit to Ireland in the famine year of 1845, Douglass likened the circumstances of Ireland's poor to those of enslaved black people. Such a tragic physiognomy of the two peoples wrenched his heart: "The open, uneducated mouth—the long, gaunt arm—the badly formed foot and ankle—the shuffling gait—the retreating forehead and vacant expression—and their petty quarrels and fights—all reminded me of the plantation, and my own cruelly abused people." The Irish needed only "black skin and wooly hair, to complete their likeness to the plantation Negro."[26] For Douglass and other abolitionists, the tragedy of both peoples lay in oppression. Neither horror stemmed from weakness rooted in race.

One group, however, utterly repudiated the notion of black-Irish similarity, and that was the Irish in the United States. Irish immigrants quickly recognized how to use the American color line to elevate white—no matter how wretched—over black. Seeking fortune on the white side of the color line, Irish voters stoutly supported the proslavery Democratic Party. By the mid-1840s, Irish American organizations actively opposed abolition with their votes and their fists. In the 1863 draft riots that broke out in New York and other northeastern cities, Irish Americans attacked African Americans with gusto in a bloody rejection of black-Irish commonality. In Ireland and in Britain, too, cultural nationalists seeking to shed racial disadvantage counterattacked, forging a Celtic Irish history commensurate with that of Anglo-Saxonists.*

---

*The long history of Anglo-Saxon denigration of the Celtic Irish race inspired pro-Celtic nationalists to turn the cultural tables. The Scots, unlike the Irish, had not lacked apologists. In the 1760s the Scottish poet James MacPherson (1736–96) published the *Poems of Ossian*, which

While Ireland's political struggle for independence from Britain delayed an Irish dimension of the Celtic literary revival until late in the nineteenth century, political Irish nationalism had flourished long before the struggle for Irish independence succeeded in 1921. Irish nationalists could turn Saxon chauvinism inside out in ways similar to those of abolitionists like David Walker. In 1839 Daniel O'Connell won over American abolitionists' hearts with a scathing condemnation of American imperialism. Abolitionists advocated peace, as expansionists were lusting after a seizure of Mexican territory: "There are your Anglo-Saxon race! Your British blood! Your civilizers of the world . . . the vilest and most lawless of races. There is a gang for you! . . . the civilizers, forsooth, of the world!"[27] For O'Connell, Anglo-Saxons were nothing but natural-born thieves. At the same time, two non-Irish litterateurs laid a basis for the study of Celtic literature.

In the mid-nineteenth century, the French philosopher Ernest Renan (1823–92) and the English cultural critic and poet Matthew Arnold (1822–88) offered admiring portraits of the mystic, romantic, and doomed Celtic race in *Poetry of the Celtic Races* (1854) and *On the Study of Celtic Literature* (1866). Renan was a highly respected philosopher of religion, Arnold, one of Britain's leading poets and literary critics. Their works, both very mixed blessings, were evidently meant to be affectionate. But in praising the Irish closeness to nature as a salutary counterweight to Anglo-Saxon and Teutonic modernity, Renan and Arnold reduced them into dumb, pathetic natives.

Witness Renan. Originally from Brittany, France's self-proclaimed Celtic homeland, Renan fondly cites the natural Christianity of "that gentle little race," the Celts. "The Teutons," in contrast, "only received

---

he claimed to be the work of Ossian, a third-century Celtic bard. MacPherson professed to have discovered and translated this ancient work, but when Samuel Johnson challenged its authenticity, MacPherson could not produce his originals. *Poems of Ossian* is now considered one of British literature's greatest frauds. Robert Burns (1759–96), in contrast, remains Scotland's national poet. Burns published *Poems, Chiefly in the Scottish Dialect* in 1786, the first of a spate of well-loved and enduring works in dialect. Although Walter Scott (1771–1832) is now better known for the Saxon-Norman racial thesis, antithesis, and synthesis of his 1819 novel *Ivanhoe*, his publishing career began in 1802–03 with a collection of ballads, *The Minstrelsy of the Scottish Border*, and carried on with a series of novels and poems set in Scotland.

Christianity tardily and in spite of themselves, by scheming or by force, after a sanguinary resistance, and with terrible throes." Compared with the brutal Teutons, the avatars of modernity, Renan's Celts are childlike and superstitious, of all nations the "least provided [with] . . . practical good sense."[28] In the face of the onrushing, mechanized world of industry, this is meant as a compliment.

Arnold's portrait drips with similar presumption. Claiming distant connection to Celts through his mother, yet identifying himself firmly as Saxon, Arnold sets the racial characteristics of Saxon-English in opposition to those of the Celtic Irish: Because "balance, measure, and patience" are ever required for success, even when a race has the most fortunate temperament "to start with," the Celtic Irish are doomed. For "balance, measure, and patience are just what the Celt has never had." Arnold extended Celtic incapacity even further: "And as in material civilisation he has been ineffectual, so has the Celt been ineffectual in politics." In fact, Arnold serenely predicts failure for the race: "For ages and ages the world has been constantly slipping, ever more and more, out of the Celt's grasp. 'They went forth to war,' Ossian says most truly, '*but they always fell.*' "[29]

Here is a puzzlement. How could any of this have pleased the Celts? And yet, believe it or not, Renan and Arnold actually counted as friends of the Celtic race at the time. Arnold's campaign for a chair in Celtic studies at Oxford University succeeded in 1877, and he and Renan were praised for encouraging the late nineteenth- and early twentieth-century flowering of an Irish renaissance. True, their depiction of Celts had a distinctly racial flavor. But race was in the air at the time, and the alternative to Renan's and Arnold's patronizing lay in insults from the likes of Thomas Carlyle.

Defenders of the Celtic Irish race replied to English Saxon chauvinism with an older and more Christian version of their racial history. The popular, multivolume *History of the Anglo-Saxons* (1799–1805) by the English historian and bookseller Sharon Turner provided the template by portraying the modern English as direct descendants of Dark Age Saxons. So Irish nationalists could do that, too—and they did—claiming their pure descent from a bevy of ancient and luminous Celtic ancestors. There were, for instance, the prehistoric Firbolgs, Tuatha de Danann, and the followers of King Milesius from Spain, said to be the invaders of Ireland 1,500 to 1,000 years before the birth of Christ. Furthermore, Milesians traced their history back to Scythia (Ukraine and Russia), via Scota, an Egyptian pharaoh's daughter who gave her name to the Scots.*

Whether friends or foes, British intellectuals seeking root causes of Irish distress rarely rose above the doubt that the Irish, as Celts and as Catholics, possessed any racial qualities for greatness. On the other side of the Atlantic, however, race functioned differently in the long run.

As we have seen, Irish people lived in disparate political cultures. In Britain and Ireland they were labeled as Catholic Celts, linked by race with the despised French. In the United States their situation was more complex. In Britain and Ireland religion carried far more weight than in the United States. Religious wars, after all, had long raged over England; for centuries Britain had dubbed Anglicanism the national, Protestant religion. In the United States no sect enjoyed constitutional recognition. The United States also lacked a long history of antagonism and entanglement with Catholic France. No wars had been fought over religion in North America, and no long history implanted religious identity at the root of American national consciousness. So while an aversion to Catholicism and Catholics was hardly a trivial facet of American life and could flare up in deadly violence, it never defined American identity over the long haul.

And then there was the ugly history of British colonialism and Ireland's situation as a colony. England was, first and foremost, a colonial power centuries before the Act of Union of 1800 purportedly united the Irish and British crowns. During the nineteenth century, a question festered—what to do with Ireland? The firm assumption that the Irish were unfit for self-government often dominated domestic politics. The United States had black people and slavery to contend with, issues so huge that they blunted anti-Irish sentiment as a source of political con-

---

* By giving her name to the Scots, Scota endowed the people of Scotland with an African origin.

flict, but not before a decade of turmoil. As we have already noted, the 1840s were a tense time in the United States, an era of rising nativism.

THE BLOODSTAINED Order of United Americans first appeared in New York City in 1844 and soon spread to Massachusetts, Pennsylvania, New Jersey, and Connecticut. Catholic churches had been torched now and then since the mid-1830s (actually black churches, too, but not on account of religion). In 1834 a nativist mob had burned the Convent of the Ursuline nuns in Charlestown, Massachusetts. Now arson became endemic, climaxing in Philadelphia in 1844, when a mob of six hundred self-proclaimed American Republicans burned down St. Michael's and St. Augustine's Catholic churches and torched many Irish residences. The rioting lasted three days, killing thirteen and wounding fifty.[30] In Pittsburgh in 1850 a candidate running on the "People's and Anti-Catholic" ticket won the mayoral race. During the 1850s Massachusetts and Connecticut enacted voter literacy tests in an attempt to curtail immigrant Democratic voting power.[31] By the mid-1850s clubs of the Order of United Americans flourished in sixteen states.[32]

Much early anti-Catholic violence was more or less spontaneous and poorly organized, driven by fear that the Irish would lower wages or increase crime. But nativism gained an important institutional basis with the founding in New York City, in about 1850, of the secret Supreme Order of the Star-Spangled Banner. Members soon became labeled "know-nothings" because they customarily responded to queries about their order with "I know nothing." Members had to be men born in the United States of native-born parents. Natives married to Catholics could not join. Know-Nothings had a broad agenda that differed according to their class and their region. They especially hated Catholics, but they also opposed liquor and political corruption. In New England, they challenged the mass voting of immigrants for the proslavery Democratic Party.

In terms of their tactics, Know-Nothing clubs like the Order of United Americans and the Supreme Order of the Star-Spangled Banner traded on patriotism. Most local chapters took the names of founding fathers or heroes and battles of the American Revolution.[33] A political party spun out of the Supreme Order of the Star-Spangled Banner was actually named the American Party. So patriotic a title encouraged members to brand opponents "anti-American." In the Midwest, for instance, where Germans had settled and voted in large numbers, refugees from the European revolutions of 1848 almost automatically seemed anti-American on account of their suspected radicalism.

Such frequent mob violence made riot the signature Know-Nothing activity: against Irish people, against Catholic churches, and against other parties' voters. Matters grew worse with the 1853 visit of a papal envoy dispatched to arbitrate disputed church property claims, which riled up anti-Catholic secret orders and societies. At every stop along the envoy's itinerary, the American and Foreign Christian Union incited mobs. In Cincinnati a crowd attempted to lynch him. Back east, in a decidedly bizarre event, a Know-Nothing mob assaulted a block of marble. The offending stone, taken from the Temple of Concord in Rome, was a gift from Pope Pius IX to be placed in the Washington Monument, still under construction. When the stone proved resistant to destruction, the mob dumped it into the Potomac River.

In 1854 a mob in Ellsworth, Maine, tarred and feathered a Catholic priest before nearly burning him to death. In Newark, New Jersey, Know-Nothings and Orangemen (Protestant Irishmen) from New York City broke the windows and statuary of St. Mary's Catholic Church and killed an Irish Catholic bystander. Elections particularly excited passions. Know-Nothing mobs beat up opposition voters in several cities, including Washington and Baltimore. After the election riots of 1855 in Louisville, a priest reported "a reign of terror surpassed only by the Philadelphia riots [of 1844]. Nearly one hundred poor Irish have been butchered or burned and some twenty houses have been consumed in the flames."[34] Here was a war of religion, deadly while it raged.

Catholic-hating fervor swept Know-Nothings into office during the fall elections of 1854, as over a million followers in ten thousand local councils seized control of entire state governments.[35] Massachusetts, New York, and six or seven other states elected Know-Nothing governors, and between seventy-five and a hundred congressmen as well as a host of state and local officials, including mayors in Boston, Philadelphia, and Chicago. (Numbers vary, owing to the difficulty of determining just who should be counted as a Know-Nothing. The movement went by an abundance of organizational names.) The future president Rutherford B. Hayes was moved to exclaim, "How people do hate Catholics."[36]

On assuming power, Know-Nothings pushed a variety of measures opposing political corruption and promoting temperance, but Catholic immigrants remained the primary target. A bill was put forward to bar people not born in the United States from holding political office and to extend the waiting period for naturalization to twenty-one years. Such barriers and extensions would obviously have prevented many in the working class from voting, precisely the Know-Nothing intent. Like most Know-Nothing measures proposed by neophyte legislators, these failed to become law. In Massachusetts, however, Know-Nothings did manage to enact a nunneries inspection bill, which empowered legislators to inspect Catholic convents and schools, a mandate the legislators pursued with questionable enthusiasm.

Several luminaries played their part. Sam Houston (1793–1863), leader of the Texas revolution, president of the Republic of Texas, then governor and senator from the state of Texas, cobbled together a theory about the difference between old and new immigrants that functioned well into the twentieth century. For Houston, the founding fathers and heroes of the American Revolution constituted the fine old immigrants, in sharp contrast to the new immigrants of the 1850s, people "spewed loathingly from the prisons of England, and from the pauper houses of Europe."[37]

Ulysses S. Grant (1822–85), only a decade from the U.S. presidency, pitied himself for his lack of "privileges" compared with German job seekers who seemed to have all the luck. During the Civil War, seizing a chance to legalize his prejudices, Grant enacted one of the rare nineteenth-century anti-Semitic policies. Called General Orders No. 11, it expelled all Jews, including families with children, from the Department of Tennessee in December of 1862. Grant's excuse? He insisted that he had to control Jewish peddlers. In fact, his directive affected all Jews in Tennessee, no matter their vocation, sex, or age. President Abraham Lincoln quickly rescinded the order, but not before several families were displaced.[38]

In the South, Know-Nothings also did well in the mid-1850s elections. An Alabama Know-Nothing congressman spoke for many when he declaimed, "I do not want the vermin-covered convicts of the European continent. . . . I do not want those swarms of paupers, with pestilence in their skins, and famine in their throats, to consume the bread of the native poor. Charity begins at home—charity forbids the coming of these groaning, limping vampires."[39] This kind of proclamation played as well in the South, with its few immigrants, as in the North, with its many.

Eventually, as we know, fundamental political tensions destroyed Know-Nothingism as slavery—the elephant in the American living room—bumped about more aggressively. In 1855 the question of slavery in the Nebraska Territory set southern Know-Nothings on one side, demanding explicit safeguards for slavery, and northerners on the other, refusing to go along. Once the slavery issue split the Know-Nothing movement along sectional lines, the newly founded Republican Party picked up northern Know-Nothings unwilling to bow to southern devotion to slavery. In the South, Know-Nothings rejoined or ceded to Democrats. The split did not signal the definitive end of nativism. For instance, the Know-Nothing candidate for president in 1856, the former Whig president Millard Fillmore, polled some 800,000 votes, or over one-fifth of those cast nationwide, although he carried only the state of Maryland. Democrats elected James Buchanan of Pennsylvania, their last successful presidential candidate until the 1884 election of Grover Cleveland. Slowly the worst violence associated with Catholic hating in the United States ended, but poor Irish Catholics remained a race apart—Celts. At the same time, nine-tenths of African Americans remained enslaved, and they were not only abused as an inferior race: they were seldom counted as Americans. Towering over the notion of two inferior races, Celt and African, the figure of the Saxon monopolized the identity of *the* American. But at least the Celts had their whiteness.

10

THE EDUCATION OF
RALPH WALDO EMERSON

Ralph Waldo Emerson (1803–82) towers over his age as the embodiment of the American renaissance, but not, though he also should, as the philosopher king of American white race theory. Widely hailed for his intellectual strength and prodigious output, Emerson wrote the earliest full-length statement of the ideology later termed Anglo-Saxonist, synthesizing all the salient nineteenth- and early twentieth-century concepts of American whiteness. (See figure 10.1, Ralph Waldo Emerson.)

A quintessential New Englander born in Boston, Emerson descended from a family of scholarly ministers whose American roots reached back to 1635. Emerson's esteemed father, the Reverend William Emerson, had delivered a Phi Beta Kappa address at Harvard—just as his son would a generation later—and served as pastor at Boston's First Church. Such a lofty perch, while conferring eminent respectability, did not guarantee financial security even while the Reverend William Emerson lived. His death, when Waldo was not quite eight years old, plunged the family into outright hardship. Luckily Waldo's diminutive aunt—she stood four feet three inches tall—Mary Moody Emerson (1774–1863) was there to fill a crucial gap in his education at home.*

---

* Under the title "Amita" ("Friend"), Ralph Waldo Emerson gave an appreciation of his aunt to the Women's Club of Boston in 1869.

Fig. 10.1. Ralph Waldo Emerson carte-de-visite.

An 1814 American edition of de Staël's *On Germany* had introduced German romanticism and the wisdom of India to intellectual Americans like Mary Moody Emerson. She kept the book at hand throughout her life and used it to transmit her enthusiasm for de Staël and German romanticism to her nephew before, during, and after his formal studies.[1] He had a good, traditional New England education, attending the Boston Latin School, then following his forebears to Harvard College, where he waited on tables to cover tuition. He taught school for four years before enrolling in the Harvard Divinity School, which he left as a Unitarian minister in 1829. That same year he married Ellen Louisa Tucker and became minister of Boston's Second Church.

EMERSON'S FASCINATION with German thought was practically foreordained. At Harvard he studied with the confirmed romanticists George Ticknor and Edward Everett, two young scholars recently returned from studies at Göttingen's Georg-August University. Well schooled by Aunt Mary, Emerson had incorporated her comments into his Harvard senior essay, winning second prize in 1821. Even his older brother, William, pitched in, going abroad to study at Göttingen in 1824–25 and writing home to Waldo urging him "to learn German as fast as you can" in order to follow him to Germany.[2]

German thought filled the air around Boston's young intellectuals.

In the 1820s Emerson read English writers like Samuel Taylor Coleridge, who had studied at Göttingen with Blumenbach,[3] and William Wordsworth, both necessary guides into things German since Emerson never gained great competence in the German language. All in all, his Harvard study, Aunt Mary Moody Emerson's keenness for German romanticism, and Germaine de Staël's *On Germany* propelled Emerson ever deeper into study of German philosophy and literature.

TRANSCENDENTALISM, THE American version of German romanticism (à la Kant, Fichte, Goethe, and the Schlegel brothers), flourished in New England, particularly in eastern Massachusetts, from the mid-1830s into the 1840s. German transcendentalism offered an odd mixture, including even a hefty dose of Indian mysticism inspired by Friedrich von Schlegel, which Mary Emerson had also found congenial.* In place of established Christian religion (particularly the then prevailing Unitarianism), transcendentalism offered a set of romantic notions about nature, intuition, genius, individualism, the workings of the Spirit, and, especially, the character of religious conviction. At bottom, it prized intuition over study and emphasized the idea of an indwelling god who unified all creation. Guided by Aunt Mary, Emerson borrowed transcendentalism's focus on nature as a spiritual force for his essay *Nature* (1836), now considered the transcendentalists' manifesto.[4†]

Most leading New England transcendentalists had attended Harvard College, and many had continued into Harvard's Divinity School preparing for the Unitarian ministry. Emerson fits the mold perfectly in several ways, as a minister and as one who resigned his pulpit after a crisis of faith. Even after leaving the ministry, however, Emerson remained

---

* Friedrich von Schlegel had studied Sanskrit in Paris and in 1808 published a book on Indian languages and knowledge: *Über die Sprache und Weisheit der Indier* (*On the Language and Wisdom of the Indians*). Emerson also shared this fascination with Indian language and philosophy with an Oxford scholar of Aryan, Max Müller, with whom he carried on an epistolary friendship for decades before meeting in person in 1873.
† Henry Hedge, an original transcendentalist and longtime Emerson familiar, had also studied in Germany.

intrigued throughout his life by the religious dimension of transcendentalism. In *Nature* he announces American transcendentalism as a new way of conceiving spirituality, amplified two years later in his classic *Divinity School Address*.*

WITHIN THIS German-driven transcendental swirl, one man, an Englishman, stood tallest: he was Thomas Carlyle (1795–1881). (See figure 10.2, Thomas Carlyle.) A reedy, stooped six-footer and a lifelong hypochondriac, Carlyle was usually half sick with a cold. The twenty-four-year-old Emerson (also tall, thin, and hypochondriac) discovered Carlyle's unsigned reviews in the *Edinburgh Review* and the *Foreign Review* in 1827 and began to hail the British author as his "German-ick new-light writer," as well as "perhaps now the best Thinker of the Saxon race."[5] Clearly Carlyle's take on German mysticism would lay the foundation for American transcendentalism.

Actually, Carlyle was, geographically speaking, just barely a "Thinker of the Saxon race," having been born in Scotland in the little town of Ecclefechan, eight miles from the English border.[†] This provenance counted heavily for Carlyle, who wished to be known as a *southern* Scot, that is, as a Saxon rather than a Celt—the northern Scots, to his mind being the latter and therefore, as we have seen in this mind-set, inferior.

After study at the University of Edinburgh, Carlyle, like many other English speakers, encountered German thought in de Staël's *On Germany* in 1817. So impressed was he that he sent his future wife, Jane Welsh, a copy of de Staël's novel *Delphine*. Furthermore, what he saw in *On Germany*—with its racial introduction, its elevation of Goethe

---

* Between these two, Emerson's *American Scholar* (1837) declares American intellectual independence from British models. American intellectual independence was not entirely complete, for in transcendentalism Germans replace the discarded British. Even the name "transcendentalism" came, via de Staël's *On Germany*, from the German philosopher Immanuel Kant's notion of "transcendental reality" in the *Critique of Pure Reason* (*Kritik der reinen Vernunft*, 1781 and 1787).

† Ecclefechan lies midway between Lockerbie (where Pan Am flight 103 went down in 1988, killing 270 people) and Gretna Green, on the border between Scotland and England, well south of Glasgow.

to mythic status, and its concluding section on German transcendental mysticism—encouraged
Carlyle to study German. This
enthusiasm for the German language and its literature gained
him employment as a German
tutor in Scotland and motivated
his translation of Goethe's *Wilhelm Meister's Apprenticeship*
in 1824, which he sent along to
Goethe in Weimar. That opening
inaugurated a respectful correspondence lasting until Goethe's
death in 1832.[6]

Fig. 10.2. Thomas Carlyle.

Carlyle actually came to think
of Goethe as "a kind of spiritual father," and took upon himself the
task of spreading the transcendental gospel.[7] And spread it he did, writing the magazine articles Emerson was reading in New England in the
late 1820s and early 1830s, many of them reviews of German authors
and essays on German thought.[8] Like Carlyle, Emerson worshipped
Goethe throughout his scholarly life. So thorough was this adoration
that Goethe's *Italienische Reise* shaped Emerson's European itinerary
of 1833, dictating a first stop in Rome.[9] Emerson even began collecting Goethe statuettes and portraits and named the Emerson family cat
"Goethe."[10]

Emerson was thirty when he first saw Europe. By then he had left his
pastorate and lost his beloved young wife to tuberculosis two years after
their marriage. Now he poured energy into seeing for himself the luminaries of this new philosophy. Coleridge and Wordsworth came first, and
both disappointed Emerson greatly. He found Coleridge "a short, thick
old man [who] took snuff freely, which presently soiled his cravat and
neat black suit." Even worse was Wordsworth who abused the beloved
Goethe and Carlyle and nattered on as though reading aloud from his

books. Wordsworth later sneered at Emerson as well, calling him "a pest of the English tongue" and lumping him with Carlyle as philosophers "who have taken a language which they suppose to be English for their vehicle . . . and it is a pity that the weakness of our age has not left them exclusively to the appropriate reward, mutual admiration." Emerson felt he had spent an hour with a parrot.[11]

The visit in Scotland with Carlyle, however, went perfectly. Much younger than Coleridge and Wordsworth, Carlyle captivated Emerson through a day and a night of passionate exchange chock full of fresh ideas expressed energetically. At this point neither man had published canonical work, but recognizing kindred spirits, they fell into each other's arms, initiating a lifelong correspondence that even weathered ideological strains over slavery and the American Civil War. Mutual support immensely enhanced both their careers.

At the time of Emerson's visit, Carlyle's novel *Sartor Resartus* had reached the public only in magazine form, and little wonder, for this ponderous, autobiographical tale drags English readers through a morass of German transcendentalism and the mysticism of Immanuel Kant, with nothing of de Staël's clarity. Carlyle's novel is clotted with German, making it a hard sell in Britain; its protagonist, for instance, bears the challenging name Diogenes Teufelsdröckh. While a later admirer would pronounce *Sartor Resartus* part of a "great spiritual awakening of the Teutonic race," at the time, only two readers that we know of lauded its magazine publication: a Father O'Shea of Cork, Ireland, and Ralph Waldo Emerson.[12]*

In fact, without Emerson's tireless promotion, Carlyle's writing career might have ended there. But Emerson took Carlyle's novel in hand, shepherding an American edition into print and contributing a preface. With this help, the thumping, clamorous, and obscure style of *Sartor Resartus* electrified the Americans becoming known as transcendentalists: Theodore Parker spoke admiringly of a "German epidemic," and William Ellery Channing experienced it as a "quickener"

---

* Given Carlyle's negative view of the Irish, he would not have appreciated Irish admiration and found American applause all the more precious.

of his own ideas.[13] Thanks to Emerson, an American edition of Carlyle's *French Revolution* soon followed. The first money—£50—that Carlyle ever earned through his writing came from Emerson, acting as Carlyle's agent in the United States over the course of several years.[14] Indeed, Emerson made Carlyle more popular by far in America than he had ever been in Great Britain. Carlyle returned the favor, launching Emerson's career in the United Kingdom with the 1841 publication of *Essays*. Carlyle's advocacy had a number of English critics calling Emerson a Yankee genius, a sterling compliment since "genius" offered the romantics' highest form of praise.

Given Emerson's inability to read German very well, Carlyle stepped in as his teacher of transcendentalism, and not always an uncritical one. Early in their friendship Carlyle recognized the derivative nature of Emerson's thought, explaining later "that Emerson had, in the first instance, taken his system out of 'Sartor' and other of [Carlyle's] writings, but he worked it out in a way of his own."[15] Before meeting Emerson, the prominent English academic Henry Crabb Robinson, a founder of University College, London, had dismissed him as "a Yankee writer who has been puffed by [Carlyle] into English notoriety" but who was "a bad imitator of Carlyle who himself imitates Coleridge ill, who is a general imitator of the Germans." (Once they met, Robinson's view of Emerson softened.) John Ruskin's estimation of Emerson wavered over time; at one point Ruskin, one of England's leading intellectuals, considered Emerson "only a sort of cobweb over Carlyle."[16]

This image of Emerson as a watered-down Carlyle-Teutonist never entirely dissipated, just as critics of Carlyle, Emerson, and transcendentalists have harped on the Teutonic opacity of their style. Southern critics, perhaps naturally, amplified these charges by tacking on an anti–New England, anti-antislavery twist. As the American sectional crisis deepened in the 1850s and Emerson spoke more pointedly against slavery and the slave power, a southern animus against him grew.[17]*

---

*A reviewer in the *Southern Literary Messenger* found Emerson's style "affectedly, studiously, and elaborately involved and obscure." Emerson's observations were not " 'apples of gold set in pictures of silver,' but rather like pearl embedded in a mudhole. . . ."

On the other hand, Americans adored Carlyle's emphatic writing style and his apparent, if vague, sympathy for ordinary people and a disdain for the elite. Even Garrisonian abolitionists and feminists who advocated civil rights for all, seemed blind to the broader tendency of his politics. By 1840 Carlyle had come to despise their movement outright and deprecate the whole notion of universal human rights. Had they read him attentively, American fans would have realized this. But they did not. Antislavery Americans visiting London for the World Anti-Slavery Conference in 1840 unwittingly sought Carlyle out, ignorant of his approval of slavery as a perfectly appropriate labor regime for those he considered inferior races. Elizabeth Cady Stanton preserved an admiration for Carlyle even after he threw the visiting abolitionists out of his house. In the late 1860s, when abolitionists were splitting over the enfranchisement of poor black men (before educated white women got the vote), Stanton turned into a mean-spirited, Saxon chauvinist more in line with Carlyle's thought. She happily quoted Carlyle's *Sartor Resartus* to the detriment of people she considered inherently inferior.[18]

One notion guiding both Carlyle and Emerson, and supposedly liberal Americans like Stanton, was their heroic figuration of what they termed the Saxon race. Many other Americans—including Thomas Jefferson, the novelist Harriet Beecher Stowe, and Sarah Josepha Hale, editor of the most popular nineteenth-century American women's magazine—proclaimed themselves Saxons.[19]* Most of these just briefly and easily looked back to "our Saxon ancestors," before moving on, but Emerson dedicated an entire book to the subject, as we shall see. Cobbled together as race history, it drew on the eighth-century English historian Bede, Norse mythology, and many prevailing versions of English history, notably the (male) historian-bookseller Sharon Turner's wildly popular *The History of the Anglo-Saxons, from Their First Appearance above the Elbe, to the Death of Egbert*, originally published in 1799 and in its seventh edition in 1852. Emerson owned a copy of the seventh edi-

---

* Jefferson's fellow Virginian Thomas Paine, did not agree that most Americans' ancestors were Saxons. In *Common Sense* Paine concluded that "not one third of the inhabitants [of America] are of English descent."

tion and eagerly absorbed its Saxon chauvinism. Digging deep into Old Norse literature, Turner lumps Saxons and Norse together to come up with a list of undying "traits" of the English race. He proclaims liberty the first and foremost of these traits, which he believes persisted from the fifth-century Saxon/Norse conquest and had remained valid ever since. Like Thomas Jefferson, Turner contrasts the Anglo-Saxon tradition of liberty with the Norman inclination toward tyranny. However, Turner's concept of a Norman "graft" onto England's original Anglo-Saxon "stock" disagrees with Jefferson's idea of permanently, racially pure Anglo-Saxons.[20]

Carlyle, who imagined himself a representative of Britain's Norse heritage, infected his followers, including Emerson, with "we Saxon" jargon. Even the cosmopolitan Margaret Fuller, a foremost American interpreter of German romanticism, fell under the spell. On meeting Carlyle in London in 1846, Fuller portrays him admiringly, just the way he liked to be seen: "Carlyle, indeed, is arrogant and overbearing, but in his arrogance there is no littleness, no self-love: it is the heroic arrogance of some old Scandinavian conqueror—it is his nature and the untamable impulse that has given him power to crush the dragons. . . . [Y]ou like him heartily, and like to see him the powerful smith, the Siegfried, melting all the old iron in his furnace."[21]

This Teutonic/Saxon race chauvinism increased in Carlyle and Emerson as they aged, but far more so in Carlyle. His identification with his Saxons as Germans seemed boundless, as he completely embraced German nationalism and Teutonic race chauvinism along the lines of Charles Villers and romantics like the two Schlegels, de Staël's friends.[22] As early as 1820, in his twenty-fifth year, Carlyle was already admiring German writers for the "muscle in their frames."[23] A decade later, he was delivering popular lectures on German themes. One of several 1837 lectures was entitled "On the Teutonic People, the German Language, the Northern Immigration, and the Nibelungen Lied," the pagan German epic that later inspired Richard Wagner's *Ring* cycle. It may seem odd to readers today, but when Carlyle spoke of "the German people," he was including much of the population of Britain. In any case, Carlyle came to sound a lot like the willfully excerpted version of *Germania* by the Roman author Tacitus, which was then beginning to circulate among German nationalists. Alert to the values of his time, Carlyle sexes his German nationalism masculine.

His Germans are "the only genuine European people, unmixed with strangers. They have in fact never been subdued; and considering the great, open, and fertile country which they inhabit, this fact at once demonstrates the masculine and indomitable character of the race. They have not only not been subdued, but been themselves by far the greatest conquerors in the world."[24] Those themes of masculinity and race purity would soon reappear in Emerson, with masculinity of far greater consequence. On the matter of racial purity Emerson would waver.

But neither of them had a good word to say for France or the French people—an "Ape-population," as Carlyle put it. France had turned revolutionary in 1789 and again in 1848, and Carlyle detested anything hinting of democracy. Such broad condemnation raised problems. What was one to make of the virile French Norman conquerors? Carlyle finessed that contradiction by pronouncing Normans to be Norsemen who had merely learned to speak French; obviously, for him, the change of language had not altered their blood, their basic nature, or their manly might. The Norman conquest had clearly benefited Britain, "entering with a strong man [William the Conqueror] . . . an immense volunteer police force . . . united, disciplined, feudally regimented, ready for action; strong Teutonic men."[25] All of this went quite a bit over the top, but American readers loved it. Carlyle might have trashed the French more lustily, but Emerson did his bit.

An 1835 lecture shows just how far Emerson would go. "Permanent Traits of the English National Genius" begins by connecting Americans to the English: "The inhabitants of the United States, especially of the Northern portion, are descended from the people of England and have inherited the traits of their national character." As for the French, their early enemies may be trusted when they hold, " 'It is common with the Franks to break their faith and laugh at it. The race of Franks is faithless.' . . . An union of laughter and crime, of deceit and politeness is the unfavorable picture of the French character as drawn by the English and Germans, and even by the French themselves."[26] The unmanly vices of frivolity, corruption, and lack of practical know-how all afflicted the French. How else to view a people who invented the ruffle, while it took the English to invent the shirt?[27]* For manly practicality, look to the "English race." For the childish, "singing and dancing nations," look south.[28] That north/south dichotomy would prove a durable theory, one Emerson trumpeted and his followers echoed, including his younger and rather priggish English admirer Matthew Arnold, ostensible defender of the beleaguered Celts.

Emerson and Carlyle outlined a transatlantic realm of Saxondom also taken up by Arnold, among many others. In his first letter after Emerson's 1833 visit, Carlyle wrote, "Let me repeat once more what I believe is already dimly the sentiment of all Englishmen, Cisoceanic and Transoceanic, that we and you are not two countries, and cannot for the life of us be; but only two <u>parishes</u> of one country, with such wholesome parish hospitalities, and dirty temporary parish feuds, as we see; both of which brave parishes <u>Vivant! vivant!</u>"[29] In the late 1830s Emerson was urging Carlyle to visit the United States, perhaps even to settle permanently: "Come, & make a home with me," Emerson wrote.[30] What a joy it would be to merge the intellects of Saxondom in their own two persons!

This rhetoric of bonding seemed to have no ceiling. In 1841 Carlyle, following Goethe's infatuation with the ancient Greeks, wrote, "By and by we shall visibly be, what I always say we virtually are, members of neighboring Parishes; paying continual visits to one another. What is to hinder huge London from being to universal Saxondom what small Mycale was to the Tribes of Greece. . . . A meeting of <u>All the English</u> ought to be as good as one of All the Ionians. . . ."[31] And Emerson agreed. Enjoying a reputation for genius in Britain as well as the United States by 1853–55, he repeated a lecture entitled "The Anglo-American." He might well have been speaking autobiographically in his comments on

---

*After his trip to France in 1848, Emerson admitted that the French had some masculinity. But throughout his life his basic inclination was Francophobic.

the "godly & grand British race": "it is right to esteem without regard to geography this industrious liberty-loving Saxon wherever he works,— the Saxon, the colossus who bestrides the narrow Atlantic. . . ."[32] But in all this mutual admiration, a rift would soon appear.

Emerson saw himself as a New Englander, virtually as an Englishman, and therefore as a "Saxon." "We Saxons" peppered his lectures, essays, and journals. In his classic 1841 essay "Self-Reliance," Emerson exhorts his readers to wake up the "courage and constancy, in our Saxon breasts," to realize that New Englanders are the final product of a process of distillation that had earlier turned Norsemen into Englishmen over the course of a millennium.* Later on, he would portray New Englanders as even more English than the English, as "double distilled English."

Carlyle would not go that far. For all his Germanicism, Carlyle saw London as the natural capital of Saxondom for the present and foreseeable future. Perhaps later—probably much later—the capital might move west: "After centuries, if Boston, if New York, have become the most convenient 'All-Saxondom,' we will right cheerfully go thither to hold such festival. . . ."[33] Before long, this boil would fester and burst, for Emerson's timetable sprang from a conviction that England was already practically worn out from excessive commercialism, labor troubles, and luxury. The Saxons on Americans' side of the ocean, woodsmen who reminded Emerson of the Germans of Tacitus, would inherit the mantle of Saxon leadership sooner rather than later.[†]

Emerson did not visit Britain between 1833 and 1847. When he later did, he found Saxon identity weakening as a glue of friendship. Britain was enduring the economic hard times and suffering that would inspire Charles Dickens's novel *Hard Times* (1854). The ever grumpy Carlyle grew more authoritarian, to the point that in 1848 he complained about Emerson's equanimity: Emerson was "content with everything" and

---

* The whole sentence reads, "If we cannot at once rise to the sanctities of obedience and faith, let us at least resist our temptations; let us enter into the state of war and wake Thor and Woden, courage and constancy, in our Saxon breasts."

† Emerson mentions Tacitus at least four times in *English Traits*, turning his prose toward themes of German nationalism.

becoming "a little wearisome" with his "pleasant <u>moonshiny</u> lectures." Emerson fired back, reporting that Carlyle "sits in his four-story house and <u>sneers</u>."[34] Basically, the friendship was over, but on one issue Emerson and Carlyle could still agree. Both looked askance at the Irish.

Carlyle termed the Irish "Human swinery," playing on the commonplace analogy between Irish people and pigs. The Irish were believed to live with their pigs, and pigs were considered quintessentially Irish, as in the saying, "as Irish as Paddy's pig." Over in Concord, Massachusetts, where Irish laborers worked in mud and lived in shanties, Emerson saw no reason to dispute this libel. One of his rare comments on the districts of the poor, where he spent very little time, reveals both prejudice and naïveté: "In Irish districts, men deteriorated in size and shape, the nose sunk, the gums were exposed, with diminished brain and brutal form."[35] Like Carlyle in *Chartism* (1840), Emerson skirts the issue of whether race alone made the Irish ugly. On such an easy topic, the two found agreement.*

Then came the American Civil War. Emerson, no radical abolitionist, nonetheless opposed American slavery, particularly after the toughening of the Fugitive Slave Law in 1850 and John Brown's raid on the Harpers Ferry, Virginia, federal arsenal in 1859. He also supported the Union during the war itself. Emerson did make a third and last trip to Europe, in 1872–73, only to find that he and Carlyle, both impaired by age, could no longer manage a meeting of the minds. Carlyle voiced a growing antipathy toward just about everybody. Gone were his youthful hints of sympathy for ordinary folk, an inclination always vaguely abstract. After his bitter pronouncements on what he called the "Nigger question" in 1850, he expressed no sympathy whatever with the poor, whether recently emancipated in the Western Hemisphere or despised and impoverished in Ireland and Britain.

But while their halcyon days may have gone, their influence lived

---

* In 1858 Carlyle published his last great work, a six-volume biography of Frederick the Great, king of Prussia from 1740 to 1786. Celebrating Teutons, Germans, and Prussians to the point of unreadability, this rambling, battle-obsessed history identified more thoroughly with Germanic militarism than Emerson could stomach.

on. Tutored in German race theory reaching back to Winckelmann and Goethe, each had become his country's national voice, eloquently equating Americans with Britons and Britons with Saxons. The Anglo-Saxon myth of racial superiority now permeated concepts of race in the United States and virtually throughout the English-speaking world. To be *American* was to be *Saxon*.

ENGLISH TRAITS

In the mid-1850s, Emerson cast about for new material and, at the same time, felt a need to get notes from his two European trips into print. Journal entries from those visits in 1833 and 1847–48 contained an abundance of raw material for a book on England and the Saxon race. But to buttress his arguments he read widely in history and science dealing with the race of men (and he did mean *men*) he considered permanent masters of the earth. Like all of Emerson's books, *English Traits*, which appeared in 1856, collects lectures delivered to various audiences over the course of a decade. Part travelogue, part autobiography, part historical ethnography, *English Traits* heightened his fame and gained appreciation as his wittiest book. Its popularity endured well into the twentieth century, when its racial theories began to fall into disrepute.[1]

Ideas about Saxons and the English people had long percolated in the United States. In his 1835 lecture "Permanent Traits of the English National Genius," Emerson called attention to the similarities in Americans' and Englishmen's appearance—the red and white complexion, blond hair, blue eyes, and tall stature—and, without doubt, ferocious manhood, all admirable traits quite unlike those of small and dark Celts, obviously (for Emerson) Asiatic in origin. These ideas reappeared in his 1843 lecture "Genius of the Anglo-Saxon Race" and in 1852–53 in "Traits and Genius of the Anglo-Saxon Race" and "The Anglo-American."[2]

These oft-repeated lectures made a ready audience for *English Traits*. Within three months of publication, 24,000 copies were in print in the United States and Great Britain, and the book was widely and positively reviewed.[3] Despite its blatant English/Saxon chauvinism—or perhaps because of it—*English Traits* attracted readers of various political persuasions and racial backgrounds. Charlotte Forten, for instance, the daughter of wealthy black Philadelphians and, at nineteen, an abolitionist in her own right, championed the book. Forten, who was living in Massachusetts at the time, bought the book and finished reading it within three weeks of its publication. In February 1857 Forten went to hear Emerson speak on the topic "Works and Days," which she found enlightening and the person of Emerson intimidating. She liked it, she said, "*very* much. The author's views of English character are far more liberal than those of American travelers generally. He evidently appreciates dear old England; and, loving her as I do, I like his book and thank him for it with all my heart."[4] The antislavery U.S. senator from Massachusetts, Charles Sumner, joined Forten and many other Americans in rampant Anglophilia. He pronounced himself attracted by "famous London town," which he considered downright "bewitching."[5] However clear-minded they might have been about the shortcomings of American society, New Englanders went gaga over the English.

Emerson himself cared little for London society, but he was obsessed with Saxon violence and manly beauty, both of which qualities he lacked. He was, in fact, a tall and skinny man, who, like his friend Thomas Carlyle, suffered from various nervous and bodily ailments throughout his life. As a house-bound intellectual when not lecturing before appreciative audiences, Emerson grew fascinated by the primeval virility of outdoor men of physical strength. Many others shared these anxieties, enough to make scenes of frontier violence staples of popular entertainment in Britain and the United States.[6]

THE CORE chapter of *English Traits*, called "Race," begins in measured tones. Emerson enumerates the three components of the English population: first the Celt, to whom he gives less than a paragraph; second, the German, also briefly noted; and third, the "Northmen." The balance of the chapter revels in ancient Viking history, dominated by traits of personal beauty and bloodthirstiness.

In the remainder of *English Traits*, race becomes ever more defined. The English race may be mixed, but, even so, racial "stock" determines national destiny: the "early history of each tribe show[s] the permanent bias. . . . In [King] Alfred [the Great of Wessex], in the Northmen, one may read the genius of the English society. . . ." Emerson's use of breeding terminology like "stock," anticipates the vocabulary of twentieth-century eugenics.

The "Race" chapter expresses two thoughts rooted in concerns Emerson shared with masses of Americans relishing his themes—two thoughts expressed as content and form. Brutality emerges as the chapter's prized quality, with manly beauty its outward appearance. As early as 1835 Emerson had praised the men he alternately termed Danes, Norsemen, Saxons, and Anglo-Saxons for their "beastly ferocity."[7] He amplifies this theme in *English Traits*. Bodily strength, vigor, manliness, and energy emerge as natural outgrowths of early Saxon bloodthirstiness, presented lovingly. Nature created Saxons/Norsemen as "a rude race, all masculine, with brutish strength," endowing their English descendants, in turn, with an "excess of virility."[8]

Homicidal history, synonymous to Emerson with gorgeous male energy, comes to life in his two quintessential "Norsemen," the brothers Horsa and Hengist, legendary founders of Saxon England. Recall that Thomas Jefferson had considered honoring them on the Great Seal of the new United States of America. According to legend, the mid-fifth-century British warlord Vortigern invited the brothers Horsa and Hengist into what is now Kent, in the southeastern tip of England, to wrest the island from its Celtic population and their Roman overlords. A century later the monk Gildas described the tribes of Horsa and Hengist as "vile unspeakable Saxons, hated of God and man alike," but their reputation rose considerably with the passage of centuries.[9]

Today Horsa and Hengist are considered Jutes from what is now Denmark, but tradition claims them as founders of the Anglo-Saxon nation that King Alfred raised to greatness in the late ninth century. Emerson ignored particularities of geography and lumped together Norsemen, Jutes, and Saxons as marvelous Scandinavian pirates, "a rude race, all masculine, with brutish strength.... Let buffalo gore buffalo, and the pasture to the strongest!"[10] Staying over the top, Emerson reveled in the Saxon/Jute/Norse brutality he had discovered in Samuel Laing's translation of *Heimskringla, or Chronicle of the Kings of Norway.** Though the term "Norsemen" usually refers to people of the far north—that is, to Dark Age Scandinavians in general—Emerson, by drawing on the *Heimskringla*, would seem finally to focus on Norway as the homeland in his theory. Actual German Saxons, in fact, hardly appear in *English Traits*, because, with the exception of Goethe, Emerson questions Germans' fitness to serve as models of any sort. Along with "the Asiatic races," he said back in 1835, Germans lack the racial constitution for political greatness, sharing as they do Asians' political impotence out of "a defect of will."[11] Norsemen supply the bonny figure of the Englishman American's ancestor.

Scandinavia might work as the ancestral home of northern whiteness, but Scandinavia of the 1850s created a dilemma: it was backward and really quite poor—a little nothing beside the British behemoth. How could Emerson reconcile that reality with his need for Scandinavian racial (hence permanent) brilliance? If the Norsemen endowed Britain with all its "Saxon" greatness, how to explain the relative obscurity of contemporary Scandinavia? Why had not Norwegians and Danes launched the industrial revolution, grown rich on worldwide commerce, and colonized the globe?

Here Emerson resorts to a favorite metaphor: the fruit tree. Scandinavia, he surmises, lost its best men during the Dark Ages—lost them to England and never recovered: "The continued draught of the best men in Norway, Sweden and Denmark to their piratical expeditions exhausted those countries, like a tree which bears much fruit when

---

* *The Heimskringla, or Chronicle of the Kings of Norway. Tr. from the Icelandic of Snorro Sturleson, with a Preliminary Dissertation, by S. Laing* had been published in London in 1844, one of the many books Emerson bought on his 1847 visit.

young, and these have been second-rate powers ever since. The power of the race migrated and left Norway permanently exhausted."[12]* It is a lame theory, and Emerson does not lean on it heavily. For his purposes, recent history of his Norsemen *in Scandinavia* need not loom large. The early days sufficed.

Consider his affection for obscure Norwegian kings and princes: "These Norsemen are excellent persons in the main," says Emerson, "with good sense, steadiness, wise speech, and prompt action. But they have a singular turn for homicide." Then, in a spirit of great good fun, he goes on to detail their amusements:

> their chief end of man is to murder, or to be murdered; oar, scythes, harpoons, crowbars, peatknives, and hayforks, are tools valued by them all the more for their charming aptitude for assassinations. A pair of kings, after dinner, will divert themselves by thrusting each his sword through the other's body, as did Yngve and Alf. Another pair ride out on a morning for a frolic, and, finding no weapon near, will take the bits out of their horses' mouths, and crush each other's heads with them, as did Alric and Eric. The sight of a tent-cord or a cloak-string puts them on hanging somebody, a wife, or a husband, or, best of all, a king. If a farmer has so much as a hayfork, he sticks it into a King Dag. King Ingiald finds it vastly amusing to burn up half a dozen kings in a hall, after getting them drunk. Never was poor gentleman so surfeited with life, so furious to be rid of it, as the Northman. If he cannot pick any other quarrel, he will get himself comfortably gored by a bull's horns, like Egil, or slain by a land-slide, like the agricultural King Onund.[13]

BEAUTY AND strength, strength and beauty. Entwined they thread through *English Traits*. On succeeding pages Emerson praises "the fair Saxon man" as "handsome" (three times) and associates him with "beauty" (four times). On one page, English and Scandinavians appear

---

* Emerson's often repeated notion that races could exhaust themselves enjoyed currency well into the twentieth century and reappears as the possibility of "unspent" races in a 1923 essay by the cultural pluralist Horace S. Kallen.

as "a handsome race" who "please by beauty" and are "distinguished for beauty" as "handsome captives" in Rome. In support, Emerson notes frequent references to the "personal beauty of its heroes" in the *Heimskringla*.

A century earlier, the Swiss physiognomist Lavater had maintained that outer beauty betokens inner qualities, and Emerson repeats this conviction in *English Traits*. The "English face," he says, combines "decision and nerve" with "the fair complexion, blue eyes, and open and florid aspect. Hence the love of truth, hence the sensibility, the fine perception, and poetic construction. The fair Saxon man, with open front, and honest meaning . . . is not the wood out of which cannibal, or inquisitor, or assassin is made, but he is moulded for law, lawful trade, civility, marriage, the nurture of children, for colleges, churches, charities, and colonies."[14] He does not explain how Norse assassins turn into loving fathers without losing their racial character of manly brutishness.

Such enthusiasm for physical attractiveness recalls Johann Friedrich Blumenbach's hymns to his lovely Georgian skull, although in Blumenbach's case, the skull was *female*. Such a progression came naturally to Emerson, educated at the hands of the Germanicists Mary Moody Emerson, George Ticknor, and Edward Everett and immersed in Goethe, all enamored of ancient Greeks as paragons of beauty.*

Likewise, Horatio Greenough, a young American artist living in Rome. Emerson had met Greenough in Florence in 1833 and gone on in *English Traits* to gush about his "face . . . so handsome, and his person so well formed," truly "a votary of the Greeks," and a good mind to go with his good looks.[15] Steeped in things Greek, Greenough had written his own *Artist's Creed*, musings on beauty à la Winckelmann, and he tutored Emerson on the Parthenon marbles in London and much else regarding Greek beauty. The friendship lasted nearly twenty years. Emerson had Greenough over for dinner shortly before the younger man died of brain fever in late 1852, at the age of only forty-seven.[16]

Emerson never fetishized Greeks the way Greenough and many

---

* Emerson read Goethe's essay on Winckelmann in 1850.

another did, but comments scattered throughout his published and unpublished work reveal an acceptance of Winckelmann's ideals. In September 1855, for instance, he dedicated a new cemetery in Concord by praising the Greeks, who "loved life and delighted in beauty." Bodily aesthetics were also central to German education and therefore to Emerson, but therein lay a problem. Blumenbach had coined the race name "Caucasian" as a concept of female beauty, full of feminine connotations of captive powerlessness.[17]

Many earlier intellectuals, certainly Immanuel Kant, Edmund Burke, and the eighteenth-century Edinburgh philosophers, had associated beauty with smallness, weakness, and women. For Emerson this would not do. He set out to wrench Saxon beauty away from female captives, away from the odalisques of the white slave trade, and away from French academic painting. He wanted the concept of beauty for his bloodthirsty, virile Norsemen. This task he took up in *English Traits*, and it led him to practically homoerotic heights.

Pondering, "Why England is England? What are the elements of that power which the English hold over other nations?" Emerson settles on race, history, and bodily might.[18] Englishmen, he asserts, show "great vigor of body and endurance. Other countrymen look slight and undersized beside them, and invalids. They are bigger men than the Americans. . . . They are round, ruddy, and handsome; at least, the whole bust is well formed; and there is a tendency to stout and powerful frames. . . . [I]n all ages, they are a handsome race."[19] Such vigor leads naturally to a fine militarism echoing Thomas Carlyle's image of the English "broad-fronted broad-bottomed Teutons . . . in solid phalanx foursquare to the points of the compass. They constitute the modern world. . . ."[20]

Such bluster may strike the reader as odd; certainly it is narrow, for no other race or nation makes much of an appearance in this book. Celts and the French emerge briefly as negative referents; American Indians make a fleeting appearance—as fast runners—in a dependent clause in chapter 2; Jews and Negroes peek through only once, as peoples defined by the concept of race. Alongside the Saxons, all others are lesser, gendered, and, by default, female.

Behind these judgments lay a fear that Americans had already fallen away from their mother country's—no, their *fatherland's*—standard of greatness. Emerson did not originate this thought. George-Louis Leclerc, Comte de Buffon, led a school of European naturalists who contended that animals degenerated in the Americas. In volume 5 of his thirty-six-volume *Histoire naturelle* (1749–88) Buffon presents a theory of American degeneracy, asserting that nature in America is "weaker, less active, and more circumscribed in the variety of her productions." This kind of slur cut deeply and cried out for refutation. Thomas Jefferson undertook the writing of *Notes on the State of Virginia* in the 1780s to disprove Buffon's contention that American horses—and, by implication, American men—lacked the virility of their Old World counterparts. Jefferson even shipped the remains of an American moose to Paris as proof that American animals grew to heroic dimensions.

As Emerson was composing *English Traits*, the Scots anatomist Robert Knox was disparaging stringy Americans: "Already the United States man differs in appearance from the European: the ladies early lose their teeth; in both sexes the adipose cellular cushion interposed between the skin and the aponeuroses [fibrous connecting tissue binding muscle to bone] and muscles disappears, or, at least, loses its adipose portion; the muscles become stringy, and show themselves; the tendons appear on the surface; symptoms of premature decay manifest themselves."[21]

Emerson shared the commonplace fear that civilization kills manhood, but Americans seemed particularly afflicted. Take his comparison of educated Englishmen and educated Americans. Weird though it seems, Emerson could see the English as more civilized and better educated than Americans, but simultaneously bigger, stronger, and tougher. In his chapter on universities, Emerson reports that at Oxford "diet and rough exercise secure a certain amount of old Norse power," while "they read better than we, and write better."[22] Emerson returns to this anxiety several times over the years in his journals:

> 1852: Englandishmen are pastureoaks; ours are pine saplings; large men here do not look architectural . . . but slight, ill-woven . . .[23]

1853: I felt the extreme poverty of American culture beside English. A mere bag of bones, was the one, sticking out in forlorn angularity; the other was fat & unctuous, shining & cheerful.[24]

1855: Tis clear that the European is a better animal than the American. Here you can only have Webster, or Parsons, or Washington, at the first descent from a farmer or people's man. Their sons will be mediocrities but in England, ~~you~~ in Europe, the privileged classes shall continue to furnish the best Specimens. The Czars of Russia shall continue to be good stock.[25]

Unwittingly, perhaps, Emerson connects the state of American masculinity to class. In "Self-Reliance," his most often quoted essay, he steps out of his own Concord- and Boston-based, Harvard-educated history to identify with those less educated and to contrast the brute rage of the multitude of common people with the "decorous and prudent" anger of the timid, feminine, college-educated and "cultivated classes." One rough, "sturdy lad from New Hampshire or Vermont" who tries everything and has no fear of failure is "worth a hundred of these city dolls," and the brutes "at the bottom of society" easily overwhelm the "feminine rage" of their betters.[26] Such philosophical noodling required a good deal of tortured analysis, even self-hatred. His definition of education, for instance, contains a regional dimension.

Emerson began teasing out the characteristics of southerners in the 1840s, when southern belligerence over slavery began to roil the nation's politics and those of his state of Massachusetts, divided as it was between upholders and opponents of slavery. Rising sectional tensions in the wake of the annexation of Texas as a slave state in 1845 and the immense territory acquired after the defeat of Mexico in 1848 pushed along Emerson's perception of innate differences between northerners and southerners. Boston, indeed all of New England, serve as synecdoche for the North, in Emerson's concept a smarter but weaker "race" than southerners. Southerners—meaning white male slaveholders—appear stronger and more brutal, but plainly lacking in intelligence.

In terms of manhood, the balance between smart and strong tips against northern opponents of slavery. In 1852, even as Emerson deplores the success of proslavery forces, he surmises that "Democrats carry the country, because they have more virility: just as certain of my neighbors rule our little town, quite ~~hon~~ legitimately, by having more courage & animal force than those whom they overbear."[27] Once again, Emerson was undermining his own claim to manliness in the construction of this nutty but commonplace notion.

Emerson may not have invented such stereotypes, but certainly his intellectual prestige lent them weight and longevity. That New Englanders were smarter and better educated than southerners appeared a reassuring fact in light of the looming conflict. But for Emerson southerners' brute strength embodied a kind of savage masculinity.

Westerners, those living beyond the Appalachian Mountains, did not figure in Emerson's philosophy until his first western tour, in 1850. His eight lectures earned him $500 each, money that drew him west several times more and engraved western men in his consciousness as a special type of Saxon. In a way Emerson saw white western American men as a sort of southern American tribe writ large, one possessed of more vitality than the eastern tribe by dint of its closeness to the land.

THE NOTION that Saxons were always free, like so many of Emerson's ideas about England, is not true. When Emerson describes liberty and freedom as English or Saxon racial characteristics, he overlooks not only the slavery issue then roiling American politics but also recent history on both sides of the Atlantic. After all, American indentured servitude, one form of bondage, reached into his own lifetime, and English convicts were still being forced into exile overseas while Emerson studied at Harvard in the 1820s. Moreover, slavery remained the rule rather than the exception in British colonies when he began his ministry at Boston's Second Church.

Nonetheless, Emerson, like Jefferson, claims in *English Traits* that the "Saxon seed" carries an "instinct for liberty," and he envisions freedom and liberty as crucial—and permanent—Saxon racial characteristics.[28] In a turn that would become commonplace, Emerson turns political practices into racial traits: racial genius (not historic or economic developments) made Anglo-Saxons both respecters of freedom within their brotherhood and natural rulers of other races. Thus political power was assumed to be a trait of the English race, emblemized in the Magna Carta of 1215, the cornerstone of English common law, and the Somerset decision of 1772, outlawing slavery within England.

The Magna Carta actually grew out of a struggle between church and state. England's King John, an avid international adventurer, had imposed heavy taxes on his subjects to fund the Third Crusade and pay a ransom demanded by the Holy Roman emperor for release of John's predecessor, Richard I, the Lionheart, taken prisoner near Vienna in 1192 as he wended his long way home from the Third Crusade. To gain Richard's release, John imposed especially heavy burdens on the churches. Those levies provoked the archbishop of Canterbury to channel unrest among the aristocracy into a demand for a formal statement of liberties—liberties of the church and liberties of the barons, who between them controlled virtually all of Britain's wealth.[29] After revisions to a first draft in June 1215, the king and the barons signed the Magna Carta at Runnymede, on the Thames River near Egham, in present-day Surrey County. In translation from the Latin, the Magna Carta begins with a clause guaranteeing the freedom of the English church: "FIRST, THAT WE HAVE GRANTED TO GOD, and by this present charter have confirmed for us and our heirs in perpetuity, that the English Church shall be free, and shall have its rights undiminished, and its liberties unimpaired." N.B.: It is a particular institution, "the English Church," that is to be free.

Use of the Magna Carta as proof of England's Saxon heritage dates back to the early seventeenth century, when Sir Edward Coke in 1610 first linked notions of a Saxon past to the Magna Carta and to English freedom, and in 1640, when John Hare added the German twist: "There is no man understands rightly what an English man is, but knows withal that we are a member of the Teutonick Nation, and descended out of Germany. . . ." David Hume and Edmund Burke lent their luster to the mix in the eighteenth century. Emerson's own authority in English history, Sharon Turner, made his contemporary Englishmen the very same people as ancient Saxons. By Emerson's time, the 1689 Bill of Rights following the Glorious Revolution of 1688–89 and the evolving English constitution (common law) had turned into talismans of English racial genius.

Emerson took for granted a religious identity of the English or Saxon race, Protestantism, of course, in sharp contradistinction to Catholicism. The notion of a historic, Protestant English church separate from the Catholic Church began with a sixteenth-century personal struggle between Henry VIII and Pope Clement VII. Henry intended to annul his marriage to Catherine of Aragon and marry Anne Boleyn, who sympathized with the Protestant Reformation under way on the European continent. When the pope would not agree to an annulment, Henry married Boleyn anyway; the pope excommunicated him; Parliament validated the new marriage; and the conflict escalated.

In addition to a power struggle over the royal marriage bed, the Catholic Church's wealth made it a tempting target. Once Parliament declared Henry head of the church in England, possessions that had been Catholic became English. As English nationalism increased, Henry's disagreement with the Catholic Church blossomed into a symbolic struggle between supposed descendants of French Catholic Normans and supposed descendants of Anglo-Saxon Protestants. Emerson picked up and amplified a chain of association linking Saxons and Protestants, Protestantism to the English church, the English church to the Magna Carta, and the Magna Carta to "liberty."[30]

The 1772 Somerset decision over slavery was also key. The case involved James Somerset, an African enslaved in the Reverend William Emerson's Boston before the American Revolution. Somerset's owner had taken him to Britain, then prepared to send him to the West Indies for resale. Here was an issue that attracted the British antislavery movement. Granville Sharp, a reformist leader, championed Somerset in the King's Bench (the English functional equivalent of today's U.S. Supreme Court), arguing before Lord Mansfield, the presiding judge, who ruled that Somerset could not be forcibly removed from Britain. Mansfield's decision quickly acquired much broader meaning, for he supposedly added that "as soon as any slave sets foot upon English territory, he becomes free" or "the air of England is too pure to be breathed by a slave."* Here was a notion pleasing to Emerson, that the air of England conferred freedom. It followed that American air would confer freedom as well—never mind the problem of existing slavery and American agitation against it. Emerson let English experts explain their history. For anthropology he also turned to Britain and Germany.

BEFORE WRITING *English Traits*, Emerson read voraciously in the anthropology of his day. Although familiar enough with the work of Johann Friedrich Blumenbach to include the word "Caucasian" once in *English Traits*, Emerson did not find Blumenbach's concept useful. Blumenbach's broad term "Caucasian" lumped together Celts and Saxons, while Emerson preferred a finer means of distinction.

In the 1850s, American race theory, never straightforward, was still chaotic. The well-regarded monogenesis of the English physician James Cowles Prichard, for instance, contradicted the hard-line racism and craniometric polygenesis of the American ethnologists Josiah Nott and George Gliddon. Nott and Gliddon published a very loose translation from the French of the splenetic Arthur de Gobineau's then obscure *Essay on the Inequality of Races*. None of these reigning experts pleased Emerson, especially not the mean-spirited, proslavery thought of Nott and Gliddon or that of their highly respected mentor, Samuel George Morton of Philadelphia. Instead, Emerson turned to Scottish scientists in vogue at the time.

---

* Popular interpretation, as phrased in 1785 by the poet William Cowper in "The Task," followed the broader rather than the actual, narrow decision based on habeas corpus:

> Slaves cannot breathe in England, if their lungs
> Receive our air, that moment they are free[.]
> They touch our country, and their shackles fall.

Cowper was protesting the existence of slavery in general ("I would not have a slave to till my ground") and in the British empire in particular. Cowper wrote five other antislavery poems, including "The Negro's Complaint" (1788).

•

DURING THE early nineteenth century, the brothers William and Robert Chambers published *Chambers's Edinburgh Journal*, a popular weekly magazine aimed at serious young men seeking to improve themselves through self-education. The Chambers boys had themselves risen the hard way after the failure of their father's cotton factory, and they only slowly began to thrive in the publishing business. As *Chambers's Edinburgh Journal* flourished in the 1850s, William Chambers stayed with the magazine, but Robert Chambers (1802–72) wrote a series of "courses" on various popular topics, such as Scottish biography, marine biology, and literature. By 1844 he was a fellow of London's Geological Society, carrying on a scholarly correspondence of international reach.

Robert Chambers realized early on that the geological record revealed an earth much older than the Bible posited, and also that living species had changed with the passage of time. "Evolution" as a term did not yet exist; rather, the theory was called "transmutation" and was associated with socialists, radicals, and Frenchmen.[31] In 1844 Chambers published *Vestiges of the Natural History of Creation* anonymously, correctly fearing reaction against his radical explanation of transmutation in place of divine creation. His theory that forms of life evolve was fundamentally sound, but the text was uneven, combining solid science, hearsay, and long-disproved theories. Emerson noted in his journal in 1845, "*Vestiges of Creation* . . . Everything in this Vestiges of Creation is good except the theology, which is civil, timid, & dull."[32] Emerson the transcendentalist did not mind that Chambers contradicted Genesis; the problem with the text lay in its lack of conviction. Chambers did, in fact, state his assertions provisionally.

Vestiges presents a unified theory of evolution encompassing the cosmos and all living things, including people. The stars and all the heavens had developed from spontaneous electrical generation, giving rise to every form of life through means of elaboration from the lowest, simplest organism to man's apex in Europeans. While only one of its twenty-one chapters deals with humans, its tone is ambivalent. Chambers is a monogenesist, seeing all people as products of the same origin. But he hesitates over the possibility of a brotherhood of man. Chambers (like the early American Samuel Stanhope Smith) stresses the influence of lifestyle on personal appearance, including beauty. Unlike Emerson, who compared Englishmen to oaks, Chambers contrasts "the soft round forms of the English" with "the lank features of their descendants, the Americans."[33]

Despite condemnation by experts, *Vestiges* leaped to best-sellerdom in Britain and the United States, with seven printings in its first year, and in the seventeen years between its publication and the appearance of Charles Darwin's *Origin of Species*, it sold 23,750 copies. Emerson's copy belongs to an 1845 American printing.[34] In some quarters, Chambers's book is carelessly cited as a precursor to Darwin. Its thesis and methods differed greatly from Darwin's, but both authors faced the criticism that their science contradicted scripture.[35]

Though Chambers wrote *Vestiges* in secrecy and published it anonymously, Emerson quickly learned the author's identity, most likely via the journalist Alexander Ireland, who knew both parties. When Emerson expressed a desire to meet the Chambers brothers, Ireland invited Emerson to Britain in 1846, sweetening his invitation with the promise of a lucrative speaking itinerary.[36] Ireland finally introduced Chambers and Emerson in London in 1848, and they evidently had a pleasant visit.[37] However, Emerson never met his other Scottish authority, Robert Knox.

EMERSON DID read Robert Knox's *The Races of Men: A Fragment* (1850) and rather liked what he saw.[38] At bottom he agreed with Knox's sense of the importance of race and his conviction that races deteriorate away from their home territory. Emerson also shared Knox's aesthetic ranking of the races and denigration of the Irish Celts. Knox, like Carlyle, was a Lowland Scot, and the "Low" counted as fully for Knox as for Carlyle and for the same reason: "Low" would make them Saxons untainted by Celtic blood.

Unlike Robert Chambers, Knox (1791–1862) had been impeccably schooled as a medical doctor in Edinburgh and France. Still young in the

1820s, he lectured on anatomy in the famous medical school of the University of Edinburgh while publishing a score of papers on animal anatomy still to be found on the shelves of the Princeton University Library.

Then, in Knox's fortieth year, scandal struck. The cadavers so essential to his anatomy lessons, it turned out, had been supplied by a notorious pair of Irish thugs named Burke and Hare, who were murdering people for the express purpose of delivering their bodies to Knox's dissection table. Although Knox escaped conviction, he left Edinburgh in disgrace and turned to translating scientific papers and lecturing on the anthropology of man, starting, naturally, with the race he deemed best: the Saxon.

For Knox "race or hereditary descent is everything; it stamps the man." Like all the other Western racists of the time, he placed the darkest-skinned and poorest people—Africans and Australians—at the bottom of his racial hierarchy.[39] That much was a given. But, as in German race theories, questions of color, indeed of any peoples outside of Europe, counted for little in Knox's racial scheme. He cared most about the locals, the Saxons and the Celts, whom he saw as permanently opposed. To enforce that view, Knox also needed to denigrate Blumenbach's "Caucasian" designation, a big tent encompassing peoples from North Africa, Spain, Europe, Russia, Turkey, and India. Far too broad, Knox grumbled, this was just "Blumenbach's Caucasian dream."[40]

Knox's prominence as an anthropologist peaked following the revolutions of 1848, which had also galvanized another political reactionary appalled by revolution, Arthur de Gobineau. The revolutions of 1848 happened to precede the time when Emerson was preparing *English Traits*.[41] In the 1850s, Knox's Saxonism accelerated a drift toward racial determinism in British and American anthropology that would dominate the field for another seventy-five years. Knox's 1850 treatise, *The Races of Man: A Fragment*, was reissued in 1862 as *The Races of Men: A Philosophical Enquiry into the Influence of Race over the Destinies of Nations*. Then, as Darwin took over center stage, Knox's work fell into relative obscurity until its return to fame in our own times, when scholars seeking a racist bogeyman in science revived his work, only to revile it.

Emerson had worked himself into a hole. He wanted to trumpet the determining force of race along the lines of Robert Knox, but he had trouble holding on to that view. In *English Traits* he waffles on purity and permanence, though in almost everything else he favors continuity, as in the traits of Norsemen constant in Saxons, Englishmen, and Americans. He proclaimed the existence of permanent "traits" in halls around the country in a popular lecture called "Permanent Traits of English National Genius," first delivered in 1835 and repeated for years to appreciative audiences.

A SHARED fascination with Englishness allowed Emerson and his readers to overlook a lot of nonsense in his ideas. Like so much race talk, the crucial "Race" chapter in *English Traits* contradicts itself in tone and in word. It makes one statement and then, without a retraction, offers conflicting information. For instance, the chapter begins by dismissing the race-determinist writing of "an ingenious anatomist" (Robert Knox), who rashly decrees races to be "imperishable." Like others before him, including Blumenbach, Emerson notes the confusion over the number of actually existing races.[42] Citing Blumenbach by name, Emerson agrees that races shade into each other imperceptibly. Then, in utter contradiction, he continues to cleanly distinguish races according to their own unique traits.

On the one hand, Emerson suspects that "the spawning force of the race" explains English imperial success. On the other hand—and this chapter contains a multitude of hands—ascribing English success to race merely flatters the English. After all, says Emerson, "Every body likes to know that his advantages cannot be attributed to air, soil, sea, or to local wealth, as mines and quarries, nor to laws and traditions, nor to fortune, but to superior brain, as it makes the praise more personal to him." Then, on yet another hand, race actually does explain a lot:

> It is race, is it not? that puts the hundred millions of India under the dominion of a remote island in the north of Europe. Race avails much, if that be true, which is alleged, that all Celts are Catholics, and

all Saxons are Protestants; that Celts love unity of power, and Saxons the representative principle. Race is a controlling influence in the Jew, who, for two millenniums, under every climate, has preserved the same character and employments. Race in the negro is of appalling importance. The French in Canada, cut off from all intercourse with the parent people, have held their national traits. I chanced to read Tacitus "on the Manners of the Germans," not long since, in Missouri, and the heart of Illinois, and I found abundant points of resemblance between the Germans of the Hercynian forest, and our *Hoosiers*, *Suckers*, and *Badgers* of the American woods.

Then, on a fifth hand, "It is easy to add to the counteracting forces to race," such as civilization. Emerson adds in the hopelessly mixed nature of the English race, consisting not simply of Celts, Normans, and Teutons. "Who can trace them historically?" he asks, quoting Daniel Defoe to the effect that the Englishman is "the mud of all races."[43]

The *true* English type inhabits only a narrowly circumscribed territory: fashionable London. Coarse, provincial, and too anxious to please, the Scots harbor too many local dialects of speech. Ireland is worse: "In Ireland, are the same climate and soil as in England, but less food, no right relation to the land, political dependence, small tenantry, and an inferior or misplaced race."[44]

In the final analysis, Emerson comes out of his welter of contradiction agreeing with Robert Knox after all. In the chapter entitled "Character," race determines history: "[It] is in the deep traits of race that the fortunes of nations are written, and however derived,—whether a happier tribe or mixture of tribes, the air, or what circumstance that mixed for them the golden mean of temperament,—here [in England] exists the best stock in the world, broad-fronted, broad bottomed, best for depth, range and equability. . . ."[45]

And this is where Emerson stood when he wrote *English Traits* in the mid-1850s. Later in the nineteenth century, scholars would trace the political genius of Saxons to the mark (land held in common by ancient Germans) or to the German forest. But for Emerson, the beautiful, bloody, virile Norsemen of the Dark Ages hold the key to American racial identity.

As AUTHOR of *English Traits* and a font of themes usually located much later in the nineteenth century, Emerson qualifies as a full contributor to white race theory. His enormous intellectual strength and prodigious output made him the source of a crucial current of thought, for he enunciated virtually all the salient nineteenth- and early twentieth-century concepts of Anglo-Saxonism. *English Traits* expressed the views of the most prestigious intellectual in the United States, elevating its formulation into American ideology. The American was the same as the Englishman, who was the same as the Saxon and the Norseman. Thus "Saxon" supplied the key word exiling the Celtic Irish—white though they may be—from American identity. Wrenching his Saxon away from Blumenbach's female beauty, Emerson created a white racial ideal that was both virile and handsome. Towering over his age, he spoke for an increasingly rich and powerful American ruling class. His thinking, as they say, became hegemonic.

EMERSON IN THE HISTORY OF AMERICAN WHITE PEOPLE

It hardly seems necessary to underline Emerson's importance in nineteenth-century American culture. One of his well-read contemporaries expressed this esteem: "I think Mr. Emerson is the greatest man—the most complete man that ever lived. . . . He is indeed a 'supernal vision.' I often think that God and his holy angels must regard him with delight."[1]* Another described him as "the most American of our writers," the embodiment of "the Idea of America, which lies at the bottom of our original institutions"—views that resonate still.[2] While so many of his nineteenth-century peers calibrated their thought according to the Bible, Emerson read everything and translated it into recognizable American terms. His enrichment of American intellectual life turned the phrase "Ralph Waldo Emerson" into a summary of Victorian America's intellectual history.

Emerson expressed the best of his age, albeit in the most restrained

---

* By 1854 Emerson was the most famous of American writers, having been reviewed an astounding 644 times. Despite a temporary dip in his standing when his sunny liberalism lost its cachet in the 1960s and 1970s, he still dominates his century. After that bout of belittlement as a mere derivative thinker, Emerson bounced back, never having lost his status as a canonical author. The Princeton University Library holds 651 imprints with "Ralph Waldo Emerson" in their titles, including twelve volumes of Houghton Mifflin's 1903–04 *Complete Works of Ralph Waldo Emerson*, Harvard University Press's seven volumes (as of 2008) of the *Collected Works of Ralph Waldo Emerson*, sixteen volumes of Emerson's *Journals and Miscellaneous Notebooks*, and innumerable volumes of Emerson poems, sermons, essays, and correspondence.

terms. Looking kindly upon progressive reform, he denounced the barbarism he saw in American slavery and befriended a woman, Margaret Fuller, one of the smartest people of her generation.* Truly, Emerson cemented the identification of liberal, antislavery New England with American intellect, while the luxury of his language—its very wealth of allusion and nuance—amazes readers to this day.[3] Much of his popularity grew out of his ability to mirror and to orchestrate the thinking of his age: as a mirror, he reflected back familiar notions already accepted, if only tacitly, by educated Americans; as an orchestrator, he arranged simple thoughts into elaborate, memorable performances. His every note seemingly rang true. But did it?

It is important to notice that when Emerson said "American," he meant male white people of a certain socioeconomic standing—his. Without his saying so directly, his definition of American excluded non-Christians and virtually all poor whites. Native American Indians and African Americans did not count. In *English Traits*, when he tallies up the American population, Emerson explicitly excludes the enslaved and skips over native peoples entirely.[4]

On the whole, Emerson's engagement with Saxon racial identity simply shut out all else. Certainly, insofar as race connects to blackness and slavery, Emerson remains outside the ranks of racial thinkers. Many others of the time were obsessed by color, but Emerson had little to say about black people. What he did say, with the exception of "Voluntaries," a poem commemorating the Civil War exploits of the Massachusetts Fifty-fourth Colored Troops, lacks sentiments of brotherhood.[5]

Musings in the journals—unpublished while he lived—are mostly what we have to judge. In the mid-1840s, before his views had hardened, Emerson preferred abstractions to empathy, on the theory that only ideas could "save races." He remained unsure, he said, of the ultimate worth of the Negro race: "[I]f the black man carries in his bosom an indispensable element of a new & coming civilization, for the sake of that element no wrong nor strength nor circumstance can hurt him,

---

*The embodiment of nationalist moderation, Emerson would not go so far as to advocate votes for either white women or black people of any sex.

he will survive & play his part." However, "if the black man is feeble & not important to the existing races, not on a par with the best race, the black man must serve & be sold & exterminated."[6] Thus *the* black man, a notion rather than an individual, remains a plaything of the forces of history.

Such confusion is not lessened by the fact that Emerson hated slavery, especially the Fugitive Slave Act of 1850. His excoriation of the law and of New Englanders who supported it takes up more space in his journals than any other political issue: eighty-six manuscript pages in his journal for 1851.[7] But, like that of Thomas Jefferson, for instance, Emerson's disapproval of slavery in no way reflected racial egalitarianism. Rather, it connected to his sense of civilization: he considered slavery a relic of barbarism that was bad for civilization, that is, bad for his kind of white people. He harbored no doubt that American indulgence of slaveholders threatened the United States as a whole: "The absence of moral feeling in the ~~country~~ whiteman is the very calamity I deplore," he notes in 1851, adding a chilling denouement: "The ~~loss of~~ captivity of a thousand negroes is nothing to me."[8]

Neither, by the mid-1850s, did it perturb Emerson that black people and Indians might become extinct; on the contrary, their eventual disappearance would improve the human race by widening the gap between "man & beast!" The black man "is created on a lower plane than the white, & eats men & kidnaps & tortures, if he can. The Negro is ~~reactionary~~ imitative, secondary, in short, reactionary merely in his successes, & there is no origination with him in mental & moral sphere."[9]

Occasional nameless black figures do appear fleetingly in the journals. One instance corroborates the multiracial nature of Emerson's Concord: his mention in 1845 of a heterogeneous church meeting where "the whole various extremes of our little village society were for once brought together. Black & white, poet & grocer, contractor & lumberman, Methodist & preacher joined with the regular congregation in rare union."[10] If race means blackness, Emerson plays the tiniest part in American intellectual history, although quite a callous one. Proud of his ability to deliver unsentimental realism in the face of a racial hierarchy decreed by natural law, Emerson deviates only briefly from his concept of permanent racial hierarchy. But ever so briefly he did deviate.

In the mid-1840s, Know-Nothing xenophobia and mob violence troubled Emerson, setting off a flirtation with the idea of hybridity. In an often quoted journal entry he moves to praise multiculturalism, envisioning a new America forged from all the different constituents that make up this new country:

> . . . in this Continent,—asylum of all nations, the energy of Irish, Germans, Swedes, Poles, & the Cossacks, & all the European tribes,—of the Africans, & of the Polynesians, will construct a new race, a new religion, a new State, a new literature, which will be as vigorous as the new Europe which came out of the smelting pot of the Dark Ages, or that which earlier emerged from the Pelasgic [ancient Greek] & Etruscan barbarism. La Nature aime les croisements.[11]

Emerson's reputation for ethnic-racial broadmindedness rests largely upon this generous and virtually unique statement of American identity.[12] Nowhere else, however, did he welcome multicultural America so warmly, despite occasional doodlings about mixture and "crossings" (usually phrased in French). His journals for 1847 contain five statements on mixture: "La Nature aime les Croismants," "Crosiements," "Croisment," twice, and "Nature loved crosses, and inoculations of barbarous races prove: and marriage is crossing."[13] But there was nothing sustained, no sentence even completed.

WHEN RACE means white blood, however, Emerson surges to the fore.[14] Since his views were already circulating in the United States and Great Britain, Emerson cannot be seen as an originator. He was what we might nowadays call an enabler. Nonetheless, by phrasing bromides in his learned and graceful prose, he endowed them with his own substantial intellectual prestige. No matter how contradictory and obtuse, they circulated as American orthodoxy.

With the rare exception of the Fugitive Slave Act, Emerson paid scant attention to any of the historical processes that spawned hardship and political upheaval. To him history served as racial prologue—as the opening scenes in a drama rather than as events that affected people's relation to one another. Economic classes existed as though decreed by Fate, not as outcomes of human interaction. Therefore, poor people, especially poor white people, native and immigrant, remain at the periphery of Emerson's field of vision. By the late 1850s, Emerson deemed an array of the poor to be poor by inherent nature. The Irish and others in the antebellum working class (the Jews, Italians, and Greeks of the turn of the twentieth century had not yet arrived in massive numbers), whom he called "guano," were fated by race to play dismal roles in a mechanistic world.

By 1860, political upheaval had further hardened Emerson's racial views. Passage of the Fugitive Slave Act, which he considered a wreck of American civilization, had prompted him to publish a book of essays intended to advise fellow Americans on how to live in the face of nasty politics. These essays, entitled *Conduct of Life* (1860), express much crueler views than any he had voiced in the 1840s. Here Emerson sounds practically as mean-spirited as Thomas Carlyle. "Fate," for instance, contains an eloquent defense of the land-grabbing enthusiasms of "manifest destiny." In it, entire races are consigned to extinction in the interest of Nature's greater good.[15]

Emerson had mulled over these issues in his journal as early as 1851: "Too much guano. The German & Irish nations, like the Negro, have a deal of guano in their destiny. They are ~~+~~ ferried over the Atlantic, & carted over America to ditch & to drudge, to make the land fertile, & corn cheap, & then to lie down prematurely to make ~~the grass~~ a spot of greener grass on the prairie."[16] The appearance of the "German" nation among Emerson's guano races recalls his distinction between wonderful "Saxons" in England and mere Germans. The sacrifice of the poor, hardworking races like the German, Irish, and African for the good of the more advanced, like the Saxon, was nothing other than the working out of inevitable—and salutary, because inevitable—laws of Nature. "Fate" transformed national opportunism into the destiny of races.

As harsh as Emerson sounds on races he thought inferior, his theories could have sunk a great deal lower. Counterparts living to the south of his beloved New England built their theoretical edifices on the foundation of African slavery. And slavery encouraged a good deal more meanness than Emerson could muster against those who were free.

THE AMERICAN SCHOOL
OF ANTHROPOLOGY

Emerson died in 1882, but his cold formulations did not die with him. Such crabbed views of American ancestry, appearance, and masculinity rolled on well into the future and actually seem mild when compared with the mean-spirited school of "American anthropology." Emerson was aware of the toxic racial thinking of his time and rejected the worst of it.

From the eighteenth century onward, racial schemes have flourished, each offering a different number of races, even a different number of Caucasian races. Emerson had to make sense of this from his perch in Concord, and, thoroughly Anglicized, he perforce looked not to his own country or to the European continent. He chose, rather, to seek reinforcement for his ideas in Great Britain, specifically in Sharon Turner's monumental, multivolume *History of the Anglo-Saxons*, which had popularized the foundational concept of racial "traits," and in the work of his Scots: the geologist Robert Chambers and the physician-anthropologist Robert Knox. Their ideas struck Emerson as cleaner and of much finer provenance.

This had to do in part with the fact that most racial thought in the United States served to justify slavery and, as such, was pretty mean-spirited. This was uncongenial to Emerson, who leaned toward abolitionism. But had he been determined to denigrate black people, he might have looked to those widely respected American scholars who were eagerly consolidating a white supremacist "American school" of anthropology.

SAMUEL GEORGE MORTON (1799–1851), the most revered American anthropologist among them, began as the hardworking son of an immigrant Quaker family from Ireland. His merchant father died in Samuel's childhood, and his mother followed in 1817, when Samuel was eighteen. When a rich uncle in the old country offered to finance his higher education, Morton seized the opportunity. He earned an M.D. degree in 1820 from the University of Pennsylvania and spent time in Edinburgh and Paris, the leading European centers for medical education. Along the way, Morton grew enamored with phrenology, then enjoying a great vogue as science.* His University of Edinburgh M.D., awarded in 1823, and his European contacts did much to burnish a growing international reputation. Back home in Philadelphia, Morton gradually established himself in the city's medical community and scholarly societies. As a professor of anatomy between 1839 and 1843 at the University of Pennsylvania, the best medical school in the United States, Morton reached a wide audience of leading American medical doctors and anthropologists.

Skulls ruled the day in American anthropology, an enthusiasm that would lead seamlessly into the fetish of craniometry early in the twentieth century and on into intelligence testing during the First World War and beyond. Morton owned a lot of skulls. At his death in 1851, his collection comprised 918 human skulls (51 more were still in transit), 278 crania of other mammals, 271 of birds, and 88 of reptiles and fish: a collection worthy of Johann Friedrich Blumenbach.[1†] Morton had diligently measured each human skull along twelve different axes—up and down, sideways, back and forth, in, around, and interior volume—and

*The actual originator of the American school was a Philadelphia medical doctor and admirer of phrenology named Charles Caldwell, who critically reviewed Samuel Stanhope Smith's *Essay on the Causes of the Variety of Complexion and Figure in the Human Species* in 1811. Caldwell directly inspired Samuel George Morton.

†Morton and his American admirers saw him as Blumenbach's successor, even as Blumenbach's superior.

written up his findings in widely praised studies of American Indians (*Crania Americana*, 1839) and ancient Egyptians (*Crania Ægyptiaca*, 1844). Morton's fame stemmed from his measurements of cranial capacity, which he judged to predict intellectual ability according to race.*

On this basis Morton ranked American Indians as a separate race somewhere midway between white and black people, thereby proving conclusively the existence of racial difference—to his own satisfaction as well as to that of his contemporaries.[2] Morton also possessed some Inuit skulls. What was to be deduced about their race? Not knowing how to answer that, he simply set them aside, just as European racial theorists had alternately expelled and accepted Lapps in jiggering European racial identity.

Clearly, these were tortured calculations, none more so than Morton's classification of different socioeconomic strata of ancient Egyptians as different races in *Crania Ægyptiaca*. He counted most Egyptians as Caucasian but a minority as Negro, while at the same time dividing them into three further types—"Pelasgic," "Semitic," and "Egyptian." Those three were suspiciously stereotypical as white, Jewish, and black racial lines. Much of this echoed Winckelmann on the beauty and symmetry of ancient Greeks and Petrus Camper's concept of the facial angle. At the top of Morton's heap were large crania and straight facial angles, denoted as Pelasgic, or Greek: the "symmetry and delicacy of the whole osteological structure" make the Pelasgic "familiar to us in the beautiful models of Grecian art."

And near the bottom were skulls Morton categorized as Semitic types resembling, he says, "Hebrew communities" characterized by "comparatively receding forehead, long, arched, and very prominent nose" and, in sum, a "strong and often harsh development of the whole facial structure." The Semitic race, he contends, ought not to be accorded

---

* *The Mismeasure of Man* (1996), Stephen Jay Gould's classic study of physical anthropology and intelligence testing, deems Morton's cranial measurements badly flawed. More recently, however, the Michigan anthropologist C. Loring Brace, in *"Race" Is a Four-Letter Word: The Genesis of the Concept*, has contested Gould's findings and vindicated Morton's measurements, but not his overall findings. Brace does not support Morton's conclusions regarding relative racial intelligence as revealed in cranial measurements. But he respects Morton's methodology, ascribing the flaws to Gould.

much respect, having been "admitted into Egypt only upon sufferance." All smaller skulls belonged to slaves, dumber, darker-skinned examples of the Egyptian type. They interest Morton even less than his Semitic types and rate hardly any description. So much for Jews and Africans in Morton's Egypt.[3]

For Morton and his many admirers (including Robert Knox in Scotland and Arthur de Gobineau in France), the greatness of ancient Egypt seals the permanence of racial hierarchies, the very bedrock of nineteenth-century racial theory. Like that of the ancient Greeks, deemed very similar to nineteenth-century Gentile northern Europeans, ancient Egypt's glory is linked to the superiority of white people, Americans included. Never mind puzzling details. What looked like wooly hair in ancient Egyptian depictions Morton deems wigs worn by Egyptians over their real hair, which surely was straight and light-colored, like that of "the fairest Europeans of the present day." (Why Egyptians would wear wooly-haired wigs does not rate an explanation.) Plunging forward, Morton pronounces the cranial formation of ancient Egyptians—at least the better-dressed and more pompously buried Egyptians—identical to that of the "modern white man."[4]*

Why did Morton's equations of prominent ancient Egyptians and the "modern white man" make sense to race theorists? The answer has everything to do with the wealth and power of nations of their own time. Again and again, racial hierarchies set the poor and powerless at the bottom and the rich and powerful at the top. The early twentieth-century sociologist Max Weber says it well. While the nobility believe their superiority grows out of their "underived, ultimate, and qualitatively distinctive *being*," no one in favored circumstances wants to admit the chanciness of privilege. "The fortunate man," Weber says, "is seldom satisfied with the fact of being fortunate. Beyond this, he needs to know that he has a

---

* Morton and his followers departed from the prevailing orthodoxy of James Cowles Prichard in *The Natural History of Man: Comprising Inquiries into the Modifying Influence of Physical and Moral Agencies on the Different Tribes of the Human Family* (1848). Prichard classified North Africans, including Egyptians, as people of African origin. Prichard, whom Arthur de Gobineau also pilloried (consistently misspelling Prichard's name), insisted on the single creation of mankind, with a subsequent elaboration of separate tribes. Prichard was the mid-nineteenth-century's monogenist par excellence.

right to his good fortune. He wants to be convinced that he 'deserves' it, and above all, that he deserves it in comparison with others. . . . Good fortune thus wants to be 'legitimate' fortune."[5] Innate qualities are needed to prove the justice—the naturalness and inalterability—of the status quo. In the United States, in Samuel George Morton's Philadelphia, where the buying and selling of laborers extended into the nineteenth century, that often turned into a justification for African slavery.*

MORTON'S WORK on skulls earned him enormous prestige in the United States and in France, where he impressed even Paul Broca, the most prominent French anthropologist, who was also a polygenesist. An 1861 controversy in French anthropology over French and German head sizes echoed Morton's notions of racial superiority. All the prominent anthropologists of the time assumed that brain size correlated with intelligence. Here lay a problem. Bigger bodies house bigger heads, and bigger heads house bigger brains. German bodies (even of professors) were bigger than French bodies; therefore German brains were bigger than French brains. What were French anthropologists to do? Were Germans simply smarter? Even French anthropologists who accepted a correlation between head size and intelligence when applied to other people reckoned uneasily that the correlation did not always hold.[6†] The debate was never resolved, only rendered trivial with the passage of time. Skulls kept their pride of place in anthropology and, with them, the owner of a world-class collection. So firmly did Morton personify the American school of anthropology that a visit with him became obligatory for ambitious young scientists. Two key visitors were Josiah Nott and Louis Agassiz.[‡]

---

* Pennsylvania emancipated the enslaved in 1780, but the law allowed the indenturing of children until they were at least twenty-eight years old. Indentures could be bought and sold in the open market.

† While anthropologists differed on the meaning of various skull measurements, their confidence that all these measurements meant something seems not to have wavered. One of them, Louis-Pierre Gratiolet, designated three human races according to the part of the brain their physiognomy expressed: frontal, parietal, and occipital.

‡ Josiah Nott studied at the University of Pennsylvania, where Samuel Morton taught in the years 1839–43, but he graduated in 1827, before Morton joined the faculty.

·

JOSIAH NOTT (1804–73), scion of a prosperous South Carolina family, received his medical degree from the University of Pennsylvania after undergraduate study at the College of South Carolina. An accomplished surgeon and founder of the University of Alabama School of Medicine, the agnostic Nott loved annoying traditional believers. As a polygenesist, he disputed the account of creation in Genesis in his first major publication, *Two Lectures on the Natural History of the Caucasian and Negro Races* (1844). The races were created separately, Nott argues, well before the beginning of biblical time.[7]* For Nott and others in the American school of anthropology, multiple creations had to mean that the history in the Pentateuch (the first five books of the Old Testament, or Torah) applies only to white Westerners. Nonwhite peoples had separate histories, told, presumably, in their own various books of Genesis. This view enjoyed international currency.

Though he lived in Mobile, Alabama, in the deepest South, Nott kept up with the latest in European anthropology. Reading Gobineau's pessimistic, 1,000-page *Essai sur l'inégalité des races humaines* (1853–55), Nott exclaimed that he had "seldom perused a work which has afforded [him] so much pleasure and instruction."[8] Right up front in his dedication to the Saxon king George V of Hanover, Gobineau proclaimed convictions—"that the racial question over-shadows all other problems of history, that it holds the key to them all, and that the inequality of the races . . ."—bound to entrance Nott.[9]†

Like many other racists, Gobineau had seemingly mastered the multilingual contents of entire libraries to formulate a universal truth that energetic races, certainly the Aryan, create national greatness. In turn, Aryan prosperity was fated to attract inferior races. Just as inevitably,

---

* Nott's most persistent opponent in the monogenesis/polygenesis dispute was a New Yorker turned South Carolinian, the Reverend John Bachman, minister of St. John's Lutheran Church in Charleston. Bachman, who had an 1848 Ph.D. from the University of Berlin, began criticizing Nott in 1849.

† Nott disregarded the way Gobineau ended his sentence: "the inequality of the races from whose fusion a people is formed is enough to explain the whole course of its destiny." *The* American was not about racial fusion.

the races would mix; the superior race would degenerate, and the nation would collapse in revolution. According to Gobineau, this inexorable process of race degeneration explained the catastrophic (to him) revolutions of 1848.

Gobineau took the concept of an Aryan "race" out of the obscure scholarship of philologists studying dead languages like Sanskrit and, eventually, made it familiar. In the 1780s William Jones, a British linguist, had discovered a resemblance between Sanskrit and classical Greek and Latin. Other scholars, such as Franz Bopp in Berlin, Friedrich Schlegel in Paris and Berlin, and Max Müller in Oxford, elaborated the relationship between languages and peoples in the early nineteenth century. They postulated the existence of a proto-Indo-European language that had spawned Indo-European languages spoken widely, from the Indian subcontinent to western Europe.

Thus, the nineteenth-century rage for races turned languages into peoples, and the word *arya*, meaning "noble" or "spiritual" in Sanskrit, came to be applied to an imagined, superior race of *Aryans*. Some resistance to the conflation of language and race did arise. Müller of Oxford, the leading English-speaking comparative philologist, ultimately backed away from the often anti-Semitic identification of Aryan with a race rather than a language, but his awakening came too late. Racial extremists like Gobineau had already applied the term to the idea of a superior race, dooming it to a racial future.[10] Even so, the term "Aryan" did not enjoy wide popularity until the early twentieth-century English publication of Gobineau's *Essai*. Nor was Aryan the most useful concept Josiah Nott discovered in Gobineau's work.

Rather, Nott found two essential points: first, races are unequal, and, second, race mixing is therefore bad. He heartily endorsed both sentiments long before Gobineau's *Essay* gained other adherents. For several years after its publication in 1853, Gobineau's *Essay* went largely unread and, when read, was not particularly appreciated. In a personal letter to Gobineau, Alexis de Tocqueville, Gobineau's mentor, denounced the work as promoting "spiritual lassitude" because its racial determinism deprived individuals of free will and destroyed any motivation to improve.[11]

But Nott had resolved to spread the word to American audiences. In 1855 he hired the twenty-one-year-old, Swiss-born Henry Hotze of Mobile to help him translate Gobineau's *Essai*, but strictly according to Nott's southern slaveholding ideology.[12]* This translation, entitled *The Moral and Intellectual Diversity of Races: With Particular Reference to Their Respective Influence in the Civil and Political History of Mankind, from the French of Count A. de Gobineau* (1856), bears Gobineau's name as author, but much of it is pure Nott. For instance, he corrects Gobineau's lack of interest in African slavery through a polygenesist appendix of his own, showing Morton's cranial measurements laid out according to Morton's taxonomy. Gobineau, interestingly, denounced this amendment as a distortion of his thought.

The denunciation was well deserved, for Gobineau says quite clearly that Africans contribute positively to the mixture of races in prosperous metropolitan centers by offering Dionysian gifts such as passion, dance, music, rhythm, lightheartedness, and sensuality. Whites, for their part, contribute energy, action, perseverance, rationality, and technical aptitude: the Apollonian gifts. In the short run, and even though the final outcome must entail utter ruin, this is all for the good, at least for Gobineau. But not for Nott. While Gobineau sees whites as obviously racially superior, they are insufficient in and of themselves and need the contributions of other races for the development of civilization.[13]† Gobineau's Africans contribute to mixture, even though mixture inevitably causes revolution. The European revolutions of 1848 terrified Gobineau, but failed to interest Nott.

Other sharp differences divided Nott and Gobineau. They lived on different continents, surrounded by different peoples, and motivated by

---

* After working for the Mobile *Register*, Hotze served briefly in Mobile's Confederate militia and as a commercial and secret agent for the Confederacy in London, where he published a Confederate newspaper through the duration of the war. One of Hotze's contacts among British people sympathetic to the Confederacy was Dr. James Hunt, a disciple of Robert Knox, who had founded the Anthropological Society to advance Negrophobic anthropology.

† In 1855, when Nott and Hotze were preparing their version of Gobineau's *Essai*, Tocqueville was proposing Gobineau to the Académie des Sciences Morales et Politiques, to which Tocqueville and his traveling companion Beaumont had been elected in the 1830s. Tocqueville disliked Gobineau's *Essai*, but was fond of Gobineau personally.

different political events. Each defined the concept of "races" in order to answer his particular needs. Gobineau was an antidemocratic reactionary explaining political revolution by pitting the Aryan race against other, inferior, white-skinned races; Nott, a slaveholding reactionary railing against abolitionists, saw a white race pitted against a black one. Race as color occupied Nott's center stage, while Gobineau kept his eye on Celts, Slavs, and Aryans. As a result, Nott's loose translation retained Gobineau's fear of race mixing but discarded whatever else did not apply: out went Gobineau's anxieties over the people of eastern Europe and his pessimistic view of white Americans.[14]* All in all, Nott's awkward translation of Gobineau never added much to America's racial bubbling, never amounted to much more than an obscure provincial publication.[15]†

EARLY ON, in 1843, Nott had published an important article on miscegenation, racial science's bugaboo. His title says it all: "The Mulatto a Hybrid—probably extermination of the two races if the Whites and Blacks are allowed to marry."[16] Why would Nott write that the mating of blacks and whites would produce infertile hybrids, when a glance around his own Alabama neighborhood would have put the lie to this notion? More to the real point, the possibility of mixed marriage doubtless annoyed Nott far more than the inevitable mixed sex. In any case, while this theory of infertile progeny made no sense in theory or practice, it did serve Nott's scholarly purposes and pushed along his fine scientific reputation.

Having made his name, Nott burnished it by compiling two antholo-

---

* The theme of Aryan beauty runs through Gobineau's thousand pages of text. Gobineau and Emerson seem to have been echoing each other in their paeans to the blond barbarian Leviathan with his red and white complexion, broad shoulders, great height, and utter fearlessness and their conviction that Anglo-Saxons stemmed from Scandinavia and conserved the vital Aryan essence.

† An unsigned review in *Putnam's Monthly* of January 1856 discusses *Moral and Intellectual Diversity of Races* with care. The reviewer regrets Holtz's (and Nott's) emasculation of Gobineau's original, while disagreeing, as had Tocqueville, with Gobineau's fatalism. The reviewer concludes that the translation is worth reading.

Gobineau's great vogue came with the late nineteenth- and early twentieth-century Teutomania of German nationalists like Richard Wagner, Houston Stewart Chamberlain, and Madison Grant. When a new English translation of Gobineau was published in 1915, it, rather than Nott's, found a growing and appreciative audience of nationalists and eugenicists. No English editions of Gobineau's *Essai* appeared between 1856 and 1915.

gies: *Types of Mankind* (1854) and *Indigenous Races of the Earth* (1857), both published with George R. Gliddon, an Englishman long resident in Egypt who had supplied Morton with skulls and Nott with inspiration. Gliddon's wife drew the illustrations in *Types of Mankind*.[17] That both of these flimsy books sold extremely well demonstrates how little rigor nineteenth-century scholarly race talk required. Cobbled together from miscellaneous pieces in various genres and lengths by a wide array of contributors, each anthology included pieces by Louis Agassiz, whose luminous European origin and Harvard affiliation gave any work a certain scientific cachet.

Louis Agassiz (1807–73), a charming, German-educated Swiss physician-scholar, had made his name as a follower of the French naturalist Georges Cuvier. Glimpsing opportunity across the sea, Agassiz sailed to the United States in 1846 on the kind of lecture tour intended to generate permanent, remunerative employ.* Stopping first in Philadelphia, Agassiz paid his respects to Samuel George Morton, then moved on to deliver lectures in 1847 in Cambridge, Massachusetts, where he found sponsors of a professorship at Harvard.

Twelve years later, Charles Darwin published *On the Origin of Species*, a book that conquered biology and changed science forever. But Darwin did not conquer Agassiz, who, famously, never accepted Darwin's concept of evolutionary change. To his very end, Agassiz preferred a polygenesist scheme in which God had created the races separately at the very beginning. Even so, with the founding of the Harvard Museum of Comparative Zoology, Agassiz presided over a scholarly institution of enormous influence. For twenty-six years, until his death, he shaped not only the world of American natural history museums but also the field of American anthropology, which natural history museums housed until well into the twentieth century. This legacy he passed on to his Harvard protégé and successor, the Kentuckian Nathaniel Southgate Shaler (1841–1906).

Shaler became a fixture at Harvard during the 1870s, often referring

* George Gliddon had come to the United States for the second time on a similar quest, but he never found steady work and became one of Nott's permanent dependents.

to Agassiz as "my master." As a professor of geology, paleontology, and scientific truth in general, Shaler taught a generation of men destined to lead the United States, including Theodore Roosevelt. Through his commentary on American life, Shaler's Anglo-Saxon chauvinism provided a bulwark to the New England–based movement against immigrants from southern and eastern Europe. Today, after the mid-twentieth-century reshuffling of race into a black/white binary, Shaler appears in history as a proponent of black inferiority. But in the 1880s and 1890s, he also—and mainly—helped elevate the figure of the white male Kentuckian into an emblem of America and took aim at southern and eastern European immigrants as menaces to American racial integrity.

THE AMERICAN school of anthropology faded after the publication of its masterworks in the 1850s.[18] One of its core tenets—that different races constitute different species and stemmed from several separate racial creations (polygenesis)—lost a good deal of credibility with the publication of Darwin's *Origin of Species* in 1859. But its racist notions served the needs of American culture too well to disappear entirely. Indeed, the American school's founding belief in permanent and unchanging racial identity has yet to expire.

By the early 1890s, the American leaders in anthropology—Morton, Nott, Agassiz—had done their work and passed from the scene. White race taxonomy was, in any case, evolving into notions of immigration restriction and eugenics. Samuel George Morton had died at fifty-two in 1851; following Confederate service and disappointment with the post-slavery South, Nott died in 1873, the same year as Louis Agassiz. After a long cognitive decline, Agassiz's friend Emerson died in 1882, as did Gobineau.

They left behind a dour legacy: the fetishization of tall, pale, blond, beautiful Anglo-Saxons; a fascination with skulls and head measurements; the drawing of racial lines and the fixing of racial types; the ranking of races along a single "evolutionary" line of development; and a preoccupation with sex, reproduction, and sexual attractiveness. All this proved not only durable but also applicable to people now considered white.

THE SECOND ENLARGEMENT
OF AMERICAN WHITENESS

Tempting though it may be to cling to a simple history of whiteness stretching back through American history, our task here is to reveal the historical record, where we find a far more complex story. Rather than a single, enduring definition of whiteness, we find multiple enlargements occurring against a backdrop of the black/white dichotomy.

Any nation founded by slaveholders finds justification for its class system, and American slavery made the inherent inferiority of black people a foundational belief, which nineteenth-century Americans rarely disputed. Very few believed that people of African descent belonged within the figure of *the* American. At the same time, Americans rarely excluded Europeans from the classification of "white," especially when it came to politics and voting. After property qualifications for voting ended in the first half of the nineteenth century—the first enlargement of American whiteness—virtually all male Europeans and their free male children could be naturalized and vote as white. Thus, matters of legal American race remained relatively clear as a question of black/white, especially in the South. "Southerner" meant white southerner; "American" required whiteness, but mere whiteness might not suffice in society. Although determining who counted as "white" for political purposes was clear, whiteness in and of itself got one only so far toward being part of *the* American.

As we have seen, enormous efforts went into enthroning the Teutonic/Saxon/Anglo-Saxons, tracing them back to a tough Germanic-Scandinavian strain, conquerors of old, never themselves conquered. This heroic depiction left out a gaggle of Celts: those millions of French, Irish, and northern Scots and their children who were assumed to lack Saxon blood. In the mid-nineteenth century, it was mostly Irish Catholics who raised the issue. For Ralph Waldo Emerson, they were not deeply, truly Americans. Nor were certain Catholic and Jewish Germans. In this sense, Emerson's time was passing.

THE CIVIL War offered a huge opening. Hundreds of thousands of immigrants volunteered for military service on both sides. Not surprisingly, the Union Army, about one-fourth of whose personnel came from abroad, benefited from immigrant support more than the Confederacy. Some immigrants were well integrated into heterogeneous Union forces as Irish and Germans scattered throughout a panoply of regiments. In addition, and quite shrewdly, the Union Army organized itself along national lines. Among its thirty-six Irish units were the New York Fighting Sixty-ninth, the Irish Zouaves, the Irish Volunteers, and the St. Patrick Brigade. Italians made up the Garibaldi Guards and the Italian Legion. The eighty-four German units included the Steuben Volunteers, the German Rifles, and the Turner Rifles.[1] Confederates looked askance at the Union's polyglot ranks, and for decades afterwards Civil War Decoration Day holidays offered embittered former Confederates occasions to characterize their side as "American" and to impugn the Union Army as "made up largely of foreigners and blacks fighting for pay."[2]

Conversely, former Unionists—and most Democrats—saw immigrants' service as a multicultural victory over Know-Nothing nativism. According to one minister, the children of the dead, thanks to the sacrifice of their immigrant fathers, are "no longer strangers and foreigners, but are, by this baptism of blood . . . consecrated citizens of America forever."[3] Union Decoration Day oratory projected the sunny side of wartime immigrant Americanization, helping to usher hundreds of thousands into the white American club. Such a view, however, was far from universal. The Republican Party and its media spokesmen initially saw such easy Irish Americanization as little more than another facet of traditional, Democratic, proslavery white supremacy.

The extremely popular and influential *Harper's Weekly* and its brilliant German cartoonist Thomas Nast (1840–1902) led the charge. Siding with southern black Republicans against northern Irish Democrats, Nast appropriated a caricature long popular in England week after week. He depicted Irishmen as brutal, drunken apes—rioting on St. Patrick's Day, overturning Reconstruction in the South, and cynically crashing their way into American politics as white men. By allying with former Confederates and fat-cat northern Democrats, Irishmen were said to be trampling the rights of loyal black southern defenders of the Union. To Nast, Irish opportunity meant the black man's defeat. Of course, both opportunity and defeat had taught the Irish how politics worked in America. Race, in black and white terms, retained its importance. (But race did not matter above all. No women could vote.)

Consider Nast's 1868 cartoon. (See figure 14.1, "This Is a White Man's Government.") A stereotypical Irishman on the left swears allegiance to the Confederate (CSA on his belt buckle) in the middle, with Horatio Seymour, a New York Democrat plutocrat, holding graft money, on the right.* The Irishman's shillelagh reads "a vote," referring to a tendency of Irish immigrants to vote the Democratic ticket and, presumably, thereby to undermine true American values. The Irishman's hat saying "5 points" recalls the bloody Saint Patrick's Day riot of 1867 in New York City's biggest slum.† Behind the Irishman, a building in flames, the "Colored Orphan Asylum," refers to its destruction by an Irish mob during the deadly 1863 draft riots. Together, these three figures trample the loyal black American veteran, whose Union soldier's hat and American flag lie in the dust, the ballot box beyond his reach. Nast's only half-ironic caption reads, "This Is a White Man's Government."

---

* In 1868 the Democratic nominating convention met in New York City. Seymour emerged as the party's presidential candidate but lost to Ulysses S. Grant in the general election.
† In 1892 New York City razed the Five Points slum for the creation of Columbus Park at Mulberry and Bayard Streets in lower Manhattan. This area, a magnet for successive waves of immigrants, is currently known as New York's Chinatown, previously Little Italy, which remains only a tourist destination.

Fig. 14.1. Thomas Nast, "This Is a White Man's
Government," Harper's Weekly, 1868.

Without a doubt, Nast's cartoon reflects a good deal of reality. Irish workers had shown little hesitation in brandishing their new-found whiteness as a tool against others. In the West of the 1880s, Irish workingmen agitated as "white men" to drive Chinese workers off their jobs and out of their homes. This anti-Chinese movement produced the country's first race-based immigration legislation, the Chinese Exclusion Act of 1882. Although not all Chinese immigrants fell under the law—merchants, teachers, students, diplomats, and other professionals were exempted—the Irish and other whites continued to attack the Chinese in a series of western pogroms called the "Driving Out."[4] As it would again, "racial" violence addressed economic competition.

In the 1870s and 1880s, politics began to serve the economic interests of Irish and German immigrants in many walks of American life.

The right to vote, for instance, opened a path to employment through government patronage and civil service jobs. Labor union control meant that their sons and brothers stood first in line for steady work and, later, skilled jobs. The figure of the Irish policeman owes its longevity to this system of public employment. Thanks to patronage jobs and government contracts, fewer in the second and third generations suffered the grinding poverty that had dogged their famine immigrant ancestors. Along the way they learned, in true American fashion of the time, to profit from the vulnerability of nonwhite Americans barred from voting—hence barred from the fruits of bloc voting.[5] Color mattered, even for Ralph Waldo Emerson, that preeminent Saxonist.

EMERSON HAD his contradictions, of course. In *English Traits* of 1856, he both denounced and embraced racial determination. In *Conduct of Life* of 1860, he again both deprecated and then echoed the racist views of Robert Knox, describing the "German and Irish millions, like the Negro," as races with "a great deal of guano in their destiny."[6] Ever a Saxon chauvinist, Emerson could nonetheless soften toward poor immigrants, presumably Irish, provided their bodies were sufficiently light in color. In 1851 Emerson cast his eye on the newcomers around him, judging them, in most cases, as suitable to join his world.

> America.   Emigration.
>
> In the distinctions of the genius of the American race it is to be considered, that, it is not indiscriminate masses of Europe, that are ~~transported~~ shipped hitherward, but the Atlantic is a sieve through which only or chiefly the liberal adventurous sensitive *America-loving* part of each city, clan, family, are brought. It is the light complexion, the blue eyes of Europe that come: the black eyes, the black drop, the Europe of Europe is left.[7]

For Emerson, as for his admirers, it was the blue eyes and the light complexion that conferred on the Irish a real-American identity. With the arrival of millions of dark-eyed new immigrants at the turn of the twentieth century, his preferences counted ever more heavily.

As many immigrants poured into the United States, a new hierarchy was under construction, one placing Anglo-Saxons at the top and the Irish just below, soon to be incorporated into the upper stratum of northwestern Europeans as "Nordics." The newest newcomers, Slavic immigrants from the Austro-Hungarian empire, Jews from Russia and Poland, and Italians, especially those from south of Rome, had still to be judged and rated. This sorting out took place within a history of older waves of immigration.

Back in the mid-nineteenth century, masses of impoverished Catholics had inspired contrasts between "old" and "new" immigrants. The Texas founding father Sam Houston had contrasted the old immigration of the colonial generation, on the one hand, and the new, midcentury Catholics, on the other. Now, at the turn of the twentieth century, Catholic Irish and Germans were assuming their place as "old" immigrants, while the "new" immigrants from southern and eastern Europe were being slotted where Houston's famine Irish had been. In their penury and apparent strangeness, the new immigrants after 1880 made Irish and German immigrants and, especially, their more prosperous, better-educated descendants seem acceptably American.

Thus occurred the second great enlargement of American whiteness. It came with such reluctance and with so many qualifications and insults that Irish Americans continued to feel excluded and aggrieved. It took a very long time for the realization of acceptance to sink in, for it had begun in the middle of the nineteenth century and stretched across the lifetimes of a generation and more. The commentary was far more likely to castigate new immigrants than to welcome the old. In the great hue and cry over this new round of immigration, the voice of one New Englander carried farthest.

IN THE 1890s, Francis Amasa Walker (1840–97), the most admired American economist and statistician of his time, laid the scientific groundwork by publishing a number of influential articles positing the need to limit the number of immigrants. (See figure 14.2, Francis Amasa Walker.) The son of a professor of economics who also served in the U.S. Congress, Walker graduated from Amherst College in 1860 and rose through Union Army ranks during the Civil War. After studies in Germany, he was appointed director of the U.S. census of 1870. He directed the census of 1880 while attached to the Sheffield Scientific School of Yale University between 1872 and 1880. In 1881 he became president of the Massachusetts Institute of Technology and in the following years presided over

Fig. 14.2. Francis Amasa Walker as president of Massachusetts Institute of Technology.

both the American Statistical Association and the American Economic Association (AEA). Until the creation of the Nobel Prize in economics in 1969, the AEA's annual Walker Prize stood as the world's highest honor accorded an economist. Having been born in Boston, moreover, Walker was almost automatically deemed smart, able, and enterprising. Who better than a Bostonian to tell Americans what they needed to know? And Walker had some help.

The idea of *New England*, as we have seen, played a pivotal role in American race thought. Ostensibly a regional identity, New England stood for racial Englishness—vide *English Traits*. In this sense, the writing of American history bristled with race talk, as the Brahmin author and congressman Henry Cabot Lodge showed in his well-regarded books.

Lodge was an expert on Anglo-Saxon law, the topic of his Harvard Ph.D. dissertation. By 1881 he had taught at Harvard for three years and was starting his political career, sped along through a series of lectures at the Lowell Institute (where we have already seen Louis Agassiz) and publication of his 560-page *Short History of the English Colonies in America*. A perfect specimen of Anglo chauvinism, this book ascribes the greatness of the United States to the "sound English stock" of the middle classes and the "fine English stock" of families like George Washington's, "good specimens of the nationality to which they belonged, and . . . a fine, sturdy, manly race."[8] Again and again, Lodge trumpets the qualities of "the English race" and bases the inevitability of American independence on the intrinsic worthiness of that race.

Ten years later, Lodge confidently presented supposedly hard proof of New Englanders' superiority, in an article quoted approvingly for the next forty years. "The Distribution of Ability in the United States" (1891) quantified the conventional wisdom of the time in pages of tables and lists purporting to prove that Massachusetts had contributed the largest number of distinguished Americans: 2,686 of the 14,243 names in the six volumes of Appleton's *Enyclopædia of American Biography*. Lodge's methodology, with its subtle means of inclusion, worked fine for just about everybody in the race business, despite glaring weaknesses. For one thing, he gauged distinction according to the size of subjects' portraits, so that a larger illustration in *Enyclopædia of American Biography* garnered two stars, while a smaller one got only one star, even after Lodge admitted that "portraits do not appear to have been distributed simply on the ground of ability and eminence." For another, while forthrightly acknowledging the impossibility of figuring "race-extraction" with any confidence and tracing it only through the paternal line, he nonetheless continued to use racial categories based upon names and places of birth.[9] Never mind these limitations; Lodge still carried on to recognize the English as the greatest American "upbuilders."

As for southerners, Lodge found them deficient, even though "no finer people ever existed than those who settled and built up our Southern States." The problem was slavery, which "dwarfed ability and retarded terribly the advance of civilization."* Southerners got shut out of regional greatness, but Lodge's summary, in a crucial gesture of inclusion, reached beyond England to include "people who came from other parts of Great Britain and Ireland."[10] New England still ruled, but the Irish now took their place within its glory.

---

* Among Lodge's rare dissenters stood John Hammond Moore, a historian from Mississippi, who objected that Lodge's sloppy methodology deprived the South of standing, which it surely did.

•

As in the case of so many immigration restrictionists, Francis Amasa Walker's New England descent seemed connected to his blood and virility. In 1923 Walker's biographer called this father of six children the "fine flowering of all that was superior and, in the best sense, peculiar in New England before the Civil War." Echoing a familiar theme of purity, the biography claims that Walker's "ancestry was extraordinarily homogeneous. Almost all [his] forebears came over in the first great wave of English immigration before 1650, and there was afterwards little or no admixture from other than British stock."[11] New England identity meant smart minds in handsome bodies, the sine qua non of Americanism. But would there be enough of them?

The census of 1880 had indicated a decline in the native white American birthrate. Since Walker firmly linked immigration to reproduction, he blamed native white Americans' "decay of reproductive vigor . . . out of the loins . . . of our own people" on the pernicious influence of slovenly foreigners. True, he conceded, native white demographic stagnation did owe something to "luxurious habits," "city life," boardinghouse "habits unfavorable to increase of numbers," and the Civil War's toll on native white bodies. Succeeding racist and eugenicist thought would consistently echo the baleful effects of city life and war, both enemies of the health of "the race."* But never mind, most trouble lay with the "monstrous total of five and a quarter millions" of recent foreign arrivals.[12] They posed the threat of racial endangerment.

Nativism and its cold-blooded, stock-breeding lexicon increased in volume, as during the 1890s Walker and others railed ever more stridently against the evils of immigration. "Degradation" joined "stock" as a leitmotif. In 1895 two articles entitled "The Restriction of Immigra-

---

* "The race" would seem to indicate the human race, but its meanings in their contexts often pointed toward only middle- and upper-class whites of English descent. Walker's demographic anxieties pertained merely to white Americans; he did not include others as Americans. Describing the American population of 1790—when Indians still lived in the Northeast and one-fifth of the enumerated population descended from Africans—Walker said that "(leaving the Africans out of account) it was all of European stock." The terminology of "stock"—as in better or poorer—evaluated people as creatures whose whole value emerged in metaphors of animal breeding.

tion" repeated "degradation" and "degraded" six times and "ignorant and brutalized peasantry" twice. "Loins" appeared often, too, euphemistically attached to both Anglo-Saxon and immigrant, as in the loins of "beaten men from beaten races; representing the worst failures in the struggle for existence." Phrases destined for greatness.

LIKE SAM HOUSTON, Walker contrasted *old* and *new* immigrants, but his chronology betrayed slipperiness between good ("old" pre–Civil War German and Irish) and bad ("new" immigrants arriving later on). Yes, the immigration problem had first appeared in the 1850s with the "degraded peasantry" needed to build the railroads and canals. Look, he warned, how the influx had reduced native whites' fertility. Clearly native-born Americans had begun to "shrink" from competition with early Irish. Now it was happening all over again, only somehow the "old" Irish immigrants were becoming Americans and, inexorably, failing demographically, too.*

Without much explanation, Walker admitted the Irish immigrants into the American fold as northern Europeans. With Americanization came demographic failure, so that the Irish as Americans were, in their turn, "shrinking" from competition with Italians and no longer reproducing mightily. But this time the Americanization process had come to a halt. Walker thought the new immigrants, unlike the old ones, had to remain inherently repulsive.[13] In no way could these new hordes evolve like northern Europeans; they would inevitably "degrade" American citizenship.

For Walker, cheap, easy transatlantic transportation was partly to blame for lowering the caliber of immigrants. In the old days, only the brave and enterprising ventured across the seas. But now "Hungarians, Bohemians, Poles, south Italians, and Russian Jews," from "every foul and stagnant pool of population of Europe," could reach the United States with ease. These "vast masses of peasantry, degraded below our utmost conceptions," lacked all "the inherited instincts and tendencies"

---

*Walker's theory of a demographic driving-out survived until its refutation in 1945 in W. Lloyd Warner and Leo Srole's *The Social Systems of American Ethnic Groups.*

of native (white) Americans. Walker did not hold back: "Their [the new immigrants'] habits of life, again, are of the most revolting kind." Moreover, and most significantly for Walker, these "masses of alien population" created problems spanning politics, the economy, and demography: laboring for low wages, they offered a harvest of ignorant workers ripe for demagogues. Lured into labor unions, they could easily be "duped" into going on strike. Such immigrant radicalism threatened the very health of American democracy.

The themes trumpeted by Walker and seconded by Lodge—New England superiority, reproductive competition, and labor radicalism— expressed a deeply conservative ideology that perverted Darwinian natural selection and feared worker autonomy. These notions would enjoy great longevity in the new language of truth: racial science. Supposedly rigorous and attentive to natural laws, racial science supplied the theory and praxis of difference among Europeans (as well as the descendants of Africans) in the United States. No longer stigmatized as inherently different, Irish and Germans entered a second enlargement of American whiteness to become constituent parts of *the* American. For now there were newcomers to toil at hard labor and be stigmatized as racially inferior.

WILLIAM Z. RIPLEY AND
THE RACES OF EUROPE

Francis Amasa Walker's famous cliché "beaten men from beaten races" played well in white race science, but Walker was hardly out there alone crying in the wilderness. Scores of others—men like the author and lecturer John Fiske and scholars from high academia, like the era's leading sociologist, Edward A. Ross, and the pioneering political scientist Francis Giddings of Columbia—joined Walker in pushing northern European racial superiority over new immigrant masses. At the other end of the spectrum, the American Federation of Labor also drew the line against the new immigrants as "beaten men of beaten races."[1] But Walker, who was to die in 1897, stood highest in influence, practically dictating how Americans would rank white peoples for decades, a period that introduced William Z. Ripley.

Originally from Medford, Massachusetts, William Z. Ripley (1867–1941), like Walker and Lodge, advertised his New England ancestry: his middle name, Zebina, he said, honored five generations of Plymouth ancestors.* Ripley contrasted "our original Anglo-Saxon ancestry in America" with that of "the motley throngs now pouring in upon us," and, like Walker, he attended to his manly and nattily dressed appearance.[2] (See figure 15.1, William Z. Ripley.) With Ripley it was smart

---

* Neither of Ripley's parents, however, bore the name Zebina.

minds in handsome bodies all over again—and, one might add, education and connections.

After gaining a bachelor's degree in engineering from MIT, Ripley took a Ph.D. in economics at Columbia, writing a dissertation on the economy of colonial Virginia. After two years' lecturing at MIT and Columbia, Ripley found himself at somewhat loose ends in 1895. He needed a better-paying job, and an aging Francis Walker needed a scientific classification of American immigrants. Walker chose Ripley, his favorite student, and Ripley seized this opportunity to codify the gaggle of immigrants.[3]*

Fig. 15.1. William Z. Ripley, professor of economics, Harvard University, ca. 1920.

Ripley later said that *The Races of Europe* took nineteen months of work. To a scholar these days that seems not very long. Working with his suffragist wife, Ida S. Davis, and librarians at the Boston Public Library, Ripley synthesized the writings of hundreds of anthropologists.[4]† John Beddoe in England and Joseph Deniker and Georges Vacher de Lapouge in France proved especially helpful. European anthropologists had been compulsively measuring their populations for decades, offering Ripley tens of thousands of detailed measurements, charts, maps, and photographs. Ripley used them all. Such exhaustive scholarship, together with the "Ph.D." attached to Ripley's Anglo-Saxon name on the title page, endowed *The Races of Europe* with a glowing scientific aura.

Ripley's work first reached the public as a series of lectures at the

---

* Ripley told the *New York Times* reporter that he had needed the extra money for his children's education.

† In his preface Ripley says that his wife performed such "a goodly share" of the book's preparation that he wanted to include her name on the title page. This did not occur.

Lowell Institute in Cambridge, Massachusetts, in 1896. Earlier in the century the Lowell Institute had offered its podium to likely speakers on race such as George Gliddon (Josiah Nott's collaborator) and Louis Agassiz (soon to join the Harvard faculty). The New York publisher Appleton issued the lectures serially in *Popular Science Monthly* and then published a generously illustrated book in 1899.*

Weighing in at 624 pages of text, 222 portraits, 86 maps, tables, and graphs, and a bibliographical supplement of more than two thousand sources in several languages, the sheer heft of *The Races of Europe* intimidated and entranced readers, blinding most of them to its incoherence. Ripley himself may have been blinded by the magnitude of his task, aiming as he did to reconcile a welter of conflicting racial classifications that could not be reconciled. (See figure 15.2, Ripley's "European Racial Types.") In this table Ripley presents "traits" he considered important—head shape, pigmentation, and height—along with the multiple taxonomies posited by various scholars.

One glaring taxonomic dilemma appears in the inclusion of "Celtic," in parentheses, beneath "Alpine." Anthropologists had long struggled to sort out the relationship between ancient and modern Celts, between the Celtic regions of Europe such as Ireland and Brittany, and between ancient and modern Celtic languages such as Gaelic. Was France a Celtic nation? Yes and no. French Republicans embraced their nation's revolutionary heritage, identifying with such glorious ancient Celtic heroes as Vercingetorix, the tragic protagonist of Caesar's *Gallic War*.[5] Royalists like Alexis de Tocqueville and his companion Gustave de Beaumont, in contrast, proudly claimed descent from Germanic conquerors. Beaumont, we remember, gave his French protagonist in *Marie* the Frankish name Ludovic rather than the more familiar French Louis.

Ripley's parenthesis does not solve the Celtic problem, and he stoops to insert Georges Vacher de Lapouge (a cranky, reactionary librarian at a provincial French university whom we will encounter again later)

---

*Two other seminal racist works also appeared in 1899: Houston Stewart Chamberlain, *Die Grundlagen des neunzehnten Jahrhunderts* (translated as *Foundations of the Nineteenth Century*), and Georges Vacher de Lapouge, *L'Aryen: Son rôle social*, translated into German in 1939, but not English. A now forgotten, then aspiring American racist scholar, Carlos C. Closson, translated Lapouge's shorter work on the Aryan.

European Racial Types.

		Head.	Face.	Hair.	Eyes.	Stature.	Nose.	Synonyms.	Used by.
1	TEUTONIC.	Long.	Long.	Very light.	Blue.	Tall.	Narrow ; aquiline.	Dolicho-lepto. Reihen-gräber. Germanic. Kymric. Nordic. Homo-Europæus.	Koll-mann. Ger-mans. English. French. Deniker. Lapouge
2	ALPINE (Celtic).	Round.	Broad.	Light chest-nut.	Hazel-gray.	Medium, stocky.	Variable ; rather broad ; heavy.	Celto-Slavic. Sarmatian. Dissentis. Arvernian. Occidental Homo-Alpinus. Lappanoid	French. Von Hölder. Germans Beddoe. Deniker. Lapouge Pruner Bey.
3	MEDITER-RANEAN.	Long.	Long.	Dark brown or bl'k	Dark.	Medium, slender.	Rather broad.	Iberian. Ligurian. Ibero-Insular Atlanto-Med.	English. Italians. Deniker.

Fig. 15.2. "European Racial Types," in William Z. Ripley,
The Races of Europe *(1899).*

into the list of authorities. Ripley thereby conferred a measure of scientific recognition, although Lapouge's fanatic Aryan/Teutonic chauvinism destroyed his standing in France. Questionable scholarship aside, Ripley had set out to transcend "the current mouthings" of the racist lunatic fringe, and his thoroughness inspired confidence for years. Ordinary readers judged his book scientific, and anthropologists hailed his methodology.

NOTHING EVER got truly settled in race science, but Ripley came close. How many European races were there? Ripley says three: Teutonic, Alpine, and Mediterranean. What criteria to use? Following accepted anthropological science, Ripley chooses the cephalic index (the shape of the head; breadth divided by length times 100), "one of the best available tests of race known."[6] Add to that information about height and pigmentation, and he has nailed each of the three white races:

Teutonics: tall, dolichocephalic (i.e., long-headed),
     and blond;
Alpines: medium in stature, brachycephalic (i.e.,
     round-headed), with medium-colored hair;
Mediterraneans: short, dolichocephalic (i.e., long-headed),
     and dark.

The cephalic index was not new. In fact, a real European scholar, the Swedish anthropologist Anders Retzius, had invented it in 1842, coining the terms "brachycephalic" to describe broad heads and "dolichocephalic" to describe long heads. The technique quickly took hold in Europe, where researchers took to measuring heads by the tens of thousands.

Anthropologists loved the cephalic index because it seemed to measure something stable, and race theorists demanded permanence. Heads supposedly remained constant across an endless succession of generations. Concentration on the head was not new. A skull, we recall, had inspired Blumenbach's naming white people "Caucasian." Samuel George Morton and Josiah Nott had backed up their assertions of white supremacy with Mrs. Gliddon's drawings of skulls. France's Paul Broca, his generation's most renowned anthropologist, also based his race theories on skull measurements.

Retzius and other fans of the cephalic index had no trouble linking head shape with "racial" qualities such as enterprise, beauty, and, of course, intelligence. Theorizing from old skulls, they envisioned primitive, ancient, Stone Age Europeans—often identified as Celts—as brachycephalic and also dark in color. Accepted theory soon held that long-headed dolichocephalics had invaded Europe and conquered these primitive, broad-headed people. A lot of the old natives were still around, people considered backward, such as the brachycephalic Basques, Finns, Lapps, and quite a few Celts; they were still assumed to be primitive natives, like peasants and other supposedly inert groups.*

---

* Paul Broca became the most enthusiastic French anthropometrist in the middle of the nineteenth century. But in the 1870 era of sharp military conflict between France and a newly united Germany, Broca pulled back from the association of long-headedness, Teutonic race, and enterprise. Now

Following the English anthropologist John Beddoe, Ripley gingerly notes "the profound contrast which exists between the temperament of the Celtic-speaking and the Teutonic strains in these [British] islands. . . . The Irish and Welsh are as different from the stolid Englishman as indeed the Italian differs from the Swede."[7] This idea of temperament as a racial trait was based on a perversion of Darwinian evolution. With a perfectly straight face anthropologists reasoned that evolution operated on entire races (not individuals or breeding populations), that races had personalities, and that physical measurements of heads betokened racial personality.

Over time the cephalic index both dominated as a symbol of race and became a two-edged sword when color was added to it. Long-headed people, "dolichocephalics," for instance, should be light and Teutonic (good) or dark and Mediterranean (bad). Alpines (maybe middling, maybe bad) were supposed to be brownish and brachycephalic. These correlations counted as "harmonic" correspondence. Rather than deal with people who did not fit the pattern, such as blond Alpines, race-minded anthropologists them deemed "disharmonic" and then just ignored them. Perfectly "harmonic" Mediterraneans with long heads and dark hair, eyes, and skin also faded from view, because anthropologists judged them to be obviously inferior and therefore of scant interest.

At first all this measuring of heads meant little to most Americans. Slavery and segregation had seen to it that race resided most obviously in skin color, or at least in physical appearance or ancestry that could be classified as black or white. But up-to-date experts stuck to their guns, proffering scientific explanation via visuals. (See figure 15.3, Ripley's brachycephalic and dolichocephalic skulls.) A caption at the lower left reads, "Brachycephalic type. Index 87. Zuid-Beveland, Holland," and refers to photographs on the left. On the lower right, "Dolichocephalic type. Index 73. Zeeland, Holland" refers to photographs on the right.*

---

taking note of the close relationship between science and jingoism, Broca pointed out that the greatest scientific admirers of dolichocephaly came from northern Europe. They had relegated France to the brachycephalic zone out of racial chauvinism.

* Even though both these skulls, brachycephalic as well as dolichocephalic, came from the Netherlands, anthropologists usually classified the Netherlands as dolicho-blond territory.

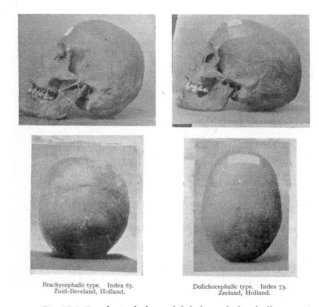

Brachycephalic type.   Index 87.
Zuid-Beveland, Holland.

Dolichocephalic type.   Index 73.
Zeeland, Holland.

Fig. 15.3. Brachycephalic and dolichocephalic skulls, in
William Z. Ripley, The Races of Europe *(1899).*

These images were intended to show the difference between a long, dolichocephalic skull with a cephalic index of 73 and a round, brachycephalic skull with a cephalic index of 87.

Since ordinary readers rarely encountered skulls in everyday life, and Ripley badly wanted them to understand, he added photographs of racial "types" along with their cephalic indices for further clarification. (See figure 15.4, Ripley's "Three European Racial Types.")

The three types are ranked vertically, with the Teutonic inevitably at the top, the Mediterranean inevitably at the bottom, and the Alpine in the middle. The Alpine type's cephalic index is noted as 88, that is, brachycephalic, and the Mediterranean type's as 77, that is, dolichocephalic, and the hair and eye color of both types is noted. The two dolichocephalic Norwegian Teutonic types are simply "pure blond," although, inexplicably, the hair color of the man on the right seems as dark as that of the brachycephalic Austrian and the Sicilian.

The four men depicted as embodiments of the "Three European

Fig. 15.4. *"The Three European Racial Types," in William Z. Ripley, The Races of Europe (1899).*

Racial Types" have no names. Anthropologists of the era saw no need for names. They dealt in ideal "types" that stood for millions of presumably interchangeable individuals.

RIPLEY'S 624 pages do contain a great deal of information—unfortunately, much of it is contradictory. He recognizes early on that his three racial traits—hair color, height, and cephalic index—are not reliably linked in real people. Short people can be blond; blond heads can be round; long heads can grow dark hair. He admits—and laments—that such complexity destroys any notion of clear racial types. Even his limited number of traits produced an infinity of races and subraces, a taxonomical nightmare.*

To further undermine notions of racial permanency, Ripley concedes that mixture and environment, which most anthropologists preferred to ignore, also affect appearance. Faced with such complexity and so many unknowns, Ripley was, he says, "tempted to turn back in despair." But

---

* No biological bases existed then, and none exist now, for cleanly differentiating the peoples of the world. Before the age of DNA testing, anthropological classification depended upon two kinds of observations: first, measurement, such as cephalic index; second, observation of outward appearance. Neither reveals the history of biological descent, whether of individuals or of groups. Today's DNA tests offer probabilities and similarities far more reliable than the observations and measurements of Ripley's time. Although often presumed infallible, DNA testing measures probabilities, not actual fact, and forensic processes include sloppiness and mistakes. In a 1997 *Sciences* article entitled "Bred in the Bone?" Alan H. Goodman analyzes the mistaken DNA racial identification of a black woman killed in the 1995 Oklahoma City bombing.

he could not let go.[8] He did, however, turn his back on the American South, where people white in appearance were discriminated against as Negroes. The U.S. Supreme Court had taken that matter up in *Plessy v. Ferguson* in 1896. Homer Plessy, a man who looked white, had been ejected as black from a newly designated white-only car. He sued and lost when the court ruled for segregation. The African American novelist Charles Chesnutt remarked on the "manifest absurdity of classifying men fifteen-sixteenths white as black," but, absurd or not, that was long to hold true.[9]* Ripley hardly cared. What happened in the South was less important than how to classify the immigrants pouring into the North. To unravel black and white would have hopelessly snarled his system.

Additional conceptual problems haunt the book's organization. Definitions—who counts as European people and what constitutes European territory—conflict from one chapter to the next. Ripley is not sure where Europe and its races begin and end. While he dismisses Blumenbach's notion of a single Caucasian race, *The Races of Europe* reaches past the territory of the Teutonic, Alpine, and Mediterranean races into Russia, eastern Europe, and western Asia as far as India. Africans appear in the chapter on Mediterranean race. Supposedly the Teutonic race belongs in Scandinavia and Germany; the Mediterranean race, in Italy, Spain, and Africa; and the Alpine race, in Switzerland, the Tyrol, and the Netherlands. Yet another, separate chapter wonders whether Britons originated in the Iberian Peninsula, given that Irish legend names the Spanish king Melisius as the father of the Irish. More taxonomical strangeness was to come.

As NOTED, Ripley's three-race system excludes many Europeans, such as Jews, Slavs, eastern Europeans, and Turks. Lapps present the usual quandary: they obviously live in Europe, but they do not look the way anthropologists wanted Europeans to look. Linguists did not face this problem; they put Lapps with Magyrs, Finns, and other speakers

---

* Chesnutt predicted that wealth would open the route to equal treatment in the public sphere.

Fig. 15.5. *"Scandinavia," in William Z. Ripley,* The Races of Europe *(1899).*

of Finnic languages. No problem there. But Ripley rejects this linguistic classification because the Lapps lack beauty: "The Magyrs, among the finest representatives of a west European type," he says, "are no more like the Lapps than the Australian bushmen." (See figure 15.5, Ripley's "Scandinavia.") The captions under photos of Lapps list only height (4' 9½" and 4' 8") and high cephalic indexes (both 87.5) as confirmation that Lapps are too short in stature and too broad of head.[10]* Piling it on, Ripley adds an unnamed German anthropologist's insult that "they [Lapps] are a 'pathological race.' " Actually, rather than documenting pathology, these photographs demonstrate a Scandinavian variety trumped by racial science's obsession with purity.

JEWS POSE another problem. Having long occupied a separate conceptual space within the races of Europe, they must be discussed as a category. At the same time, they are too varied to fit into one of Ripley's three European races. Recognizing this shortcoming early, Ripley had added a "supplement" on Jews to his Lowell Institute Lectures and articles published in *Popular Science Monthly*. *The Races of Europe* allots Jews and Semites a separate chapter.

---

* The captions read, "SCANDINAVIA. Teutonic types. 55: Vaage, index 75. 56: Hedalen, index 76. 57: Jøderen. 58: Norwegian. Lapps. 59: Stature 1.46 m. Index 87.5. 60: Index 87.5. Stature 1.43 m."

Fig. 15.6. "Jewish Types," in William Z. Ripley, The Races of Europe (1899).

Anti-Semitic writers had long posited a permanent Jewish race. But Ripley does not like that. Rather, he calls them a "people," since Jews conform closely to others among whom they live. His photographs of Jewish faces confirm regional variation.[11]* (See figure 15.6, Ripley's "Jewish Types.")

Then consider their noses. Ripley's bizarre discussion of the stereotypical Jewish nose betrays his uneasiness. He draws three figures to demonstrate how easily "the Jew" may be turned into a Roman. (See figure 15.7, Ripley's "Behold the Transformation!") A tortured paragraph explains this conceptual nose job:

The truly Jewish nose is not so often truly convex in profile. Nevertheless, it must be confessed that it gives a hooked impression. This seems to be due to a peculiar "tucking up of the wings," as Dr. Beddoe expresses it. . . . Jacobs has ingeniously described this "nostrality," as he calls it, by the accompanying diagrams: Write, he says, a figure 6 with a long tail (Fig. 1); now remove the turn of the twist, and much of the Jewishness disappears; and it vanishes entirely when we draw the lower continuation horizontally, as in Fig. 3. Behold the transformation!

---

* The *National Geographic*'s reviewer of *The Races of Europe* found Ripley's separate treatment of Jews anti-Semitic, because it treated Jews as though they did not fully belong in Europe.

Throwing up his hands, Ripley also explains that Jewish noses do not prevail among urban Jews; besides, many non-Jews have noses that look Jewish.[12]

Fig. 1.   Fig. 2.   Fig. 3.

Fig. 15.7. "Behold the Transformation!" in William Z. Ripley, The Races of Europe *(1899).*

TODAY'S READERS might find intriguing Ripley's use of a measure of blackness for people of the British Isles. His tool, the "Index of Nigrescence," had originated with the respected British anthropologist John Beddoe. Over the course of thirty years, Beddoe measured thousands of British heads. Employing impeccable methodology, he analyzed their cephalic indexes, hair, eye, and skin color. Those measurements grounded his classic *Races of Britain* (1885), whose countless pages of tables convinced Ripley and his generation of scientists that the Irish were dark. Beddoe's maps and photographs slipped easily into Ripley's chapter on Britons in *The Races of Europe*.[13] (See figure 15.8, Ripley's "Relative Brunetness.")

The text reads, "RELATIVE BRUNETNESS BRITISH ISLES, after Beddoe '85 [*Races of Britain*] 13,088 observations." On the right the scale ranks the "INDEX OF NIGRESCENCE," with light skin and hair at the top and dark skin and hair at the bottom.

This map also attempts to define linguistic groups: a line between highland and lowland Scotland traces the boundary of the Gaelic speech of Scotland and Ireland ("Gaelic Celtic"); another line separates English from the Gaelic of Wales and the Channel Islands ("Kymric Celtic"); a line through Ireland demarcates the eastern borderline of Irish Gaelic. These unreliable linguistic boundaries often reappeared as racial boundaries between Briton and Celt. Lowland Scots such as Thomas Carlyle and Robert Knox, you may recall, were delighted to be British Saxons rather than highland Scottish Celts.

RACES OF EUROPE vaulted to success immediately on publication in 1899. The *New York Times* devoted two full pages to a glowing review,

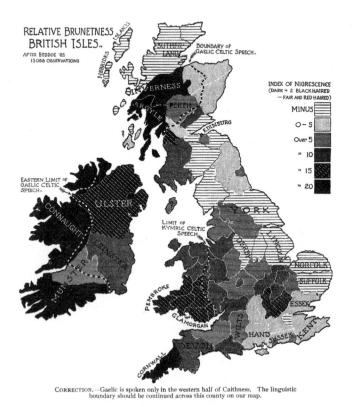

Fig. 15.8. "Relative Brunetness British Isles," in William Z. Ripley,
The Races of Europe (1899).

reproducing several of the book's photographs. The *Times* reviewer
(identified simply as W.L.) raves about Ripley's "great work" of "elaborate scope and exhaustive treatment." Best of all, Ripley demolished
the "schoolroom fallacy that there is such a thing as a single European
or white race."[14] Addressing general readers, the *Times* underlines this
telling point in an era of alarming European immigration. Scholars also
loved *Races of Europe*. The sheer amount of labor it required delighted
the *American Anthropologist*'s reviewer, who gushed over "the best
results of the last twenty years in physical anthropology."[15]

The British edition of 1900 prompted the Royal Anthropological

Society to give Ripley anthropology's crowning honors, the Huxley Medal and an invitation to deliver the Huxley Lecture of 1902. Occupied with a move from part-time appointments at MIT and Columbia to a permanent post at Harvard, Ripley was unable to accept for 1902. Later he remarked with youthful hubris that Sir Francis Galton, the world's most famous statistician—and the father of eugenics—had substituted for him.[16] Ripley did finally deliver the 1908 Huxley Lecture, the first American to achieve this singular mark of distinction. The *New York Times* reported his lecture under the pithy headline of "Future Americans Will Be Swarthy."[17]

Like *Races of Europe*, Ripley's Huxley Lecture delivers racist notions in scholarly tones.* He predicts a "complete submergence" of Anglo-Saxon Americans to follow the "forcible dislocation and abnormal intermixture" of many races and the low Anglo-Saxon birthrate. He also frets that Jews ("both Russian and Polish") were dying at too slow a rate, "only one-half that of the native-born American," despite living in abysmal circumstances. While Anglo-Saxons avoided having children, short, dark, round-headed Jews in the tenements multiplied alarmingly. Echoing his mentor Francis Amasa Walker's phrasing, Ripley warns that immigration was now tapping "the political sinks of Europe," bringing a "great horde of Slavs, Huns and Jews, and drawing large numbers of Greeks, Armenians and Syrians. No people is too mean or lowly to seek an asylum on our shores."

Reiterating favorite themes in European racial science, Ripley warns that the tendency of city people to be darker "can not but profoundly affect the future complexion of the European and American populations." Ripley's surmise that these dark-haired men were more sexually potent than blonds repeats speculations of Emerson and others, adding a note of anxiety. Ending ruefully, Ripley posits that all might not be lost. Even if Anglo-Saxon Americans followed American Indians and the buffalo into extinction, surely their mixture with others would mean a

---

* "Racist" here does not refer to people of color, who were not part of Ripley's concern. He spoke the lexicon of biological racial difference—with regard only to people now considered white.

continued, worthy life. After all, there exists a "primary physical brotherhood of all branches of the white race." *The* white race?

Dancing about the hot coals of theory in 1908, Ripley says there might be only one white race, not the three of 1899. Even further, perhaps, "all the races of men" belong to the same human brotherhood, and "it is only in their degree of physical and mental evolution that the races of men are different."[18] If so, nevertheless, some races (the white) are more advanced—more "evolved"—than others (the dark).

This cloudy perversion of Darwinian evolution and Mendelian inheritance thrived in the early twentieth century. Like most of his scholarly peers, Ripley believed that races of people, like Gregor Mendel's garden peas, inherited gross "unit" traits, such as intelligence, head shape, pigmentation, and height. Because Ripley believed that the original Europeans—those primitive, Stone Age Celts fated for displacement— were dark, he concludes that the "abnormal intermixture" of peoples in the United States would lead to a "reversion to the original stock." The hybrids might be even darker than the dark parent because of "the greater divergence" of stocks. If Italian men mated with Irish women, they would produce "the more powerful . . . the reversionary tendency" toward darkness. There could be no intermediate pigmentation.

Harvard's prestige played a large part in the longevity of such nonsense as scientific truth. But mostly *The Races of Europe* spoke to a race-obsessed nation by delivering the right opinions dressed up as science. Never mind that the book could not survive a careful reading, that it bulged with internal contradiction, or that its tables and maps offered a Babel of conflicting taxonomies. William Z. Ripley's *Races of Europe* remained definitive for the next quarter century.

ALTHOUGH *Races of Europe* defined Ripley's reputation over the long run, it represented a detour in his scholarship, for the young Ripley had first been a promising economist rather than an anthropologist. True, *Races of Europe* brought him excellent job offers from Cornell, Columbia, Yale, and Harvard. But the position he accepted in 1902 took him into Harvard's Department of Political Economy, where he remained until his retirement in 1933, when, like his mentor Francis Amasa Walker, he served as president of the American Economic Association.[19]

In these many years Ripley's reputation shone brightly. He appeared regularly in the *New York Times*. In the mid-1920s he warned President Calvin Coolidge, investors, and politicians of the dangers of unsound railroad financing and appeared as a cartoon character measuring railroad financial soundness. (See figure 15.9, Ripley measuring the railroads.) During the Hoover years of the Great Depression, he advocated government regulation along lines that would become President Franklin D. Roosevelt's New Deal. In fact, Ripley had taught Roosevelt at Harvard, delivering lectures that apparently inspired the reform of the American economy.[20]

Through it all the *New York Times* covered him diligently, printing his warnings and reviewing his books. It reported Ripley's auto accident, his nervous breakdowns, his retirement, his death, and, a quarter of a century later, the

Fig. 15.9. The New York Times *shows Ripley measuring the railroads.*

death of his wife.[21] All this attention signified a scholar at the top of the heap. But an immigrant of an original turn of mind was rising to challenge his preeminence.

FRANZ BOAS, DISSENTER

Born in Minden in Prussian Westphalia to middle-class parents, Franz Boas (1858–1942) had a sound German education. After attending a Protestant gymnasium, he studied at Heidelberg, Germany's oldest university.* (See figure 16.1, Franz Boas.) Like many German undergraduates, he joined a fraternity (*Burschenschaft*) known for dueling and drinking. Interestingly, being Jewish did not stand in his way, for during the 1870s his Burschenschaft Allemannia accepted Jewish students; not until later in the century did Allemannia and other fraternities become exclusive anti-Semitic centers of German nationalism. After a semester at Heidelberg, Boas moved on to Bonn, then completed his graduate work at Kiel University, earning a Ph.D. in physics in 1881. Not that Boas escaped the barbs of German bigotry. In both Heidelberg and Kiel he had encountered Germany's burgeoning anti-Semitism, from the "damned Jew baiters" who provoked "quarrel and fighting."[1] By the 1880s such harassment was becoming endemic, but Boas was able to avenge these insults, at least in part, through duels that left scars on his face, symbols of honorable, upper-class German manhood.

---

* Had he sought a Saxon identity, the Westphalian Franz Boas might have been considered a Saxon. Given the continual remapping of kingdoms and provinces in the German-speaking lands, any relationship between western ("Lower") Saxony and Westphalia had to be vague. Having actually grown up in Germany and not being much of a Teutomaniac, he pressed no such claim.

In 1881 Boas moved on to post-graduate work at Berlin with the pioneering German anthropologists Adolf Bastian and Rudolf Virchow (the latter considered a father of German anthropology), who taught him the physical anthropology of bodily measurement and alerted him to the possible influence of environment on head shape.[2] No finer training could be had in Germany, but with anti-Semitism now closing in, his homeland hardly offered Boas a promising career. The German nationalist Berlin movement, led by its intellectual avatar, Professor Heinrich von

Fig. 16.1. Franz Boas.

Treitschke, had made overt hatred of Jews so widespread and respectable that Boas began to ponder emigration.[3]

An opportunity arose in 1883 to pursue his study of psychophysics (the relationship between physical sensation and psychological perception) far from Germany, in Anarniturg in the Arctic Cumberland Sound. There, living with the Inuit, he sought to perceive the environment as they did and to think like them. Those two years of fieldwork were useful and enjoyable. Even the hardships and strange food came to hold an appeal. Raw seal liver, he discovered, "didn't taste badly once [he] overcame a certain resistance."[4]

Late nineteenth-century European anthropologists were typically both provincial and arrogant. They operated from two basic assumptions: the natural superiority of white peoples and the infallibility of elite modern science. Supposedly, scientific methodology endowed European scholars with universal knowledge. Boas might have accepted such dogma as a student, but during his time with the Inuit his independent streak took him toward diametrically opposite conclusions. Trying, for instance, to record and understand the Inuit language and failing, Boas realized that the fault lay not in the Inuit but in his own limitations. He began to see how hallowed European ways had disabled its scholars. "We [civilized people] have no right to look down on them," he said of the Inuit, an almost unique, even heretical, thought at the time.

This breakthrough took Boas well toward the cultural relativism that would dominate twentieth-century anthropology. All knowledge, even Western knowledge, was relative and circumscribed: "our ideas and conceptions are true only so far as our civilization [i.e., our culture] goes."[5] To know everything worth knowing was impossible. And to know anything about other people required immersion in their world, to become, in a sense, one of them.

In the decade following 1885, Boas made several fieldwork trips to the Pacific Northwest and held a series of temporary positions, including stints at the American Museum of Natural History in New York, the World's Columbian Exposition in Chicago in 1893, and G. Stanley Hall's Clark University in Worcester, Massachusetts, then in its heady early years. Such wandering afforded refuge from Germany and sufficient time for research, but no financial security. Finally, in 1896, at the relatively advanced age of thirty-eight, he gained an appointment as lecturer in anthropology at Columbia University, joining a faculty that included the young luminary William Z. Ripley. Not that life had suddenly become cushy for Boas. Whereas Ripley had a choice of jobs and enjoyed generous remuneration, Boas began with temporary employment and a paltry salary at Columbia, evidently made possible only by his rich uncle's underwriting. American anti-Semitism, then on the increase, doubtless played a role in such disparity.[6]

Even so, Boas quickly forged an international reputation as a careful yet innovative scholar. His colleagues soon came to respect his fieldwork and publications—they granted him tenure in 1899, when he was forty-one—even as he questioned their conventional notions of racial superiority and civilization. One such innovation appeared in Boas's 1894 address to the Anthropology Division of the American Association for the Advancement of Science, called "Human Faculty as Determined by Race." Its premises—that race, culture, and language are separate, independent variables and should not be confused—undergirded Boas's classic book, *The Mind of Primitive Man,* first published in 1911 and revised in the late 1930s. But as statements applying to Americans, these points began to enter popular consciousness only in the 1930s, when anthropologists were becoming the experts on race. Boas's *Anthropology and Modern Life* (1932) then emerged as a major scientific declaration.

One theme of the 1894 lecture questioned the evolutionary view of human races that equated whiteness with development and civilization. Downplaying anatomical differences between races, Boas looked to environment and culture rather than to race as shapers of people's bodies and psyches. Here was the radical germ of cultural relativism, one fast attracting adherents, among them Paul Topinard, successor to Paul Broca and then the leading French anthropologist. Topinard applauded Boas's thinking, declaring him "the man, the anthropologist [he] wished for in the United States" and with whom "American anthropology enters into a new phase." Boas, though he had not found a home in Europe, did retain some European chauvinism. He enjoyed outshining American anthropologists, who lacked his Old World education. "Actually," he conceded, "it is very easy to be one of the first among anthropologists over here."[7]

For all its originality, Boas's 1894 address contained a number of dated ideas. One of them was the validity of comparing numbers of "great men," in the fashion of Sir Francis Galton in England and Henry Cabot Lodge's "Distribution of Ability in the United States." And Boas remained tentative, closing with: "Although, as I have tried to show, the distribution of faculty among the races of man is far from being known, we can say this much: the average faculty of the white race is found to the same degree in a large proportion of individuals of all other races, and [even though] it is probable that some of these races may not produce as large a proportion of great men as our own race." Counting up great men might be forgiven in Boas, even inferring failure in other races and cultures. After all, such was the tenor of impeccable scholarship at the time. Everyone else was doing it, but he was moving on. Boas soon jettisoned notions of comparative intelligence, as well as designations of "higher" and "lower" races.[8]

In 1906 he made another brave gesture toward racial tolerance by accepting an invitation from the pioneering African American social scientist W. E. B. Du Bois (1868–1963) to deliver a commencement address at Atlanta University. Not only was Boas a white scholar willing to go to a black institution; he came with a message of encouragement for young people about to enter a hostile America. Quite amazingly for 1906, he assured them they had nothing to be ashamed of. Other races—the ancestors of imperial Romans and the northern European barbarians— had endured their own dark ages. Now, if educated young black people could understand the "capabilities of [their] own race," they could attack "the feeling of contempt of [their] race at its very roots," and thereby "work out its own salvation."[9]

In these Atlanta remarks, Boas draws intriguing parallels. For instance, he likens the differences between European Jews and Gentiles to imagined racial differences between European nobles and peasants. At this time French authors like Gobineau and Lapouge, along with many other European writers, considered France's nobility Teutonic and the common people Celts, a supposedly different and inferior race. Not so, Boas declared. European nobles were "of the same descent as the people." So were European Jews, "a people slightly distinct in type" from the Gentiles they live among.[10] By "European" Jews, Boas doubtless had Germans in mind. In other commentary he did distance himself from Jewish immigrants newly arrived from Poland and Russia, people he termed "east European Hebrews."

Thinking of himself as German American, Franz Boas neither hid nor proclaimed his Jewishness, and why should he have? For him, Judaism was a religion. His family, he said, had "broken through the shackles of dogma." He had, therefore, been freed from the restraints "that tradition has laid upon us," and could strive toward an ethical rather than a religious life.[11] There could be no such thing as a Jewish *race*, because, for Boas, race resided in the physical body, something to be measured and weighed. He placed no faith in the notions of racial temperament so dear to Ripley and his English authority John Beddoe. Boas assumed that Jewishness might eventually disappear into American society through assimilation; he and most other German Jews in the United States lived by that belief. The new Jews from Russia and Poland, however, he judged differently. Their appearance in the early twentieth century caused him some consternation.

Unable to cast out every prejudice of the time, Boas dealt with the issue of immigrant strangeness in two ways, one inclusive, the other exclusive. Obviously, American society had over many decades worked its magic, as American-born generations assimilated physically and culturally. But could it Americanize these new immigrants, "Italians, the various Slavic people of Austria, Russia, and the Balkan Peninsula, Hungarians, Roumanians, east European Hebrews, not to mention the numerous other nationalities," and bring them closer to "the physical type of northwestern Europe"? For Boas, "these people," so distinct in many ways, were a worrisome "influx of types distinct from our own."[12]

Here we have a contradiction. Boas did not support immigration restriction. Too much racism there. And yet his use of the language of "we" points straight to an "us" and "them" ideology. Not even this most liberal thinker could escape divisions of self and other inherent in racial ideology. The early 1900s were a particularly tough time to think about racial equality, and, as a result, such tension echoes across Boas's work.

"HUMAN FACULTY as Determined by Race" might strike a twenty-first-century reader as timid, even retrograde. And "your own people" addressed to a black audience in Atlanta might ring uncomfortably close to the odious "you people." But it was dramatic to hear Boas speak warmly across the black/white color line in an era of naked racial antagonism. During the late nineteenth century, poor, dark-skinned people often fell victim to bloodthirsty attack, with lynching only the worst of it. Against a backdrop of rampant white supremacy, shrill Anglo-Saxonism, and flagrant abuse of non-Anglo-Saxon workers, Boas appears amazingly brave.

It mattered little in those times that lynching remained outside the law. More than twelve hundred men and women of all races were lynched in the 1890s while authorities looked the other way. Within the law, state and local statutes mandating racial segregation actually expelled people of color from the public realm. On a national level, the U.S. Supreme Court decided *Plessy v. Ferguson* in 1896, validating Louisiana's railroad segregation statute and opening the way to the segregation of virtually all aspects of southern life. Such laws and decisions, allied with local practice, disenfranchised hundreds of thousands, tightening a southern grip on federal power that racialized all of national politics.

Federal policy toward Native American Indians and people from Asia also signaled their vulnerability to white cupidity. In 1882 the Chinese Exclusion Act, passed after loud demands from organized labor, barred any sizable immigration of Chinese workers. Samuel Gompers, head of the American Federation of Labor and himself a Jewish immigrant from England, clamored for Asian exclusion when the legislation first passed and when it was up for renewal ten years later. Gompers even pressed for exclusion of Chinese from settling in American Pacific island possessions and from working on the Panama Canal.[13] Before and after initial passage of Chinese exclusion, Indians and Asians in the West fell victim to whites lusting after their land and their jobs, as locals harried, attacked, and expulsed their Chinese neighbors. In 1887 the Dawes Severalty Act halved the land that Indians controlled by dividing up tribal territory among individuals and opening the so-called surplus Indian lands to white settlement. Southern states, beginning with Mississippi and South Carolina, revised their constitutions in the 1890s, encouraging the enactment of poll taxes, literacy and property qualifications, and grandfather clauses that ended black political life in the South.

Economic hard times further aggravated labor tensions. In the 1870s Slavic and Italian coal miners in western Pennsylvania suffered abuse, ostracism, cheating, incarceration, and attack. The U.S. Army massacred Lakota (Sioux) at Wounded Knee, South Dakota, in 1890, as lynching, that scourge of black Americans, took the lives of eleven Italians in New

Orleans in 1891. Elsewhere labor conflict brought out company private militia (such as the Pinkertons) and state and national guards to coerce striking workers, as in the Homestead, Pennsylvania, steelworks in 1892.[14] Doing the bidding of employers, local police and sheriffs and injunctions mandated by the Sherman Anti-Trust Act of 1890 broke labor unions, forcing striking workers back to work. Ugliness of spirit reached well beyond workers into the upper strata of American society.

A notable instance of anti-Semitism occurred in 1877 when a Saratoga Springs hotel refused to admit the New York financier Joseph Seligman, whose bank had helped finance the Union during the Civil War. Organized outbreaks of anti-Jewish violence occurred for the first time during the depression of the 1890s. In Louisiana and Mississippi, night riders attacked Jewish families and businesses. Personal abuse like stone throwing, hitherto occasional, became common throughout the North. When their employer hired fourteen Russian Jews, five hundred New Jersey workers rioted for three days in 1891, forcing Jewish workers and residents to flee. Educated Americans like the Boston Brahmin Henry Adams had long harbored anti-Semitic feelings. Now they felt free to voice stereotypical notions of Jewish control of the nation.

As mobs rampaged and learned opinion asserted the absolute superiority of Anglo-Saxon Americans, imperialist expansion put theory into practice. The Anglo-Saxon identity of "manifest destiny" had been obvious since 1845, when the journalist John O'Sullivan (despite his Celtic name) coined the phrase savoring the image of "the Anglo-Saxon foot" on Mexico's borders and "the irresistible army of Anglo-Saxon emigration" pouring down upon the entire western portion of North America. Surely, the Anglo-Saxon would take over the Caribbean and Asia. Not least, the Spanish-American-Cuban War of 1898, a fairly transparent grab for empire, promised new frontiers for the American ruling class. The now virtually deified Theodore Roosevelt certainly had his say. Of Dutch ancestry, he preferred to speak of "the American race," or "our race," sometimes echoing Thomas Carlyle and Ralph Waldo Emerson.[15]

Racism permeated scholarship. Within Boas's own field, the older leaders quickly rejected his racial relativism. Daniel Brinton, a prominent evolutionist, used his 1895 presidential address to the American Association for the Advancement of Science to reject Boas's 1894 theory. For Brinton, the "black, the brown and red races differ anatomically so much from the white . . . that even with equal cerebral capacity, they could never rival the results by equal efforts."[16] Assertions of Anglo-Saxon superiority continued pouring out, as from Boas's Columbia colleague John W. Burgess. Writing in the *Political Science Quarterly* in 1895, Burgess denounced the ignorance and wickedness of those supporting open immigration to the United States. They sought, he maintained in newly fashionable racial terminology, "to pollute [the United States] with non-Aryan elements."[17] This kind of meanness far outshouted Boas's careful edging away from racial chauvinism.

WILLIAM Z. RIPLEY'S *The Races of Europe* appeared in 1899, the same year his Columbia colleague Franz Boas received a professorship. In a singular turn of events, Boas reviewed the book for *Science*, the respected journal of the American Association for the Advancement of Science. Boas's criticism departs sharply from the prevailing chorus of acclaim in three important aspects. First, Boas questioned Ripley's conceptualization of ideal racial types. To Boas, that made no sense. Furthermore, he doubted that three (or more) races existed in Europe, and, last, he harbored serious reservations on the robustness of the cephalic index as a test of race.[18]

Such skepticism undermined the truth value of Ripley's book and pointed toward where Boas would take anthropology in the new century. At the same time, though, here was a matter of interpretation, for in 1899 Boas was himself still measuring heads. (Two of his best-known students, the anthropologist Margaret Mead and folklorist-novelist Zora Neale Hurston, came along later to assist in this research.) While at Clark University, Boas had begun a Virchow-style study of the cephalic indexes of schoolchildren. In this he was merely carrying on the work of his mentor in Germany, who had measured tens of thousands of schoolchildren and categorized them according to their pigmentation and cephalic index in the 1870s. By the mid-1890s, however, Virchow had grown skeptical. Such measurements, even by the thousands, had not yielded much of anything beyond the fact that language, culture, and physical body did not neatly coincide. Virchow concluded that "Indo-Europeans," another contemporary term for northern Europeans, exhibited no uniform physical type.[19] Boas, for his part, was not yet ready to go that far. Perhaps more research on the concepts of racial type and cephalic index would shed light on the pressing new immigrant question.

THAT RESEARCH turned him to data compiled by Maurice Fishberg, a medical doctor practicing in New York's heavily Jewish Lower East Side. Fishberg had measured forty-nine Jewish families over the course of two generations, producing intriguing results, but in a sample too small to support convincing conclusions.* To enlarge the sample size would require new funding, so Fishberg suggested that Boas approach the U.S. Immigration Commission, created by Congress in 1907. In the late eighteenth century, St. Jean de Crèvecoeur and Samuel Stanhope Smith had posited the creation of a new and particularly American physical type, and Ralph Waldo Emerson had voiced doubts along that line decades later. Taking up this idea, Boas proposed to study the effect of "change of environment upon the physical characteristics of man." He specifically wished to discover whether immigrants from southern and eastern Europe could adjust to their American environment.

The Immigration Commission funded Boas's application—such questions were in the air—and through 1908–09 he directed the measurement of some eighteen thousand eastern European and Russian Jews, Bohemians, Neapolitans, Sicilians, Poles, Hungarians, and Scots.[20] The tens of thousands of northern Europeans, mostly Irish and Germans, still immigrating to the United States caused no alarm and therefore

---

* Maurice Fishberg, an immigrant from southwest Ukraine, taught medicine at his alma mater, New York University. After several papers on the Jews of New York City, he published *The Jews: A Study of Race and Environment* in 1911, in which he contended, like Boas, that Jewish physiognomy varied widely and that Jews were not physically different from other Europeans. His unnamed *New York Times* reviewer remained unconvinced, wondering why, if "the Jewish race" is not pure, "Jews and Jewesses from quite different quarters of the globe resemble one another so markedly."

hardly figured in this research. Here was another token of the second enlargement of American whiteness.

The Immigration Commission of 1907 was also known as the Dillingham Commission, its chair being Senator William P. Dillingham, Republican from Vermont. Shortly after being formed, it took a big step toward immigration restriction. President Grover Cleveland, a Democrat, had frustrated restrictionists in 1897 by vetoing a bill (supported by the American Federation of Labor) limiting entry to immigrants who passed a literacy test. Southern states had begun to use literacy tests as a means of curbing black and poor white voting, and the Dillingham Commission took up the restrictionist cause with a vengeance. By the time it closed down in 1910, it had sponsored eighteen immigrant reports in forty-one volumes, most of them encouraging restriction. But one dealt with Boas's measurements of immigrants and their children.

Nearly 600 pages long, Boas's *Changes in Bodily Form of Descendants of Immigrants* consists largely of graphs, illustrations, and tables, the very scientific apparatus Ripley and others had employed to convey methodological soundness. Details of stature and weight figured, but were minor compared with the cephalic index, the king of race measurements. Among Boas's several immigrant populations, some heads attracted more attention than others, and his most famous conclusions concerned the scariest immigrants: southern Italians ("Sicilians and Neapolitans") and Russian/Polish Jews ("east European Hebrews").

Boas presents his findings in conventional tabular form. (See figure 16.2, Boas's "Table 8.") Table 8, for instance, indicates differences in the head shapes of Jewish youngsters of three types: those born outside the United States, those born less than ten years after the immigrant mother's arrival in the country, and those born subsequently. The bombshell lay in the columns on the right. They show that the longer the mother had lived in the United States, the more her American-born son's head shape differed from that of her sons born abroad.[21] These findings were nothing short of revolutionary.

Boas found that head shape, supposed never to change, was indeed changing. The round-headed "east European Hebrew" was becoming

TABLE 8.—*Differences in head form of Hebrew males, between foreign-born, those born in America within 10 years after arrival of mother, and those born 10 years or more after arrival of mother—Continued.*

CEPHALIC INDEX.

Age.	Average of total series.		Differences in cephalic index of total series and those—					
			Foreign-born.		Born in America—			
					Less than 10 years after arrival of mother.		Ten years or more after arrival of mother.	
		Cases.		Cases.		Cases.		Cases.
5 years	83.5	71	+1.5	18	±0.0	29	−1.1	24
6 years	84.1	57	±0.0	16	+0.4	28	−0.8	15
7 years	83.3	75	+0.7	18	+0.2	32	−0.7	25
8 years	83.3	98	+1.0	27	+0.2	45	−1.6	26
9 years	83.0	185	+1.7	51	−0.5	54	−1.0	100
10 years	83.0	359	+1.6	83	−0.4	137	−0.6	139
11 years	82.9	442	+1.6	114	−0.2	189	−1.1	139
12 years	82.9	521	+1.7	133	−0.2	225	−1.2	163
13 years	82.8	498	+1.2	137	−0.2	208	−0.9	153
14 years	82.5	477	+1.6	120	−0.2	223	−1.0	134
15 years	82.4	331	+1.7	94	−0.4	174	−1.6	63
16 years	82.6	73	+1.1	36	−0.8	23	−1.6	14
17 years	82.2	40	+0.8	24	−1.4	10	−1.2	6
18 years	82.4	27	+0.6	22	−0.7	3	−5.4	2
19 years	82.8	37	+0.1	31	+1.0	4	−4.3	2
20 years and over	82.9	803	+0.1	764				

WIDTH OF FACE.

Age.	Mm.	Cases.	Mm.	Cases.	Mm.	Cases.	Mm.	Cases.
5 years	116.3	68	+1.0	15	−1.0	29	+0.6	24
6 years	116.5	53	−0.4	15	+0.3	23	±0.0	15
7 years	118.2	61	+1.1	15	+0.2	32	−1.0	24
8 years	121.1	95	+0.8	25	+0.3	44	−1.9	26
9 years	122.1	194	±0.0	50	+0.5	62	−0.4	82
10 years	123.4	358	+1.3	82	−0.3	141	−0.3	135
11 years	124.8	441	+0.9	113	−0.2	184	−0.4	144
12 years	124.8	520	+1.8	132	−1.0	225	±0.0	163
13 years	127.5	497	+0.1	136	−0.1	208	−0.1	153
14 years	129.8	475	+0.2	118	+0.3	215	−0.7	142
15 years	131.2	329	+1.1	93	−0.3	153	−0.1	85
16 years	131.9	72	+1.5	35	−1.3	23	−1.5	14
17 years	133.2	40	+0.8	24	−1.7	10	−0.7	6
18 years	135.0	27	+0.1	22			−0.4	5
19 years	135.1	36	−0.2	30			+1.2	6
20 years and over	138.4	793	+0.1	755			−1.5	38

Fig. 16.2. Franz Boas, "Table 8. Differences in head form of Hebrew males, between foreign-born, those born in America within 10 years after arrival of mother, and those born 10 years or more after arrival of mother—*Continued,"* in Reports of the United States Immigration Commission *(New York: Columbia University Press, 1912).*

more long-headed, while "the south Italian, who in Italy has an exceedingly long head" was becoming more short-headed. All in all, it appeared "that in this country both approach a uniform type, as far as the roundness of the head is concerned." Having found what he perhaps was looking for, Boas read enormous significance into these changes, even though they were modest. He concluded that "when these features of the body change, the whole bodily and mental make-up of the immigrants may change." Thus, Alpines, Mediterraneans, and Jews would join Anglo-Saxons as real Americans in body and therefore in mind and spirit. For "the adaptability of the immigrant seems to be very much greater than we had a right to suppose before our investigations were instituted." At bottom Boas's study denied the need for hysteria over the new immigrants.*

The Dillingham Commission, not surprisingly, came to the opposite conclusion, one favoring the idea of permanent type. While duly noting the scholarly import of Boas's work, just one report in a thickening fray, the commission declined to incorporate his findings in its report; deeming them incomplete, it vaguely recommended further study.[22] In the long run, however, Boas won. Social scientists and the educated lay public took note of his study, increasing his stature internationally.[23] The possibility that races from southern and eastern Europe might change physically began to circulate in enlightened discussions of immigration and American identity. Ultimately, Boas's research on immigrants' heads cast the cephalic index into anthropology's waste bin and tipped the heredity versus environment balance toward environment, at least for a while. That tipping took a long time.

In the short run, U.S. immigration policy hardly changed. Rather, the restrictionist campaign petered out in the face of opposition in the form of the power generated by immigrant organizations and their allies. Immigrant neighborhoods created a panoply of institutions, starting with stores and saloons and extending into newspapers and political organizations. Their names reveal their provenance—the Penn-

---

*It should be noted, however, that Clarence C. Gravlee, Richard L. Jantz, and Corey S. Sparks reexamined Boas's immigrant study in 2001 and 2003 and concluded that the changes Boas found were too slight and contradictory to sustain his claims for a possible change in "type."

sylvania Slovak Catholic Union, the Ukrainian Workingmen's Association, the Polish Women's Alliance, the Sons of Italy, the Serbian National Federation, the *Chicagoer Arbeiter Zeitung*, and the *Irish World* newspaper—and their numbers were legion; fraternal organizations, mutual-aid societies, burial societies, nationalist clubs, saloons and taverns, and foreign-language newspapers kept immigrants in touch with their homelands and supplied the news that mattered in native languages.[24] A popular Italian language newspaper, *Il Progresso Italo-Americano*, a New York daily founded in 1880, reached more than 100,000 readers, and the Yiddish *Jewish Daily Forward*, founded in 1897, had a circulation of 175,000. Political clubs delivered the votes that elected the representatives who served the needs of immigrant constituencies.

Postponement of immigration restriction from the 1880s to the 1920s, for example, testifies to the clout of congressional representatives of immigrant communities, particularly in New York. The first Italian American U.S. representative was elected in 1890, after serving in the California State Assembly from 1882 to 1890. While a token number of Jews had entered in the U.S. House of Representatives during the nineteenth century, their numbers increased impressively after 1900. More than twenty Jewish representatives served in Congress before the First World War, the great majority as Democrats from New York.[25]

In addition, an articulate liberal-minded cohort of freethinkers, social workers, and settlement house workers had firsthand knowledge of the poor European immigrants who were being racialized and denigrated. Living out the promise of progressivism, liberals were gaining influence in the public sphere. Immigrants, their children, their institutions, and their friends—and their employers—together created a climate more favorable to immigration, even toward working people and the poor.[26] Shying from controversy and content to leave well enough alone, Presidents William Taft and Woodrow Wilson each vetoed bills containing literacy tests.

American political culture was moving into the Progressive Era, and Boas's own circle reflected the change. Boas had long prided himself on his family's "Forty-eighter"* liberalism, and his wife came from a free-thinking Austrian Catholic family. A friend, Felix Adler, had founded the Society for Ethical Culture, and Boas's Forty-eighter uncle Abraham Jacobi and his friend Carl Schurz championed reform, especially address-ing the needs of poor children. Boas's friends also included feminist pro-gressives like Frances Kellor, Victoria Earle Matthews, and Mary White Ovington. His students, such as Melville Herskovits, Otto Klineberg, Ruth Benedict, Zora Neale Hurston, Margaret Mead, and Ashley Mon-tagu, investigated non-Anglo-Saxons and stressed the crucial role of environment in human culture.[27]

It mattered that so many of the settlement house workers and moral reformers advocating public health and social services for the poor were educated women—the very women Theodore Roosevelt hectored over their duty to breed. Turning away from the nineteenth-century pat-tern of charity intended to correct personal weaknesses, they recognized the structural causes of poverty. Localities, states, and even the federal government, they said, owed the population certain services as rights, because environment, not inherent weakness, made people poor. When the environment changed for the better, then people would improve.

POPULAR CULTURE played a leading role in this high point of progres-sivism. While the Immigration Commission gathered data and Boas measured heads, the American theater rode a wave of fascination with settlement houses and immigrants. A play called *The Melting Pot* opened in Washington, D.C., in October 1908 to Theodore Roosevelt's praise, and moved on to long runs in Chicago and New York. Its author, the English Jewish immigrant Israel Zangwill, celebrates the creation of Americans out of immigrants in a melodramatic version of Boas's graphs and tables of immigrant assimilation.[†]

The plot of *The Melting Pot* revolves around two characters who, unbeknownst to each other, have emigrated from the same Russian vil-

* The aftermath of the European revolutions of 1848 had sent hundreds of liberal-minded Germans into exile. They retained their progressive ideals as "Forty-eighters," much as the revolutionaries of 1968 identified themselves according to their activist year.
† Zangwill said his experience as president of a committee to rescue Russian Jews from the pogroms and resettle them in the United States inspired the play.

lage of Kishinev (in modern Moldova, between Romania and Ukraine). Vera Ravendal, an aristocratic, revolutionary Christian, now works in a New York settlement house; David Quixano, a Jewish musician and composer, has witnessed the slaughter of his parents in the most infamous of the Russian pogroms, the trauma that drove him to the United States. The supporting cast includes David's Orthodox uncle and aunt, a German symphony conductor, the Quixano family's Irish domestic servant, and a nouveau riche American playboy. Although Zangwill places the Quixanos among the despised Ashkenazi "east European Hebrew" masses of early twentieth-century immigrants, he gives them a Sephardic name evoking a more prestigious Iberian history. Benjamin Disraeli, the late British prime minister, had given his characters Sephardic ancestry in novels written before his prime ministership in 1868.[28]*

When Vera and David fall in love in *The Melting Pot*, they find that old country rages are still boiling. Vera's father, it turns out, had led the pogrom that killed David's parents, and David's uncle Mendel cannot forgive either the assailant or the descendant of a murderer. In America, however, Vera is free to understand David's feelings better than his uncle, and the New World allows the young people to transcend their pasts. Vera and David agree to marry without sacrificing either of their religions.

The play ends on the Fourth of July with a rousing performance of David's "American Symphony." As David and Vera watch the sun set behind the Statue of Liberty, they celebrate the American melting pot:

DAVID [Prophetically exalted by the spectacle]
    It is the fires of God round His Crucible.
    [He drops her hand and points downward.]
    There she lies, the great Melting Pot—listen! Can't you hear the
    roaring and the bubbling? There gapes her mouth
    [He points east]
    —the harbour where a thousand mammoth feeders come from the
    ends of the world to pour in their human freight. Ah, what a stir-

---

* Disraeli's "Young England" novels are *Vivian Grey* (1827), *The Young Duke* (1831), *Contarini Fleming* (1832), *Henrietta Temple* (1837), *Venetia* (1837), *Coningsby, or the New Generation* (1844), *Sybil, or the Two Nations* (1845), and *Tancred, or the New Crusade* (1847).

ring and a seething! Celt and Latin, Slav and Teuton, Greek and
Syrian,—black and yellow—

VERA [Softly, nestling to him]

Jew and Gentile—

DAVID Yes, East and West, and North and South, the palm and the pine,
the pole and the equator, the crescent and the cross—how the great
Alchemist melts and fuses them with his purging flame! Here shall
they all unite to build the Republic of Man and the Kingdom of God.

Ah, Vera, what is the glory of Rome and Jerusalem where all
nations and races come to worship and look back, compared with the
glory of America, where all races and nations come to Labor and look
forward! [He raises his hands in benediction over the shining city.]
Peace, peace, to all ye unborn millions, fated to fill this giant
continent—the God of our children give you Peace.

[An instant's solemn pause. The sunset is swiftly fading, and the
vast panorama is suffused with a more restful twilight, to which
the many-gleaming lights of the town add the tender poetry of the
night. Far back, like a lonely, guiding star, twinkles over the darken-
ing water the torch of the Statue of Liberty. From below comes up
the softened sound of voices and instruments joining in "My Country, 'tis of Thee." The curtain falls slowly.][29]

ALL IN all, questions of immigration and assimilation were a mud-
dle between 1890 and 1914. The promise of assimilation exemplified
by Boas and Zangwill encouraged Americans of a welcoming turn of
mind. Conversely, Ripley's idea of three separate European races, with
lines deeply etched between them, held more power. Two emblematic
figures, the patrician president Theodore Roosevelt and the scholar
Edward A. Ross, enunciated the thinking of most educated early
twentieth-century Americans who feared that immigrants would
defile their America. This was thoroughly racist thinking, directed
toward races that were white.

17

ROOSEVELT, ROSS,
AND RACE SUICIDE

Well-born, impeccably educated, and a master communicator, Theodore Roosevelt (1858–1919) never lost sight of race as the driving force of human history, especially of his "American race." (See figure 17.1, Theodore Roosevelt.) In books and articles throughout his public life, Roosevelt could alter his emphases depending on the political context, but he was always a leading race thinker of his times.* And he got started early.

As a youngster, Roosevelt admired the heroics depicted in Henry Wadsworth Longfellow's "Saga of King Olaf" in *Tales of a Wayside Inn* (1863). During a summer in Dresden, Germany, when he was fourteen, Roosevelt was exposed to the *Nibelungenlied* (that pagan German saga of Siegfried the dragon slayer), deepening his sense of Teutonic heritage.[1] Later, as an undergraduate at Harvard, he absorbed the ideas of American racial greatness and immigrant inferiority from Professor Nathaniel Southgate Shaler of Kentucky and came to agree with Shaler on a popular tenet of American race talk. Like so many other old-line Americans, Roosevelt easily saw the figure of this tall, slender Kentuckian as the quintessential native American. And in graduate studies

---

* Another representative American opinion maker, Horace M. Kallen, quite aptly termed Roosevelt "a drum-major and a prophet."

Fig. 17.1. Theodore Roosevelt as Master of the World.

at Columbia, Roosevelt also absorbed the Teutonist notions of John W. Burgess, another conservative admirer of all things German.

Roosevelt's rise in politics proved vertiginous. A Republican by birth, he was appointed assistant secretary of the navy in 1898, at age thirty, a stint followed by volunteer service in Cuba during the Spanish-American War. His well-publicized war record helped him get elected governor of New York and, in 1900, placed as vice president on a Republican ticket headed by William McKinley. Roosevelt was forty-two years old when he became president after McKinley's assassination in 1901. Serving as a progressive, even a trust-busting president between 1901 and 1909, he returned to politics as the presidential nominee of the Progressive Party in the 1912 campaign that brought the Democrat Woodrow Wilson to the White House.

During this entire time Roosevelt spoke and wrote tirelessly, starting off with a series of Teutonist histories and biographies: *The Naval*

War of 1812 (1882), *Thomas Hart Benton* (1887), *Gouverneur Morris* (1888), and *The Winning of the West* (1889–96).[2] The American Historical Association (AHA) acknowledged his contribution to the writing of history by electing him president in 1912. This selection was unsurprising, since Roosevelt had succeeded wildly as a historian. Moreover, as a strident Teutonist, he fit in well with his AHA predecessors: the Boston Brahmin-statesman-historian George Bancroft in 1886, the industrialist turned award-winning historian James Ford Rhodes in 1899, the Boston Brahmin grandson and great-grandson of presidents Charles Francis Adams in 1901, the Anglo-Saxonist, imperialist historian Alfred Thayer Mahan in 1902, and Roosevelt's Harvard classmate and friend the Harvard history professor Albert Bushnell Hart in 1909.[*]

Echoing Carlyle's Norse theme in the 1880s, Roosevelt's *Thomas Hart Benton* hails the "most war-like race" those hardy frontiersmen, conquerors of the West like "so many Norse Vikings." Echoing Emerson in *English Traits*, Roosevelt practically savors the "hideous brutality" of warfare against the Indians. Indeed, Roosevelt's enthusiasm for virile violence knows few bounds. Intrepid Americans who take over Texas merge into Emersonian Norsemen as "Norse sea-rovers," "a ship-load of Knut's followers," and "Rolf's Norsemen on the seacoast of France." Roosevelt pictures Sam Houston as an "old world Viking" whose life as a whole emerges "as picturesque and romantic as that of Harold Hardraada himself."[3†]

Thus, early on, Roosevelt bought into much of the Teutonic hypothesis of American governmental institutions, but not quite all of it. Others, such as the Reverend Josiah Strong, were jubilantly predicting the

---

[*] There was a gap. Fredrick Jackson Turner's election in 1910 signaled a hiatus in the Teutonist idea. Turner espoused a "frontier thesis," making the American frontier, not medieval Germans in their forests, the wellspring of American identity. Like Crèvecoeur, Turner envisioned Americans as a mixture of northern Europeans—still only northern Europeans—but as a mixture occurring in the Western Hemisphere rather than in Emerson's version of England. Such views placed Turner outside the club of pure Teutonists.

[†] Harold Hardraada (1015–66), king of Norway, also Harald III Sigurdsson, led an international life, in Norway, Scotland, and England and in Russia, Sicily, and Bulgaria, perhaps even in Jerusalem. Attempting to enforce his claim to the English throne, he died in battle at Stamford Bridge, Yorkshire, England, at the hands of the English king Harold II. Less than a month later Harold II died at Hastings, and William of Normandy became king of England.

universal reign of the Anglo-Saxon at the expense of all other races. Strong's book *Our Country: Its Possible Future and Its Present Crisis* (1886) primed Americans for a final conflict between Anglo-Saxons and others, with, presumably, Irish and other Celts on the losing side.[4] It sold 175,000 copies in a generation.

Not quite so narrow, Roosevelt acknowledged the mixed racial nature of Britons and Americans—race, of course, meaning the European races alone. In what today seem like trivial nuances, Roosevelt usually termed his superior race "English-speaking," rather than simply "English." Nonetheless, his reasoning made "native Americans"— that is, Anglo-Saxon Protestants—uniquely suited racially for self-government, thanks to their Teutonic heritage. Everybody who was anybody could agree on that. Of course, as with all race talk, conflicting assumptions and disparate conclusions arose. A century ago they could draw blood.

Controversy reigned over whether Americans or Englishmen or even Germans had inherited the self-governing genius of medieval German forests. The English Anglo-Saxonist E. A. Freeman chose his own England, but accepted Americans into his race club. Herbert Baxter Adams, holder of a Ph.D. from Heidelberg (most American race theorists studied in Germany at one time or another), taught at Johns Hopkins. A prideful New Englander, he planted medieval Germans' descendants in New England, rather bypassing England itself. The Harvard Ph.D. and young congressman Henry Cabot Lodge, a New Englander of self-proclaimed Norman French heritage, saw much virtue in the Norman contribution to England, yet spoke often and easily of "the English race." Following Carlyle, Lodge saw Normans as Saxons who happened to speak French and therefore as full-blooded Teutons. John W. Burgess, a political scientist at Columbia University, had spent 1870–73 studying at Göttingen. Burgess held that Germans monopolized racial and political superiority, even down to his own times.

More than a little distrust crept into race theory with regard to present-day Germans. As imperial rivalries raged in early twentieth-century Europe, Burgess pushed for a political alliance of the "Teutonic" powers of Germany, England, and the United States against France. But Lodge distrusted both Britain and Germany. Roosevelt, meanwhile, shied away from Germany, calling it the land of "swinish German kinglets who let out their subjects to do hired murder, and battened on the blood and sweat of the wretched beings under them."[5] The lawyer, philosopher, and social Darwinist historian John Fiske, the leading American popularizer of Anglo-Saxonism, held, "We New Englanders are the offsprings of Alfred's England," but nonetheless, "we—the English—are at least three-quarters Celtic. . . . I believe that in blood, we are quite as near to the French as to the German—probably more so." Most other turn-of-the-century Teutonists (like Emerson earlier) thought the French stood for all that was alien to the democratic, but not revolutionary, Anglo-Saxon genius. Even Henry Cabot Lodge, the self-proclaimed Cabot descendant, made his French ancestors into Saxons, the better to admire the Germans of Tacitus and Caesar.[6] And so it went. Tempests we now set in a teapot, but at the time a big, important pot of tea.

Like the majority of his contemporaries, Roosevelt made race (not, say, class) the major force of human history, but his notion of American race changed over time. In his early work, Americans and Englishmen are much the same race, a product of German, Irish, and Norse combining in the British Isles. In admitting the Irish admixture, Roosevelt parted ways with some of his fellow Teutonists. His teacher Burgess, for instance, had locked the Irish out of the Teutonic race, and Roosevelt's friend Henry Cabot Lodge initially had hard words for the Irish. Politics, where the Irish represented a potent force, made all the difference. After Lodge entered politics, he like Roosevelt came around as his Irish American constituents forced him to soften this critique.

Darwinian evolution proved more problematic. A progressive thinker, Roosevelt accepted the validity of evolution but gave it his own, racial spin. As he pondered the great sweep of English and American history, he agreed with other modern scientific thinkers, including Ripley, that Darwin had to be right. But any evolutionary change would occur only very, very, very slowly and, crucially, in terms of what we now more easily see as culture: a race must surely require a thousand years or more to develop temperamentally to the level of Teutons. But once thus formed, fine traits would be passed along within the race. Thus, Americans of Teutonic descent possessed "that union of strong, virile qualities . . . that inestimable quality, so characteristic of their race, hard-headed common sense." Perhaps other races, even southern Italians, would evolve in their turn, but evolution to a superior level could not take place anytime soon. Woodrow Wilson, the Princeton political scientist and future president, agreed. The superior "English race" had risen through "slow circumstance."[7]* So must all the others, by patiently waiting their turn.

According to this psycho-cultural notion of evolution, temperament trumped all, but the right temperament was under siege, as the census of 1890 made clear. The wrong people were increasing, and the right people were not.

Roosevelt first glimpsed danger in the early 1890s, as did Francis Amasa Walker, in the declining birthrate among old-stock New Englanders. French Canadians migrating to jobs in the American textile industry struck Roosevelt as a dangerous mass "swarming into New England with ominous rapidity." By 1895 what Roosevelt called the "warfare of the cradle" had intensified. It was becoming ever more difficult to "prevent the higher races from losing their nobler traits and from being overwhelmed by the lower races."[8]

"RACE SUICIDE" loomed as an issue "fundamentally infinitely more important than any other question in this country."[9] For Roosevelt, this was not a matter of workers versus capital or the poor versus the rich. It was a kind of race war pitting the higher races of his native Americans against two groups deemed inferior by dint of their heredity: "degenerate" poor white families of native descent and immigrant workers from southern and eastern Europe. (African Americans hardly figured in this discussion, as prominent race thinkers had convinced themselves that *the Negro* was dying out, unfitted as *he* was to

---

*When Roosevelt and others spoke of "native Americans" at the turn of the twentieth century, they excluded people not of northern European descent. Indians, Negroes, Asians, and immigrants from southern and eastern Europe did not count as "native Americans."

live outside of slavery.) As a race publicist in the era of rising worker unrest, Roosevelt dedicated the last decades of his life to exhorting the better classes to reproduce more lustily in order to meet and, he hoped, overcome the demographic competition of their inferiors.

Great slogans are rare, and this one—"race suicide"—though co-opted by Theodore Roosevelt, was not of his invention. Rather, it was coined by the popular and distinguished sociologist Edward A. Ross (1866–1951) in 1901. (See figure 17.2, Edward A. Ross.) In "The Causes of Racial Superiority," both an address to his colleagues in the social sciences and a widely quoted article in the *Annals of the American Academy of Political and Social Science*, Ross stresses something he terms *racial temperament* over biological race.[10]* He puts it all together— the dominance of racial temperament, the minor role of biological race, disastrous demographics—producing the catastrophe of "race suicide" looming on the horizon. His emblematic phrase picks up Francis Amasa Walker's unfavorable demographics and echoes Walker's wording.

Well before his sloganeering, Ross had scaled the heights of American academia. Receiving his B.S. from Coe College in 1886, he went on to study at the University of Berlin and Johns Hopkins Universities (Ph.D. 1891), then moved around quite a bit. After posts at the Universities of Indiana, Cornell, Stanford, and Nebraska, he capped off a fine career at the University of Wisconsin, the leading American institution in social science.† A founder of sociology in U.S. universities, Ross was elected presi-

Fig. 17.2. Edward A. Ross.

---

* Ross belonged to the mass of progressives like Roosevelt who termed the opponents of involuntary sterilization—such as social workers, immigrants, and African Americans—"sentimentalists."

† For publicly criticizing the power of corporations and unrestricted immigration, Ross had run afoul of Mrs. Leland Stanford, a founder of the university. She forced President David Starr Jordan to fire Ross in 1900.

dent of the American Sociological Association in 1914 and 1915. He also excelled as a popularizer of social scientific truth; his books sold half a million copies during his lifetime.[11]

Like other declarations on race, "The Causes of Racial Superiority" contradicts itself from one statement to the next. Ross opens by denigrating the old-fashioned concept of race as "the watchword of the vulgar." What the craniometricians measure—head shape as a racial trait—interested him not at all. Ross's racial characteristics are temperamental: "climatic adaptability," "energy," "self-reliance," "foresight," "stability of character," and "pride of blood."[12] These were the concepts to focus on.

In page after page, Ross beats his drum: "the Celtic and Mediterranean races," "domesticated races" and "economic races," "the higher races," "the great races," "the higher blood," "the Superior Race" with capital letters, and, echoing Emerson's "singing and dancing nations," "the childishness or frivolousness of the cheaply-gotten-up, *mañana* races." "The economic virtues," he concludes in italics, "are a function of *race*."[13]* All this appears in a lecture aimed at an audience of scholars of the American Academy of Political and Social Science.

Writing for a popular audience in the *Independent*, Ross echoes Emerson's and Roosevelt's image of American pioneers as Vikings, selected "not for the brainiest or noblest or highest bred" but for the "strongest and most energetic."[14] Like Ripley and the Teutonists, Ross prizes height and denigrates by name the people he thinks too short. Sardinians did not make the cut, nor did those "masses of fecund but beaten humanity from the hovels of far Lombardy and Galicia," and "cheap stucco manikins from Southeastern Europe . . . from Croatia and Dalmatia and Sicily and Armenia, they throng to us, the beaten members of beaten breeds . . . Slovaks and Syrians . . . as undersized in spirit, no doubt, as they are in body."[15]

Finally, willing to use any weapon at hand, Ross accepts the reasoning of then fashionable, self-styled European "anthroposociologists,"

---

*While cherishing "climatic adaptability" as a dimension of race superiority, Ross laments the debility of hardy northerners once they move to warmer places.

physical anthropologists Otto Ammon and Georges Vacher de Lapouge, who bent Darwinian natural selection to their mania of craniometry and had also made their way into William Z. Ripley's influential *Races of Europe*. Ammon and Lapouge were spinning out fantastical theories of race temperament based on the cephalic index, famously pronouncing European townspeople more long-headed (meaning, for them, more Teutonic and superior) than the people of the surrounding countryside (those more Celto-Slav and inferior). Following them, Ross concludes that the "city is a magnet for the more venturesome, and it draws to it more of the long-skulled race than of the broad-skulled race. . . . [T]he Teuton's superior migrancy takes him to the foci of prosperity, and procures him a higher reward and a higher social status." For someone dismissing race as superstition, Ross bought right into the mumbo jumbo of racial skull shapes.[16]*

In lockstep with Ross, Roosevelt opined, "If all our nice friends in Beacon Street, and Newport, and Fifth Avenue, and Philadelphia, have one child, or no child at all, while all the Finnegans, Hooligans, Antonios, Mandelbaums and Rabinskis have eight, or nine, or ten—it's simply a question of the multiplication table. How are you going to get away from it?"[17] But Roosevelt did not have the public sphere to himself. While he was nagging educated women of "our own type" to bear babies, a less articulate, but nonetheless oppositional, discourse arose that undercut his fundamental assumptions. Worker-oriented commentary, especially (but not exclusively) in the foreign-language press, disputed both the notion of upper-class racial superiority and the logic of racial determinism. Their point was well taken, for the so-called beaten men from beaten races were doing most of the work. In the garment, iron, and steel industries, in the mines and mills that kept the amazing American economy running, immigrants supplied the necessary brawn. The rhetoric flowing from the country's Roosevelts and the Rosses might

---

* Ross did not agree, however, with other anthropologists (e.g., Sir Arthur Keith in England) that war served eugenic purposes. According to Ross, modern warfare had become so industrialized that it no longer served manly ends. In the twentieth century, warfare was more like "an extra-hazardous branch of engineering" with little material payoff.

harp on race—the Italian race, the Jewish or Hebrew race, the Anglo-Saxon race. Such blather only obscured—in words, at least—the gaping chasm between the classes, and the working classes were beginning to have their say.

THE INDUSTRIAL Workers of the World (IWW, or Wobblies), founded in 1905, became the most visible sign of working-class mobilization. Repudiating the American Federation of Labor's business model of organizing only skilled workers (now monopolized by English-speaking northwestern Europeans, especially Irish Americans), the IWW welcomed all kinds with an "industrial" model that sought to bring the unskilled, immigrant masses into unions by stressing their interests as workers.[18]*

With their working-class readership, Italian and Yiddish newspapers came to reflect the anarchist and socialist views of their readers. The earliest Italian and Yiddish newspapers sprang up in New York in the 1880s, with the left press appearing in the following decade. The anarchist *Il Proletario* was founded in Hoboken, New Jersey, in 1902, as the organ of the Italian Socialist Federation, joining the socialist *Jewish Daily Forward* founded in 1897. Such papers depicted American society quite differently from the tony journals that couched their race theory in quasi-scientific, quasi-historical terms.

Italian anarchists especially heaped scorn on American self-righteous blindness, above all when it came to injustices inflicted on blacks in the South. True, other immigrant workers had become targets of labor abuse, but Italians had suffered a special wound, the lynching of eleven Italians in New Orleans in 1891. As though to echo David Walker's 1835 accusations, *Il Proletario* skipped over the idea of white races and stressed the injustices of black Americans at the hands of native-born whites. A blast from *Il Proletario* in 1909 asked,

---

*The IWW manifested a split between its leadership and its rank and file. The latter consisted of a mix of races and ethnicities, varying by location and industry, while the leadership consisted largely of Irish Americans.

Who do they think they are as a race, these arrogant whites? From where do they think they come? The blacks are at least a race, but the whites . . . how many of them are bastards? How much mixing is their "pure" blood? And how many kisses have their women asked for from the strong and virile black servants? As have they, the white males, desired to enjoy the warm pleasures of the black women of the sensual lips and sinuous bodily movements? But the white knights care little for the honor and decency of the black women, whom they use and abuse as they please. For these, race hatred is a national duty.

Sounding a note that grew louder and louder, *Il Proletario* reached a ringing conclusion: "Not race struggle but class struggle."[19]

BUT IT was too early, and *Il Proletario*'s exhortation fell on ears attuned to another sort of analysis, one that interpreted class status as permanent racial difference with African Americans largely cornered in the South; the "race" in this race question was as much white as black.

THE DISCOVERY OF
DEGENERATE FAMILIES

As the nineteenth century drew to a close, American race theory had settled into a four and a half part scheme. On top, where they had been since Emerson, were the stout, pure, and admirable Anglo-Saxons. Catholics—Irish and German—were on their way into the club of the select as northern Europeans. A separate category contained the European "beaten men of beaten races." Swarthy and round-headed, they were easy enough to see, for recent European scholarship guided Americans into the science that found them inferior. Black people—segregated, impoverished, and disfranchised—generated a good deal of southern commentary, but for the majority, they quite obviously did not—could not—be included within *the* American. American Indians and Asians, largely disappeared from racial calculation.

So far, so good for the theorists, but what was to be done with the poor whites, those unsavory millions of native-born Anglo-Saxons? Many of them were drifters or hunters or hardscrabble farmers living out in the country—often in the South—or scratching a livelihood on the edges of town. Anglo-Saxon of race, but manifestly inferior in lifestyle, they did not fit into the American racial plan. They needed to be put into a racial box and theorists found one: "degenerate families."

•

HIGH-MINDED RICHARD L. Dugdale laid the cornerstone of the "degenerate family" edifice.[1] Born in England, Dugdale (1841–83) lived on an inheritance in New York City and served as corresponding secretary of the Prison Association of New York and secretary of the National Prison Association in the 1870s. He was a man described as "so quiet, so modest, so full of love for all men . . . engaged not only in the cause of prison reform, but in all the great reforms that made themselves felt in his day and generation . . . [and] much attached to his sister, Jane Margaret, an invalid. He was never attracted to other women, and was very shy and retiring in their presence." Dugdale therefore heads the long list of men anxious about bad heredity (including Francis Galton, Henry H. Goddard, Madison Grant, and Charles Benedict Davenport) who never had children of their own.[2] After Dugdale died at age forty-two, his sister, Jane Margaret, established the Richard L. Dugdale Fund for the Promotion in the United States of Sound Political Knowledge and Opinions." She died a year later.*

For some years Dugdale had been concerned with prisons. Then the hard times following the panic of 1873 aggravated social conditions. Two European criminologists, Cesare Lombroso and Martino Beltrani-Scalia, had recently taken up the scientific study of crime "in its perpetrators" in order to formulate means of prevention. Their work attracted Dugdale, who sought to apply their recommendations in New York State.[3] In 1874 he visited thirteen county jails and in 1877 published his report analyzing the inmates as *"The Jukes": A Study in Crime, Pauperism, Disease and Heredity, also Further Studies of Criminals.* A resounding success, it was reprinted five times by 1895.

A multitude of tables lent an aura of reliability to the data. Dugdale described not only particular individuals but also a type of family as a huge social problem. In seventy-five years, by Dugdale's calculation, the 1,200 "Jukes" (a pseudonym) had cost the state of New York $1,308,000, "without reckoning the cash paid for whiskey, or taking into account

---

* In 1900 the $1,311.72 balance of the fund was turned over to the New York Public Library for the purchase of books on "economic subjects."

the entailment of pauperism and crime of the survivors in succeeding generations and the incurable disease, idiocy and insanity growing out of this debauchery, and reaching further than we can calculate."[4] This entire malediction, according to Dugdale, stemmed largely—though not entirely—from defective heredity.

Trying to pin down the provenance of such a dire outcome, Dugdale traces the Jukes' descent back to a "jolly and companionable," hard-drinking, early eighteenth-century ancestor named Max, a person with no last name who lived by hunting, fishing, and casual labor. Max sired children aplenty "some of them almost certainly illegitimate." The pseudonym "Juke" comes from the family of sisters Max's sons married, a family Dugdale also suspects of illegitimacy.

This tale of crime, pauperism, and consanguinity Dugdale presents not "as a generalization" but as hard facts supporting dramatic conclusions:

> In other words, *fornication*, either consanguineous or not, is the backbone of their habits, flanked on one side by *pauperism*, on the other by *crime*. The secondary features are *prostitution*, with its compliment of *bastardy*, and its resultant neglected and miseducated childhood; *exhaustion*, with its complement *intemperance* and its resultant unbalanced minds; and *disease* with its complement *extinction*.[5]

The text, replete with mentions of Juke "blood" and "stock," dedicates many pages to "harlotry" as "the distinctive tendency of the Juke family." The foremost cause of "hereditary pauperism" is disease, and the "most common" disease among the Jukes is syphilis, which, according to the shy little Dugdale, ignorant male Jukes regard as a sign of virility.[6]

What, then, was to be done about the Jukes and their ilk? Following Lombroso and Beltrani-Scalia, Dugdale offers solutions: solid industrial training for skills, industriousness, and chastity would be good steps, but most important would be the removal of the Juke children from their own degenerate homes into good families.[7] Although torn between "THE HEREDITY" and "THE ENVIRONMENT" as determinants of criminality, Dugdale favors heredity. Despite his vision of environment as a means of mitigating bad heredity, readers drew more emphatic conclusions. In the wake of *"The Jukes,"* nature overshadowed nurture in the creation of degenerate families, and the way toward drastic measures began to open.

After the 1877 publication of *"The Jukes,"* a kind of quiet standoff prevailed between the two camps of nature and nurture. They agreed that hereditary weakness in poor whites was a serious, even endemic problem. But differences surfaced among proposals for dealing with it. Those favoring correction through training and resettlement made some headway, as in the case of another wealthy New York social reformer, Josephine Shaw Lowell (1843–1905).

In 1879 Lowell seized upon Dugdale's depiction of Juke family harlotry.* If harlotry, poverty, and illegitimacy were inherited products of weak-mindedness, then weak-mindedness itself must not be allowed to breed. In a real sense, Lowell put herself in the place of the state, calling "promiscuous and criminalistic" women carriers of a "deadly poison," which they passed on "even to the third and fourth generations." Lowell went on to indict charity organizations, accusing them of allowing "men and women who are diseased and vicious to reproduce their kind."[8] The thought took hold and led to Lowell's creation of the Custodial Asylum for Feeble-Minded Women, in Newark, New York (not New Jersey), designed to prevent mentally handicapped young women from having children.

Thus began what is called "negative eugenics," a system seeking to prevent a class of people from reproducing. Meanwhile, Theodore Roosevelt got busy encouraging motherhood among his own superior stocks, an approach counted as "positive eugenics." Though controversial on account of its expense in the late 1870s, the custodial asylum

---

*Although Lowell appears here as a link in the degenerate-family chain leading to eugenic sterilization, she played a much broader role in the history of social work in New York State. A founder of the New York Charity Organization Society and the Consumers' League of New York and other organizations devoted to poor and working-class women, she was pro-labor and anti-imperialist. Lowell formulated social work's theoretical basis in her book *Public Relief and Private Charity* (1884).

remained a remedy of choice. By the late 1880s fourteen states housed fifteen institutions caring for over four thousand children.[9] But far less gentle approaches to Americans widely considered dysgenic were coming under review.

LET US remember that social reformers like Richard Dugdale and Josephine Shaw Lowell meant to do just that—reform the social landscape by focusing on families they considered hereditarily degenerate and, therefore, a threat to the well-being of society in general. As Christians, they meant first to do good. If scientific validity lay on their side, then so much the better, as a means of gaining support for eugenic remedies. Dugdale's *"The Jukes"* had reaped an abundant harvest among penologists and social workers as well as among "social gospelers" whose humanitarian commitment to the poor could not be doubted.

One such, Oscar Carleton McCulloch (1843–91), an influential student of hereditary degeneracy, drew his initial inspiration directly from *"The Jukes."* (See figure 18.1, Oscar McCulloch.) His research on a large, itinerant Indiana family slid so easily into the literature of eugenics and social welfare as to became another classic.

McCulloch had been a traveling salesman before forsaking commerce for religion. After graduating from the Chicago Theological Seminary in 1870, he made his way to the Plymouth Congregational Church in Indianapolis in 1877, the very year Dugdale's *"Jukes"* appeared. In Plymouth Church, McCulloch welcomed all sorts of people, offered lectures and classes, and even created a savings and loan institution to meet a variety of needs. Here was a go-getter, and reformers from throughout Indiana flocked to McCulloch and made his church a center of Christian charity.[10] Popularity did not suffice for McCulloch, who longed for theoretical justification for his good works. Inspired by Dugdale's example, he set out to place his own philanthropy on a more scientific basis by pursuing, over a decade, deep research on the Indiana poor.

An impoverished family, more especially its "pauper history of several generations," provided an excellent case study. In *The Tribe of Ishmael: A Study in Social Degradation* (1889), McCulloch traced the family back to early English settlers migrating from Virginia into Ken-

Fig. 18.1. Oscar McCulloch, frontispiece, The Open Door: Sermons and Prayers by Oscar C. McCulloch *(1892).*

tucky and southern Indiana. Here, though unquestionably English, lay a different sort of heritage, for the "Ishmaelites" descended from the wrong English blood. Ishmaelite ancestors came from "the old convict stock which England threw into this country in the seventeenth century," a great tide of antisocial men and lewd women shipped out of England in the seventeenth and eighteenth centuries.* McCulloch's science proved lasting. In "The Tribe of Ishmael" of 1923, the eugenicist Arthur H. Estabrook brought McCulloch's findings from the 1880s up

---

*The belief that poor whites descended from antisocial English indentured servants was widely accepted well into the twentieth century. As late as 1941, the Harvard-educated Mississippi Delta planter William Alexander Percy described the "river rat" of the lower Mississippi River as a descendant of English debt prisoners. Percy characterized the Anglo-Saxon river rat of "pure English stock" as "illiterate, suspicious, intensely clannish, blond, and usually ugly . . . the most unprepossessing [breed] on the face of the ill-populated earth." Like many elite white southerners, Percy blamed racial violence on these poor whites, whom he considered inferior to "the Negro."

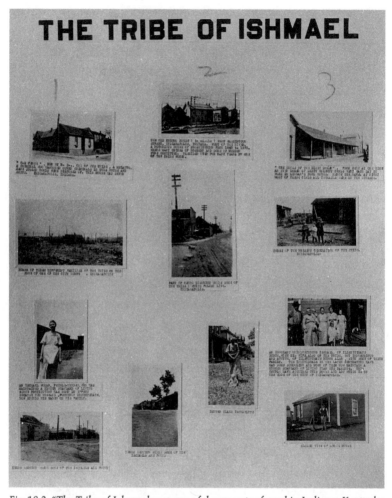

Fig. 18.2. "The Tribe of Ishmael, a group of degenerates found in Indiana, Kentucky, Ohio, Illinois, Missouri, and Iowa—with individual photos and captions."

to date: "The men were shiftless; the women, immoral, and the children, ill-fed and clothed, the typical feeble-minded people who are so easily recognized today."[11] (See figure 18.2, Arthur Estabrook's illustrations of the Ishmaelites.)

McCulloch figured that bad heredity had endowed the Ishmaelites with three outstanding traits: "pauperism, licentiousness and gypsy-ing." They refused steady work, he said, preferring to vagabond, beg, steal, and breed; "general unchastity" characterized them. "The prostitu-tion and illegitimacy are large, the tendency shows itself in incests [sic], and relations lower than the animals go." Following his logic, McCulloch concluded that "so-called charity" merely encouraged the Ishmaelites' parasitism on society and should not, therefore, be offered.[12] The environ-ment no longer contributes to the problem, as with Dugdale's Jukes. Now "degradation" and "parasitism" spring from the fatal combination of bad heredity and wrongheaded charity. The bad-blood theory was not new.

Poor people actually had been shipped to British North America dur-ing the colonial era, and the label of criminal was broad. As we have seen, British and Irish street children, the homeless, criminals, and indentured servants accounted for a sizable percentage of seventeenth- and eighteenth-century settlers, especially in Virginia. Great numbers of these forced immigrants actually had committed small-time thievery, the petty crimes of poverty, such as stealing food or flitching a pig. For others, the crime, so to speak, lay only in being poor or vulnerable to the kidnapping for export that amounted to organized crime.[13]

It was true that if they survived the transatlantic voyage, sale, resale, and many years of servitude, freedpeople and their descendants tended to remain poor. But survivors occasionally rose into the ranks of the landowning. Of the 5,000 indentured servants transported to Virginia between 1670 and 1680, 241 managed to acquire their own land. A dra-matic instance of upward mobility lay in the person of the Irish-born Matthew Lyon (1749–1822). One of Ethan Allen's Green Mountain Boy heroes of the American Revolutionary Battle of Ticonderoga, Lyon had begun his American career in servitude, ascending to the status of founder of the state of Vermont, member of the Vermont assembly, and U.S. congressman.[14] Such exceptions—there were many more—did not make a dent in race theory.

People at the top of society have always been quick to condemn those at the bottom to perpetual service. Never mind that with time there often came improvement. In early America, the notion of hereditary criminality was already circulating among the favored classes. One Anthony Stokes in 1783 spoke for many when he wrote of "a swarm of men" he called "Crackers," who were overrunning western Virginia and North Carolina: "Many of these people are descended from convicts that were transported from Great Britain to Virginia at different times, and inherit so much profligacy from their ancestors, that they are the most abandoned set of men on earth. . . ."[15] Here were ideas that stayed strong all the way to Theodore Roosevelt.

Roosevelt's immensely popular, multivolume hymn to Manifest Destiny, *The Winning of the West* (1889), picked up on the bad-heredity theme. Chronicling the settlement of the South, Roosevelt recognizes some in the backwoods as "stern, manly, and honest"; that was the best of them. But others were unsavory:

> people drawn from the worst immigrants that perhaps ever were brought to America—the mass of convict servants, redemptioners, and the like, who formed such an excessively undesirable substratum to the otherwise excellent population of the tidewater regions in Virginia and the Carolinas. Many of the Southern crackers or poor whites spring from this class, which also in the backwoods gave birth to generations of violent and hardened criminals, and to an even greater number of shiftless, lazy, cowardly cumberers of the earth's surface.[16]

DUGDALE AND McCulloch, both social gospelers working closely with the poor, might seem far removed from the science of, say, William Z. Ripley on the Harvard University faculty. Actually little distance lay between eastern academia and midwestern local science, for Dugdale and McCulloch agreed with Roosevelt and got very good at deploying scientific rhetorical strategies. Exhibiting table after table, they modeled their presentations on the U.S. census then becoming the apogee of exact demographic science.[17] In a paper at the 1888 meeting of the National Conference of Charities and Corrections, McCulloch illustrated his findings with striking visuals that included a diagram 3' by 12' showing 250 biologically connected pauper households. McCulloch succeeded brilliantly. Elected president of the National Conference of Charities and Corrections, he presided over the annual meeting in May 1891 in Baltimore. It was his last public appearance before his death the same year.[18]

Such diagrams of descent soon became a staple feature of eugenic publications fond of photographs of paupers, the feebleminded, and their unkempt children hanging around filthy, broken-down lodgings. While religion, charity, science, and prejudice had become

Fig. 18.3. David Starr Jordan as president of Stanford University.

comfortable bedfellows, reformers posing as scientists could go only so far, however. As eugenics hardened, real scholars stepped in.

McCulloch's church had attracted an academic follower. The early career of David Starr Jordan (1851–1931) took him from Cornell to Indiana, where he taught high school science in Indianapolis and natural history at Northwestern Christian University (later Butler University). Within ten years Jordan had become the youngest college president in the United States—of Indiana University—at age thirty-four, and then first president of Stanford University. (See figure 18.3, David Starr Jordan.) Two related movements occupied Jordan: peace and eugenics. His belief in peace stemmed from a conviction that warfare and the celibate (Catholic) clergy were "dysgenic," because they prevented "the best of the race"—soldier-warriors and scholars—from passing on their gifts. For Jordan, their loss became doubly catastrophic in light of what he saw as the heedless multiplication of so-called degenerate families and immigrant, or "alien," races.

While living in Indianapolis, Jordan had joined McCulloch's Plymouth Congregational Church; even after moving on, he continued to quote and praise McCulloch in his own books on eugenics and religion.* (In another merger of religion, morals, and hereditarian thought, the American Unitarian Association published Jordan's eugenics books aimed at the general public.)

Here was a bridge. Jordan's impeccable scholarly credentials boosted degenerate-family studies into widely recognized intellectual respectability. In *The Heredity of Richard Roe* (1911), for instance, Jordan quotes Dugdale and McCulloch alongside Harvard's Charles Benedict Davenport and the luminous Francis Galton of the University of London.

Jordan, like Dugdale, McCulloch, and Theodore Roosevelt, effortlessly wrapped himself in the mantle of dispassionate fact as he dissected a mass of degenerate Anglo-Saxons. Pity, for example, the poor whites of the North Carolina mountains consigned by Jordan "to the lineage of England's pauperism transported first to her colonies, afterward driven from the plains to the mountains." England's defectives, he announced, left a "trail of pauperism and crime from Virginia across Carolina, Kentucky, Indiana, Missouri, even to California and Oregon." And it was still happening in the early twentieth century, when Jordan lamented that European nations continued to ship their defectives to the United States to reproduce "the same inefficient men, sickly women, frowsy children, starved horses, barking cur dogs, carelessness, vindictiveness, and neglect of decency."[19] Generation after generation, century after century, Jordan warned, these poor white people passed down faults as indelible as race was assumed to be. So perilous a situation demanded vigorous action, vigorous science. Quantification was on its way.

---

* Jordan's eugenic publications include *The Religion of a Sensible American* (1909), *Blood of the Nation: A Study of the Decay of Races through the Survival of the Unfit* (1910), and *The Heredity of Richard Roe: A Discussion of the Principles of Eugenics* (1911). *Blood of the Nation: A Study of the Decay of Races through the Survival of the Unfit* is still in print, for sale for $19.50 through the *Forbes Magazine* book club. Two high schools and two middle schools in California are named for Jordan.

FROM DEGENERATE FAMILIES
TO STERILIZATION

Henry H. Goddard, Ph.D., a sweet-tempered Quaker from Maine, directed research at the Vineland Training School for Feeble-Minded Girls and Boys in New Jersey from 1906 to 1918. In the larger history of racial ideas, he bridges two critical fields—degenerate-family studies and immigrant intelligence testing—by connecting the charities and corrections community of Dugdale and McCulloch to the hereditarian and eugenicist.[1]*

A scholar and humanitarian, Goddard (1866–1957) received his doctorate from Clark University in 1899.† After study at the University of Leipzig and a stint at the West Chester, Pennsylvania, Normal School, Goddard moved to Vineland in 1906 and took that institution to the cutting edge of the child-study movement for the scientific study of pedagogy.‡ Renowned for his personal touch, Goddard treated his young charges with the utmost kindness. All reported that he respected each

---

* Goddard also served as the first football coach at the University of Southern California.
† Clark, then headed by the psychologist G. Stanley Hall, was at its peak as an institution dedicated to the ideals of German scholarship. Franz Boas was leaving Clark as Goddard was receiving his doctorate. Like many of the men interested in race and heredity in the late nineteenth and early twentieth centuries, Goddard was another Yankee who loved the outdoors. Although married for many years, he had no children.
‡ The child-study movement professionalized social-gospeler impulses and plugged them into the vast spread of childhood institutions as all the states mandated compulsory education between 1880 and 1918.

and every one as a uniquely valuable individual. Goddard would there-fore seem a most unlikely candidate to recommend a policy later associ-ated with the Nazis. Even so, it is to Goddard and the Vineland school that this story leads. Tender care of the "feebleminded" was part of that care, but so were the implications of family ancestry.

Who better to suggest the study of those implications than Charles Benedict Davenport (1866–1944), the independently wealthy scion of a Connecticut family who claimed Puritan descent and whose father had traced the family back to England in 1066? Davenport had taught at Harvard and the University of Chicago, making a reputation with his studies of chicken breeding, then moving—in what seemed a natu-ral progression—to look into "heredity in the human race." He placed particular emphasis on "the value of superior blood and the menace to society of inferior blood."[2]

In 1898 Davenport had become director of the summer school of the biological laboratory of the Brooklyn Institute of Arts and Sciences at Cold Spring Harbor, on Long Island, not far from Theodore Roosevelt's country place at Oyster Bay. From there he gained grants from the recently created Carnegie Institution of Washington and founded the Carnegie Institution Station for Experimental Evolution at Cold Spring Harbor in 1904. In 1910, having secured access to Mrs. E. H. Harriman's railroad fortune, Davenport established the Eugenics Record Office (ERO). Between 1910 and 1918 the Harriman contribution to the ERO grew to half a million dollars.[3]*

Inspiration for such wide ambition came from London. As a bright young Harvard professor, Davenport in 1901 had visited Francis Galton (1822–1911), the founding father of eugenics and a deep thinker on the matter of controlled human breeding.

Galton had written *Hereditary Genius: An Inquiry into Its Laws and Consequences* (1869), the urtext of eugenics tying heredity to social prominence, or "genius."[4]† Nowadays Galton is remembered

---

*The Cold Spring Harbor institution serves currently as a center of research on the human genome.
†In *Inquiries into Human Faculty* (1883) Galton praised the founding study of hereditary degeneracy, "*The Jukes.*"

mainly as a founder of statistics, especially for his theory of correlations and statistical deviation recognized in the bell curve. But being a scholar of many interests, he also founded eugenics with his protégé in mathematical statistics, Karl Pearson, an ardent eugenicist in his own right and another giant of twentieth-century statistics.* Even the word "eugenics" was Galton's invention, combining the Greek words for "good" and "inheritance." Like so many hereditarians, Galton (the cousin of Charles Darwin) was independently wealthy; also like other rich men interested in human reproduction, he had no children. Like Carlyle and Emerson, Galton combined a fragile constitution— nervous breakdowns, dizziness, and palpitations—with a glorification of masculine strength.

Along with his admiration of "vigorous [male] animals," Galton appreciated feminine beauty. Traveling around Great Britain, he surreptitiously compiled a "beauty map" locating the ugliest British women in industrial, working-class, Celtic Scotland and the most beautiful in wealthy, Anglo-Saxon London.[5] Galton describes his methodology in his autobiography:

> Whenever I have occasion to classify the persons I meet into three classes, "good, medium, bad," I use a needle mounted as a pricker, wherewith to prick holes, unseen, in a piece of paper, torn rudely into a cross with a long leg. I use its upper end for "good," the cross-arm for "medium," the lower end for "bad." The prick-holes keep distinct, and are easily read off at leisure. The object, place, and date are written on the paper. I used this plan for my beauty data, classifying the girls I passed in streets or elsewhere as attractive, indifferent, or repellent. Of course this was a purely individual estimate, but it was consistent, judging from the conformity of different attempts in the same population. I found London to rank highest for beauty; Aberdeen lowest.[6]

---

* Pearson, with his own example of a degenerate family, mentions "a certain bad stock as far back as 1680" that was still producing "drunkenness, insanity, and physical breakdown" in 1900, proof that "this law of inheritance is as inevitable as the law of gravity, we shall cease to struggle against it." In *National Life from the Standpoint of Science* (1905), Pearson also declared, "Lunacy is one of the things which we may quite definitely accept as an inherited character."

Interestingly enough, given turn-of-the-century correlations of race and head shape, photographs of Galton show him to have had dark hair and a flat back of the head; that is, he was brachycephalic, not dolichocephalic, which counted heavily for some of his contemporaries.

Galton also mistrusted democracy, figuring the "average citizen . . . too base . . . for the everyday work of modern civilization."[7] His version of evolution made natural selection into an engine for determining the characteristics of races as well as classes. *Hereditary Genius* proclaims that "Jews are specialized for a *parasitical* existence."[8] So powerful was Galton's reputation and influence that, after the First World War, this bigoted view circulated as a scientific commonplace.

Convinced the "brains of the nation lie in the higher of our classes," Galton advocated procreation between people of the upper crust. At the same time, while frowning on the heedless breeding of the poor, he did not advocate its curtailment. That would be left for others. Galton, ever the patrician, shared Roosevelt's concentration on his own, higher class. From his Eugenics Record Office at the University of London, Galton offered a treasure trove to American eugenicists and to Charles Davenport in particular.

Not that Galton and Davenport agreed totally. With his ability to combine variables (i.e., regression and correlation analysis), Galton's theories of human heredity could take several factors into account at the same time. Davenport and most American eugenicists rejected complexity, preferring to believe that human inheritance acted in a simple on-off fashion, like the height, color, and wrinkling of Gregor Mendel's sweet peas. Intelligence could then be mapped and numbered along a single yardstick, allowing Davenport to speak of intelligence as a "unit character" or "unit trait."[9] In today's parlance, he saw intelligence as a single heritable gene. It followed that unit characters decreed an individual to be either normal or feebleminded. Unit traits—genes, if you will—also determined shiftlessness, nomadism, or "thalassophilia" (love of the sea), all, as in the degenerate-family studies, hereditary. Thalassophilia, Davenport thought, was a sex-linked, recessive trait like color blindness, because he had always found it only in males. This kind of theorizing moved Karl Pearson to confide to Galton, "[O]ur friend Davenport is not a clear strong thinker."[10] One cannot but wonder how Davenport would have correlated his weird category of thalassophilia with, say, shiftlessness.

Galton and Davenport were creatures of their cultures. Class ruled Galton's Britain and his classification; race ruled Davenport's United States and his classification. For Davenport, Poles, Irish, Italians, Hebrews, and others behaved differently, each according to their race. He believed, as did William Z. Ripley, that immigrants from southern and eastern Europe would make the American population "darker in pigmentation, smaller in stature, more mercurial . . . more given to crimes of larceny, kidnapping, assault, murder, rape, and sex immorality."[11] Davenport passed this twisted racial theory, co-opted in part from Francis Galton, to Henry Goddard in New Jersey at the Vineland Training School for Feeble-Minded Girls and Boys. In the Garden State it fell on fertile ground, for Goddard had spotted the perfect case, a "feeble-minded" Vineland resident he called Deborah Kallikak.

This was an invented name. Goddard had joined two Greek words—*kallos*, meaning "beauty," and *kakos*, meaning "bad"—to come up with it.[12] Deborah Kallikak, the child of an impoverished, unwed mother, had come to Vineland in 1897 at age eight.[13] The child's progress was uneven. By age twenty-three she was a nice-looking young person skilled in sewing but slow in reading and writing. For Goddard, her skills were practically beside the point. She and the thousands like her represented a threat to the welfare of the race.

Indeed, the great menace of someone like Deborah Kallikak lay in her normal, even attractive appearance and the likelihood, should she ever leave Vineland, of her having sex and, consequently, of bearing children. Once beyond institutional protection, "she would at once become a prey to the designs of evil men or evil women and would lead a life that would be vicious, immoral, and criminal." Goddard tested her on the Binet-Simon scale in 1910 and gave her a mental age of nine—low intelligence of "moron" grade—which, he concluded, would deprive her of moral judgment.

The Binet-Simon intelligence tests are the second half of Goddard's contribution to the literature of the "warfare of the cradle." He had discovered the work of the French researchers Alfred Binet and his associate Theodore Simon on a European trip in 1908.* Employed by the French Ministry of Public Instruction, they had devised a mental test, whose results they figured on a numerical scale. The numbers were meant to help schools identify pupils in need of special education. Goddard adapted Binet's tests for use in English and immediately began testing the Vineland inmates. With its nicely quantified results, the test rapidly gained popularity. By 1910 Goddard was giving it to New Jersey schoolchildren, a year later to New York City children, and by 1913 to immigrants at Ellis Island. The intelligence test had labeled Deborah Kallikak, in Goddard's invented terminology, a "moron." How, Davenport asked Goddard, did she get to be that way?†

Goddard worked backward, tracing Deborah Kallikak's genealogy to the American Revolution. There he found two Kallikak families. One consisted of upstanding citizens with "a marked tendency toward professional careers." They had married into the best families of New Jersey and produced "nothing but good representative citizenship. There are doctors, lawyers, judges, educators, traders, landholders, in short, respectable citizens, men and women prominent in every phase of social life."

The other branch had produced Deborah Kallikak. Her family branch, some 480 of them, included 36 illegitimate children, 33 "sexually immoral persons, mostly prostitutes," 3 epileptics (epilepsy was then considered hereditary), 82 dead babies, 3 criminals, and 8 keepers of "houses of ill fame." Both branches descended from the same man, Martin Kallikak Sr., but from two different women. Therein lay the difference. The bad Kallikaks derived from Martin Kallikak's unmarried sex with "a feeble-minded girl" who worked in a tavern.

Goddard's book *The Kallikak Family* appeared in 1912 to a fine critical reception and excellent sales. Social scientists heralded its impor-

* Binet died in 1911, before the great American vogue in intelligence testing and the controversies it aroused. He had never meant his tests as means to rank adults.
† "Morons" were rated as smarter than "imbeciles," who, in turn, were considered more intelligent than "idiots."

tance, applauding the "authenticity of its data and the correctness of the work."* In the child-study field and beyond, its research had an enormous effect in pushing a growing hereditarian belief that ancestry was everything, environment nothing.† Its message rang loud and clear: for the public good, the feebleminded must not breed; otherwise society will suffer. "There are Kallikak families all about us," Goddard warned. "They are multiplying at twice the rate of the general population."[14] In the "warfare of the cradle," the inferior would always outbreed superior stocks, and "no amount of education or good environment can change a feeble-minded individual into a normal one." Like slavery on the black side of the color line, indenture, crime, or illegitimacy on the white side means permanent damnation. Slum clearance and other palliative remedies are equally useless, for "these mentally defective people who can never be taught to live otherwise than as they have been living" are promiscuously breeding squalor.[15]

How, then, is society to protect itself? At first Goddard cast a vote for segregation of the mentally impaired, but segregation was immensely expensive. To sequester the feebleminded until they passed breeding age, as Goddard knew well, cost dearly. Harking back to Josephine Shaw Lowell, he finally broached the alternative, sterilization, and the die was cast. Many in the United States were more than ready, even eager, to stem the degenerate tide threatening to swamp its Anglo-Saxon genetic pool.

By 1912, when Goddard published *The Kallikak Family*, several states had already turned to compulsory sterilization as a cheap means of controlling the reproduction of undesirables. Eugenicists spearheaded this movement, but they had support from liberals in the charities and corrections wing of humanitarian reform. Leading social reformers were quite willing to deplore the "debasing and demoralizing influence of an unrestrained feebleminded woman."[16]

---

* Even early on, however, the book's positive reception contained a hint of reservation regarding Goddard's assumption that intelligence was a single Mendelian unit trait.
† Goddard's reasoning regarding feeblemindedness (though not by that name) reappears as the source of social ills and defective human beings in the best-selling analysis of intelligence and human destiny of the late twentieth century: *The Bell Curve: Intelligence and Class Structure in American Life* (1994), by Richard J. Herrnstein and Charles Murray.

Thanks to medical advances that made sterilization relatively easy and safe, Indiana had led off the sterilization wave in 1907 with a law proclaiming, "WHEREAS, heredity plays a most important part in the transmission of crime, idiocy, and imbecility . . ."[17]* Other states followed, but with mixed results, for involuntary sterilization remained controversial. The courts invalidated such laws on the basis of cruel and inhumane punishment, for lack of due process, and for failures in equal protection under the law. New Jersey's state supreme court quickly struck down a compulsory sterilization law in 1913, and governors in Vermont, Nebraska, and Idaho vetoed others.[18]

If sterilization were to prevail, expert guidance was called for. Undaunted, in 1922 Davenport's Eugenics Record Office offered a model eugenical sterilization law meant to assist states in crafting involuntary sterilization laws that could withstand court challenge. In 1924 Virginia passed the first such act, stating that "heredity plays an important part in the transmission of insanity, idiocy, and imbecility, epilepsy, and crime."[19] The court test that followed increased the visibility of "degenerate families" and, in light of the long-standing prejudice against poor white southerners, gave degeneracy a poor and female southern face.

THE FIRST person slated for sterilization under Virginia's sterilization law was eighteen-year-old Carrie Buck.[20] (See figure 19.1, Carrie Buck and her mother.) Buck had not been accused of a crime; she was described as a pregnant, unmarried, feebleminded daughter of an unmarried, feebleminded mother living in Virginia's State Colony for Epileptics and Feeble-Minded. Prominent eugenicists entered the case against her to halt the propagation of "these people [who] belong to the shiftless, ignorant and worthless class of anti-social whites of the South."[21]

The U.S. Supreme Court upheld Virginia's sterilization law 8–1, led by American law's eminence grise, the eighty-one-year-old Oliver Wendell Holmes, who wrote the majority opinion. Holmes accepted

---

*Vasectomy for men, tubal ligation for women. The earliest vasectomy had been performed in Chicago in 1897.

Fig. 19.1. Carrie Buck and her mother, Emma Buck, at the Virginia State Colony for Epileptics and Feeble-Minded, just before going to trial in 1924.

Goddard's argument that Buck's weaknesses were hereditary. He also agreed with the prevailing logic that criminals were born, not made, and that society could protect itself by preventing their birth. Holmes decreed it "better for all the world, if instead of waiting to execute degenerate offspring for crime, or to let them starve for their imbecility, society can prevent those who are manifestly unfit from continuing their kind." His famous conclusion—"Three generations of imbeciles are enough"—echoed throughout American law.[22] The associate justices former president William Howard Taft and Louis D. Brandeis concurred. And so sterilization became settled law in many states, an acceptable means of dealing with people designated feebleminded—especially of poor women of all races bearing children out of wedlock.[23]

During the 1930s, following *Buck v. Bell*, local law enforcement and welfare officials rounded up the poor and sterilized them practically en masse: by 1968, some 65,000 Americans had been sterilized against their will, with California far in the lead and Virginia a distant second.[24]* The American model eugenical sterilization law that had inspired Vir-

---

*Between 1907 and 1956, 60,166 people had been sterilized as mentally deficient, insane, or epileptic. California led the way with 19,998; Virginia followed with 6,811, North Carolina with 4,777, Michigan with 3,597, and Kansas with 3,025.

ginia's 1924 law also worked in Germany. On gaining power in 1933, National Socialists quickly enacted a law for the prevention of progeny with hereditary diseases, which included deafness and blindness as well as mental handicap and chronic mental or physical illness. In Germany, as in the early twentieth-century United States, the prime targets of involuntary sterilization were poor people. Anglo-Saxon, Teutonic, or Nordic ancestry did not spare poor whites stigmatized as Jukes, Ishmaelites, Kallikaks, and Bucks.

As it turned out, Carrie Buck represents an all too common case of personal vulnerability. At about age eight, she had been placed in a foster home. Some years later a member of that family raped her. Pregnant as a result of the rape, she was sent to the Virginia State Colony for Epileptics and Feeble-Minded to be sterilized as soon as she gave birth. Primitive, haphazardly administered Stanford-Binet intelligence tests rated her and her mother as imbeciles, but as an adult, Carrie showed no signs of impairment. Against a backdrop of degenerate-family studies demonizing poor white people, Carrie Buck's sterilization had resulted from sexual abuse, not mental weakness.[25]

Despite its promise of preventing social ills on the cheap, sterilization never attained total acceptance, for doubts over who should make such intimate decisions never subsided, and bias characterized their execution. Opponents' arguments mounted: Catholics objected to this breach of the human body, socialists pointed to the class bias of eugenics, and anthropologists argued that culture, not biology, explained characteristics that sterilization was supposed to extinguish.

Eugenic sterilization ultimately fell out of favor, but the fall was slow and gradual. During the 1930s, when German National Socialists took it up, demonstrating the deadly and perverse workings out of eugenics, the field lost its standing as objective science. Civil rights protests in the 1960s and 1970s against the involuntary sterilization of black, American Indian, and Latina women effectively stripped the practice of respectability as public policy. Different morals demanded different policies. Virginia repealed its sterilization law in 1974, but Carrie Buck died in 1983, before her vindication. On the seventy-fifth anniversary of the *Buck v. Bell* decision, in 2002, the state placed a commemorative marker in her hometown of Charlottesville, and the governor issued a formal apology. Oregon, North Carolina, and South Carolina followed Virginia's repudiation.

And here ends the compulsory sterilization story that began with degenerate-family research. Another story with shared roots unfolded at the same time, leading to the mental testing of immigrants and to immigration restriction.

20

INTELLIGENCE TESTING OF
NEW IMMIGRANTS

Mental tests: such a simple and accurate means of rating human intelligence, even, as Robert Yerkes, a leading tester claimed, of appraising "the value of a man."[1] Once Henry H. Goddard had imported Alfred Binet and Theodore Simon's mental tests into the United States, it became apparent that their usefulness reached far beyond their limited role in France. There, the tests designated schoolchildren for special education; in the United States, they rated the children at the Vineland school for the feebleminded and then went on to serve other, much wider purposes. Officials at Ellis Island figured Goddard's tests in Vineland could help them decide who, among immigrants streaming into the country, could stay and who had to return.

What were these tests like? In 1917 masses of U.S. Army draftees who could read answered questions like these:

Why do soldiers wear wrist watches rather than pocket watches?
Because
☐ they keep better time.
☐ they are harder to break.
☐ they are handier.

Glass insulators are used to fasten telegraph wires because
☐ the glass keeps the pole from being burned.

☐ the glass keeps the current from escaping.
☐ the glass is cheap and attractive.

Why should we have Congressmen? Because
☐ the people must be ruled.
☐ it insures truly representative government.
☐ the people are too many to meet and make their laws.[2]

Men who could not read answered pictorial questions. Soldiers were to say what was missing from each picture:[3]* (See figure 20.1, "Test 6.")

TEST 6

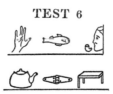

Figure 20. Black-board chart for demonstrating the Picture Completion Test.

Fig. 20.1. "Test 6," in Carl C. Brigham, A Study of American Intelligence *(1923).*

Testers aimed high, promising to measure innate intelligence, not simply years of education or immersion in a particular cultural milieu. This claim was obviously absurd, but no matter. The allure of mental testing proved irresistible, because demand for ranking people was high, and the process was cheap and, best of all, apparently scientific. The juxtaposition of congressional mandates and the ambitions of early twentieth-century social scientists explains how Goddard went from degenerate families to intelligence testing of immigrants.

NATIVISTS HAD long denigrated immigrants on the grounds of their supposed inferiority. Prescott Farnsworth Hall, one of the then recent

---

* In his course on biology as a social weapon, the Harvard professor Stephen Jay Gould administered the Army test for illiterates to fifty-three of his students. The students did very well: thirty-one scored A; sixteen scored B; but six scored C, placing them at what Gould called the intellectual borderline and fit only for buck private duties.

Harvard graduates founding the Immigration Restriction League in 1894, mashed together degenerate families, immigrants, and competitive breeding: "The same arguments which induce us to segregate criminals and feebleminded and thus prevent their breeding apply to excluding from our borders individuals whose multiplying here is likely to lower the average of our people."[4] This logic steadily gained ground.

From the 1890s onward, federal legislation toughened standards for excluding "lunatics," "idiots," people likely to become public charges, the insane, epileptics, beggars, anarchists, "imbeciles, feeble-minded and persons with physical or mental defects which might affect their ability to earn a living."[5] But with five thousand immigrants passing through Ellis Island daily, sorting through them imposed an impossible task on ten or so Public Health Service physicians. Something had to be done. Learning of Goddard's methods, the commissioner of immigration concluded that help lay at hand right there in New Jersey. He invited Goddard to use his newfangled intelligence tests to speed up the exclusion process, an assignment Goddard carried out with the help of his lady testers from Vineland.[6]* Certain alarming conclusions leaped off the pages of Goddard's report:

The intelligence of the average "third class" immigrant is low, perhaps of moron grade. . . .

Each test taken by itself seems to indicate a very high percentage of defectness. There is no exception to this. . . .

The immigration of recent years is of a decidedly different character from the earlier immigration. . . . It is admitted on all sides that we are getting now the poorest of each race. . . . "of every 1000 Polish immigrants all but 103 are laborers and servants." . . .

---

* Not everyone agreed with Goddard. Public Health Service M.D.s at Ellis Island regarded his Binet-inspired tests skeptically; they altered or ignored them as they thought necessary.

According to TABLE II. INTELLIGENCE CLASSIFICATION OF IMMIGRANTS OF DIFFERENT NATIONALITIES, 83 percent of the Jews, 80 percent of the Hungarians, 79 percent of the Italians, 87 percent of the Russians were feebleminded. Sixty percent of the Jews were morons.[7]

In sum: most of the immigrants currently passing through Ellis Island were mentally defective. With this crucial point made and quantified, intelligence testing took a further step, as the new field of psychology seized wartime opportunities.

By 1917 Goddard had joined a new group of immigration opponents who had no connection to charitable institutions. Based in academia, Robert Yerkes and Lewis Terman did not associate with the poor or feel concern for their well-being. As scholars, they shaped their truths—drawn, they said, from science—toward their preferred results. Not compulsory sterilization this time, but the classification of the American population according to intelligence and race on the basis of quantifiable methodology. Once again, Charles Benedict Davenport of the Eugenics Record Office at Cold Spring Harbor, New York, supplied the missing link.

In the prewar years, Davenport's institution had diligently compiled hereditary studies of defective families. His statistics dovetailed nicely with omnibus characteristics Davenport considered Mendelian unit traits: pauperism, low intelligence test scores, epilepsy, criminalism, insanity, height, and sexual immorality. While the First World War interrupted such degenerate-family work and sterilization, wartime conscription presented eugenicists with great new opportunities in mass mental testing. Robert Yerkes (1876–1956), Davenport's erstwhile student at Harvard, moved to the fore.

Yerkes was no vaunted New Englander. His humble provenance does not get much attention from his biographers, in stark contrast to works by and about proud Yankees like Davenport. Perhaps in an elite environment, his farm-boy background contributed to his early reputation for ordinary intellectual ability, coupled with rigidity, stubbornness, and a tee-totaler's lack of bonhomie. Indifferent to wealth, power, fame, popularity, and personal beauty, he was not the sort to win popularity polls. Born on a farm in Bucks County, Pennsylvania, Yerkes had attended an ungraded rural school, then the State Normal School at West Chester, where Goddard had begun his professional career. With the support of an uncle willing to trade tuition money for chores, Yerkes was able to transfer to Ursinus College, in the greater Philadelphia area, before going on to Harvard, where he took an A.B. in 1898 and a Ph.D. in 1902.[8] Once again, the nation's most prestigious center of learning would play a pivotal role in race theory.

Harvard's importance in eugenics does not imply some nefarious scheme or even a mean-spirited ambiance. Rather, Harvard's import in this story attests to the scholarly respectability of eugenic ideas at the time. Yerkes's most influential teachers at Harvard were the German philosopher Hugo Münsterberg—a great believer in the importance of mental testing, ranking people hierarchically, and letting elites make society's decisions—and Charles Benedict Davenport, that venerator of Francis Galton.[9]

Yerkes began teaching at Harvard in 1902 and published his first book in 1907. Entitled *The Dancing Mouse and the Mind of a Gorilla*, it dealt with animal sexuality considered in the light of evolution.[10] He also worked half-time at the Boston Psychopathic Hospital alongside the esteemed Elmer Ernest Southard, inventor of "cacogenics," the clumsily named study of racial deterioration. Yerkes and Southard started administering mental tests in 1913, just when Goddard began testing immigrants on Ellis Island. Yerkes's rise was rapid—he was elected president of the American Psychological Association (APA) in 1916—but it was also uncertain, since he had been denied tenure at Harvard, which evidently held a low estimate of the new field of psychology.[11] An odd situation.

As president of the APA, but still lacking tenure, Yerkes chafed at his field's lack of scholarly standing. Not that the prejudice lacked merit. Still separating from philosophy in the 1910s, psychology seemed soft and lacking in scholarly rigor. The beautifully quantified results of mental testing, so Yerkes and others realized, offered a promising route to academic respectability. As the United States prepared to enter the First

World War, Yerkes sought to extend intelligence testing to millions of servicemen. Such a mass of statistical data, unique in its comprehensiveness, would doubtless command respect in academe.

But gathering a data bank of this magnitude would obviously be a huge undertaking. Yerkes found a route in the National Academy of Sciences, which in 1916 created the National Research Council to bring scientists into the war effort. In May of 1917 Yerkes convened a committee of testers that included Goddard and Lewis Terman of Stanford. Working at Goddard's Vineland Training School, the team had by July 1917 created three sets of tests for use on Army recruits.[12] The Army Alpha was directed toward men who could read; the Army Beta served illiterates; and individual tests filled in where needed in special cases—in theory, at least.

When the project closed down in January of 1919, some 1,750,000 men had been tested, generating a huge body of data and further encouraging wide-scale use of intelligence tests. Before the war, intelligence testing had sometimes inspired ridicule, not infrequently as leading citizens tested out as imbeciles. The patina of science, however, had carried the day, securing the Army tests' role as science's last word on intelligence. This prestige was something new. That word contained overweening ambition. Henry Goddard kindly pronounced intelligence testing "the most valuable piece of information which mankind has ever acquired about itself . . . a unitary mental process [that is] the chief determiner of human conduct."[13]

In a 1923 *Atlantic Monthly* article Yerkes confidently assumed that intelligence testing could gauge much more than mental capacity. The tests, he maintained, could determine a man's entire human worth. Yerkes was thinking about the immigrants who, he thought, diminished the effectiveness of the Army and, by extension, the overall health of American society: "Whereas the mental age of the American-born soldier is between thirteen and fourteen years, according to army statistics, that of the soldier of foreign birth serving in our army is less than twelve years. . . ." These numbers would echo loudly in hereditarian circles. Yerkes warned of the recently arrived foreign-born, "Altogether they

are markedly inferior in mental alertness to the native-born American."
He explained that differences between the white racial groups were
"[a]lmost as great as the intellectual difference between negro and white
in the army."[14] Once again, a scientist was speaking of "white racial
groups" as a means of classification.

OVERALL, YERKES'S testing project pegged the average mental age of
recruits at least eighteen years old at 13.08 years—accurate, it was
claimed, to the second decimal place, though nonsensical as arithmetic:
how could the average be below average? No matter. For Yerkes, with
his unit-trait-unalterable-inherent-mental-ability concept of intelligence, this meant no further intellectual growth was possible, for the
tests revealed *innate* native intelligence. Nothing in life after birth
would make any difference whatsoever, not heightened language facil-
ity, more effective schooling, or increased familiarity with American
culture. Furthermore, mental worth varied by race, as the term was
understood in the early twentieth century: as a categorization applicable to peoples from various parts of Europe and its outlying areas.
Yerkes and his colleagues drew many lines of race within the American population; one of the deepest separated so-called natives, whose
ancestors had immigrated long ago, from recent arrivals.

Not that all was clear sailing. The Army, with war needs uppermost,
never supported the testing project, and training procedures aimed at
making effective soldiers severely interfered with the tests' administration. Officers complained that men given the Beta tests' two lowest
grades, D and E, frequently turned into excellent soldiers once taught
to read. Another commander dismissed the psychologists as a needless
"board of art critics to advise me which of my men were the most handsome or a board of prelates to designate the true Christians."[15]

OUTSIDE THE Army, however, intelligence testing succeeded spectacu-
larly. After the war, Yerkes stayed on in Washington, D.C., into the
mid-1920s, then moved on to his own laboratory at Yale, where he
made a brilliant career in primate research. The National Academy of

Sciences' official report of Yerkes's Army IQ tests, an unreadable, 890-page document featuring many charts and diagrams, reached only a tiny readership of specialists.[16] In light of the controversy over immigration then raging, Yerkes encouraged one of the team of Army IQ testers, his protégé Carl Campbell Brigham of Princeton, to publish a readable digest for the general public.

Like many scholars seeking to place intelligence tests, eugenics, and race on a scientific basis, Brigham (1890–1943) sprang from prosperity and lofty New England breeding. He especially savored his descent from a signer of the Mayflower Compact in 1630. "Socially gifted," according to his admiring biographer, Brigham "retain[ed] throughout his life the poise, bearing, and social graces derived from the environment of an old and esteemed New England family."[17] Toward the end of his undergraduate career, Brigham fell under the spell of the new methodology of mental tests. His well-regarded 1916 Ph.D. dissertation on the use of Binet tests on Princeton schoolchildren earned him an appointment on the Princeton University faculty. In 1917 Robert Yerkes discovered Brigham's work and enlisted him to help administer intelligence tests to Army recruits.[18]

After the war Brigham rejoined the Princeton faculty, plunging once more into mental testing. Testing was now quite popular among educators as a means of ranking college applicants, and among nativists as scientific justification for cutting off immigration from southern and eastern Europe. The cause enjoyed prestigious support. Madison Grant and Charles W. Gould, two wealthy lawyers and Yale alumni, friends and eugenic opponents of immigration, underwrote Brigham's project of putting Yerkes's findings in accessible form for general readers, including, not least, members of Congress.[19]*

Princeton University Press published Brigham's *A Study of American Intelligence* in 1923. Robert Yerkes wrote the foreword, assuring readers "no one of us as a citizen can afford to ignore the menace of

---

* Grant's and Gould's own books fared differently among the general public. Grant's *Passing of the Great Race* became a sensation, whereas Gould's *America: A Family Matter* (1922), which argued, according to Yerkes's foreword, "for pure-bred races," never gained a large following.

race deterioration or the evident relations of immigration to national progress and welfare." Brigham, Yerkes contended, was presenting "not theories or opinions but facts."[20]

A Study of American Intelligence displayed an abundance of charts and graphs. Brigham divided the population into nearly a score of categories and illustrated numerous relative mental ages: atop the scale, American officers rated a mental age of 18.84 years; at the bottom, "U.S. (Colored)" came in at only 10.41 years. Native white Americans were roughly halfway between the two, achieving a mental age of 13.77 years, lower than immigrants from England, Scotland, the Netherlands, and Germany.[21] Native American Indians and Asians did not count.

A dramatic bar graph arranged according to low scores compared racial and national groups in another way, with A the highest, C the average, and E the lowest score (see figure 20.2, Brigham's bar graph.) Lumping black men of all backgrounds into a single unit, Brigham was respecting the traditional American black white dichotomy. At the same time, he distributed white people across nineteen overlapping categories reflecting current antagonism toward immigrants from southern and eastern Europe. His four major groups consisted of native-born whites, total whites, foreign-born whites, and Negroes. Within these groups, Brigham differentiated between the above-average foreigners and the below-average foreigners. Turks and Greeks just barely improved on the foreign-born average, while men from Russia, Italy, and Poland ranked at the bottom with the "Negro draft." Northwestern Europeans topped the chart.[22]

Among Brigham's noteworthy illustrations was table 33. (See figure 20.3, Brigham's "Table No. 33.") This feat of statistics achieved the seemingly impossible task of reconciling the racial groups (William Z. Ripley's still influential *Races of Europe* classification of Teutonic, Alpine, and Mediterranean on the basis of cephalic index) with the Immigration Service's national origins assigned to immigrants.

It is not by accident that Brigham substitutes "Nordic" for Ripley's "Teutonic," because Brigham owed a substantial debt to Madison Grant's *Passing of the Great Race, or The Racial Basis of European History.* First published in 1916, substantially revised in 1918 and in 1921, *The*

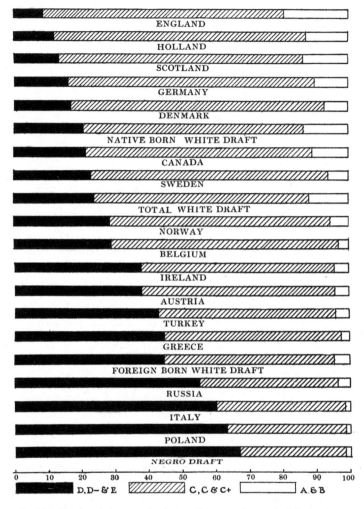

Fig. 20.2. Brigham's bar graph of mental test results, in Carl C. Brigham,
A Study of American Intelligence (1923).

Passing of the Great Race sold well over a million and a half copies by
the mid-1930s. Grant uses "Nordic" instead of "Teutonic" in order to
include Irish and Germans within the superior category but not Slavs,
Jews, and Italians.[23]

This astonishing table offers nonsensical estimates of national

TABLE No. 33

Tentative estimates of the proportion of Nordic, Alpine and Mediterranean blood in each of the European countries.

	PER CENT. NORDIC	PER CENT. ALPINE	PER CENT. MEDITERRANEAN
Austria-Hungary..................	10	90	0
Belgium.........................	60	40	0
Denmark........................	85	15	0
France..........................	30	55	15
Germany........................	40	60	0
Greece..........................	0	15	85
Italy............................	5	25	70
Netherlands.....................	85	15	0
Norway.........................	90	10	0
Sweden.........................	100	0	0
Russia (including Poland).........	5	95	0
Poland..........................	10	90	0
Spain...........................	10	5	85
Portugal........................	5	0	95
Roumania.......................	0	100	0
Switzerland......................	35	65	0
Turkey (unclassified).............	0	20	80
Turkey (in Europe) (including Serbia, Montenegro and Bulgaria).......	0	60	40
Turkey (in Asia).................	0	10	90
England.........................	80	0	20
Ireland..........................	30	0	70
Scotland	85	0	15
Wales...........................	40	0	60
British North America............	60	40	0

Fig. 20.3. Brigham, "Table No. 33. Tentative estimates of the proportion of Nordic, Alpine and Mediterranean blood in each of the European countries," in Carl C. Brigham, A Study of American Intelligence *(1923).*

"blood," presumably on the basis of cephalic indices, without explaining its methodology, which Brigham drew from one of eugenicists' favorite theorists, Georges Vacher de Lapouge. Lapouge had displayed a similar table showing "proportions of blood" according to cephalic indexes in several countries (distinguishing northern Germans from southern Germans) in his *L'Aryen: Son rôle social (The Aryan: His Social Role)* in 1899.[24]* For his part, Brigham in 1923 tabulated the

---

* Lapouge called 70 percent of northern Germans and 70 percent of Americans, but only 20 percent of southern Germans, dolichocephalic (i.e., superior). He located the highest proportion of dolichocephalics—85 percent—in Spain, but he would have dismissed them as Mediterraneans rather than Nordics. His next highest proportions of dolichocephalics were in England and Scandinavia, where they were safely Nordic.

(European?) population of "Russia (including Poland)" at 5 percent Nordic and 95 percent Alpine, while "Poland" is 10 percent Nordic and 90 percent Alpine. With three different subject lines, Turkey is 40, 80, and 90 percent Mediterranean, as though its regions could be demarcated according to "blood" and nobody ever migrated anywhere. Ireland and Wales are 70 and 60 percent Mediterranean, while England is only 20 percent Mediterranean. The high Mediterranean percentages allotted to Ireland and Wales presumably reflect the racist assumptions of John Beddoe and William Z. Ripley that the Irish and Welsh belong to a more primitive and therefore shorter, darker, and long-headed population than the English. After a war in which Germans had been stereotyped as "the Hun," German "blood" was downgraded from heavily Nordic to majority Alpine. Given the value judgments assigned to "Nordic," "Alpine," and "Mediterranean," table 33 emerges as an exquisite example of scientific racism, one of a series of attempts to combine "blood" with nation. This table intrigued social scientists, whether accepting or skeptical.

In 1911 the U.S. Immigration Commission, under Senator William P. Dillingham of Vermont, had issued the *Dictionary of Races or Peoples*, a handbook intended to clear up the "true racial status" of immigrants, on the basis of Ripley's *Races of Europe* and reprinting many of his maps. Like Ripley, *Dictionary of Races or Peoples* appealed to questionable authorities like Lapouge and his German anthroposociologist colleague Otto Ammon.[25] Like most attempts to codify racial classification, the *Dictionary of Races or Peoples* tried to reconcile the warring categories of several different experts through lists of "race," "stock," "group," "people," and Ripley's and other scholars' races. Its mishmash of categories had left open the gap that Brigham tried to fill.

In addition to these European racial "blood" measurements, Brigham reinterpreted the correlation between immigrant test scores and length of residence in the United States. As might be expected, given the questions, the longer immigrants had resided in the United States, the higher their scores. But Brigham followed Yerkes's reasoning, noting, then rejecting, the obvious causal relationship:

Instead of considering that our curve . . . indicates a growth of intelligence with increasing length of residence, we are forced to take the reverse of the picture and accept the hypothesis that the curve indicates a gradual deterioration in the class of immigrants examined in the army, who came to this country in each succeeding five year period since 1902.[26]

In other words, immigrants who had been in the United States longer scored higher because they were inherently smarter, the cream of the crop, as it were, self-starters who had set out from the old country early on, while the way was still hard. Later arrivals had no such pluck. They scored lower because they belonged to inferior races who let shipping companies deliver them the easy way across the ocean. Anthroposociology's cockamamie notions about headshape differences between urban and rural dwellers were now applied to conditions in the United States.

ARRIVING IN the jittery postwar era, *Study of American Intelligence* enjoyed a wide popularity that overwhelmed a few critical reviews in liberal journals. Brigham's credibility rode on a handsome set of advantages—his Princeton Ph.D., his Princeton University Press publication, his Princeton faculty position, and financial backing from Grant and Gould. With this kind of high-level support, his book enjoyed much currency in the early 1920s as scientific proof that immigrants from southern and eastern Europe were as inherently defective as whole races of Jukes and Kallikaks. The idea played well in a country—and its Congress—roiled by economic, political, and social unrest.*

---

* After the war Americans embraced intelligence testing more enthusiastically than people in other countries, but mental testing took place largely in the private sector. Yerkes complained in 1941 of the U.S. military's neglect: "Germany has a long lead in the development of military psychology. . . . The Nazis have achieved something that is entirely without parallel in military history. . . . What has happened in Germany is the logical sequel to the psychological and personnel services in our own Army during 1917–1918."

21

THE GREAT UNREST

The United States stayed out of the European charnel house of war until 1917, when the conflict was already three years old. But even as American troops went to fight in Europe, the United States experienced the war less as a tragedy of trench warfare and more as a time of spiraling labor unrest and anti-immigrant paranoia. Between 1917 and 1919, a growing cycle of strikes and labor tension alarmed Americans across the political spectrum. A cartoon from the *Saturday Evening Post*, the nation's most popular magazine, captured the all too facile coupling of immigrants, and radicalism, and race. (See figure 21.1, Johnson, "Look Out for the Undertow!") Here Herbert Johnson, the *Post*'s regular cartoonist, depicts an American family dashing into the waves of "immigration," grinning innocently.[1]* The mother wears the "sentimentalist" label that hardheaded, science-minded race theorists routinely attributed to anyone—especially women—who believed that the environment played a role in human destiny. The smiling father, equally clueless, leads his family into the wave as "employer of cheap labor." Only the child, the "future of America," hangs back, sensing the peril ahead. Rolling in with the "immigration" wave are fatal threats to the nation—"lowered

---

*Herbert Johnson (ca. 1880–1947), a Nebraskan, drew for the *Saturday Evening Post* from 1915 until his death. A stout foe of Franklin Roosevelt's policies, Johnson saw the New Deal as "Government in Business," an octopus strangling honest business.

Fig. 21.1. Herbert Johnson, "Look Out for the Undertow!"
Saturday Evening Post, *1921.*

standards," "race degeneration," "bolshevism," and "disease." In this cartoon, the race in question was white, as was the menace.

Republicans in Congress had been trying to restrict immigration on more or less racial grounds since the 1880s, but with limited success. Their party was, in fact, divided. Although normally allied with the Republicans, manufacturers employing cheap immigrant labor lobbied diligently against legislation to curtail it. Their economic interests weighed against a tightening of the labor market and the certainty of rising wages. The result was an unexpected alliance. Democratic presidents and congressmen representing large numbers of immigrants also resisted anti-immigration legislation as racist and discriminatory. So long as immigrants could vote—before or after naturalization—their representatives, usually Democrats, blocked much restrictive legislation.

At the center of these legislative storms were not the Irish or the Germans—they had mostly been accepted and assimilated (during the war, Germans sometimes through anxiety or intimidation). Rather, the main targets hailed from southern and eastern Europe, the masses of Slavs, Italians, and Jews, many said to be mentally handicapped, prone to disease and un-American ideologies. Therein lay the threat. Where in all this were Asians? Nowhere, for since 1882, after Chinese workers had completed the western portion of the transcontinental railroad, they had, one and all, been declared ineligible for citizenship. Not being part of the new American political economy meant that Asians lacked any influence in Congress. It took them a long time to gain parity.* A fundamental issue was labor: the stigmatized immigrants came as workers to feed American industry.

During the late nineteenth century, the United States had industrialized impressively. After recovery from the deep depression of the 1890s, American industrial output rivaled Europe's. More than 14.5 million immigrants, mostly from southern and eastern Europe, entered the country between 1900 and 1920, their numbers far exceeding even the lowly Irish and Germans disdained by Ralph Waldo Emerson as "guano races."[2] In Emerson's time the Irish had found paying work on the canals and the eastern railroads; now immigrants poured into manufacturing, rather than farming and transportation, generating the profits of twentieth-century America.[3]

By the 1890s industrialization had given rise to giant corporations like Standard Oil of John D. Rockefeller, U.S. Steel under Andrew Carnegie, and the combined Union Pacific, Southern Pacific, and Illinois Central railroads run by E. H. Harriman. The wealth of these corporations depended upon friendly state and federal legislators and a multitude of local corporation lawyers in the state legislatures that elected U.S. sena-

---

*The 1882 ruling In re Ah Yup declared Chinese not to be white, and therefore not eligible for naturalization under the 1790 Naturalization Act. Although the language of the 1790 act deemed only free white (males) eligible, the Fifteenth Amendment in 1870 made black people eligible for naturalized citizenship. The Chinese Exclusion Act of 1882 enacted the prohibition against Chinese naturalization into federal law. The "Gentlemen's Agreement" President Theodore Roosevelt negotiated with the government of Japan in 1907 permitted the entry of Japanese gentlemen—scholars, diplomats—but prohibited the immigration of working-class Japanese.

tors until 1913. Corporate-minded officeholders shaped a legal context friendly to corporations and hostile toward labor. Free to squelch workers' attempts to organize and quick to exert the power of the state against strikers, corporations rewarded themselves with salaries, bonuses, and profits and their shareholders with dividends, rather than accord their workers wage increases. Inevitably, workers came to resent such exploitation. In the popular mind, their resentment wore an immigrant face.

Soon disruptive actions, such as the great steel strike in Homestead, Pennsylvania, in 1892 and the 1894 Pullman strike near Chicago, broke out regularly. Even voters who may have felt no particular warmth toward labor began to cast protest votes against the two major parties, both very dedicated to serving capital. In consequence, during the so-called Progressive Era before 1915, left-wing policies more attuned to the needs of people than to the wishes of powerful corporations gained favor.

The Socialist Party (SP), founded in 1901, led the way, powered by voters unhappy with the lockstep Republican and Democratic probusiness status quo. Throughout the country the SP grew quickly from around 1910, attracting some 100,000 members. One stronghold, New York City's 1.4 million Yiddish-speaking, working-class immigrants, elected a series of socialist candidates, including ten state assemblymen, seven city councilmen, one municipal judge, and one congressman.[4] The SP candidate for president, Eugene Debs, polled a million votes in 1912, the SP's high-water mark.

The far more revolutionary labor organization, the Industrial Workers of the World, also seized the moment, waging a media-savvy textile strike in Lawrence, Massachusetts, birthplace of American industry in the heart of symbol-laden New England. The IWW had broken away from the SP in 1905 to pursue more radical, worker-centered policies. For many anxious Americans, the SP and IWW merged into a huge revolutionary threat to American society, one identified with immigrant "alien races." In the tense, hyper-patriotic atmosphere of wartime, any hint of labor militancy did not play well across the country.

ONCE THE United States became a belligerent in April 1917, war production shot up, and the labor was in many cases supplied by immigrants.

Long working hours and soaring inflation ensued. Everyone complained about the high cost of living, for wages did not keep pace with spectacular price increases. The result was a tsunami wave of strikes, peaking in 1917. The IWW, though small in number, staged highly publicized actions in the West, home to large numbers of Mexican immigrants. Although native-born lumberjacks and mineworkers vastly outnumbered Mexicans in the IWW, true to the hysteria of the moment, many Americans assumed the whole organization to be aliens. It was but a short step to draconian legislation. The Immigration Act passed in February 1917 targeted the IWW specifically and labor radicalism generally, barring entry into the United States of all "anarchists, or persons who believe in or advocate the overthrow by force or violence of the Government of the United States."[5] Vigilantes quickly took the law into their own hands; they lynched a Wobbly organizer in Butte, Montana, and in the fall federal agents raided IWW headquarters in forty-eight cities. Such federal action kept the IWW in court and on the defensive, even as strikes for more pay continued around the nation.

Meanwhile, in February and October 1917 Russia experienced a first and then a second revolution in the name of the working class. The second one, proclaiming itself Marxist, Bolshevik, and Soviet, took Russia out of the European slaughterhouse of war. Furthermore, it increased the attraction of socialism as an alternative to senseless, belligerent politics and bolstered the appeal of Marxism as a sweeping explanation for the human condition.

At bottom, Marxism touted class conflict, rather than race conflict, as the motor of history. Such a substitution of class for race did not alter Americans' social ideology, for foundational law and the organization of government data (such as the census) still relied on categories of race. The Russian revolution did not persuade Americans to think about labor and politics in terms of class; they continued to interpret all sorts of human difference as race.

Therein lay a crisis of race ideology. If the Teutonic white peoples of Europe represented humanity's apex, how had they reverted to savagery so easily? The African American sociologist W. E. B. Du Bois had an answer: "This is not Europe gone mad; this is not aberration nor insanity; this *is* Europe; this seeming Terrible is the real soul of white culture . . . stripped and visible today."[6] In the face of the first great crisis of whiteness, saving the "real soul of white culture" became Americans' task after the war, one imposed and accepted amid a clash of ideas and events. The Russian revolution and wave after wave of strikes converged on hereditarian concepts of permanent racial traits à la Ripley's *Races of Europe*. The idea of the "melting pot" was already under stress when wartime anxieties tested it further.

By the armistice of November 1918, "bolshevism" in the American public mind meant the world turned upside down. In Germany a socialist revolution followed the abdication of Emperor Wilhelm II, evidently spreading the red tide. Many in the United States felt themselves stuck in a bad dream, in which Bolshevik Wobblies were running things, foreign strikers were fomenting chaos, and an insurrectionary proletariat threatened to seize government, murder citizens, burn churches, and in general destroy civilization. The end of civilization meant ugly, ignorant, unwashed immigrants breeding freely—their defects innate, hereditary, and permanent—and native Americans trodden underfoot. Events of 1919 simply made things worse.

The whole world seemed in convulsion. Strikes and revolutions raged on every continent, in France and even in England. In the United States, 1919 began with a general strike of 100,000 workers in Seattle, an event that seemed so unthinkably un-American that it had to have foreign causes. Another *Saturday Evening Post* cartoon explains where strikes come from and offers a solution to the labor crisis.[7] (See figure 21.2, Roun, "100% Impure.") A grubby, dark-skinned "undesirable alien" with a red flag in his hat for socialism, offers a potent, tempting drug, "100% proof strike" to befuddled "labor." According to race theory's prevailing wisdom, labor's head shape tells a tale. It is flat in the back, thus marking him as a brachycephalic Alpine, hence bovine of intelligence and easily misled by "undesirable alien." The valise of "undesirable alien" contains four other bottles of poison, three labeled "discontent," "labor trouble," and "strife." Arriving in the nick of time to save poor, dumbfounded "labor" is a policeman labeled "US." The solution to the labor problem caused by "undesirable alien" must therefore come from stringent federal governance.

Fig. 21.2. Ray Roun, "100% Impure," Saturday Evening Post, 1921.

Seattle's general strike lasted only a week, but it was long enough to offer conservatives time to trumpet Bolshevik infiltration right here at home, which mounting strikes seemed to prove: 175 in March, 248 in April, 388 in May, 303 in June, 360 in July, and 373 in August. More strikes had taken place in 1917, but more workers had gone out in 1919's climate of hysteria. This was also the summer of bloody attacks on African Americans who had come up from the South to jobs in northern industry. Antiblack pogroms made 1919 the Red Summer: red for bloodshed as well as labor conflict.[8]

Strikes rolled into the fall: some in places where famous strikes had occurred before and some where striking seemed unthinkable. In September 350,000 steelworkers struck U.S. Steel factories in six states, climaxing a decades-long campaign for an eight-hour-day and recognition of the steelworkers' union. In November 600,000 railroad workers in twenty states walked off the job, and wildcat strikes paralyzed transportation locally. Nearly half a million coal miners threatened to strike in November, when coal heated American homes and schools.

Even the police played a part. In Boston 1,200 police struck for higher wages and union recognition, throwing the city into chaos. Calvin Coolidge, governor of Massachusetts, announced that the police had no right to strike, called in the state national guard, and emerged an instant hero. Commentators likened striking Boston police to Bolsheviks. Coolidge became the Republican vice presidential candidate in the fall of 1920 and president after President Warren G. Harding's death in 1923.

Popular hysteria bred confused thought. Most strikes had centered on wages or conditions on the shop floor, but now labor militancy merged with socialism and anarchism, notions deemed foreign and un-American. A poem published in a steel industry magazine linked politics to nativity:

> Said Dan McGann to a foreign man who worked at the
>   self-same bench.
> "Let me tell you this," and for emphasis, he flourished
>   a monkey wrench,
> "Don't talk to me of this bourgoissee, don't open your
>   mouth to speak
> "Of your socialists or your anarchists, don't mention
>   the bolshevik,
> "For I've had enough of this foreign stuff, I'm sick as a
>   man can be
> "Of the speech of hate, and I'm telling you straight,
>   that this is the land for me."[9]*

Anarchists had presented a popular target since the late nineteenth century, and in the present unrest a murder in Massachusetts offered opportunity to clobber anarchism in the persons of Nicola Sacco and Bartolomeo Vanzetti, Italian laborers associated with Luigi Galleani, publisher of the revolutionary *Cronaca Sovversiva (Subversive Chronicle)*. Sacco and Vanzetti, convicted of murdering two security guards in the course of a robbery in Braintree, became a cause célèbre on account of the questionable conduct of their trials, which ended with the hanging of both men in 1927, after enormous controversy.[†]

---

* Dan McGann, with an Irish name, now stands for the real American.
† In 1977 then governor Michael Dukakis signed a declaration removing "any stigma and disgrace" from Vanzetti and Sacco, because of the shoddy conduct of their trials.

•

INVESTIGATIONS PROLIFERATED. The *Saturday Evening Post*, which reached some ten million Americans, ran a series of "fire alarm" articles warning of the intertwined immigrant-bolshevik menace.[10] The U.S. Senate took up investigations of domestic bolshevism, hearing testimony that Jews had caused the Russian revolution. With the *Post*'s amplification, claims that Jews caused strikes and revolutions, bolshevism, socialism, syndicalism, strikes, and the melting pot ricocheted through a jumpy society.

Bombs and bomb scares joined strikes as sowers of disorder. Bombs were sent to prominent men in the federal government and to post offices countrywide, aimed especially at proponents of immigration restriction. Although the identity of the bombers was not known, foreign radicals and labor organizers got the blame. American Legionnaires broke into IWW halls and beat up whomever they found, and the U.S. Justice Department began raiding socialist meeting halls far and wide in the fall. Dragnets in November yielded 249 deportable (i.e., noncitizen) radicals and took them on a "Red Special" to Ellis Island for deportation. The deportees included the famous anarchist Emma Goldman. No socialist, and certainly not Russian, Goldman was nevertheless shipped to Russia as a bolshevik.*

The specter of a bolshevism hagriding Americans made suspect any departure from conventional thought, political or cultural. Before and during the war "Americanization" projects had attempted to teach immigrants English and turn them into Americans. But wartime fears of espionage and sedition intensified this campaign into a press for "One-hundred percent Americanism." One hundred percent Americanism meant not simply unstinting support for the war and the closing of radical newspapers such as *Il Proletario*, with its sharp criticism of American public life, but also a renunciation of old-country ways of living and speaking. Cities and employers coerced employees into Americanization courses, where the English language, civics, and an upstanding way of

---

* Emma Goldman (1869–1940) was born in Lithuania and immigrated to the United States when she was seventeen.

life were strictly encouraged. The National Americanization Committee, led by the New York labor reformer Frances Kellor, was nominally a federal organization but functioned according to Kellor's vision. The committee defined its work as "the interpretation of American ideals, traditions, and standards and institutions to foreign-born peoples," "the combating of anti-American propaganda activities and schemes and the stamping out of sedition and disloyalty wherever found," "the elimination of causes of disorder, unrest, and disloyalty which make fruitful soil for un-American propagandists and disloyal agitators," and "the creation of an understanding of and love for America and the desire of immigrants to remain in America, and have a home here, and support American institutions and laws." These often intense classes met several times per week and were closely monitored by the authorities.[11]

Before the war Henry Ford had set up one of the longest-lived one hundred percent Americanism systems in his Michigan automobile plants. Ford's Sociological Department, a model of Americanization, taught autoworkers "how to live a clean and wholesome life," according to Ford's own idea of "living aright." Speaking English, passing regular home inspections, remaining sober, keeping a savings account, and sticking to "good habits" were mandatory, while riotous living and roomers were strictly forbidden.

The Ford school was intended to Anglo-Saxonize an immigrant workforce, as symbolized at graduation. At center stage stood a huge, papier-mâché melting pot with stairs on both sides. As the band struck up a rousing tune, graduates in their national clothing went up the stairs on one side, entered the melting pot, and came out on the other side singing "The Star-Spangled Banner" and waving American flags. They were now dressed in derby hats, pants, vests, jackets, stiff white collars, polka-dot ties, and a Ford Motor Company badge in each lapel.[12] For women, Americanization meant conforming to social workers' notions of proper housekeeping, cooking, dressing, and child rearing. In sum, Americanization imposed the use of English and patriotic conformity. Socialistic notions were nowhere to be found here or, indeed, anywhere in the American power structure.

THE MELTING POT
A FAILURE?

Every national tenet needs its stentorian voice, and for well over half a century the *Saturday Evening Post* spoke for American anti-immigrant racism. Founded in 1821, it was by the 1920s, with more than two million subscribers, the nation's most popular periodical, as well as an excellent platform for a well-illustrated, coldhearted, nativist campaign against immigrants from eastern and southern Europe.

Declaring immigration restriction a matter of life and death for the American people, the *Post* editor George H. Lorimer (1868–1937) so powerfully shaped public opinion that his magazine influenced American lawmakers all too eager to assuage panicky constituents. The House Committee on Immigration heard Lorimer's *Saturday Evening Post* editorial of 7 February 1920 read aloud: "The matter of race must be given more attention. . . . [T]hese alien peoples are temperamentally and racially unfitted for easy assimilation. . . . The rank and file of these unassimilated aliens still live mentally in the ghetto. . . . In thought they are still stoned by the gentile. . . . They are serfs to tradition—narrow, suspicious, timid, brutal, rapacious. . . ."[1] The races in question, of course, were white.

Part of Lorimer's genius was his ability to blend his message with a great gift for recruiting talented writers and artists. In 1916, for instance, he hired a green young painter on the strength of two covers painted on spec; Norman Rockwell subsequently painted *Post* covers for forty-five years. And although Lorimer's personal politics leaned far to the right, he did not hesitate to employ writers like Sinclair Lewis, F. Scott Fitzgerald, Theodore Dreiser, Jack London, and Stephen Crane, who stood more to his left. But Lorimer did make sure that one man bigger than all the foregoing agreed with him right down the line.[2]

Kenneth L. Roberts (1885–1957) harbored a great distaste for southern and eastern Europeans—especially Jews—and an abhorrence for racial "mongrelization." Both Roberts and Lorimer believed that immigration would extinguish the race of native Americans, because "races cannot be crossbred without mongrelization any more than dogs." A proud Maine Yankee whose ancestors, he claimed loudly, came to Maine in 1639, Roberts graduated from Cornell University in 1908.[3] During the First World War, he served in the U.S. Army's Siberian Expeditionary Force. He joined the *Saturday Evening Post* staff in 1919 and quickly succeeded. In the first seven months of 1919 alone, he earned $7,700, at a time when doctors and lawyers earned around $2,000 a year.[4]

Roberts stayed with the *Post* for ten years, before leaving in 1928 to write historical fiction, books that are still read and appreciated, especially by the listeners of North Country Radio in northern New York State and the guests on Garrison Keillor's *Prairie Home Companion* cruises.* Therefore, the best portrait of Roberts appeared some two decades after his *Post* pieces on immigration. In 1940, on the occasion of the publication of his new novel *Oliver Wiswell, Time* magazine celebrated his best-selling novelist's career with a cover story.[5]

His *Northwest Passage* (1937), a novel celebrating his ancestors in the French and Indian wars, was made into a well-received 1940 movie vehicle for Spencer Tracy. Universally popular, Roberts received honorary degrees from Colby, Dartmouth, Bowdoin, and Middlebury Colleges and shortly before his death, in 1957, a special Pulitzer Prize citation for historical fiction. *Time* called him "the finest U.S. historical novelist

---

*A summer 2004 North Country Radio reading list included Roberts's best-known novel, *Northwest Passage*. A list of suggested reading for the August 2005 *Prairie Home Companion* cruise recommends "any of the historical novels by Kenneth Roberts."

since James Fenimore Cooper."
(See figure 22.1, Kenneth Roberts.) But our interest in Roberts
lies in the context of the 1920s.

Even friends admitted that
Roberts was a "difficult human
being . . . among the most irascible
men alive, whose conversation
was profusely decorated with pro-
fanity."[6] But, at bottom, he—like
his editor Lorimer and the *Post*
cartoonist Herbert Johnson—
detested anything having to do
with progressive reform. Roberts
came to hate the New Deal and its
architect, Franklin D. Roosevelt,
so much that "he glued Roosevelt
dimes to the clamshells he used as
ashtrays, the better to grind ashes

Fig. 22.1. Kenneth Roberts, "Angry Man's
Romance," cover story, Time magazine,
25 November 1940.

into FDR's face."[7] Even Lorimer, no friend of immigrants or Jews, had to
tone down Roberts's blatant racism before his articles could appear in the
Post. In his books Roberts speaks freely about "damned half-negro Italians,
half-Mongol Jews, and thoroughly bastardized Greeks and Levantines."[8]

DURING THE great unrest following the First World War, Lorimer asked
Roberts to investigate postwar immigrants. The upshot, in 1920–21,
was Roberts's pungent, firsthand reports from Europe, eventually
gathered from his *Saturday Evening Post* pieces into a 1922 volume
called *Why Europe Leaves Home.*

Immigration had reached crisis proportions, Roberts howled. It absolutely had to be stopped. Agreeing with his editor Lorimer three times in
one article, Roberts termed immigration restriction "a matter of life and
death for the American people." The threat was racial: either the United
States would break up into a series of racial groups, fighting, bickering,

haggling "over their alien racial differences," or, worse, "a new composite race of people wholly different from the Americans of the present day" would emerge, a motley, inefficient, mongrelized race.[9] Having roamed far and wide on the *Post*'s dime, Roberts described Czechs as "backward, illiterate, dirty, thick-headed," and English workingmen as "runty, stunted, malformed, buck-toothed, obviously mal-nourished, diseased and generally wretched specimens." Southern Italians had descended from the mongrelized slaves of the Roman empire. Because the American nation, like ancient Greece and Rome, grew out of blond Nordic genius, mongrelization would ruin the United States as surely as it ruined the ancients.[10] And so it went.

The intensity and widespread circulation of Roberts's anti-Semitic venom merged into an ugly tide of hatred. Pounding away at the Jews as "mean-faced, shifty-eyed," and "unassimilatable [*sic*]" "human parasites," "a poisoned emigration from Europe," and the natural agents of bolshevism, Roberts's articles herald a deepening preoccupation with Jews in popular discourse.[11] Anti-Semitism was already well established in the United States but grew increasingly abusive in the early twentieth century. Before the war Jews had figured as only one in a list of inferior Europeans, along with Slavs and Italians. Now Jews moved to the top, personifying the menace of immigration and bolshevism in racial terms.*

One example of the stereotypes assigned to Jewish immigrants, often termed "Hebrews," lay in the popular work of the Wisconsin professor Edward A. Ross. Deemed an expert on immigration since his 1901 lecture on race suicide, Ross repeated familiar stereotypes in his widely read and influential *The Old World in the New: The Significance of Past and Present Immigration to the American People* (1914): Jews are loud and pushy; they lie and cheat; Jewish men pursue Gentile rather than Jewish girls. Ross repeated the familiar orthodoxy of the time that immigrants were lowering the level of American intelligence and American beauty. In a famous phrase echoing Shakespeare's *The Tempest*, Ross called new immigrants "the Caliban type" who "belong in skins, in wattled huts

* In 1915 vigilante Georgians raided a prison, kidnapped Leo Frank, an Atlanta Jewish businessman, and lynched him.

at the close of the Great Ice Age. These oxlike men are descendants of those *who always stayed behind.*"[12] Ross maintains, with many others at the time, that race purity produces beauty. As we know, William Z. Ripley had in 1908 also predicted that the crossing of heterogeneous strains would make Americans ugly. Ross foresees "a good many faces of a 'chaotic constitution,' " the outcome of the blending of "dissimilar" European races.

The most "dissimilar" for Ross are the "Hebrews," polar opposites of "our" pioneer breed. Jews are "undersized and weak-muscled." Shrinking from outdoor activity and screaming at the slightest injury, they cannot be made into Boy Scouts, iconic symbols of hardy young manhood. Indeed, at the turn of the twentieth century, the outdoors functioned as the symbolic Nordic setting, whereas inferior races were thought to inhabit the teeming city slums where they could perpetually stay indoors.

For Ross, Jewish shortcomings, however prominent, were not permanent or innate. Granted, it would take eons for Jews to turn into pioneer stock, he hinted, but that time might eventually arrive.[13] Kenneth Roberts disagreed: to him immigrant shortcomings were inborn and permanent, and he defined immigration in terms of race.

Quotas should therefore severely limit the numbers of immigrants of certain races, never mind nationality. Like Carl C. Brigham in *A Study of American Intelligence*, Roberts used the increasingly fashionable term "Nordic" to designate a superior race. In turn, Brigham's book leans on the authority of the prominent eugenicist Madison Grant, who inserted the term "Nordic" into public discourse in *Passing of the Great Race*. Roberts knew Madison Grant and his acolyte Lothrop Stoddard personally and echoed their warnings directly. In *Why Europe Leaves Home*, Roberts quotes, cites, and recommends both Grant and Stoddard and makes Grant's Nordic a household name.[14]

OBITUARIES OF Madison Grant (1865–1937) remembered this quintessential patrician racist as a pioneering conservationist, which was true.[15] His New England Puritan descent ever in evidence, Madison Grant con-

Fig. 22.2. Madison Grant.

sidered American nature his patrimony, and in many ways it was. (See figure 22.2, Madison Grant.) He saved various endangered species, ranging from California redwood trees to American bison, and founded the Bronx Zoo. Along with Theodore Roosevelt—his longtime correspondent, fellow outdoors enthusiast, and book blurber—Grant played an active role in the Boone and Crockett Club of wealthy New Yorkers interested in the early phases of conservation. Without this club and Grant in particular, Glacier National Park, Everglades National Park, and Olympic National Park might not have come into being. Grant's education at Yale (his family's institution), enhanced by four years of study in Dresden, allowed him to read European anthropology in its original languages.[16]* He was an accomplished man, but his accomplishments led him in odd, even pernicious, directions. His understanding, for instance, of animals and trees took Grant to the conservation of the races through eugenics and immigration restriction. As a prime hereditarian of the 1910s and 1920s, Grant exerted enormous influence at Cold Spring Harbor's Eugenics Record Office.

William Z. Ripley's *Races of Europe* lay at the foundation of Grant's science. And Grant did consider his work brutally, objectively scientific, even at the cost of rejecting fundamental American values. The introduction to his pessimistic masterwork, *The Passing of the Great Race* (1916; 4th edition, 1921) warns, "[T]his generation must completely repudiate the proud boast of our fathers that they acknowledged no distinction in 'race, creed, or color' or else the native American must turn the page of history and write: 'FINIS AMERICAE.' "[17] To Grant, the melting

---

*Grant's fellow students in Dresden included the future *Saturday Evening Post* editor Horace Lorimer.

pot might have worked in the olden days of Nordic immigrants—who for Grant and Roberts now include the Catholic Irish—but the current surge of non-Nordic immigrants dooms the melting pot to "absolute failure."[18] No more melting pot, and no more democratic human rights. The "sentimentalists" must be put down along with the alien races.

Resolutely hereditarian, *The Passing of the Great Race* combines the commonplaces of degenerate-family studies, Galtonian eugenics, race suicide, history, and polygenesis (rejection of the idea of the same origin for people of all races).[19] One remedy for race deterioration came from his eugenics colleague Harry Latimer. One might, Grant muses, designate the

> least desirable, let us say, ten per cent of the community. When this unemployed and unemployable human residuum has been eliminated together with the great mass of crime, poverty, alcoholism and feeblemindedness associated therewith it would be easy to consider the advisability of further restricting the perpetuation of the then remaining least valuable types.

By progressively "eliminating" inferior types, "the most vital and intellectual strains" could finally be chosen "to carry on the race."[20] Grant and other eugenicists envisioned negative eugenics as the glorious future of evolution. If this sounds Nazi-like, it most certainly was, and Nazis in Germany took lessons from Grant.

Grant, Ripley, and all the other Teutonists fetishized height. Once again, the Sardinians are racially "dwarfed," like "the Polish Jew, whose dwarf stature, peculiar mentality and ruthless concentration on self-interest are being engrafted upon the stock of the nation." Perhaps, Grant admits, some peoples he includes among his Nordics may actually be short. To explain this departure from theory, he surmises that the natural height of the Irish, and even some English, may be lowered by the continued existence of "a considerable population of primitive short stock"—"primitive stock" always being short and dark. His example of the influence of "primitive short stock" on Nordics contrasts Englishmen of different "races" that happen to coincide with class difference:

"the Piccadilly gentleman of Nordic race and the cockney costermonger of the old Neolithic type." Hair and eye color count, but skin color less so in *The Passing of the Great Race*, because skin color is unreliable. Pure Nordics have "absolutely fair skin," making the Nordic "the white man par excellence." But, unfortunately, many real Nordics, even Scandinavians, may not be sufficiently pale.[21]

Short Englishmen, swarthy Nordics, and poor whites in the U.S. South or London's East End all compromise Grant's tortured attempt at a coherent hereditarian classification. Grant also rejects the notion of the Kentuckian as the quintessential Nordic American popularized by Theodore Roosevelt's professor Nathaniel Southgate Shaler. No better than poor whites—whether "crackers" or the shiftless whites of Georgia, the Bahamas, and Barbados—Kentuckians lack even the excuse of living at low altitudes, when high altitudes were thought to foster superior races. More befuddlement follows. Grant reckons that the Cumberland Mountains should favor "men of the Nordic breed," but mountains of the South were notorious for producing degenerate families. Lacking an answer, Grant seems to shrug and walk away, concluding, "There are probably other hereditary forces at work there as yet little understood."[22]

Grant may have sunk into obscurity, but the biggest name in American letters, Theodore Roosevelt, loved the first edition of *The Passing of the Great Race*, going so far as to supply a blurb proclaiming it "a capital book; in purpose, in vision, in grasp of the facts our people most need to realize. . . . It shows a fine fearlessness in assailing the popular and mischievous sentimentalities and attractive and corroding falsehoods which few men dare assail. It is the work of an American scholar and gentleman."

Academic reviews were also largely positive, though criticism did arise from liberals and Jews, both easily brushed off because of their origins. Franz Boas grasped the danger of a spiteful, racist account coming from an author with sound scientific credentials. Credentials be damned, Boas condemned Grant's work as "practically a modern edition of Gobineau" based on "dogmatic assumptions." Boas recognized the

Fig. 22.3. John Singer Sargent, Apollo and the Muses, *1921, blond Apollo, Museum of Fine Arts, Boston.*

fanciful nature of Grant's maps, which had dazzled most other reviewers.[23] Young Horace Kallen's negative review prompted Grant to dismiss it as the work "of a Jew and just what [he] expected from the followers of Boas."[24] So cavalier a dismissal sufficed to tamp down dissent during the heyday of the blond, long-headed Nordic.

The dolichocephalic (long-headed), light-haired "dolicho-blond" embodies Grant's beau ideal, a figure now practically forgotten but one cutting quite a swath in the 1920s. According to Grant, Nordics have not only given the world civilization, enterprise, and bravery; they also possess heavenly beauty: the gods of lovely ancient Greece were, of course, blond. In 1921, the same year the best-selling revision of *The Passing of the Great Race* appeared, the American society painter John Singer Sargent depicted ancient Greeks and their gods as quintessential dolichoblonds in *Apollo and the Muses,* a mural in the Museum of Fine Arts, Boston. (See figure 22.3, Sargent, *Apollo and the Muses,* blond Apollo.) Even Sargent's horses are blond. (See figure 22.4, Sargent, *Apollo and the Muses,* blond horses.)

Fig. 22.4. John Singer Sargent, Apollo and the Muses, *1921, blond horses, Museum of Fine Arts, Boston.*

Without equivocation, Grant maintains that no artist depicting the crucifixion "hesitates to make the two thieves brunet in contrast to the blond Saviour," perhaps because the great artists of the Renaissance, Dante, Raphael, Titian, Michelangelo, and Leonardo da Vinci, "were all the Nordic type."[25] The astonishing version of history in *The Passing of the Great Race* advances the then accepted explanation for the fall of Rome: dolicho-blond Roman patricians committed race suicide by not having children, by marching off to war, and by leaving their slaves at home to breed freely.[26] It was not for nothing that Grant and David Starr Jordan, Stanford University's president and a leading peace advocate, worked together on committees at the Eugenics Record Office. Jordan, for instance, deplored the war in Europe for wreaking "unparalleled havoc in the best racial elements in each nation concerned . . . thereby exhausting the near future and entailing impoverishment, both physical and mental."[27]

ANTHROPOSOCIOLOGY:
THE SCIENCE OF ALIEN RACES

"These books are all scientific." So insists F. Scott Fitzgerald's Tom Buchanan in *The Great Gatsby* (1925). A former Yale football star and member of a secret society, Tom, now thirty and immensely rich, lives in posh "East Egg" on the north shore of Long Island, well insulated from most of American life.[1] To him and others of his ilk, Lothrop Stoddard ("Goddard") figures as a purveyor of "scientific stuff" that has "been proved."

Buchanan has a point, for all these race theoreticians cheerfully called upon scientific research, often European. Following this scholarship into obscure nooks and crannies may seem odd today, but in the early twentieth century, it surged to the fore in a seductive mix of eugenics' degenerate families and Ripley's cephalic-index-driven race classification. Thus *The Passing of the Great Race* grows directly out of a body of work inspired by Georges Vacher de Lapouge (1854–1936), a French scholar mentioned earlier as an inventor of "anthroposociology" who was a librarian at the Universities of Montpellier, Rennes, and Poitiers and author of the anti-Semitic *L'Aryen: Son rôle social* (1899).

In theory, anthroposociology analyzes the relationship between human bodies and society. But for Lapouge, Ammon, Beddoe, Grant, and other anthroposociologists, heredity—conceived of as racial heredity— was everything. Environment, class status, individual variation, migration, and wealth, on the other hand, counted for naught, as determined by their science of unit traits.* In the United States in the 1920s, such pernicious ideas made sense to racial thinkers whose dogma meshed nicely with that of the German National Socialists. The Nazis adopted Lapouge as an iconic philosopher, styling him as a count or a marquis, whether or not his family in Poitiers was actually aristocratic.[2]

Lapouge, in turn, had proclaimed himself the acolyte of another French racist of uncertain nobility, Arthur de Gobineau (1816–82), whose masterwork remained largely unread for decades. A prolific author, Gobineau had published his *Essai sur l'inégalité des races humaines* (*An Essay on the Inequality of the Human Races*) in two volumes in 1853–54 to near-complete silence—only like-minded racists savored the book.[3] Another pessimistic racist, Gobineau interpreted history as the rise and fall of the blond, blue-eyed Aryan race: Aryans rose out of racial genius, but the race mixing that inevitably follows economic development brought it down.[†] When Gobineau excoriated race mixing, he meant the mixing of different races of whites.

Gobineau and Lapouge both abhorred race mixing, though they gave it different meanings. For Gobineau, race mixing meant the mating of Aryans with non-Aryans; for Lapouge, it meant the mating of dolicho-blonds with brachy-browns. Lapouge even went so far as to predict a conflict of the races over cephalic indices: "I am convinced that in the next century people will slaughter each other by the millions because of a difference of a degree or two in the cephalic index."[4] Today these head-shape theories seem bizarre, confusing, and muddled. But it was all perfectly rational to them, for Lapouge, like Gobineau, observed race mixing in modern France and despaired. Their theories enjoyed increasing credibility.

---

* Karl Pearson, Galton's successor in statistics and eugenics in London, embodied this appropriation of science. Preaching empire and racial cleansing in the name of science in *National Life from the Standpoint of Science* (1905), Pearson said, "[M]y view—and I think it may be called the scientific view of a nation—is that of an organized whole, kept up to a high pitch of internal efficiency by insuring that its numbers are substantially recruited from the better stocks, and kept up to a high pitch of external efficiency by contest, chiefly by way of war with inferior races."
† Gobineau, like the other infamous Aryan chauvinist Adolph Hitler, evidently had brown hair and brown eyes.

Gobineau cannot be counted as a classic anti-Semite, for he admired Jews as he appreciated blacks, in a stereotypical fashion. As a racist thinker, Gobineau could have been a great deal meaner. As we have seen, applause came to Gobineau from Mobile, Alabama, in the 1850s, when Josiah C. Nott sponsored an edited translation under the title *The Moral and Intellectual Diversity of Races.* When Lapouge flattered himself to be the "first prophet of the Nordic race after Gobineau," he was ignoring the mid-nineteenth-century American racists' translation. Lapouge's ignorance is understandable, for the Nott translation, like the original, went largely unnoticed at the time. Who could have known that such arcane weirdness would flourish in the twentieth century as science?

Gobineau's great breakthrough in the English-speaking world came long after his death when a Dr. Oscar Levy, whose motives remain obscure, sponsored a new and more faithful translation, published in London and the United States.* It was this 1915 translation that brought Gobineau to the attention of racists in the United States and made "Aryan" a favorite racist term. Like Gobineau, Lapouge believed that two antagonistic races lived in France—long-headed (dolichocephalic) Nordic/Aryan aristocrats and round-headed (brachycephalic) Alpine peasants.[5]

Such racist theory swirled throughout the West, with oceans no barrier. Madison Grant and William Z. Ripley shared an enthusiasm for Lapouge's anthroposociology. The bibliography of Ripley's *Races of Europe* cites Lapouge twenty-five times, and Lapouge's statistics appear repeatedly in Ripley's tables.[6] In February 1908, Ripley gave his Huxley lecture in New York to Grant's patrician Half Moon Club. By 1912 Grant was in regular correspondence with Lapouge, whom he called, in wild exaggeration, "the most distinguished anthropologist in France."[7†]

Glimpsed in a certain light, Lapouge did seem impressive. He had

---

*Oscar Levy (1866–1946), a German living in Oxford, had edited an English translation of the complete works of Friedrich Nietzsche in 1911 and is connected to the publication of the anti-Semitic and fabricated *Protocols of the Elders of Zion.*
†Lapouge also shared with Grant and other Nordic race chauvinists an enthusiasm for the outdoors and healthy, natural living.

published eighty-seven articles collected in three books. In the early 1890s his work appeared in the respected journal *Revue d'anthropologie*, edited by Paul Topinard, who had inherited the considerable intellectual prestige of Paul Broca's French school of anthropology.[8] The influential Yale sociologist William Graham Sumner cited Lapouge in the notes and bibliography of his widely read social Darwinist book *Folkways*.[9] There ended Lapouge's scholarly glory, for he twice failed competitions for the *agrégation** and was never able to secure a professorship. By the mid-1890s, Lapouge was limited to publication in obscure, provincial journals. His best-known book, *L'Aryen*, sold only 430 of the 1,000 copies printed and was never translated into English.[10] Germanophilic anthroposociology and lack of judgment cost him dearly at home.

By the turn of the twentieth century, Lapouge was totally marginalized in France. His racist screed *L'Aryen* appeared during the uproar over the Dreyfus Affair, and his strident anti-Semitism alienated him from the French social science mainstream of Emile Durkheim.[11] Henceforth, Lapouge influenced only American hereditarians in the 1920s and Nazi Germans in the 1930s. Eugenicists around Grant invited Lapouge to join their Galton Society in 1920 and to present a paper at the highly publicized Second Eugenics Conference at the American Museum of Natural History in 1921. Even Margaret Sanger, the much admired feminist advocate of birth control, extended a hand by inviting Lapouge to participate in the Sixth International Birth Control Conference in New York in 1925.[12] Lapouge, in turn, arranged the French publication of Grant's *Passing of the Great Race*. *Le Déclin de la grande race*, published in 1926 and featuring a long introduction by Lapouge, flopped. Of the 2,000 copies printed, a mere 1,000 were sold. Only in Nazi Germany did Lapouge remain an intellectual hero. German schools used selections of his and Gobineau's work as readings in the French language. *L'Aryen* came out in a German edition as late as 1939.

No wonder Hitler's Nazis admired *L'Aryen*. It contained, as a sum-

---

*The *agrégation* is a French postcollegiate qualification for secondary school and college teaching. Its difficulty and prestige vary by field, from the equivalent of an American master's degree to the equivalent of an American doctorate.

mation, a long section on "the Jew" as the Aryan's primary competitor for world domination. (Lapouge did not envision competition from people of color as much of a problem. Perhaps in the distant future the Japanese and the Negroes of the United States and the Caribbean might constitute a danger, but not very soon.)[13] These seventeen pages on the Jewish menace repeat every anti-Semitic canard: Jews are smart and have bamboozled the ignorant brachy-brown masses with tales of democracy; Jews are a bastard population; Jews have chased out the Nordics; Jews are specialized for parasitism and incapable of productive work; Jews lack military spirit, etc., etc., etc. Page after page of Lapouge's calumny ends with the defeat of Jewish domination, for, he maintains, Jews have no gift for politics; in any event, increasing numbers are converting to Christianity.

Ultimately for Lapouge as for Grant, brachycephalic Alpines pose the biggest problem because they multiply rapidly, "covering the earth with their docile and mediocre posterity."[14] In the United States, a toxic mix of Lapougian anthroposociology, degenerate-family studies, and attacks on the Jews came together in the circle of Madison Grant.

Grant pretended that his science would stand the tests of time, but in practice *The Passing of the Great Race* had to be revised in successive editions to adjust to the facts of the First World War. The 1918 edition toned down the original's admiration of Teutons and corrected Grant's confusion over which numbers in the cephalic index are brachycephalic and which dolichocephalic. Anti-German sentiment also encouraged Grant to alter Ripley's terminology.[15] Ripley had called his three European races Teutonic, Alpine, and Mediterranean. In the midst of a conflict pitting Americans against Germans, Grant replaced Teutonic with Nordic, further muddying the racial identity of Germans.*

This question of German racial identity divided two of Grant's main European influences, Houston Stewart Chamberlain and Lapouge, both future Nazi racial godfathers. Originally from England but settled in Germany, Chamberlain was married to the daughter of the nationalist

---

* The French classifier of races Joseph Deniker used "Nordic." Grant would have been aware of Deniker's work, well respected in Europe but not well known in the United States.

composer Richard Wagner. In his Teutonist, anti-Semitic jeremiad, *Die Grundlagen des neunzehnten Jahrhunderts* (*The Foundations of the Nineteenth Century*) of 1899, Chamberlain praised Germans, ancient and modern.* Dispensing with science to prove Nordic superiority, Chamberlain argued that all the great men of history, including Jesus, were actually Nordic. Of a less mystical and Pan-German *völkisch* turn of mind than Chamberlain, Lapouge put his faith in the science of the cephalic index, even though his theories led him into a morass of measurements that, amazingly, racial science accepted without a qualm.

Whereas Chamberlain adored all Germans, Lapouge prized the dolichocephalic, blond Nordic he called *Homo Europæus*, who was hardly the same as modern Germans. Lapouge classified 70 percent of northern Germans as dolichocephalic and only 20 percent as pure *Homo Europæus*. In southern Germany, he counted 20 percent as dolichocephalic and only 3 percent as pure *Homo Europæus*. The rest were hopelessly brachycephalic Alpines. Only a few dolicho-blonds still existed in France, he lamented, while—thank heaven—Americans were as Nordic as northern Germans.[16†] This was supposed to be bad for the French but good for Americans, since Alpines were acquiring a mean reputation.

Grant belonged to the side that made Germans more Alpine than Teutonic or Nordic. For Grant, moderns and ancients were entirely separate populations. Just as modern Greeks were said not to have descended from beautiful ancient Greeks and modern Italians supposedly bore little relationship to imperial ancient Romans, anthroposociologists denied modern Germans any claim to the virtues of "the ancient Teutonic tribes." This rendered German claims to Teutonic racial identity "one of their [modern Germans'] most grandiose pretensions."[17] Adopting the long-standing assumption that Alpines were slavish but brutal peasants,

---

* *The Foundations of the Nineteenth Century* achieved broad popular and critical success, going into three editions in its first year and selling some 100,000 copies by the outbreak of the war. The editor of the *Atlantic Monthly*, Albert Schweitzer, George Bernard Shaw, and many other intellectuals lavished praise on Chamberlain's book. Despite Chamberlain's belief that Germanic greatness required no supposedly scientific proof, Shaw called it "a masterpiece of really scientific history."

†The English topped Lapouge's chart with 80 percent dolichocephalic and 25 percent pure *Homo Europæus*. Lapouge considered France "denordicized" after the French Revolution's uprising of the servile, brachycephalic, Alpine masses. According to this theory, the revolution killed off the aristocracy, members of the Nordic race, and doomed France to mediocrity.

Grant was going along with prevailing racist orthodoxy to explain how Germans could commit war crimes such as the "rape of Belgium."*
The answer: Germany was no longer Nordic, but Alpine. Preserving their ideal of Teutons as a progressive and intelligent race, racists redefined Alpines. Unlike the docile, peasant sluggards of old, Alpines now emerged as inherently vicious rapists. This supposed change in German race temperament was thought to date back to the seventeenth century. According to Madison Grant, the Thirty Years' War killed off Germany's "finest manhood . . . the big blond fighting man." That generation's bloodletting created a population vacuum, which inferior Alpines, "Wendish and the Polish types," rushed in to fill.[18]

What, then, were racial theorists to say about German Americans, who were fast gaining American "old stock" identity? Between 1900 and 1920, Germans never exceeded 4 percent of immigrants to the United States, and their political profile remained low. When German Americans did not rally to Germany's side in 1914, and the United States entered the war against Germany in 1917, German American newspapers and associations proclaimed their pro-American, anti-German loyalty.[19]

Even so, during a late 1917–early 1918 bout of anti-German sentiment, German Americans endured a good deal of harassment. Localities and states banned use of the German language, local vigilante groups burned German books, and a German immigrant was lynched in Illinois in 1918. In response to these attacks, many German American newspapers shut down, and churches began to conduct services exclusively in English. By the war's end, German American institutions had fallen drastically in number and importance, furthering assimilation.[20] Germans, whether in Germany or in the United States, did not hold the attention of patrician American racists, who preferred their own version of class analysis.

---

*French anthropologists like Jean-Louis-Armand de Quatrefages and like-minded Americans envisioned fundamental changes in the population of Germany since the Middle Ages. W. S. Sadler—a health advocate, Seventh-Day Adventist, and cranky Chicago psychiatrist who had studied in Vienna with Sigmund Freud and Alfred Adler—adopted this view in *Long Heads and Round Heads, or What's the Matter with Germany* (1918). The infusion of round-headed Alpines into Germany changed the racial balance and provides "the real explanation of the unparalleled brutality, the shocking atrocities, and otherwise inexplicably barbarous behavior of the German armies in the present European conflict."

•

LIKE SO many hereditarians in this long and dour story, Lothrop Stoddard (1883–1950) was of old New England stock, apparently sharing an ancestor with the Reverend Jonathan Edwards of Northampton, Massachusetts. After a period of study in Dresden, Stoddard graduated from Harvard, read law at Columbia, and then left the legal profession to earn a Ph.D. in history at Harvard. Early on, Stoddard's instincts warned against the threat posed by people of color. Houghton Mifflin published his Ph.D. dissertation in 1914 as *The French Revolution in San Domingo*, a work that obsessively chronicles the birth of independent black and brown Haiti by dint of a massacre of all but a score of its whites.[21] Stoddard became Madison Grant's protégé in eugenics, and, in turn, Grant wrote the introduction to Stoddard's first widely read book, *The Rising Tide of Color against White World Supremacy* (1920). At that point, the two focused their demographic anxieties somewhat differently; Grant worried far more about inferior European races, while Stoddard warned of a yellow peril.[22]

Next came Stoddard's frenzied contribution to white race theory—

really an attack on the working class—*The Revolt against Civilization: The Menace of the Under Man*, in 1922. *The Revolt Against Civilization* announces its target as communism—the movement of the proletariat—by placing the hammer and sickle on its cover. (See figure 23.1, *Revolt against Civilization* cover, 1922.) The title page announces the author's impeccable academic qualifications: "Lothrop Stoddard, A. M., Ph.D. (Harv.)." But open the book, and hordes of vicious, stupid, fast-breeding, Alpine brachy-browns

Fig. 23.1. Cover of Lothrop Stoddard, The Revolt against Civilization (1922).

```
Americans of social status (1)............I. Q. = 125
    "      "    "     "    (2)............I. Q. = 118
    "      "    "     "    (3)............I. Q. = 107
    "      "    "     "    (4)............I. Q. =  92
All Americans grouped together..........I. Q. = 106
Italians...............................I. Q. =  84
Colored................................I. Q. =  83
```

Fig. 23.2. IQ results by class and race, in Lothrop Stoddard,
The Revolt against Civilization (1922).

pour out of Stoddard's mishmash of degenerate-families-Jews-Bolshe-
vism-intelligence-test hereditarianism.

Stoddard brings class into the picture, a category on a par with his
idea of race. On the authority of Goddard, Yerkes, and the Army IQ
tests, Stoddard declares intelligence to be "predetermined by heredity"
and race. Intelligence also accompanies class standing—the higher the
class, the higher the intelligence. Of course. In Stoddard's arrangement,
the classification of "Americans" excludes "Italians" and "Colored," two
catchall categories one IQ point apart.[23] (See figure 23.2, Stoddard's IQ
results by class and race.)

Stoddard agreed with Grant and the anthroposociologists on the
fundamentally determining role of heredity: "Racial impoverishment,"
according to Stoddard, is "irreparable."[24] His remedy: eugenic "race
cleansing," mentioned eight times in five pages, "race purification," and
"race perfecting," through sterilization of the "Under-Man."[25]

Nothing if not a vivid writer, Stoddard paints a cinematic word picture
of the feebleminded Juke-Kallikak-Polish-Russian-Jewish-French-Cana-
dian-mongrelized-Alpine Under-Man: the Under-Man is in "instinctive
and natural *revolt against civilization.*" The potential for revolt is permanent, but in normal conditions society restrains the Under-Man. Still,
"he remains; he multiplies; he bides his time." In chaotic times such as the
postwar present, the Under-Man breaks out, wreaking havoc on civilization, as the Russian revolution proved. "The philosophy of the Under-Man
is to-day called Bolshevism," says Stoddard, and bolshevism is a product

Country of Birth		Country of Birth	
England...........	19.7	Ireland...........	4.1
Scotland..........	13.0	Turkey............	3.4
Holland...........	10.7	Austria...........	3.4
Canada............	10.5	Russia............	2.7
Germany...........	8.3	Greece............	2.1
Denmark...........	5.4	Italy.............	.8
Sweden............	4.3	Belgium...........	.8
Norway............	4.1	Poland............	.5

Fig. 23.3. "Table II: Percentage of Superiority," in Lothrop Stoddard,
The Revolt against Civilization (1922).

of "the Jewish mind."[26] Among white race chauvinists, the belief that Jews manipulate the ignorant working masses—whether Alpine, Under-Man, or colored—has proved extremely durable.*

For Stoddard, the Under-Man is stupid. Americans as a whole might have a mental age of less than fourteen (as Yerkes's Army IQ tests supposedly revealed), but he makes recent immigrants dumber still. Stoddard's tables rank immigrants from all parts of Europe to demonstrate their relative capacity. His table showing "Percentage of Superiority" puts the English at the top and the Poles at the bottom. (See figure 23.3, Stoddard, "Table II: Percentage of Superiority.") As though to prove Italians and Portuguese equally feebleminded, Stoddard compares unidentified IQ test results of American, northern European, Italian, and Portuguese immigrant schoolchildren.[27] (See figure 23.4, Stoddard, Comparative IQs.)

Charts, tables, and lurid prose carried Stoddard far in the early 1920s; Horace Lorimer's editorials in the *Saturday Evening Post* urged "every American" to read Grant and Stoddard "if he wishes to understand the full gravity of our immigration problems."[28] Lorimer backed up their warnings with Kenneth Roberts's illustrated articles.

Visual aids played a clinching role in hereditarian literature, starting

---

*The Turner Diaries (1978), the wildly popular, dystopian, white nationalist novel by William Luther Pierce, leader of the National Alliance, is set in a ruined world in which Jews have incited blacks into fiery rebellion.

American	I. Q. = 106
North European	I. Q. = 105
Italian	I. Q. = 84
Portuguese	I. Q. = 84

Fig. 23.4. *Comparative IQs, in Lothrop Stoddard,*
The Revolt against Civilization *(1922).*

with Dugdale's many pages of statistical tables in the 1870s. As print technology improved, magazines increased their use of illustration, with the *Saturday Evening Post* in the lead. Kenneth Roberts's anti-immigration articles in the *Post* exploited the power of images, showing potential immigrants, particularly nameless eastern European Jews, as inherently alien types, not named individuals. (See figure 23.5, Roberts, "A Polish Jew.")

To illustrate a contrast, hereditarians of self-proclaimed Nordic descent proffered their own images. William McDougall, an Englishman teaching at Harvard, asked in the title of his 1921 book *Is America Safe for Democracy?* Should the wrong kind of immigrants continue to pour into the United States? For McDougall, the answer to both questions was obviously no. As support of his contentions, he offered a photograph of his own five healthy, outdoorsy, dolicho-blond, and presumably tall children.[29] (See figure 23.6, McDougall's children.) They pose in profile, the better to show off the length of their heads. Clearly McDougall was doing his part to counter race suicide.

Fig. 23.5. *"A Polish Jew," in*
Kenneth Roberts, Why Europe
Leaves Home *(1922).*

Fig. 23.6. William McDougall's children, in William McDougall,
Is America Safe for Democracy? (1921).

•

As NOTED, the U.S. Congress had already legislated immigration restriction, and it returned to the issue in 1920, led by Madison Grant's colleague Harry H. Laughlin, head of the Eugenics Record Office's research program, who served Congress as an official "expert eugenics agent." Facing the prospect of renewed immigration, and following continual lobbying by Laughlin, Kenneth Roberts, and other race-minded restrictionists, Congress acted. The Emergency Immigration Act of 1921 limited each country's quota of immigrants to 3 percent of that country's population in the United States in 1910. But with anti-immigrant sentiment running high, temporary measures seemed inadequate to address a permanent threat. Congress began holding hearings on further restricting immigration.

The only countertestimony came at the behest of New York's liberal Jewish congressman Emanuel Celler, who represented a heavily immigrant district. And even that was rushed and qualified. Herbert S. Jennings, a biology professor at Johns Hopkins, had studied with Charles Davenport at Harvard and, as a graduate student, had even rented a room in Davenport's house. Repeatedly postponed until November 1923, Jennings's testimony on Laughlin's materials showed that the region sending the most people into insane asylums was not any place in southern or eastern Europe; it was Ireland—now nestled within the Nordic fold.[30]

Paying Jennings no heed, the immigration committee passed its draconian measure. The Immigration Restriction Act of 1924, aimed particularly at Italians and Jews, limited immigration to 2 percent of the 1890 census, which had been taken before the great southern and eastern European increase. These quotas remained in force until 1965. Looking back, the commissioner general of immigration credited Roberts's articles and books and the *Saturday Evening Post*'s coverage of the immigration issue as definitive in persuading Congress to curtail immigration.[31]

IN THE early 1920s Americans at the summit of American politics and industry popularized the science of white alien races. In "Whose Country Is This?" (1921), Vice President Calvin Coolidge spoke to readers of *Good Housekeeping*—the most popular American women's magazine in the era—warning that the United States must allow only the right sort of immigrant in, one with "a capacity for assimilation" to the America of the Pilgrims, Plymouth Rock, Harvard College. The wrong sort, who comes expressly to "tear down," must be barred by limitations according to "racial tradition or a national experience." Coolidge mixes up races, nationalities, and politics in a manner thoroughly characteristic of the times, inveighing against racial "deterioration" from the mixing of peoples of divergent races, that is, Italians and Jews: "we must face the situation unflinchingly . . . [not be] so sentimental. . . . There are racial considerations too grave to be brushed aside for any sentimental reasons."[32] In October of the following year, President Warren G. Harding recommended Stoddard's *Rising Tide of Color* by name in a speech, bolstering its esteem.

The *Saturday Evening Post* editor George Horace Lorimer had already been pushing the work of Madison Grant and Lothrop Stoddard and publishing Kenneth Roberts's reports on immigration as a national catastrophe. In 1924 Lorimer upped the ante with a series of articles on new immigrants from Europe by Stoddard, who wrapped himself in the mantle of science by importing entire hunks of Grant's *Passing of the Great Race*, complete with Ripley's photos of Nordic, Alpine, and Mediterranean racial types, cephalic indices, and Grant's ridiculous maps of the European races, showing Germany with alternating Nordic and

Alpine stripes. Stoddard located "the racial factor" as the root cause "of the world's problems."[33] "Racial" as in Europeans and Japanese. Building on this published onslaught of Nordic chauvinism, real life added the specter of a newly invigorated Ku Klux Klan.

The original Ku Klux Klan, founded after the Civil War as an antiblack, anti-Republican militia, had withered during Reconstruction under federal antiterrorist prosecution. However, the hysteria of the First World War years gave it a new foundation in 1915 on Stone Mountain, Georgia. This new Klan of the 1920s cast a wider net than the old, no longer limiting its attacks to black people with political ambitions. In the 1920s its five million members—spread from Maine to Oregon and from Indiana to Florida—took out after "Katholics, Kikes, and Koloreds," or, less poetically and more accurately, after Catholics, Jews, black people, foreigners, organized labor, and the odd loose woman.[34] In Tulsa, Oklahoma, in 1921 police and sheriff's deputies joined Klansmen in a pogrom against African Americans, destroying homes, businesses, and lives in an attack hardly mourned as an assault on Americans. It was as though black Americans constituted some kind of alien race living outside the category of Americans. Thinking along Klan lines was just that widespread.

Klansmen came very close to taking over the Democratic Party in the ten-day-long Democratic presidential nominating convention in New York City in 1924. With Governor Alfred E. Smith of New York, a Catholic grandson of immigrants, one of the two most likely nominees (the other was Woodrow Wilson's son-in-law, the Georgian William McAdoo), anti-Catholic, pro-Klan delegates blocked the incorporation of an anti-Klan plank in the party platform.* McAdoo forces fought the anti-Klan plank with the support of William Jennings Bryan, three-

---

* The defeated anti-Klan plank read,

> We condemn, as opposed to the genesis of free government, secret political societies of any kind whatsoever, wherever any such society undertakes to destroy free political action and fosters racial and religious hatreds.
> We denounce its activities as contravening the spirit, if not the letter of the Constitution, and as a pregnant menace to the perpetuity of American institutions.
> We declare that no member of such a society can justly claim to be a disciple of Thomas Jefferson.
> We pledge the Democratic Party to oppose the activities of the Ku Klux Klan, or any similar organization which undertakes to control or interfere with free political action or due process of law.

time Democratic presidential candidate, a fight that included Bryan's kneeling in prayer for unity on the convention floor.[35] By the end, a *New York Times* editorial lamented, "The Southern States have lifted up their hand against Governor Smith not on personal but on religious grounds. . . . They are against him simply and solely because he is a Catholic, and because the Klan has made itself such a political power in their States that they dare not go against its command to exclude Catholics from public office in the United States."[36] The following year witnessed the spectacle of thousands of Klansmen in full hooded regalia marching down Pennsylvania Avenue in Washington, D.C.

For Coolidge, Harding, and others of their ilk, race and nation equaled political ideology, with the right races and nations assimilating into middle-class, Anglo-Saxon America, and the alien races and nations kicking up sand in their demands for workers' rights. Coolidge extended the peril across the generations: "The unassimilated alien child menaces our children" just as surely "as the alien industrial worker . . . menaces our industry."[37] From father to son and mother to daughter, alien races remained alien.

THE EARLY 1920s also witnessed the most brazen anti-Semitic publications, coming not from some weird fringe but from Henry Ford, the heroic symbol of American industry and an admirer of Ralph Waldo Emerson's *English Traits*.[38] Ford embodied twentieth-century American technological progress as the "Flivver King," who was mass-producing Model T automobiles for the great American middle class. By the end of 1913, his Dearborn, Michigan, assembly line had produced 500,000 cars.[39] A self-proclaimed pacifist, Ford had attempted to end the war by sponsoring a hastily organized "peace ship" to Europe in 1915.[40] By then he had also embraced a notion gaining credence in Europe, the belief that "the Jew" had caused the war. That conviction moved Ford to create a means of publicizing this idea in the form of a newspaper that came in every new Model T automobile.

Ford's *Dearborn Independent* played a new role in American culture by spewing anti-Semitism and putting notoriously false documents into international circulation. In an era of mounting race talk,

Henry Ford domesticated European anti-Semitism's "the international Jew" in a manner worthy of Georges Vacher de Lapouge's anthroposociology, even adding an English fillip. The ghostwriter of "Mr. Ford's Own Page," one W. J. Cameron, purveyed the beliefs of an obscure but persistent current in English and American religion, Anglo-Israelitsm. According to this sect, Anglo-Saxons were the real descendants of the Ten Lost Tribes of Israel, and England and the United States were the real Holy Land. This logic made Anglo-Saxons into the chosen people and "Modern Hebrews" into impostors. Jesus was not really Jewish; in fact, he was the Nordic ancestor of modern Germans, Scandinavians, and English people.[41] Ford's own obsessions imagined the Jews less as impostors than as the international financiers he believed to be building up the labor unions he hated in order to reduce competition and raise prices. That this made no sense whatever did not give him pause.[42]

The *Dearborn Independent* ran its first series of anti-Semitic articles in 1920 and 1921. These pieces, collected in four volumes as *The International Jew: The World's Foremost Problem* (1920–22), circulated internationally and, with German support, were translated into sixteen languages. The *Dearborn Independent* created additional mischief by publishing the fraudulent *Protocols of the Learned Elders of Zion*. Originally published in Russia in 1917, this document was purported to be the minutes of a secret 1897 meeting of Jewish leaders planning to take over the world. The *Dearborn Independent* also gave an American twist to the European anthroposociological theory that the Jews had incited dumb Alpines into committing atrocities during the war. For Ford, the Jews were committing yet another crime by duping southern black people into migrating out of the South into his territory in the North.[43] This new twist to the politics of race would soon bear fruit in the shape of changing definitions of race. For the time being, though, the "racial problem" still meant immigrants from southern and eastern Europe— white people.

24

REFUTING RACIAL SCIENCE

R acial science roared on for decades in the United States, and it might have continued much longer but for European events. Not until Nazi Germany awakened American geneticists and social scientists to the import of their scholarship did many realize that what called itself racial *science* was merely prejudice. The passing from the scene of key figures also vitiated hereditarianism. George Horace Lorimer, editor of the *Saturday Evening Post*, and Madison Grant, the eugenics mogul, both died in 1937. More important, figures with real scholarly bona fides started speaking up loud enough to be heard.

Not that dissent had been lacking entirely. The reassessment had begun quietly as early as the First World War, when a cadre of Columbia University geneticists resigned from the prime eugenics organization, still called the American Breeders' Association. In 1921 Franz Boas had published an article in the *Yale Review* questioning the racial interpretation of Army IQ tests, and in 1922 Walter Lippmann in the *New Republic* had denounced mental testers' claim to measure permanent, intrinsic intelligence. That kind of mental testing, he wrote, "has no more scientific foundation than a hundred other fads, vitamins and glands and amateur psychoanalysis and correspondence courses in will power, and it will pass with them into that limbo where phrenology and palmistry and characterology and the other Babu sciences are to be found."[1]

But hard-minded IQ testers hung on, dismissing such objections as mere emotion and claiming that no Jewish critic could think objectively about racial matters.[2] As noted earlier, the Johns Hopkins professor Herbert Jennings's scrutiny of the anti-immigration material of the House Immigration and Naturalization Committee revealed that data used to discredit immigrants from southern or eastern Europe had been misinterpreted and that, among immigrants, the Irish (now considered good Nordic "old immigrants") were most likely to land in institutions. This was not what the House committee wanted to hear, and it buried these findings. Jennings published his views in two journals with limited circulation: the *Survey*, the journal of social and charity workers, and *Science*, which, was aimed at academicians. "It is particularly in connection with racial questions in man that there has been a great throwing about of false biology," he concluded quietly.[3]

African American social scientists also attacked Carl Brigham's classification of soldiers' test scores by race and nation. Horace Mann Bond, director of the School of Education at Langston University, a predominately black institution in Oklahoma, was a doctoral student of the distinguished Chicago sociologist Robert Park. In 1924 Bond refuted Brigham's reasoning in the *Crisis*, the organ of the National Association for the Advancement of Colored People (edited by W. E. B. Du Bois), by showing that test scores correlated with funding for education. The key to test scores, therefore, lay not in race but in state policy, that is, in the environment.[4] In *Opportunity*, the organ of the National Urban League, Bond added that if Brigham were correct that Nordics were smartest, then men from the South "with the purest racial stock of the so-called Nordic branch now existent in America" should have scored highest.* Instead, white southerners achieved a mental age of only twelve and a half, a year less than the overall national average.[5]

Criticism of racial science continued with an article in the November 1927 issue of *American Mercury* by Raymond Pearl, a professor of biometry and vital statistics at Johns Hopkins. Pearl called eugenics "a mingled mess of ill-grounded and uncritical sociology, economics,

---

*The National Urban League had been founded by an interracial group of social workers and philanthropists in 1911 to find jobs and housing for black southerners migrating to the North.

anthropology, and politics, full of emotional appeals to class and race prejudices, solemnly put forth as science, and unfortunately accepted as such by the general public."[6] Another change was in the air of academia. Earlier studies had taken for granted the factual existence of races (as in "races of Europe"). Therefore, studies of racial mental differences were considered interesting as scientific research topics that could be studied objectively. But by the late 1920s psychology and sociology had begun focusing on the subjective nature of racial differences in society. Soon race prejudice became a subject worth analyzing.[7] Here Robert Park, Bond's dissertation adviser, pioneered. Park's classic 1928 essay, "Human Migration and the Marginal Man," emphatically separated race from culture. The migrant was to be seen as a person emancipated, enlightened, and even cosmopolitan. Recent immigrants to the United States were creating, not injuring, civilization. This migrant might be a man living "on the margin of two cultures and two societies, which never completely interpenetrated and fused." But that was a good thing. Take as an example an emancipated Jew like the Berlin-born, South Carolina–raised novelist and critic Ludwig Lewisohn, who had published his autobiography *Up Stream: An American Chronicle* in 1922. For Park, Lewisohn bridged two cultures, offering the best example of "the processes of civilization and progress."[8] Here notions of change and promise replaced the frozen biological determinism of eugenics. E. A. Ross, who had trashed immigrants before the war, could by 1936 write, "*Difference of race* means far less to me now than it once did."[9] Even Vineland's Henry H. Goddard was having second thoughts. Perhaps he had put too much faith in intelligence tests. In a 1927 article for *Scientific Monthly* he admitted that his feebleminded students who had tested badly should be allowed to live in the general population, even to have children.[10]

No voice for common sense spoke louder than that of Franz Boas, by the 1920s an elder statesman in his sixties who had been in the United States forty years. When he arrived in 1887, anthropology had been dominated by Mayflower gentlemen in museums stockpiling ancient bones and artifacts. Boas had gone forward to train most mid-twentieth-century leaders of the field, many immigrant-descended Ph.D.s teaching in universities just at the point when anthropology was delivering new scientific truths about race. For Boas, scientific racism, especially the supposedly premier test of race, had never seemed sound. The unchanging cephalic index, he pointed out, could, in fact, change quite quickly as a person's environment changed. It was culture that mattered, and culture changed by generation. Culture, race, and language were three independent—and equal—qualities. Boas never gave up on the idea of race, but he continually opposed racism.[11]

By the early 1920s Alfred L. Kroeber, a former Boas student, now a professor at the University of California at Berkeley, pointed out that northern blacks scored higher than southern whites on the Army IQ tests.[12] Another Boas student, Otto Klineberg (1899–1992), pressed the investigation in two important directions.

The son of immigrants to Canada, Klineberg held a B.A. in philosophy from McGill, an M.A. in psychology from Harvard, an M.D. from McGill, and a Ph.D. in psychology from Columbia. Having entered the Boas circle in 1926, Klineberg soon realized, as did the anthropologists, that human behavior could not be abstracted from its cultural context. Throughout a long life of international experience—in his research, in UNESCO, and through professorships in Brazil and France—Klineberg continued to study racial differences, prejudices, and discrimination.[13]

After discovering disparities in test scores between northwestern Kwakiutl Indians who lived on the reservation and those who lived off it, Klineberg tested Carl C. Brigham's correlations in *A Study of American Intelligence* (1924) between race and IQ in Europe. In Italy, France, and Germany in the mid-1920s, he found no differences in the performance of Mediterraneans, Alpines, and Nordics.[14] Returning to the United States in 1929, Klineberg was delighted to meet Brigham at a psychological meeting and eager to confront the older scholar: "I told him how pleased I was to meet him, since I had just completed research related to his study. His reaction rather took the wind out of my sails. 'Oh,' he said, 'I don't stand by a word of that book.' "[15]

Indeed, in 1930 Brigham published an article retreating from the claim that test scores represented "a single unitary thing" called "intelligence."* Psychologists claiming to test "intelligence," Brigham conceded, "have been guilty of a *naming fallacy*" (Brigham's emphasis). Taking aim at his own book, *A Study of American Intelligence*, he called his methods "absurd," adding that his and Yerkes's methodology "with its entire hypothetical superstructure of racial differences collapses completely." Looking back at his book, Brigham called it "one of the most pretentious of these comparative racial studies" and pronounced it "without foundation."[16] But the restricted circulation of Brigham's article meant that *A Study of American Intelligence* carried on as a racist authority for many more years.

Klineberg's second major publication dealt another blow to racial science. Yerkes and the mental testers of the 1910s and 1920s had always claimed to test innate intelligence, not the influence of schooling or environment.† Northern black men scored higher than southern black men, and the longer black men had lived outside the South, the higher their scores. When some northern black men scored higher than southern white men, what might that portend?‡

More and more anthropologists used Klineberg's analysis to high-

---

* One of Brigham's most trenchant academic critics was Truman Lee Kelley, a professor of statistics and education at Stanford, where he was a colleague of Louis Terman, one of the more enthusiastic testers of the era. Kelley's *Interpretation of Educational Measurement* (1927) criticized the technique of comparing tests administered to a large population of whites lacking "racial homogeneity" and then lumping the results of several different tests together to produce a single set of grades. Kelley also questioned the prevalence of scores of zero or 100.

† Race theorists also adopted the European anthroposociologists' theory that "selective" migration explained differences between head shapes in the country and those in the city—that superior, long-headed Europeans chose to migrate out of the country, leaving broad-headed laggards. Although Boas had demonstrated the malleability of head shape, the idea of selective migration held on into the 1920s. When the Army IQ tests showed that African Americans in cities and in the North scored higher than African Americans in the country and in the South, race theorists explained that the smarter ones—or those with more "white blood"—migrated out of the South and out of the countryside. Klineberg's results in his *Negro Intelligence and Selective Migration* (1935) disproved both contentions, effectively knocking the selective migration theory into the dustbin.

‡ Klineberg's table of IQ scores by race and region: median scores *whites:* Mississippi (41.25); Kentucky (41.50); Arkansas (41.55); Georgia (42.12); median scores *negroes:* Pennsylvania (42.00); New York (45.02); Illinois (47.35); Ohio (49.50).

Fig. 24.1. Ruth Fulton Benedict.

light the role of environment in intelligence and to weaken the biological determinism of racial science as applied also to non-blacks. Culture was gaining on race, sped along by German Nazi aggression. Then along came another student of Franz Boas.

THE "FIRST Child" of her mother's Vassar College class of 1885, Ruth Fulton Benedict (1887–1948) was born in New York City to a life that promised upper-class ease. (See figure 24.1, Ruth Benedict.) Her father was a doctor, and both parents were Mayflower descendants. However, her father's death when she was not quite two plunged her mother into financial distress and a long bereavement. Then a childhood bout of measles rendered Ruth partially deaf.

Frequent moves followed in pursuit of paying employment for her mother, tantrums, and depressions blighted young Ruth Fulton's childhood. Around 1900 the family ended up in Buffalo, where her mother worked as the city librarian, and Ruth and her younger sister, Margery, attended a tony Episcopal private school on scholarships. In the fall of 1905, thanks to the charity of strangers, the two sisters entered Vassar. One of the prestigious Seven Sisters eastern women's colleges, Vassar prided itself on developing both brain and bosom.[17] Certainly Ruth had plenty of the former; she and her sister followed their mother into Phi Beta Kappa. An English major, she continued to write and publish poetry for several more decades.*

After graduating in 1909, Ruth Fulton embarked on the obligatory

---

* During the 1920s, before she gained a permanent appointment in Columbia's anthropology department, Benedict published poetry under the pseudonym Anne Singleton, but she set the pseudonym aside in the 1930s.

upper-class European tour, which included three months in Germany, two of them in Dresden.[18] Returning to Buffalo, she joined the local Charity Organization Society as a "friendly visitor" to Polish and Italian families, teaching them "American behavior." At twenty-four, realizing the arrogance and futility of this work, she joined her younger sister, now married to a minister, in Pasadena, California, and taught in girls' high schools for two years.[19] Teaching, too, however, failed to fulfill her intellectually or emotionally. At this point, Stanley Rossiter Benedict, the brother of one of her Vassar classmates, was courting her aggressively. They married in 1914.

Three years older than his wife and another Mayflower descendant, Stanley Benedict had earned a Ph.D. in biochemistry from Yale in 1908. He was a single-minded, persistent, and rigid man who opposed her working outside their home. On vacations at Lake Winnipesaukee, in New Hampshire, Stanley was wont to race about in a motorboat; Ruth preferred paddling a canoe.[20] Nor did home life suit her. Sitting about their suburban home while he commuted to Cornell Medical School in New York City, she wrote biographies of feminist authors that went nowhere. Houghton Mifflin's rejection of her life of Mary Wollstonecraft in 1919 only steeled her resolve for further study, first a class with the philosopher John Dewey at Columbia, then more at the fledgling New School for Social Research.

At the New School, Benedict studied gender in many different cultures with the wealthy and well-connected anthropologist Elsie Clews Parsons, a Columbia Ph.D. and a member of the Boas circle. Benedict's abilities impressed Parsons, and she and another of Benedict's New School instructors took her to meet Boas. Waiving the regular requirements, he admitted Benedict into Columbia's Ph.D. program in anthropology during the spring of 1921. Benedict was thirty-three; Boas, sixty-three.[21] The two remained close collaborators, running the Columbia Department of Anthropology together until his (forced) retirement in 1936.

By the fall of 1922, Benedict was serving as Boas's teaching assistant, often guiding Barnard undergraduates around the American Museum of Natural History. One such student was Margaret Mead (1901–78), who had moved to New York City to be near her fiancé, a student at the Union Theological Seminary. But Benedict's enthusiasm for anthropology galvanized Mead. She became Mead's mentor, and she and Boas persuaded Mead to switch from psychology to anthropology for graduate school, to do work "that matters." The Benedict-Mead relationship steadily deepened, moving from teacher-student to colleague-colleague to friends, lovers, and lifelong intellectual collaborators. When Mead's daughter was born in December 1939, Benedict was in California writing her book on race and had been separated from her husband for nine years. She crocheted booties and sent them to the baby.[22] The bond between Mead and Benedict even outlasted Benedict's death in 1948.[23] Mead served as Benedict's literary executor and published two books about her.[24]

Looking back, Mead recalled Benedict as a "very shy, almost distrait [absentminded], middle-aged woman [she was thirty-four years old] whose fine, mouse-colored hair never stayed quite pinned up. Week after week she wore a very prosaic hat and the same drab dress. . . . She stammered a little when she talked with us and sometimes blushed scarlet."[25] Benedict always thought of herself as a misfit but also suspected that her deviance nourished her intellectual creativity.[26] As Mead reports in her autobiography, *Blackberry Winter: My Earlier Years*, Benedict was subject to depressions and migraines. She "expected the worst from people and steeled herself against it."[27]

And Benedict was indeed a misfit, but not one of her own making. There was the question of gender: here was a Columbia professor with a Columbia doctorate who was not appointed assistant professor until 1931, after a dozen years of teaching, advising dissertations, and publishing a best-selling book. She had also served as editor of the *Journal of American Folklore* for seven years. In 1936 she finally rose to associate professor, but not to full professor until 1948, after being elected president of the American Anthropological Association.

Outside of Columbia, by contrast, Benedict reigned as a leader in her scholarly field and as the public face of anthropology. She wielded enormous power both across the United States and especially among New York's intelligentsia.[28] In the 1920s she had begun an active career explaining anthropology to non-anthropologists, publishing articles in the *Nation,* the *New Republic, American Mercury, Scribner's,* and *Harper's.* Mead saw her as anthropology's "press committee," a one-woman popularizing force.[29] No wonder she felt conflicted!

Actually, Mead arrived first. Fifteen years younger than Benedict, Mead jumped onto best-seller lists in 1928 with *Coming of Age in Samoa,* a study of women's adolescence stressing cooperation over competition, but also offering sexual titillation. Six years later, Benedict's first book, *Patterns of Culture,* also thrived, particularly after publication of a cheap paperback edition in 1946. By the 1980s it had sold nearly two million copies and been translated into twenty-one other languages. Even today, *Patterns of Culture* introduces anthropology to the lay public by touting the importance of culture over biology and of culture as learned behavior, as "personality writ big."

The book describes three cultures, the Zuni of the American Southwest, the Kwakiutl of the American Northwest, and the Dobu of the Pacific Islands. Borrowing terminology from Friedrich Nietzsche, Benedict labels the Zuni as serenely Apollonian; the Kwakiutl she saw as violently Dionysian; and the Dobu were just plain paranoid.* Starkly contrasting behaviors, Benedict divides these groups according to culture, not by race. This message, then, focuses on the possibility of change, for culture, not transmitted biologically, changes over time, while race presumably is a permanent condition. Intriguingly, however, Benedict could not escape her own class and culture. She slips phrases into *Patterns of Culture* that place herself and her presumptive readers squarely in the Nordic column. Arguing generally against race prejudice in her introductory pages, she deplores the drawing of "the so-called race line" against "our blood brothers the Irish." Across this imagined race line, French face off against Germans, "though in bodily form they alike belong to the Alpine sub-race."[30] Old habits of thought died hard, even within the Boas circle.

---

* Benedict pioneered the culture and personality school of anthropology. In *Patterns of Culture* she had used her own research on the Zuni, Boas's on the Kwakiutl, and Reo Fortune's on the Dobu. Fortune was Mead's second husband. Benedict got along well with all three of Mead's husbands.

During the 1930s Benedict did all the work of a senior scholar. She also ran the Columbia anthropology department, though without a title, since the university administration could not imagine a woman as departmental chair. Things worsened under Boas's replacement, Ralph Linton, who disliked Benedict and soured the department's atmosphere against her. (After she died, Linton flashed a Melanesian charm, bragging that he had used it to cause her death.)[31] Old, exhausted, and ill, Boas still came to the department once or twice a week, but events in Germany increasingly preoccupied him. At first Benedict deplored his giving up "science for good works," calling it a waste of scholarly energy. But as the Nazis stepped up their anti-Semitic persecution, she came to share Boas's distress and joined his antiracist activism.[32] Nazi violence awakened many an American intellectual, so Benedict's antiracist work stands for a gathering tendency among scholars. More and more, Nazi anti-Semitism wrenched them away from the idea of a Jewish race, and even from drawing racial lines among any Europeans and their progeny.

While on sabbatical in Pasadena in 1939, Benedict wrote *Race: Science and Politics* (1940), a book widely praised for its clear explanation of anthropology's thinking about race but ultimately confused and confusing. In the first edition, Benedict speaks as an anthropologist sorting out for laymen the differences between race and racism. "Race," Benedict explains on the foreword's first page, "is a matter for careful scientific study; Racism is an unproved assumption." The text carefully distinguishes hereditary, biological race from the learned behavior of culture and language. Culture does not depend on race, and Italians, Jews, and the British are not races. There is no such thing as Nordic civilization.[33]

Given the continuing allure of scientific racism, Benedict is presenting a useful summary. But *Race: Science and Politics* is very much of a piece with its time, a statement crafted in the long shadow of the anthroposociology of Georges Vacher de Lapouge—whom Benedict confronts by name on the first page of the main text—and totally in the thrall of cephalic indices, Nordics, Alpines, and Mediterraneans.[34] She was trying to dig out of a very deep race hole, and she could get only halfway into clarity, as befit the confusions of her era.

For all its fine intentions, this book contains predictable contradictions. As in the early twentieth-century ways of thinking about race, *Race: Science and Politics* hardly touches on non-Europeans. The "races" in question are mainly white, as though all Americans descended from Europeans and African Americans hardly counted. Benedict translates "white race" as *Nordics* and "other varieties" as "*Alpines, Mediterraneans.*" She says Europeans are too mixed to be separated by race, then continues to separate the three "subdivisions" of the Caucasian race as Nordic, Alpine, Mediterranean, as distinguished by hair texture, head form, skin pigment.

This echoes William Z. Ripley in 1899, but with a difference that poses a problem: Benedict admits that none of these traits actually correlates with these subdivisions. So Ripley's categories no longer apply. For Benedict, only three great races actually exist, "Caucasoid, Mongoloid, and Negroid." They are most "definite," but—oh-oh—Boas, she admits, has his doubts and sees just two: Mongoloid, which includes "Caucasic," and Negroid.[35] Later editions grew even murkier.

After the United States entered the war in December 1941, Benedict revised *Race* by taking nonwhites more fully into account. Now Benedict speaks as the citizen of a belligerent power whose allies include Asians and Africans.[36] Nazism has heightened her awareness of American racism, which she mentions in the foreword to the 1945 edition. By now "race" in her eyes includes African Americans as well as the descendants of Europeans.

In all three editions of *Race: Science and Politics*, Benedict speaks as a Mayflower descendant, a stance Boas had actually recommended in order to lend her book an aura of disinterested fairness. In 1940 she writes as "those of us who are members of the vaunted races and descendants of the American Revolution." In 1943 and 1945 she says, "We of the white race, we of the Nordic race, must make it clear that we do not want the kind of cheap and arrogant superiority the Racists promise us."[37] This assumed bond between author and readers harks back to the early 1900s, when New England ancestry was supposed to confer intellectual soundness and readers were thought to belong to the same elevated class. That would mean a narrower, rather than a wider, readership. With the war, however, widening the readership for antiracist thinking became more important.

Between new editions of *Race: Science and Politics,* Benedict collaborated with a Columbia colleague, Gene Weltfish, on a 32-page, ten-cent pamphlet, *The Races of Mankind* (1943). Aimed at schools, churches, YMCAs, and USOs, *Races of Mankind* denounces racial chauvinism, quoting both racists and antiracist experts and explaining that "no European is a pure anything" and that "Aryans, Jews, Italians are *not* races."

Describing the actual existence of race as a meaningful category of analysis, Benedict and Weltfish were not willing to go as far as the literary critic Jacques Barzun and the anthropologist Ashley Montague. In 1937 Barzun had published *Race: A Study in Superstition,* whose title says it all.* Montague's 1942 *Man's Most Dangerous Myth: The Fallacy of Race* called the idea of race "the witchcraft of our time."[38] Both these books sold well in multiple editions, but social scientists worldwide could not agree. (Even the antiracist UNESCO statement on race [1952] retained the notion that races actually do exist.)[39] Benedict and Weltfish were writing from within the scientific mainstream, confused as it was at the time.

For Benedict and Weltfish there were three and only three races: the Caucasian race (A), the Mongoloid race (B), and the Negroid race (C). Their map shows where these three races are located. (See figure 24.2, "Most people in the world have in-between-color skin.") The Caucasoids are in northwestern Europe (not Mediterranean Europe); the Mongoloids occupy a semicircle in eastern Asia (but not Southeast Asia, Siberia, or Mongolia); Negroids are grouped around the Bight of Benin (not the rest of northern, Saharan, southern, or eastern Africa). Everyone else, presumably, has "in-between-color skin." Attractive though it might be, this map leaves everything to be explained about race in America, where

---

* Barzun felt the need for a new edition in 1965 because "the idea it treats of, although repeatedly killed, is nevertheless undying." He deplored the endless measuring and ranking of races as a "waste of intellect."

Fig. 24.2. "Most people in the world have in-between-color skin,"
in Ruth Benedict and Gene Weltfish, Races of Mankind *(1943).*

people from four continents were having sex and producing American babies.[40]

As if the peoples of the Western Hemisphere did not exist and belonged to no races, the map omits them entirely. A further explanation does not help: "American Indians are Mongoloid, though they differ physically both among themselves and from the Mongols of China. The natives of Australia are sometimes called a fourth primary race. They are as hairy as Europeans, and yet they live in an area where other peoples have very little body hair."[41] These glaring contradictions existed beside the pamphlet's main points: "All Peoples Much the Same," "Customs Not Racial," "Character Not Inborn," "Civilization Not Caused by Race," and "Race Prejudice Not Inevitable." Today the contradictions would seem to consign Benedict and Weltfish to the dustbin of racism. But such a judgment is too hasty. Within the context of their times, their antiracist main points needed badly to be made and even raised some hackles.

Another main point—"What About Intelligence?"—created a brouhaha that got the pamphlet banned from USOs. To disprove the racial character of intelligence, Benedict and Weltfish include two pages from Otto Klineberg's work and a table showing the much higher IQ scores of northern black men compared with those of southern white men. The aim was to illustrate a lesson—the crucial influence of environment on intelligence.[42] But this lesson fared badly in Congress.

Representative Andrew J. May of Kentucky, chair of the House Military Affairs Committee, barred the pamphlet's distribution to the Army, because the Klineberg table assigned whites from his state of Kentucky lower scores than northern blacks. Here May spied "communistic" influence. But the publicity following his censorship made the pamphlet much more widely known. It sold almost a million copies in a decade and was translated into French, German, and Japanese and inspired a comic book, a little movie, and a children's book entitled *In Henry's Backyard* (1948). Benedict admitted not having enjoyed the work on the two books on race, for both had called for synthesis rather than original scholarship. But they nevertheless made her—a nonspecialist in this field—an authority on race in America along the lines of the economist William Z. Ripley almost half a century earlier.

Benedict's books were meant to deny scientific legitimacy to the "races of Europe," but other scholars still leaned the other way. In 1939, the Harvard anthropologist Carleton S. Coon (1904–81) published a successor volume to Ripley's classic. In 1934 Coon's former professor and now Harvard colleague Earnest Hooton had suggested an update, and the flattered Coon, then an assistant professor, took on the plum assignment after speaking with Ripley, who was still teaching economics at Harvard and up to his ears in analysis of railroads.[43]

It was a weird undertaking. Coon began by trivializing Ripley's taxonomy, dismissing him as "a lumper, not a splitter," and one with only three criteria: cephalic index, stature, and pigmentation. This would not do for a twentieth-century physical anthropologist like Coon. The task took five years, and when finally published in 1939, Coon's version of *Races of Europe* included a near-infinity of measurements and photographs of Europeans shown frontally and in profile, arrayed in categories called "Carpathian and Balkan Borreby-like types," "Upper Palaeolithic

Survivals in Ireland," "The Alpine Race in Germany," "Aberrant Alpine Forms in Western and Central Europe," "Long-Faced Mediterraneans of the Western Asiatic Highlands," etc., etc.

Coon's ideas about classification were more aesthetic than scientific, which he confessed in an anecdote about his rejection of one subject because the fellow did not look right. The person in question, a "consul of a European nation," had "hardly any chin." That would not do for the type he was supposed to represent. And so it went. Realizing that the book was ridiculous, Coon's publisher tried unsuccessfully to suppress it before publication. The book remains an embarrassing, old-timey artifact.[44]

AFTER ITS heyday among race theorists in the 1910s and 1920s, Anglo-Saxonism declined during the Great Depression and the Second World War. A new generation of social scientists had outgrown such blather on race. Now scholars were questioning the very meanings of any and all concepts of race and studying the troubling fact of racial prejudice.[45]* Ruth Benedict, along with Franz Boas and their like, were beginning to carry the day.

Both Boas and Benedict supported the Republican side in the Spanish Civil War, and they battled for academic freedom at Columbia in the late 1930s, where an association with the American Committee for Democracy and Intellectual Freedom, which Boas chaired, got them accused of harboring communist sympathies.[46] Boas died before Benedict, holding a glass of wine and a freshly lit cigarette in his hands. He was about to announce "a new theory of race" when he keeled over dead at lunch in the Columbia faculty club in 1942.

Benedict went on, using her knowledge of non-Western peoples in the Office of War Information during the Second World War, to explain foreign cultures to officials assigned to deal with them when peace returned. Her study of Japan led to *The Chrysanthemum and the Sword,*

---

* In 1946 the *Annals of the Academy of Political and Social Science*, which had published Francis A. Walker and E. A. Ross's anti-immigrant screeds, devoted the whole issue of March 1946 to the topic "Controlling Group Prejudice."

a book analyzing Japanese culture that became her third best seller, in 1946. She died of a heart attack right at the start of the academic year in September 1948.

Benedict's role had been significant in popularizing new scientific views of race, altering, if not obliterating, the notion that Europeans belonged to different races and that the children of European immigrants posed insurmountable social problems. Hers was a critical transition away from "the races of Europe," reinforced by fundamental changes in American life.

25

A NEW WHITE RACE POLITICS

Though gratifyingly sensible, the fact that scholars changed their minds about the number of white races did not transform society as a whole. While anthropologists like Ruth Benedict were modifying the science of race, changes were occurring outside the ivory tower, even in the race-obsessed twenties. After publication of Henry Ford's second "international Jew" article in 1920, for instance, Louis Marshall, a prominent German Jewish lawyer in New York, seconded by other well-educated, well-respected German Jews, telegraphed Ford that his articles constituted libel.[1] The American Jewish Committee circulated a pamphlet by Marshall in November 1920 refuting Ford's allegations. The English-born socialist John Spargo published a book-length refutation, *The Jew and American Ideals*, and a statement in newspapers across the country in January 1921. Under the banner "President Wilson Heads Protest against Anti-Semitism," a shining list of Americans signed their names: William Jennings Bryan, Clarence Darrow, W. E. B. Du Bois, the settlement movement leader Jane Addams, the Columbia historian Charles A. Beard, the muckraking journalist Ida Tarbell, the Stanford University president David Starr Jordan, and many others.[2]

Even more important, immigrants and their children were speaking for themselves, telling stories of their transit from outsider to American in picturesque terms. Mary Antin's *The Promised Land*

(1912) and Abraham Cahan's *The Rise of David Levinsky* (1917) came early. Many other autobiographies humanizing immigrants followed, including Samuel Ornitz's *Haunch, Paunch and Jowl* (1923) and Anzia Yezierska's *The Bread Givers* (1925). True, collegiate English departments were still loath to invite American writing of any sort into the canon of English literature, and these immigrants' works did remain marginal as "minority" literature. But popular culture knew no such divide. America's best-known immigrant in the mid-1920s was a movie star, Rodolfo Valentino. Though Valentino, born in the southern Italian Puglia region, the home of many an immigrant to the United States at the turn of the century, died at thirty-one in 1926, he remains an iconic figure.

Even in politics, a silver lining peeped through. While a Democratic Party fight over the 1924 anti-Klan plank had been long and hard, many a delegate, even from the South, had proved ready to denounce the Klan by name. The effort had failed, but by only one vote. The 1920 Democratic candidate for vice president, Franklin Roosevelt of New York, had coordinated the Smith forces, struggling about the floor of Madison Square Garden on crutches after a bout with polio. Four years later, Democrats did nominate the Catholic Al Smith. Fiction, as we have seen, also faced the question of "alien races," as in F. Scott Fitzgerald's *The Great Gatsby*.

> "Civilization's going to pieces," broke out Tom violently. "I've gotten to be a terrible pessimist about things. Have you read *The Rise of the Colored Empires* by this man Goddard?"
>
> "Why no," I answered, rather surprised by his tone.
>
> "Well, it's a fine book, and everybody ought to read it. The idea is if we don't look out the white race will be—will be utterly submerged. It's all scientific stuff; it's been proved."
>
> "Tom's getting very profound," said Daisy, with an expression of unthoughtful sadness. "He reads deep books with long words in them. What was that word we——"

"Well, these books are all scientific," insisted Tom, glancing at her impatiently. "This fellow has worked out the whole thing. It's up to us, who are the dominant race, to watch out or these other races will have control of things."

"We've got to beat them down," whispered Daisy, winking ferociously toward the fervent sun. . . .

"This idea is that we're Nordics. I am, and you are, and you are, and——" After an infinitesimal hesitation he included Daisy with a slight nod, and she winked at me again. "——And we've produced all the things that go to make civilization—oh, science and art, and all that. Do you see?"[3]

But Tom Buchanan is no hero. He is nothing but a boor whose Nordic chauvinism signals his boorishness. The year after Lothrop Stoddard's appearance in *The Great Gatsby* as "this man Goddard," Fitzgerald's friend and rival Ernest Hemingway published a novella entitled *The Torrents of Spring: A Romantic Novel in Honor of the Passing of a Great Race*, quoting the title of Madison Grant's book. But once again the meaning pokes fun, for the quotation appears as parody. Race hysteria has become the sign of the weak-minded. Or of hypocrites.

Racists did their part to bring themselves down. David Stephenson, grand dragon of the Ku Klux Klan so powerful in Indiana, kidnapped and raped a white schoolteacher in 1925, mauling her to death—this atrocity after the Klan had made its reputation by attacking race mixing, loose women, Catholics, and Jews in a self-proclaimed moral crusade. Stephenson went to prison, and the Klan began to sputter out, weakened by increasingly effective opposition by antidiscrimination organizations like the Anti-Defamation League and the National Association for the Advancement of Colored People, creations of the same decade that had seen the refounding of the Klan.* The crisis of the Great Depression of the 1930s shook things up even more.

---

*The National Association for the Advancement of Colored People had been founded in 1909–10, and the Anti-Defamation League grew out of the Leo Frank trial in 1913.

•

The change from 1920s hysteria to 1940s cultural pluralism occurred simultaneously in politics and in culture. As the Irish experience had illustrated, voting played a crucial role in the making of Americans out of the despised race of Celts. Though now snuggled into the Nordic race fold, Irish Americans continued to face discrimination as Catholics. But their difference no longer seemed as intrinsic and permanent as when they were disdained as members of the Celtic race. Indeed, voting made all the difference in the world.

Overall voting participation had fallen steadily since its high point in 1896, when about 80 percent of all eligible voters had cast their ballots. After the turn of the century, none of the political parties—Republican, Democratic, or Socialist—mobilized voters at the grass roots. Immigrants and, increasingly, their children hardly voted at all. The effect of the 1920 Nineteenth Amendment to the U.S. Constitution, allowing women to vote, was simply to aggravate low voter participation by doubling the number of eligible voters without mobilizing women to come to the polls. Poor and working-class women outside of college suffrage clubs seldom overcame social obstacles to their voting. In 1924, only about 49 percent of eligible voters actually voted.[4]

People who did vote were more likely native-born of native parentage and economically prosperous. Since both Republicans and Democrats in Congress supported immigration restriction and prohibition, political parties, as the journalist Walter Lippmann noted, remained "irrelevant." Consequently, as immigrants from southern and eastern Europe gradually naturalized (a process that usually took a decade or more) and their American-born children came of age, they lacked motivation to go to the polls. Only the Irish and their children took full advantage of politics, being well acquainted with the distribution of patronage jobs.[5] In *Laughing in the Jungle* (1932) the Slovenian-born journalist Louis Adamic describes the immigrant state of political consciousness even after settling permanently in the United States: "the Bohunks . . . had little interest in American events, institutions, and politics. . . . Saturday evenings and Sunday afternoons, when they came together, the talk was largely about affairs in their native villages. Their newspapers devoted a good part of their space to clippings from the small-town sheets of southeastern Europe."[6] But things began to change in the late 1920s.

The 1928 presidential race of New York's Democratic governor, Al Smith, created much controversy, dividing the citizenry over prohibition and religion—especially Protestant versus Catholic. While the losing Smith campaign brought more voters to the polls in immigrant neighborhoods, the victory of the cold-fish, ultra-Anglo-Saxon Herbert Hoover hardly kept them mobilized. The outcome might have been different if the colorful, down-to-earth Smith had won, but his Catholicism and immigrant background proved too great an obstacle, given the shape of the electorate in 1928.[7] For working-class voters of all backgrounds, only the policies of the New Deal made politics engaging.

THE NEW DEAL policies of the first hundred days in 1933, notably the Civilian Conservation Corps and the Works Progress Administration, did bring new voters out in droves. For the first time, the federal government was addressing the crisis facing working people, so many of them from immigrant backgrounds.[8] In 1934 and, especially, in 1936, masses of young voters flocked to the polls. People who had not voted, voted now, and they voted Democratic. In Chicago, for instance, the electorate was 100 percent larger in 1936 than in 1920.[9]

The New Deal coalition supporting Franklin D. Roosevelt was solidly working-class. During the First World War hundreds of thousands of black southerners had moved to jobs in industrial centers of the North and Midwest, and they represented one of the four members of the coalition. Well-educated, middle-class intellectuals of progressive politics represented the second. White southerners who traditionally voted for the Democratic party of the Solid South were a third, and last came a coalition of immigrants and their children, often oriented toward organized labor.

Organized labor reaped enormous benefit from the New Deal, with an upsurge of industrial (as opposed to skilled) organizing that brought millions into the labor fold in the mid-1930s, under the aegis of the surging new Congress of Industrial Organizations (CIO). Emboldened unions meant labor power, in the form of protection from arbitrary shop floor management and, potent in the long run, increased wages. For the immigrant working class—and outside the South the working class consisted overwhelmingly of immigrants and their children—better wages laid the groundwork for economic mobility. This is not to say that the whole New Deal coalition was prolabor. Not at all.

The New Deal coalition, in fact, was as lumpy as could be, with certain parts working against the interests of others. The needs of working-class northern black voters, for instance, took a backseat to the powerful southern Democrats' obsession with white supremacy and abhorrence of labor unions.[10] Southerners in Congress kept the New Deal segregated, so that black people were largely excluded from policies regarding labor, housing, education. The newly created Social Security Administration, for example, excluded the two largest categories of black workers, those laboring on farms and in domestic service. The military, of course, remained either segregated (Army, Navy) or exclusionary (Marines, Air Force). African Americans got the worst of it, and President Roosevelt also balanced the interests of his Jewish constituencies against the preferences of his Catholics, as in the case of the radio priest Father Charles Coughlin.

COUGHLIN BROADCAST from Royal Oak, Michigan, a former Klan stronghold not far from Henry Ford's Dearborn, both near Detroit. In the late 1920s Ford, in his seventies, had folded his newspaper and largely withdrawn his anti-Semitic crusade, handing his mantle to the nationally popular Coughlin, with whom he lunched monthly.[11] At first Coughlin supported the New Deal, and Roosevelt envisioned Coughlin as a conduit to Catholic voters. Two influential Irish Catholic intermediaries smoothed Roosevelt's approach to Coughlin: the wealthy Joseph P. Kennedy of Massachusetts (father of John, Robert, and Edward Kennedy) and Frank Murphy, the mayor of Detroit.[12] The approach did not yield lasting fruit, however, for Coughlin soured on the New Deal and stepped up his anti-Semitic broadcasts.[13] Anti-Semitism increased in visibility in the United States with the National Socialists' seizure of power in Germany in 1933.

German Nazis did not lack supporters in the United States, although the Nuremberg Laws of 1935, which expelled Jewish Germans from a wide range of jobs and institutions, made pro-German sentiments increasingly controversial. Prominent Americans such as William Randolph Hearst, who had extolled Benito Mussolini, Italy's Fascist dictator since 1922, did back away from Hitler's more toxic Germany, with its internecine violence, negative eugenics, Jew-baiting, and illegal rearmament.[14] Nonetheless, Henry Ford and another hero of American technology found ways to admire Germany. Charles Lindbergh had soared into legend in 1927 as the "Lone Eagle" by flying across the Atlantic alone in a tiny airplane. He remained a hero in the 1930s—indeed, he remains a hero today, thanks to his amazing feat of individual skill and bravery.

After his triumphant return from France, Lindbergh had taken Ford, then sixty-four, on a plane ride in August 1927. Ford, in turn, made Lindbergh a technological consultant, and the two stayed in close touch until the Lindberghs left the United States in 1935 after the highly publicized kidnapping and murder of their son. Ford remembered later, "When Charles comes out here, we only talk about the Jews." As a resumption of the European war loomed in 1939, Lindbergh published a screamingly racist article in *Readers' Digest*, in which he cited aviation as "another barrier between the teeming millions of Asia and the Grecian inheritance of Europe . . . priceless possessions which permit the White race to live at all in a pressing sea of Yellow, Black, and Brown. . . . We, the heirs of European culture, are on the verge of a disastrous war, a war within our own family of nations, a war which will reduce the strength and destroy the treasures of the White race. . . . [I]t is time to turn from our quarrels and to build our White ramparts again."[15] Ford nodded in agreement.

Ford and Lindbergh also had German honors in common. Both received the Grand Service Cross of the Supreme Order of the German Eagle, the highest honor to a distinguished foreigner, in 1938—Lindbergh in Germany, Ford in Detroit before an audience of fifteen hundred prominent citizens.[16] It was not until the pogrom of *Kristallnacht* in 1938 and the onset of ever more violent attacks on Jews in Germany and Austria that the tide truly turned, and it became more difficult to find anything good to say about the Nazis.

Once the United States entered the war that had resumed in 1939, Americans, led by President Franklin Roosevelt and his New Dealers, drew sharper contrasts between Nazi racism and American inclusion. They pointed out that whereas Germany and Japan, the country's two prime enemies, based their national identities in race, the United States had become a nation of nations—Walt Whitman's words in *Leaves of Grass* of 1855—a nation united in its diversity. This version of the society had been heard earlier in the twentieth century.

BEFORE THE hysteria associated with the First World War snuffed it out, a nascent and similar cultural pluralism had been taking shape. One early example was the *Menorah Journal,* a magazine created in 1915 by Jewish students at Harvard seeking a middle road between their religious and their national identities, between living as Jews and living as Americans. One of them, Horace M. Kallen (1882–1974), answered Edward A. Ross's intemperate *The Old World in the New* (1914), first in two articles for the *Nation* in February 1915, then in a book, *Culture and Democracy in the United States: Studies in the Group Psychology of the American Peoples* (1924).[17] His repudiation of the purely Anglo-Saxon character of the United States came to be known as "cultural pluralism."*

Kallen chronicled wave after wave of European immigrants, beginning with the British, Irish, Germans, and Scandinavians, and continuing with others long denigrated as "new immigrants": French Canadians, Italians, Slavs, Jews. They deserved to be integrated, whereas the Anglo-

---

* Kallen had first used cultural pluralism ideas while teaching at Harvard in 1906 or 1907, but these ideas did not appear in print until 1915. Kallen went on to a fine academic career. He was a professor of philosophy at the University of Wisconsin at Madison before moving to New York City as a founder of the New School for Social Research in 1919. Active as an international citizen and supporter of Zionism, he continued teaching at the New School until his death in 1974.

Saxon stock was highly overrated, whether in burnt-out New England or in the South, where "the native white stock, often degenerate and backward, prevail among the whites . . . [who] live among nine million negroes, whose own mode of living tends, by its mere massiveness [to contaminate the whites]."[18] Note that non-Europeans do not figure as immigrants or as constituents of Kallen's ideal America. Confusingly, nor do the children of European immigrants come off very well. Kallen belonged to the numerous throng of would-be friends of the immigrant who looked askance at their American-born children. The second generation, he regretted, "devotes itself feverishly to the attainment of similarity [to Anglo-Saxons]. The older social tradition is lost by attrition or thrown off for advantage." Crime and vice appeal as routes to wealth and shallow amusement.[19] Better they should return to the picturesque immigrant ways of their parents. So much for a melting pot.

Rather than proposing, à la Henry Ford, an Americanizing melting pot, in which immigrant "ethnic types" would melt into ersatz Anglo-Saxons or be forced to leave the United States, Kallen envisioned American culture as "a great and truly democratic commonwealth," as "an orchestration of mankind. As in an orchestra, every type of instrument has its specific timbre and tonality, founded in its substance and form; as every type has its appropriate theme and melody in the whole symphony, so in society each ethnic group is the natural instrument, its spirit and culture are its theme and melody, and the harmony and dissonances and discords of them all make the symphony of civilization."[20] But Kallen's was a symphony of purely European civilization.

The progressive intellectuals Randolph Bourne and John Dewey quickly echoed Kallen's preference for ethnic color in 1916 and 1917. Bourne welcomed "our aliens" into American culture as equal partners with the Anglo-Saxon, heralding a new United States: "we have all unawares been building up the first international nation. . . . America is already the world-federation in miniature . . . the peaceful living side by side." Dewey admitted, "[T]he theory of the Melting Pot always gave me rather a pang," because he disliked the idea of "a uniform and unchanging product." Speaking to Jewish college students, Dewey much appreciates difference, and is willing to support the cause of Zionism.[21] These sentiments had been a promising start, but such welcoming words largely went silent during the 1920s. Then, in the 1930s, a defender of the immigrants' American children appeared in popular culture.

LOUIS ADAMIC (1898 or 1899–1951) was born in Blato, Slovenia, then an Austrian possession.* After his prosperous peasant parents sent him to high school, he immigrated to the United States in 1913, a self-described "young Bohunk." Settling in New York City, Adamic did unskilled labor in the offices of the *Narodni Glas*, a Slovenian-language newspaper, one of thousands of institutions immigrants had created to serve their communities. Ambitious and hardworking, he began translating articles from the *New York World* into Slovenian, then graduated to writing about Slovenians in America. When *Narodni Glas* folded in 1916, a victim of the persecution of foreign-language periodicals during the First World War, Adamic joined the Army, where he gained U.S. citizenship. Demobilized in 1923 in San Pedro, California, the port of Los Angeles, he spent the next six years there, working and writing colorfully about himself and the Croatian workers in San Pedro.[22]

These articles so charmed California literati, notably Cary McWilliams, Mary Austin, and Upton Sinclair, that they eased Adamic's approach to H. L. Mencken, who in 1928 began publishing the first of eight of Adamic's articles in the *American Mercury*, the most fashionable literary magazine of the 1920s.[23] (See figure 25.1, Louis Adamic.)

After relocating to New York City in 1929, Adamic began to publish at a furious rate. His first real book, *Dynamite: The Story of Class Violence in America*, appeared in 1931 to favorable reviews and a boost from the Nobel prize–winning novelist Sinclair Lewis.[24†] *Dynamite* sig-

---

* The independent nation of Slovenia lies between Italy, Austria, Hungary, and Croatia. Its Adriatic port is Trieste, its largest city Ljubljana, where Adamic went to high school.
† Adamic revised *Dynamite* in 1934, to further acclaim. His first book, *Robinson Jeffers: A Portrait*, just a pamphlet on the reclusive California poet, was published by the bookstore of the University of Washington in Seattle in 1929. It appears in *My America*.

naled Adamic's abiding sympathy for workers, which soon made him a supporter of the CIO, the great industrial labor federation born of the New Deal. His 1932 autobiography, *Laughing in the Jungle*, a series of satirical sketches, also well received, earned him a prestigious Guggenheim literary fellowship in 1932.

As a Guggenheim Fellow, Adamic was able to visit his former home—part of Yugoslavia since the end of the First World War—for the first time since leaving it nearly two decades ear-

Fig. 25.1. *Louis Adamic on his book tour, 1934.*

lier, bringing along his non-Slav American wife, Stella. In Split, Dalmatia, Adamic met Ivo (John) F. Lupis-Vukich, formerly publisher of a foreign-language newspaper in Chicago, who lectured Adamic on the importance of second-generation immigrants in the United States, the "strangers" most Americans did not understand. Adamic took this idea to heart.[25]

A chronicle of his stay in Yugoslavia, *The Native's Return* (1934) became a Book-of-the-Month Club main selection, quickly sold fifty thousand books, and remained a best seller for nearly two years. It brought Adamic twenty or more letters a day from Slavs living in the United States. In the course of promoting his book in heavily Slav industrial centers, Adamic delivered his "Ellis Island and Plymouth Rock" lecture hundreds of times, becoming the prime spokesman for immigrants and their children. His response to the crowds and to yet another nativist editorial by George Horace Lorimer of the *Saturday Evening Post* coalesced into "Thirty Million New Americans" in *Harper's Magazine* in November 1934. Despite its patronizing tone, this piece quickly became a classic statement of 1930s cultural pluralism.

"Thirty Million New Americans" and Adamic's subsequent books and articles sought to recast the fundamental identity of Americans. His main points were simple: the U.S. population is diverse, not essentially Anglo-Saxon, and immigrants are full-fledged Americans. As he said often, Ellis Island deserves a place at the center of American origins, right next to Plymouth Rock. As the product of so many regions and cultures, the children of immigrants carried a vast potential to "enrich the civilization and deepen the culture in this New World."[26]

In many ways Adamic unwittingly picked up themes from the nineteenth and very early twentieth centuries. His view of immigrants even shared a point with Ralph Waldo Emerson. Whereas Emerson had blithely consigned these "guano races" to faceless hard work, death, then service to the greater American good as mere fertilizer, Adamic paused lovingly with immigrant workers while they survived. He gave them names, such as Peter Molek, and listened to their wisdom. Broken after decades of dangerous work in American mines and steel mills, they recognized their alternating role as both builders of American progress and—their own word—"dung."

"The Bohunks indeed were 'dung,' " Adamic agrees in his autobiography, but he loved "their natural health, virility, and ability to laugh" and the way they saw themselves as working-class in their adopted country. A Slav without formal education, like the fictional Molek, would see injustice where "millionaires who wore diamonds in their teeth and had bands playing while they bathed in champagne." Living in miserable slums, impoverished immigrant laborers recognized that the fundamental flaw of American society lay in the maldistribution of wealth.[27]

In fact, ambivalence dominated Adamic's attitude toward his immigrant peers. Though Kallen was writing two decades earlier from Harvard, and Adamic focused on working-class neighborhoods in Pennsylvania and the industrial Midwest, both authors depict American-born children of immigrants somewhat unfavorably.* As Adamic describes

---

* Adamic seems not to have been aware of the round of cultural pluralism that Horace Kallen had initiated in 1915.

them, most in the second generation are ashamed of their parents and filled with feelings of inferiority, rendering them "invariably hollow, absurd, objectionable persons," whose "limp handshakes" give him the "creeps."[28] In time they may contribute to society, but at the moment they constitute a problem, and here Adamic's ambivalence emerges full-blown. The children of immigrants present "one of the greatest and most basic problems in this country; in some respects, greater and more basic [than] the problem of unemployment, and almost as urgent." They are a "problem" thirteen times in the article's eleven pages, on account of their "feelings of inferiority" (sixteen times). Their "racial" identities (ten times) separated them from "old [Anglo-Saxon] stock" Americans (nine times). Even their champion was using the language of races to paint a dismal picture.

But while Adamic might join Kallen in the language of race in 1934, he departs from him in two important ways: Adamic usually links race to culture, as if to hedge his bets on permanence. Members of his second generation are distinctive by "race and culture," whereas for Kallen a generation earlier, race was the same thing as culture. Adamic glimpses the possibility of change in the thirty million new Americans, for he notes the ability of a few young people to become attractive and successful. They simply need encouragement to become full-fledged Americans.

ENCOURAGEMENT CAME from several quarters, notably from a New Jersey Quaker, Rachel Davis DuBois (1892–1993), a Woodbury high school teacher inspired by W. E. B. Du Bois and angered by Father Charles Coughlin's broadcast anti-Semitism. DuBois pioneered what was called "intercultural education" by establishing the (nongovernmental) Service Bureau for Intercultural Education in 1934 to help other teachers reach out to their second- and third-generation immigrant students and incorporate information about them in their curricula—multiculturalism *avant la lettre*.[29]* As she approached

---

* DuBois lived to 101 and continued serving human rights into the late 1980s. She joined the Southern Christian Leadership Council, where she conducted Quaker dialogues in the mid-1960s.

the federal government and radio broadcasters with a plan to counter derogatory images of alien races, Adamic was one of her supporters.* By 1940, some 83 percent of American homes had a radio, which the Office of Education in the U.S. Department of the Interior was willing to use if an outlet could be found to carry DuBois's programs on American history integrating the contributions of (virtually) all groups of Americans.† The National Broadcasting Corporation turned DuBois down. Speaking for NBC, James R. Angell, former president of Yale University, found her topic too controversial, concluding, "I think I should let this dog sleep. Certainly I am not disposed to stir up the menagerie just at the moment." The Columbia Broadcasting Corporation, however, welcomed the project and broadcast *Americans All, Immigrants All* in twenty-six weekly radio segments between November 1938 and May 1939. (See figure 25.2, *Americans All, Immigrants All*.)

The series title came from a 1938 Franklin Roosevelt speech to the Daughters of the American Revolution, in which he announced, "We *are* all immigrants." In broadcast order, the programs focused on English, Hispanic, Scotch-Irish and Welsh, Negro, French-speaking, Irish, German-speaking, Scandinavian, Jewish, Slavic, Oriental, Italian, and Near Eastern Americans.[30] Success stories all, the various outsiders made their way into American mainstream success via dedicated, hard work. Well, not quite all. Negroes, scrunched down in the lower left-hand corner of the advertisement and dwarfed by talismans of the old slaveholding South, were still struggling for inclusion. Even so, by including African Americans as Americans, *Americans All, Immigrants All* marked a turning point. For most Americans, seeing Negroes as Americans meant something new under the sun.

FROM ST. Jean de Crèvecoeur in 1782 to Horace Kallen in 1915 and into the late 1930s, to speak of American "races" was to speak of Americans

---

*Adamic died distraught in his New Jersey farmhouse in 1951 after having been red-baited and criticized for his unwavering support of Josip Tito in Yugoslavia. Adamic's death was judged a suicide, but doubts remain as to its cause.

† *Americans All, Immigrants All* ignored Native American Indians, East Indians, West Indians, and Puerto Ricans.

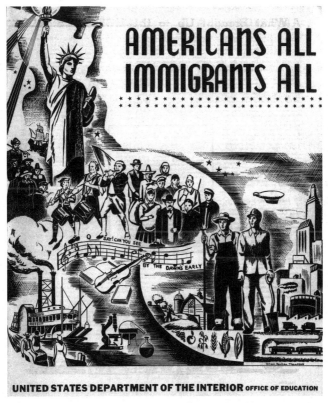

Fig. 25.2. Cover of advertising brochure for
Americans All, Immigrants All, 1938.

of Jewish, Slavic, Italian, Irish, German, and, even, "Anglo-Saxon" and
"Teutonic" background, identities assumed to be more or less permanent. Black people were relegated to a separate and lower racial com-
partment along with Native American Indians and Asians, not entirely
American, if not completely alien. *The* American was a figure of European heritage.

By the late 1930s, however, the prospect of war with the racial state
of Nazi Germany was enlarging the concept of American, so that nonwhites, notably black people, began to gain a toehold. One of the most
popular radio broadcasts of the era reflected a new inclusiveness. The

broadcast in question was not America's all-time most popular radio program, the blackface *Amos 'n' Andy Show*, but a special broadcast starring an honest-to-goodness black person.

The African American lawyer, actor, and singer Paul Robeson (1898–1976) performed this broader version of American identity by debuting *Ballad for Americans* in November 1939 before a CBS radio audience. An eleven-minute cantata originally composed for a left-leaning Federal Theater Project review in 1937, *Ballad for Americans* asks, "Am I an American?" and answers resoundingly, "I'm just an Irish, Negro, Jewish, Italian, French and English, Spanish, Russian, Chinese, Polish, Scotch, Hungarian, Litvak, Swedish, Finnish, Canadian, Greek and Turk, and Czech and double Czech American. And that ain't all. I was baptized Baptist, Methodist, Congregationalist, Lutheran, Atheist, Roman Catholic, Orthodox Jewish, Presbyterian, Seventh Day Adventist, Mormon, Quaker, Christian Scientist and lots more."

A twenty-minute ovation erupted at the song's end, and appreciative callers jammed the network's switchboard for two hours. A runaway hit, *Ballad for Americans* went on to serve as the theme song for the 1940 Republican nominating convention.[31] The two racial systems— one for the races of Europe and the "alien" races, one for the black/white dichotomy—were beginning to collide, and Robeson's generous list of American roots began an ever so slow and bumpy process of substitution of a multiple for a singular—*the* American—national identity.

THE THIRD ENLARGEMENT
OF AMERICAN WHITENESS

The Second World War rearranged Americans by the millions. Some 12 percent among a population of 131.7 million—roughly 16 million people—served in the armed forces, which threw together people whose parents hailed from all over Europe.[1] Millions of civilians migrated to jobs around the country, further diluting parochial habits. Some 2.5 million southerners left the South, and northerners went south to training camps and war work.[2] Louis Adamic had dreamed of a second, more homogenized immigrant generation, and one had already started in the Civilian Conservation Corps, fruit of the New Deal's earliest days. Now, a decade later, millions rather than tens of thousands left home.

Let us remember that this mixing occurred with several notable exceptions. Black Americans—who numbered some 13.3 million in 1940—were, of course, largely excluded. Their time would come much later, and with revolutionary urgency. But also excluded were Asian Americans. Even so, other Americans—provided they qualified as white for federal purposes—experienced a revolution of their own. Indeed, the white category itself had expanded enormously, well beyond European immigrants and their children. Included now were Mexicans and Mexican Americans.

The handsome Julio Martinez from San Antonio plays a leading role in the multicultural Army squad of Normal Mailer's best-selling war novel *The Naked and the Dead* (1948). No bit player, Martinez, like Red Valsen, the Swede from Montana, and Sam Croft, the Anglo-Saxon hunter from Texas, rates a chapter of his own.[3] Since the mid-1930s, federal and Texas state laws had defined Mexicans as white and allowed them to vote in Texas's white primary.[4] While Asian American and African American service personnel were routinely segregated and mistreated, Mexican Americans fought in white units and appeared in the media of the war, witness the boom in popular war movies like *Bataan* (1944), starring the Cuban Desi Arnaz (who in the 1950s would become a television star as Lucille Ball's husband in the long-running *I Love Lucy* series).

Meeting new people in new places broke down barriers. The novelist Joseph Heller (1923–99) left his Jewish corner of Brooklyn's Coney Island and went south to the Norfolk Navy Yard in Portsmouth, Virginia. Heller was not surprised to find that local whites studiously ignored their black fellow workers in the navy yard. But the "uniform virulence with which Protestants regarded Catholics" amazed him. Luckily for Heller, such hostility was not his problem; as a Jewish New Yorker, he became a novelty, treated well and chatted up warmly in lunchtime breaks—with a single exception.

One discussion, he wrote in his memoir, "turned to religion and I chose to volunteer the information that Jesus was in fact Jewish and of presumed Jewish parentage. The immediate and united stiffening of the entire circle of white faces was an instantaneous warning that they had never been told this before and did not want to be told it now, or ever. Even my closest pals bristled."[5] Similar lessons in cultural difference occurred countless times.

It was federal policy that supplied lessons in diversity, and federal policy also defined its limits, by means of a rigidly enforced segregation that imprisoned 110,000 Japanese Americans and counted up fractions of Negro "blood" in order to separate black servicemen from white.[6] By and large, only those being kept apart and their allies noticed the segregation for quite a long while.* The loudest notes of wartime stressed inclusion, and the song of brotherhood echoed over the years.

THIS THEME of inclusion had emerged during the New Deal of the 1930s as a means of strengthening the Democratic allegiance of new voters in immigrant neighborhoods. President Roosevelt addressed immigrants and their children in a spirit of oneness. The outbreak of war in Europe in 1939 intensified American condemnation of intolerance. One of the president's "four freedoms" defining the goals of the war was freedom of religion.[7†] In 1940, the popular picture magazine *Look* showed how far religious prejudice had fallen out of favor by publishing a special issue denouncing anti-Semitism. When Charles Lindbergh in September 1941 blamed the war on the British, the Roosevelt administration, and the Jews, the normally cautious *New York Times* denounced his anti-Semitism.[8‡] An example of official wartime Americanism appears in the seven propaganda movies the U.S. Army Signal Corps commissioned. Entitled *Why We Fight* and directed by Hollywood's Frank Capra (1897–1991). These films sought to teach enlisted men the democratic basis of the war.

The Capra family's story, one of Sicilian immigrants, presents a cogent example of two experiences, one older and one newer. As eventually a fabulously successful filmmaker, Frank Capra stands out from the crowd. His older brother, Ben, was not so lucky. Frank and the rest of his family immigrated to California in 1903 to join Ben, whose life had been more representative of Italian immigrants' misadventures.

Ben Capra had contracted malaria while working in the sugarcane fields of Louisiana with other Italians and African Americans. A black

---

* Discrimination against African American airmen was a major theme of a little-noticed war novel from 1948, James Gould Cozzens's *Guard of Honor*, in which the commander, realizing the justice of the black men's demands for an end to segregation, nevertheless sides with the more numerous, antiblack whites to avoid confrontation.

† In his 1941 annual message to Congress, Roosevelt outlined four freedoms owed everyone in the world: freedom of speech and expression, freedom of religion, freedom from want, and freedom from fear.

‡ In its editorial deploring Lindbergh's speech, the *New York Times* doubted "whether a religious group whose members come from almost every civilized country and speak almost every Western language can be called a 'race.' "

woman had nursed him back to health, and he stayed with the black family for two years. Later, in New Orleans, Ben fell victim to the beating, kidnapping, and transport that ensnared many a vulnerable immigrant of the time. Shipped to a sugar island in the Pacific Ocean, he and a buddy escaped peonage in a rowboat and were miraculously rescued by an Australian liner and taken on to California. There Ben settled,* and there his younger brother Frank spent, as he reports, a miserable American childhood: "I hated being poor. Hated being a peasant. Hated being a scrounging newskid trapped in the sleazy Sicilian ghetto of Los Angeles. My family couldn't read or write. I wanted out. A quick out."[9] The military offered a route of escape.

Frank Capra served in the U.S. Army in the First World War and was naturalized a U.S. citizen in 1920. His extraordinary film career began in the 1930s, culminating in iconic films such as *It Happened One Night* (1934), *Mr. Deeds Goes to Town* (1936), *You Can't Take It with You* (1938), and *Mr. Smith Goes to Washington* (1939). In *Mr. Deeds Goes to Town* and *Mr. Smith Goes to Washington,* ordinary Americans defeat the nefarious forces of financial and political corruption, confirming the power of upstanding, small-town individuals. The good guys were always unquestionably Anglo-Saxon.† Even scenes set in cities and on farms show exclusively Anglo-Saxon crowds forming an all-American, Anglo-Saxon backdrop to the all-American, Anglo-Saxon protagonists played by, say, Gary Cooper or Jimmy Stewart.‡ Omnipresent Nordicism characterized Hollywood feature films throughout the period, even though most filmmakers—writers, directors, producers—came from immigrant backgrounds, both Jewish and Catholic.

Frank Capra's screenwriters Robert Riskin and Sidney Buchman were eastern European Jews. Buchman, a communist, would be black-

---

* And there Ben Capra fell out of history. The rest of his life is not known.
† Movie stars routinely changed their names (or had them changed) into something more Anglo-Saxon sounding, hence Kirk Douglas (born Issur Demsky), Anne Bancroft (born Anna Maria Italiano), Rita Hayworth (born Margarita Cansino), George Burns (born Nathan Birnbaum), Alan Alda (Alphonso D'Abruzzo), and Fred Astaire (Frederick Austerlitz).
‡ Capra won an Academy Award (his second) for directing for *Mr. Deeds Goes to Town*, which was nominated for three other Academy Awards. *Mr. Smith Goes to Washington* was nominated for eleven Academy Awards and won for best screenplay. Capra also directed *The Negro Soldier*, intended to raise the morale of African Americans in the segregated U.S. armed forces.

listed during the anticommunist 1950s. Not that the Left would have offered Capra, Riskin, and Buchman ready examples of ethnic multiculturalism, for the Communist Party took its cues from the movies. Prominent communists in the United States routinely exchanged their European ethnic names for anodyne English-sounding ones: the Finnish American Avro Halberg became Gus Hall; the Jewish American Solomon Israel Regenstreif became Johnny Gates; the Croatian Stjepan Mesaros became Steve Nelson; Dorothy Rosenblum became Dorothy Ray Healey. Even the CP's worker iconography gave *the* American worker a Nordic face and a tall, muscular body.[10]

Popular literature also mirrored the movies, even as the war effort stressed diversity. A 1945 study by Columbia's Bureau of Applied Social Research found that stories published between 1937 and 1943 in magazines reaching twenty million readers featured 889 characters, of whom 90.8 percent were Anglo-Saxon. The rare non-Anglo-Saxons were stereotyped as menial workers, gangsters, crooked fight promoters, and thieving nightclub owners, while Anglo-Saxons in central roles were honest and admirable, their superiority taken for granted.[11] The advertising seeping into every corner of American popular culture beamed out smiling Nordics free, beautiful, and desirable.

With real American identity coded according to race, being a real American often meant joining antiblack racism and seeing oneself as white against the blacks. Looking back to the war years, an Italian American recalled a tempting invitation to take sides during the Harlem riot of 1943: "I remember standing on a corner, a guy would throw the door open and say, 'Come on down.' They were goin' to Harlem to get in the riot. They'd say, 'Let's beat up some niggers.' It was wonderful. It was new. The Italo-Americans stopped being Italo and started becoming Americans. We joined the group. Now we're like you guys, right?"[12] The temptation and the decision to succumb did not pass unnoticed. Malcolm X, spokesman of the black nationalist Nation of Islam, and Toni Morrison, a Nobel Prize laureate in literature, later noted that the first English word out of the mouths of European immigrants was frequently "nigger." Actually, Morrison said it was the second, after "okay."[13]

Much—too much—of 1940s American culture stayed stuck in the

racist 1920s, although some code words fell out of fashion. The roots of "Nordic" in Madison Grant's Nazi-like eugenics disabled it for use in the 1940s. Prewar names of the categories of dolichocephalic and brachycephalic also disappeared, though FBI "wanted" posters and mug shots continued to depict miscreants in profile as well as full-face. The shape of the head, it seems, still said a good deal. Nor did the cephalic index fade as in *the* American's ideal face shape—the dolichocephalic, long-headed oval of Norman Rockwell's quintessential Americans, rather than the brachycephalic square or round. Be tall, be blue-eyed, and, if a woman, be blond.

Autobiographical statements of Americans born in the 1940s reveal a keen awareness of the difference between *American* standards of beauty and the bodies of women increasingly being called "ethnic." This term dated back to the 1920s, but it came into common discourse only after the Second World War as a way to label the children and grandchildren of Louis Adamic's second immigrant generation. English, German, Scandinavian, and Irish Americans did not fall under the "ethnic" rubric, which had become a new marker for the former "alien races." An Italian American recalled his mother, in the 1940s, "referring to the Irish families on the block as 'the Americans.' "[14] For quite some time, ethnic Americans looked from afar on the "blond people," the term of the anthropologist Karen Brodkin for the "mythical, 'normal' America" of magazines and television. In quest of the tall, slender "normal" American silhouette, she wrote, "my mother and I were always dieting. Dieting was about my and my mother's aspirations to blond-people standards of feminine beauty."[15]

Much nose bobbing, hair straightening, and bleaching ensued. Anglo-Saxon ideals fell particularly hard on women and girls, for the strength and assertion of working-class women of the immigrant generations were out of place in middle-class femininity. Not only was the tall, slim Anglo-Saxon body preeminent, the body must look middle- rather than working-class.

And the middle class *was* growing in actual fact. Once again, Joseph Heller explains the economic transformation that began with military service: "My total income upon entering the air force as a private was as much as I'd been able to command outside, and as an officer on flight status was greater than I was able to earn afterward when starting out in my civilian pursuits." After the war, the money just got better.[16]

Here is Heller again, on top of the world in 1945: "I felt myself walking around on easy street, in a state of fine rapture. What more could I ask for? I was in love and engaged to be married (to the same young woman I was in love with). I was twenty-two years old. I would be entering college as a freshman at the University of Southern California, with tuition and related costs paid for by the government." And the guys from his neighborhood were doing all right, too:

> After the war, Marty Kapp [a Heller neighbor] continued what technical education had begun in the navy V-12 program and graduated as a soil engineer (yet another thing I'd not heard of before). For all his career he worked as a soil engineer with the Port Authority of New York— on airfields and buildings, I know and perhaps on bridges and tunnels, too—and had risen to some kind of executive status before he died. He did well enough to die on a golf course. . . . I was able to go to college. Lou Berkman left the junk shop to start a plumbing supply company in Middletown, New York, and looked into real estate with the profits from that successful venture. . . . Sy Ostrow, who was taught Russian in the service so that he could function as an interpreter, returned to college and, with pained resignation, saw realistically that he had no better alternative than to study law.[17]

For Italian Americans, highly segregated in slum neighborhoods and routinely called "wops," "dagoes," and "guineas" before the war, the 1940s brought brand-new money for college and homes. Before the war, Italian Americans had rarely achieved a higher education. But around 1940 their rates of college attendance quickly approached the national norm. Educational mobility led to economic mobility, which fostered political clout. Rhode Island, with its large proportion of Italian Americans, elected John Pastore its first Italian American governor in 1946.

Italian Americans in Rhode Island's state house numbered four before 1948, when their number doubled. By the late 1960s they numbered sixteen.[18] Less numerous, Slavic Americans did not succeed as brilliantly in politics, although their timetable for gaining office was similar. The first Slovenian governor of a state, Frank J. Lausche of Ohio, got elected in 1945 and was sent to the U.S. Senate in 1956.[19]

POSTWAR PROSPERITY drove the motor of mobility, and federal spending fueled the economy, most obviously in the form of the Servicemen's Readjustment Act of 1944, commonly called the GI Bill of Rights or simply the GI Bill. This multifaceted benefits program offered unemployment compensation, financing for education, and low-interest, fixed-rate, long-term loans for starting businesses and buying homes. Between 1944 and 1956, the GI Bill spent $14.5 billion to subsidize education for about half the veterans, some 7.8 million people all told.[20]*

The Federal Housing Authority (FHA), along with the Veterans Mortgage Guarantee program, offered veterans and developers federally insured mortgages and loans on terms far more favorable than those of savings and loan institutions and banks. The FHA and the Veterans Administration (VA) required only 10 percent down, and their attractively low interest rates were fixed for thirty years; people with modest incomes could pay for their homes over the long term, with no balloon payment at the end. Now it was cheaper to buy than to rent in the cities.[21] An increase in home values would underlie family wealth and middle-class status in coming generations.

The FHA and VA financed more than $120 billion in housing between 1934 and 1964, peaking in the fifties and early sixties. By then, the FHA had become the nation's prime mortgage lender, holding about one-half the home mortgages, and the VA had insured mortgages for nearly five million more.[22] Those homes were largely in new suburbs,

---

*Elite institutions were not always thrilled at the prospect of hordes of veterans invading their campuses. The president of the University of Chicago envisioned institutions like his "converted into educational hobo jungles."

Fig. 26.1. Levittown, Pennsylvania, mid-1950s.

early and famously the two Levittowns in Nassau County, Long Island, New York (built between 1947 and 1951), and in Bucks County, Pennsylvania (built in 1951).[23]* (See figure 26.1, Levittown, Pennsylvania.)

Sameness marked the suburban theme. Even the Holocaust seldom got mention, though popular culture recognized Jews obliquely. In 1945 the first (and only) Jew was crowned Miss America after a tussle over her Jewish-sounding name—Bess Meyerson (b. 1924). The Miss America organizers had always preferred Mayflower girls and pressured Meyerson to change her name to something more One Hundred Percent American.[24] But Meyerson resisted the pressure and won the crown.† Success also came to Laura Z. Hobson (1900–86), whose 1947

---

* The Levitt family was Jewish, but its first suburban community, "Strathmore-at-Manhasset," barred Jews. William Levitt noted, "No one realizes better then Levitt that an undesirable class can quickly ruin a community."
† Rule number 7 long required that Miss America contestants "be of good health and of the white race." The first African American contestant was Cheryl Brown, Miss Iowa, in 1970.

novel *Gentleman's Agreement* became a number one best seller and an Academy Award–winning movie starring Gregory Peck as a Gentile journalist who passes for a Jew in order to expose American anti-Semitism. Biblical movies of the 1950s cast Gentiles as Jews: Charlton Heston (of English and Scottish descent) as Moses in *The Ten Commandments* (1956) and Victor Mature (of Italian and Swiss descent) as Samson in *Samson and Delilah* (1950). The war for independence of the scrappy republic of Israel in 1948 made Israelis into American revolutionaries and solidified the notion of the United States as a Judeo-Christian nation.[25]

Still primarily working-class, Italian Americans hovered longer on the fringes of American whiteness, longer than Jews, but the 1950s made individuals such as the singer Frank Sinatra (1915–98) and Annette Funicello (b. 1942), the star Mouseketeer of Walt Disney's *Mickey Mouse Club*, into One Hundred Percent Americans who happened to be Italian. The simple and welcome point of these blockbusting books, movies, and figures—the essential sameness of Protestant, Catholic, and Jew (in the phrase of Will Herberg's popular book)—was a theme that played well in the postwar era.* Some pointed out, however, that sameness could appear as conformity, a much less comforting idea.

David Riesman's *The Lonely Crowd: A Study of the Changing American Character* (1950) and William W. Whyte's *The Organization Man* (1956) called attention to the anomie and conformity of *the* American of the postwar era on a best-selling scale. In its hardcover publication by Yale University Press and subsequent paperback abridgments, *The Lonely Crowd* sold more than a million copies, never mind that its *American*—white, northern, and middle-class—inhabited a constricted territory. Black Americans, poor Americans, and southerners of any race appear only in passing, as "remnants" of older traditions. To most Americans, these limitations seemed inconsequential. Riesman appeared

---

* Herberg's *Protestant, Catholic, Jew: An Essay in American Religious Sociology* (1955) does not include black Protestantism as a constituent of American religion. In September 1965 Herberg published an article in *National Review* criticizing the civil rights movement for "deliberately undermining the foundations of internal order in this country. With their rabble-rousing demagoguery. . . ."

on the cover of *Time* magazine, the first social scientist to receive this sign of national import.[26]

Jewish American writers—Philip Roth most notably—chronicled a transit from the old city neighborhood into the suburbs as an American, not merely a Jewish, tale. In Herman Wouk's best-selling 1947 novel, Marjorie Morgenstern translates her quintessentially Jewish last name, into Morningstar, just as name changes, nose jobs, hair straightening, and dieting proliferated among would-be American Americans living in their "little boxes made of ticky-tacky, and they all look just the same."

Not that sameness and conformity seemed all bad. That line from Malvina Reynolds's 1963 hit song, "Little Boxes," culminates a process of going to university to be doctors and lawyers and business executives. Those who "came out all the same" did so in nice, new neighborhoods, with good, new schools.[27] In 1960, a quarter of the American housing stock was less than a decade old, and suburban residents in single-family homes outnumbered people living in the country or in what was coming to be denigrated as the "inner city."[28] Suburbia might be monotone, but it was a sameness to be striven toward.

Not surprisingly, suburbanization changed culture as well as residence. The literary critic Louise DeSalvo spoke for millions of postwar Jewish, Italian, and other working-class white ethnic families who used GI Bill loans to move out of the city. Her family left a fourth-floor tenement apartment in Hoboken for a home in suburban Ridgefield, New Jersey. Soon Louise's mother began refusing to eat her immigrant mother's homemade peasant bread, "a bread," DeSalvo recalled, "that my mother disdains because it is everything that my grandmother is, and everything that my mother, in 1950s suburban New Jersey, is trying very hard not to be." DeSalvo's mother prefers commercial sliced white bread.

> Maybe my mother thinks that if she eats enough of this other bread, she will stop being Italian American and she will become American American. Maybe . . . people will stop thinking that a relative of my father's, who comes to visit us from Brooklyn once in a while, is a Mafioso, because he's Italian American and has New York license plates

on his new black car, and sports a black tie and pointy shoes and a shiny suit and a Borsalino hat tipped way down over his forehead so you can hardly see his eyes.[29]

Nor does DeSalvo, like so many of her generation, speak the European language of her immigrant grandparents. She has more in common with her Jewish and Irish American peers in the suburbs than with her cousins back in Puglia, which she did not visit until she was sixty years old. The GI Bill, the FHA, and the suburbs made her a middle-class American confronting American American ideals.

To be American American had rapidly come to mean being "middle class" and therefore white, as in the facile equation of "white" with "middle-class." It was as though to be the one was automatically to be the other. Such a conflation of class and race had popped right out of postwar politics' weakened organized labor, and led to dwindling visibility of the working class.

Passed after a nationwide wave of strikes in 1946, the Taft-Hartley Act of 1947 severely curbed the power of organized labor by barring sympathy strikes, secondary boycotts, and mass picketing. These tactics had stood at the heart of worker power in many a shop or industry. Now employers had the whip hand, and union growth languished. Prohibiting communists from working for unions, Taft-Hartley had also stripped organized labor of many dedicated rank-and-file organizers.[30] To be prolabor came to smell like being a communist or at least a pinko, dangerous charges during the 1950s postwar red scare. Even the very image of "the working man" came to seem old-timey, as artists turned their backs on the worker as a theme. Painters invented nonfigurative abstract expressionism in a reaction against socialist realism and shopped it around internationally as proof that American art had come of age. Noteworthy prosperity inaugurated a fat new American era that generated its own mythology.

In the twilight of their years, members of the GI Bill–FHA generation looked back on their economic success with a good deal of self-congratulation. One Leonard Giuliano presented his history of his peo-

ple: "With determination and perseverance . . . the Italian was able to
. . . pull himself up by his own bootstraps. . . . His greatest desire, of
course, was for his children and his family to have a better life than he
had left in Italy, but he did not expect this for nothing. He had to work."
Al Riccardi told a similar story: "My people had a rough time, too. But
nobody gave us something."[31] A daughter of Jewish garment workers
agreed: "My grandparents were like Russian serfs, but we climbed our
way out of poverty, we worked our way up. We were poor when we were
growing up, but we were never on home relief, and our family still had
closeness and warmth!"[32] Hard work, yes, but pushed along nicely by
government assistance rarely acknowledged in the aftermath.

WERE ALL boats lifted by the government's largesse? No, they were
not. Economic subsidies reached few African Americans still segregated behind a veil created and constantly mended in Washington.
Those lovely new suburbs, creatures of FHA and VA mortgages, were
for white people only. Federal policy made and kept them all white—
on purpose.[33]

As in the New Deal, postwar policies crafted by a southern-dom-
inated Congress were intended to bypass the very poor, which meant
southern blacks in particular. John Rankin of Mississippi chaired the
Committee on World War Legislation in the House of Representatives.
He made sure that the servicemen's bill included no antidiscrimination
clause and that every provision would be administered locally along Jim
Crow lines.[34]

In 1940, 77 percent of black Americans lived in the South. They were
leaving as fast as work opened up elsewhere, but 68 percent still remained
in the South in 1950. A few aggressive blacks had pushed their way into
GI programs, but local agents, invariably white, had obstructed the great
mass. As early as 1947 it was clear—as investigations by black newspapers and a metastudy revealed—that the GI Bill was being administered
along racially discriminatory lines. It was, the report *Our Negro Veteran*
concluded, as though the GI Bill had been intended "For White Veterans
Only."[35] This color line appeared sharply in the suburbs.

The Levittowns, for instance, managed to lock out African Americans by way of "restrictive covenants," deeds and codicils that barred an owner from selling or renting to anyone not white. (Where the rare black buyer did succeed in purchasing a house, as in Levittown in Pennsylvania, neighbors resorted to violence.) Not one of the 82,000 new inhabitants of Levittown, New York, was black, a lily-white policy that held on well into the 1960s. No matter. *Time* magazine featured William Levitt on its cover of 3 July 1950, and for decades discussion of suburbs like his made no mention of white-lining.[36]

Not that the Levittowns of America had to persuade the FHA and VA to look the other way. They had crafted federal policies advocating racial restrictions precisely in order to "preserve neighborhood stability" and prevent "Negro invasion."[37] As a result, the inner-city boroughs of New York City, for instance, received drastically less in housing subsidies than Nassau County on Long Island, where Levittown was located. Per capita lending by the FHA for mortgages was eleven times higher on Long Island than in Brooklyn and sixty times more than in the working-class Bronx. This kind of federal funding inequity affected urban families of all races, leaving cities to decay for lack of credit and to be wracked by "urban renewal" that demolished more housing than it created.[38] Black families, prohibited from moving to the suburbs, had to stay behind.

By the 1960s America's deteriorating "chocolate" cities were ringed by fresh "vanilla" suburbs. Deindustrialization aggravated conditions, as industries that had offered well-paid, union jobs to the children of immigrants in the 1940s and 1950s headed overseas. Soon the image of the "black ghetto" appeared in American commentary, and the figure of *the* Negro became virtually conflated with those "degenerate families" and "alien races" of the century's first half. The civil rights movement of the 1950s and 1960s as well as the urban riots of the 1960s were protests against a long, dismal history of racial discrimination, segregation, unemployment, and blight, economic as well as social. Looking on from afar, comfortable suburbanites saw little more than black people acting out, despite the 1968 Kerner Commission Report, which laid it all out clearly and offered very worthy recommendations.

One of them, a Fair Housing Act, Congress passed the following year, outlawing discrimination in housing.

THE FAIR Housing Act had followed two landmark pieces of civil rights legislation—the Civil Rights Act of 1964 and the Voting Rights Act of 1965. These were products of a black civil rights movement that had gone unnoticed by most Americans since the First World War. The March on Washington Movement of 1941 and the Second World War "Double Vee" campaign (against fascism abroad and discrimination at home) had pushed President Roosevelt into issuing Executive Order 8802 (calling for fair employment practices). In 1948 President Truman appointed the Civil Rights Commission and ran for reelection on a platform including a civil rights plank.* Of late the civil rights movement had garnered more attention when television began to cover it.

By 1960 the civil rights movement had high visibility and undoubted justice on its side. How could any American president, leader of the free world, live with segregation and disenfranchisement? John F. Kennedy did not. Rather, he embraced the cause of black civil rights. So did his successor Lyndon B. Johnson, who pushed through the mid-1960s legislation that began redressing government practices as old as the nation itself. But redress came with much pain.

By the mid-1960s the whole world watched as Americans played out their race drama on television. The angrier the speaker, the more rapt the attention. And no voice was angrier than that of Malcolm X.

---

* The 1948 civil rights plank enraged southern Democrats, who walked out of the convention and formed their own States' Rights ("Dixiecrat") Party with J. Strom Thurmond, governor of South Carolina, as its presidential candidate.

BLACK NATIONALISM AND
WHITE ETHNICS

M alcolm X (1925–65), uniquely eloquent as spokesman for the
black nationalist Nation of Islam (NOI), was born Malcolm Little
in Omaha, Nebraska, to a black nationalist father who had migrated from
Georgia and a mother from the Caribbean Island of Grenada. (See figure
27.1, Malcolm X, 1964.) The family was poor and already peripatetic.[1]
After a hell-raising early youth, Malcolm landed in a Massachusetts
prison with an excellent library, where he educated himself through
reading and debating, honing the already popular black notion of a
unitary American whiteness he called "the white man." Released in 1952,
he joined the NOI, rising quickly through its ranks as speaker, journalist,
and organizer. In 1961, at age thirty-six and having changed his name to
a richly symbolic Malcolm X,* he founded the NOI's national weekly
newspaper, *Muhammad Speaks,* initially publishing out of the basement
of his home in Queens. The newspaper grew right along with the NOI
movement and America's civil rights movement in general.

Concurrently, Malcolm X's Harlem Temple No. 7 became an intellectual as well as a religious center, and a bully pulpit for this peer-
less speaker. "All Negroes are angry and I am the angriest of all," he

---

* Members of the NOI exchanged their "slave names" for "X," which stood for the loss of their
unknown African families and names. After Malcolm X left the NOI and made the pilgrimage to
Mecca in 1964, he took the name El-Hajj Malik El-Shabazz.

acknowledged proudly, castigating "the white man" in no uncertain terms.[2] It was a message that thrilled and chilled Americans of all sorts. Never mind, for the time being, that Malcolm's skill in debate obscured the plain fact that NOI theory belonged to a long history of flagrantly nonsensical race thought.

The Nation of Islam considered white people—undifferentiated by class, region, or circumstance—as "devils," "a devil race" of "bleached-out white people," a single, monolithic entity. NOI

Fig. 27.1. Malcolm X, 1964.

theory held that some six thousand years ago an evil black scientist named Yakub had created the white devils through selective breeding out of the original Blackman. Yakub's white devils would rule for six thousand years, but their time would begin to end in 1914, at the onset of the First World War. Meanwhile, black people should separate from whites, and certainly not seek integration into American society. Because blacks were the targets of racist violence, they should organize into militia for self-defense, such groups to be called the "Fruit of Islam" and dedicated to achieving self-determination.[3]

Malcolm X's charisma clearly mattered more than ideology, pulling tens of thousands of black people into the NOI, besotting along the way journalists and scholars of every stripe. In July 1959 Mike Wallace's five-part television documentary *The Hate That Hate Produced* considerably amplified media fascination with the Malcolm X story and went on to spawn a Boston University dissertation, scholarly books, a phenomenally best-selling autobiography, and a feature film and commentary that continues to grow. Constantly in demand as a speaker after 1959, Malcolm X became the darling of academia.

By the early 1960s, Malcolm X was the second most sought-after speaker on American college campuses. (The most popular of all was the conservative Republican senator from Arizona, Barry Goldwater, who ran for president in 1964 against labor unions, the New Deal, and the Civil Rights Act.)[4] *Playboy* magazine introduced hipsters to Malcolm through an interview with Alex Haley (Malcolm's biographer) in May 1963, and the *Saturday Evening Post* enlightened the masses with a fourteen-page excerpt from *The Autobiography of Malcolm X* in 1964, a large story opening with a full-page color illustration and the title "I'm Talking to You, White Man."

Here are a few of Malcolm X's iconic statements: "When I say the white man is a devil, I speak with the authority of history. . . . The record of history shows that the white man, as a people, have never done good. . . . He stole our fathers and mothers from their culture of silk and satins and brought them to this land in the belly of a ship. . . . He has kept us in chains ever since we have been here. . . . Now this blue-eyed devil's time has about run out."[5] To this blanket of blame, descendants of European immigrants, the children of Louis Adamic's Peter Malek, answered, "Racists? Our ancestors owned no slaves. Most of us ceased being serfs only in the last two hundred years."[6] But few heard them. For the time being, black power garnered all the attention.

Very importantly, Malcolm X brought to blaze the love affair between academia and black nationalists, an attraction that continued after Malcolm's departure from the NOI in 1964 and his assassination in 1965. The black power movement he inspired propelled Black Panthers onto campuses and encouraged black intellectuals like the novelist James Baldwin to speak their minds openly. In *The Fire Next Time*, a brilliant essay that troubled white readers, Baldwin called white Americans' relationship to Europe "spurious"; they were hypocrites for Anglicizing their names, pretending to be real white Americans in recognition that the real America never could be only white. Embracing white supremacy and losing their ethnic identities, Baldwin maintained, were the price second-generation immigrants paid for the ticket to American whiteness.[7] In 1970 Baldwin and Margaret Mead's *Rap on Race*, a best seller, was eclipsed only when black power's most glamorous symbol, the Black Panther Party founder Huey P. Newton, held a conversation at Yale—later published—with America's most famous postwar psychologist, Erik H. Erikson.[8]

Pushed along by an avid media, the black power movement remade the notion of American racial identity.[9] Now the most fascinating racial identity was black, not white, a flip certain to disturb those who had struggled so hard to measure up to Anglo-Saxon standards. Working-class whites who resented being ignored, Catholics who felt vulnerable in academia, and Jews who were used to having the last word were all deeply offended. And white people pushed back. The rise of the "white ethnic" identity arose in direct response to Malcolm X and his black power successors.

IF BLACK people could proclaim themselves black and proud, white people could trumpet their whiteness. But therein lay a gigantic problem embedded in the long-standing American tradition of white nationalism. The Ku Klux Klans and white nationalists had already co-opted the white label, leaving "ethnic" for the aggrieved third and fourth European immigrant generations. They were innocent, they maintained, having had nothing to do with slavery or Jim Crow. And they embraced identities rooted in Europe as though it were still the early twentieth century.

But that time had passed. White ethnics could not reenact Horace Kallen's 1915 version of cultural pluralism, for they no longer spoke the old languages, wore their ancestors' clothes, or respected their grandparents' outmoded conventions of gender. The white ethnicity of the late twentieth century was little more than a leisure activity, one that American entrepreneurs embraced. Ethnic consumers could buy T-shirts imprinted with European flags, take tours of the old country, and parade in the street on ethnic holidays. This "symbolic ethnicity" seemed to offer a warm, family-oriented middle ground between stereotypes of plastic, uptight, middle-class Protestant Anglo-Saxons and violent, disorganized impoverished blacks.[10]

•

IN THE 1970s the term "ethnicity" shouldered aside older concepts of the white races. To be sure, the distinction between race and ethnicity still remains unclear. As a leading sociologist confessed, "it is true that systems of race and systems of ethnic relations have much in common."[11] To this day scholars and lay people find it difficult to tell race and ethnicity apart. Even the *Oxford English Dictionary* lists a second meaning for "ethnic": "Pertaining to race; peculiar to a race or nation; ethnological." Nowadays race leads directly to race as black, as in the black/white scheme of the South where the civil rights revolution became visible.[12] Black power took the concept even further, making black race a positive sign and white race the mark of guilty malfeasance. A correction to the guilty malfeasance part of the equation quickly appeared in print.

MICHAEL NOVAK'S *Rise of the Unmeltable Ethnics* (1972) became the national anthem of lower-middle-class whites. Born the grandson of Slovak immigrants in the Johnstown, Pennsylvania, steelmaking region, Novak (b. 1933) graduated from Stonehill College in North Easton, Massachusetts, and the Gregorian University in Rome, where he studied for the Catholic priesthood.

Staying with theology, he pursued graduate work at Catholic University and at Harvard, earning an M.A. in 1966. In 1961 he published a novel, *The Tiber Was Silver*, in which a young seminarian wrestles with ideas of God and tenets of the Catholic Church. As a freelance journalist between 1962 and 1965, Novak covered the Second Vatican Council's deliberations on the postwar world, then taught at Stanford University and the experimental college of the State University of New York at Old Westbury. In *The Rise of the Unmeltable Ethnics*, perfectly suited to the times, Novak concentrates on those unmeltable "PIGS," Poles, Italians, Greeks, and Slavs, in their view so long reviled: "The liberals always have despised us. We've got these mostly little jobs, and we drink beer and, my God, we bowl and watch television and we don't read. It's goddamn vicious snobbery. We're sick of all these phoney integrated TV commercials with these upper-class Negroes. We know they're phoney." Though they felt detested, the ethnics gloried in judging themselves smarter and harder-working than Negroes and tougher than the college crowd. Novak went along, deploring the "bigotry" he saw in Protestant and Jewish intellectuals so prejudiced against the ethnics and so in awe of black militants.[13]

Among Novak's heroes were the straight-talking vice president Spiro Agnew, born Spiro T. Anagnostopoulos in Baltimore, and the Alabama governor George Wallace.* Those tough guys reminded Novak of Slovak men arguing in Johnstown barbershops or his "uncle drinking so much beer he threatened to lay his dick upon the porch rail and wash the whole damn street with steaming piss—while cursing the niggers in the mill below, and the Yankees in the mill above—millstones he felt pressing him."[14] Newly elected governor in 1963, George Wallace had proclaimed "segregation now, segregation tomorrow, segregation forever," and backed up his words by "standing in the schoolhouse door" to protect the University of Alabama from two black students.[15] The university did finally admit the students (who eventually became honored alumni), but Wallace won, too, going on to pesky runs for the presidency in 1964, 1968, 1972, and 1976.†

Richard Nixon picked up the theme, running on the Wallace-inspired, antiblack "southern strategy" in 1968, a ploy that served Republicans well past the Ronald Reagan era. Novak reports with pride that Reagan's pollster had lifted "work, family, neighborhood, peace, strength" from him and used the slogan to rally Democrats for Reagan.[16]‡ Clearly, as they had for a century, races were still assumed to have racial temperaments, so the depiction of ethnic whites as tem-

---

*Agnew resigned the vice presidency after being indicted for bribery, becoming the first to leave office under the threat of criminal conviction.

†In 1965 Vivian Malone (1942–2005) became the first African American to graduate from the University of Alabama. James A. Hood (b. 1943), had entered with her in 1963, but left the university with an ulcer after a few months of harassment. He earned a doctorate in education from the university in 1997.

‡Novak went on to honors. Since 1978 he has held the George Frederick Jewett Chair in Religion and Public Policy at the conservative American Enterprise Institute in Washington, D.C. He received the million-dollar Templeton Prize for Progress in Religion, awarded at Buckingham Palace, in 1994 and delivered the Templeton address in Westminster Abbey.

peramentally honest and hardworking enjoyed a very long life. At bottom, the southern strategy pitted white people—*Americans*—against an alien *race* of black degenerate families judged lacking those self-same virtues. How things had changed from a promising brotherhood of the postwar era to a time of black/white tensions in the 1970s! A classic text soon spanned the two eras, capturing the mood of each moment from an academic point of view.

IN THE late 1950s the sociologists Nathan Glazer (b. 1923) and Daniel Patrick Moynihan (1927–2003) saw a trend and conceived a study of the various racial and ethnic groups in their own New York City. Glazer came from a Yiddish-speaking immigrant background and grew up in working-class East Harlem and the Bronx. He attended City College (where tuition was free); graduating in 1944, he went on to the University of Pennsylvania and to Columbia University, where he earned a Ph.D. in sociology and collaborated with David Riesman on *The Lonely Crowd*.* During the Kennedy administration of the early 1960s, Glazer worked in the War on Poverty in Washington, D.C., and got to know Daniel Patrick Moynihan, an assistant secretary of labor.

Born in Tulsa, Oklahoma, Moynihan had moved to New York with his family when he was six. Like Glazer, he lived in poor neighborhoods and studied at City College. However, Moynihan joined the Navy's officer-training program at Tufts University and received M.A. and Ph.D. degrees from Tufts after the war. In Washington, Moynihan and Glazer decided to work together, with Moynihan adding an essay on New York's Irish community and a general conclusion to Glazer's articles on ethnic groups in New York. Their 1963 book, *Beyond the Melting Pot: The Negroes, Puerto Ricans, Jews, Italians, and Irish of New York City*, became one of the most influential sociological studies of its time.[17] Glazer joined the Harvard University faculty in 1969, where

---

* Glazer is featured in *Arguing the World*, a film about the Jewish New York intellectuals who attended the City College of New York in the 1930s and 1940s and became leading American public intellectuals. Having started out as Trotskyites, they often became strong anticommunists in the 1950s and 1960s and leading neoconservatives following the turmoil of the 1960s.

Moynihan—soon to be elected U.S. senator from New York—had been since 1964.*

In its first edition, *Beyond the Melting Pot* painted an optimistic picture of various New York ethnic groups (including Negroes and Puerto Ricans) who were competing for power in the city and accommodating one another's claims. Glazer and Moynihan denied that any of the ethnic groups had melted into a bland Americanness. Ethnic groups were "not a purely biological phenomenon," and while old country languages and cultures had largely disappeared, ethnic groups were being "continually recreated by new experiences in America."[18]

Much of the book's readability rested on its ready resort to shaky generalization, which occasionally veered awfully close to stereotype.[19] The Jews were coming out on top by dint of intelligence and hard work; the bewildered Puerto Ricans could not figure out how to work the system; the Negroes were struggling against a heritage of discrimination, but the urban policies of the Kennedy administration would provide the assistance they needed. The Italians were losing ground, on account of "a failure of intellect."[20] In a mean-spirited aside, Glazer and Moynihan quote "a world-famous Yale professor who, at dinner, 'on the day an Italian American announced his candidacy for Mayor of New York,' remarked that 'If Italians aren't actually an inferior race, they do the best imitation of one I've seen.' (It was later also said of Mario Procaccino that he was so sure of being elected that he had ordered new *linoleum* for Gracie Mansion.)" Never mind the Italians; all in all, the future seemed hopeful.

Beyond the Melting Pot appeared in a second edition in 1970 with a very different feel. In a new long introduction, Glazer regretted the rise of black militants who insisted on their uniqueness. Now, he lamented, "we seem to be moving to a new set of categories, black and white, and that is ominous."[21] And that was where American white-

---

*In 1965 Moynihan published *The Negro Family: The Case for National Action*, also known as "The Moynihan Report," which added African Americans to the literature of degenerate families. From 1973 to 1975 he served as U.S. ambassador to India and in 1976 was elected to the U.S. Senate, where he served four terms.

ness stood three-quarters of the way through the twentieth century. The civil rights movement, it seemed, had spawned the ugly specter of black power, a source of alienation for white people. Rejecting the burden of white guilt that Malcolm X laid on them, white Americans were morphing into Italian Americans and Jewish Americans and Irish Americans. What they had in common was not being black.* Basically, white versus black now sufficed as an American racial scheme—for the moment.

---

*Nathan Glazer published the first full-length denunciation of affirmative action in 1975, *Affirmative Discrimination: Ethnic Inequality and Public Policy.* By 1997 he had come around to a grudging acceptance of multiculturalism (provided it was temporary) in *We Are All Multiculturalists Now.*

THE FOURTH ENLARGEMENT
OF AMERICAN WHITENESS

Agitating and media-dominating as America's civil rights and black power movements were, most of the country's white people might have doubted that the upheaval had much to do with them. They might have thought that they were individuals who had succeeded by themselves and that "race" had always meant black people, who had not. In fact, by the 1960s the whole "races of Europe" discourse had fallen completely out of fashion. Books such as William Z. Ripley's *Races of Europe*, once essential reading on race, were now remaindered as useless, and if you were not Jewish, calling Jews a race would send you straight into the anti-Semitic column.

Reminders that Jews and Italians had been labeled as "races" a generation earlier might have prompted a retort that "race" was used more loosely in the past. This is true. But *every* use of "race" has always been loose, whether applied to black, white, yellow, brown, red, or other. No consensus has ever formed on the number of human races or even on the number of white races. Criteria constantly shift according to individual taste and political need. It was clear, however, that in the olden days, Jim Crow had kept the "colored" races apart from whites and African Americans largely hidden behind segregation's veil. Shortly after the end of the Second World War, the end of legalized segregation began to propel black people into national visibility as never before.

Concurrently, other changes were soon to deeply alter Americans' sense of the very meanings of "race." Little noticed at the time, the openness of the mid-1960s went well beyond the black/white color line. The Immigration and Nationality (Hart-Celler) Act of 1965 was specifically crafted to counter earlier Nordic-minded immigration statutes, especially in terms of Asians. It also allowed for wider immigration from the Western Hemisphere and Africa. Therein lay the seeds of demographic revolution.

New new immigrants of the post-1965 era, overwhelmingly from outside Europe, were upending American racial conventions. Asians, greatly rising in number, were rapidly being judged to be smarter and, eventually, to be richer than native-born whites. Latinos formed 13 percent of the population by 2000, edging out African Americans as the most numerous minority.

The U.S. census, without peer in scoring the nation's racial makeup, had begun to notice Latin Americans in the 1940s by counting up heterogeneous peoples with Spanish surnames and hastily lumping them together as "Hispanics." Though an impossibly crude measurement, it survived until 1977. By that point, the federal government needed more precise racial statistics to enforce civil rights legislation. To this end, the Office of Management and Budget issued Statistical Policy Directive no. 15.

Here was a change worth noting: in the racially charged decades of the early twentieth century, governments at all levels had passed laws to separate Americans by race. Though Jim Crow segregation was supposed to be separate but equal, in practice it worked to discriminate, by excluding nonwhites from public institutions, whether from libraries, schools, swimming pools, or the ballot box. The Civil Rights Act of 1964 and the Voting Rights Act of 1965 began to change all that, so that by the late twentieth century the rationale for counting people by race had morphed into a means of keeping track of civil rights enforcement. Statistical Policy Directive no. 15 set the terms for racial and ethnic classification throughout American society by directing federal agencies— including the U.S. census—to collect data according to four races (black,

white, American Indian/Alaskan Native, and Asian/Pacific Islander—
Hawaiian was added later as a concession to protests) and one ethnic
category (Hispanic/Latino, which is not racial). Elaboration was good for
civil rights, but it opened the way to chaos.

Under these guidelines the Hispanic/Latino classification portended
enormous turmoil. Now that there was a "non-Hispanic white" category,
did there not also exist Hispanic white people? Yes, no, and other. Faced
with the given racial choices on the census of 2000, fully 42.2 percent of
Latinos checked "some other race," rather than "black" or "white," throwing nearly 6 percent of Americans into a kind of racial limbo.[1]

In addition, the U.S. census of 2000 had to increase a deeper and
more personal recognition of multiracial identities. For the first time,
respondents were allowed to describe themselves as belonging to one
or more of fifteen "racial" identities. As so often in the past—and adding confusion—the list of races included nationalities.[2] (See figure 28.1,
Question 6 from 2000 U.S. Census.) This expansion now allowed for 126
ethnoracial groups or, for purists, 63 races. It did not take much analytical ability to see that any notion of race lay so diluted as to lose much of
its punch. And taxonomy was rapidly buckling much further under the
weight of interracial sex.

Nothing new here. Americans' disorderly sexual habits have always
overflowed neat racial lines and driven race thinkers crazy. Asians and
Native American Indians had the highest rates of interracial marriage,
but others, including African Americans, now often married and had
children with people from outside their racial-ethnic group. By 1990,
American families were so heterogeneous that 1/7 of whites, 1/3 of blacks,
4/5 of Asians, and 19/20 Native American Indians were closely related to
someone of a different racial group. With some 12 percent of young
people now calling themselves multiracial, it is expected that, by 2050,
10 percent of whites and blacks and more than 50 percent of Latinos,
Asians, and Native American Indians will be married to someone outside their racial group.[3]

With so many nonwhite and white Americans marrying willy-nilly,
barriers between the progeny of European immigrants have largely dis-

☞ ❻ **What is this person's race?** *Mark* ☒ *one or more races to indicate that this person considers himself/herself to be.*

☐ White
☐ Black, African Am., or Negro
☐ American Indian or Alaska Native—*Print name of enrolled or principal tribe.* ❚

_____

☐ Asian Indian   ☐ Native Hawaiian
☐ Chinese   ☐ Guamanian or
☐ Filipino   Chamorro
☐ Japanese   ☐ Samoan
☐ Korean   ☐ Other Pacific
☐ Vietnamese   Islander—
☐ Other Asian—*Print race.* ❚   *Print race.* ❚

_____   _____

☐ Some other race—*Print race.* ❚

_____

Fig. 28.1. Question 6 from 2000 U.S. Census.

appeared. Among white people, three out of four marriages had already crossed ethnic boundaries by 1980. A generation later, very few white Americans had four grandparents from the same country.[4] Crèvecoeur's European-derived "American, this new man," had arrived. William Z. Ripley had predicted this outcome in 1908, fearing, above all, the "inharmonious" mixing of Italian men and Irish women. But he now would have been forced to reconsider his prediction that such a "racial" mix would make Americans ugly.

We have already seen the lowering of racial boundaries starting in the

1940s, when "ethnic" began replacing "race" as applied to the descendants of European immigrants. The use of "racial groups" for white people has become a moribund category, too, partly because white people are so mixed up. Finally, the perquisites of mere whiteness count for less in the present situation, while the stigma of blackness—once just one drop sufficed to curse the white-looking individual—also seems less mortal.

Back in the twentieth century, white people were assumed to be rich or at least middle-class, as well as more beautiful, powerful, and smart. As citizens and scholars, they said what needed to be known and monopolized the study of other people—with themselves hardly being marked or scrutinized in return. Think of Francis A. Walker and William Z. Ripley, for whom formal education, New England ancestry, and useful connections assured authority. Half a century later, the upheaval of the civil rights era turned the looking glass around, bringing white people under scrutiny. Think of Malcolm X and James Baldwin.

WITH THE American South so fully in the spotlight during the civil rights revolution, one of the earliest scrutinizers of whiteness came from north Georgia. Lillian Smith (1897–1966), a white southern essayist, novelist, and (with her lifetime partner Paula Schnelling) operator of a fancy summer camp for girls, powerfully described her South in *Killers of the Dream* (1949 and 1961). The book pilloried southern culture as pathological and white supremacist southerners as caught in a spiral of sex, sin, and segregation.[5]* Here was a book of wide influence that portrayed whiteness as morally diseased.

Following Smith, two white Texan journalists turned a critical gaze on white people by passing as black. John Howard Griffin (1920–80) dyed his skin black and traveled throughout the South, researching a magazine series published as *Black like Me* in 1961. An international bestseller, *Black like Me* became a feature film in 1964. (Gerda Lerner,

---

* *Killers of the Dream* includes a sequence of mistaken racial identity reminiscent of Gustave de Beaumont's *Marie*, when young Lillian's mother rejects a child initially thought white but discovered to be colored.

then a writer, later a pioneering historian of women, wrote the screen-play.) White southerners in *Black like Me* were indeed a perverted, disgusting crowd. The women dehumanized their black neighbors with the "hate stare"; the men's notions of blackness began and ended pornographically.[6] Griffin, in turn, inspired Grace Halsell (1923–2000), whose dyed skin turned her into a strange-looking black woman, but black enough to pass and to attract racist insult, in the North and the South, as she chronicled in *Soul Sister* (1964).[7]* By the 1990s, whiteness was no longer the invisible norm, and the critical study of white people was burgeoning into an academic field in the mold of black studies.[8]

Critical white studies began with David R. Roediger's *The Wages of Whiteness: Race and the Making of the American Working Class* in 1991 and Noel Ignatiev's *How the Irish Became White* in 1995. Seeing slavery and black people as central in creating nineteenth-century white identity, these two books show how working-class European immigrants, Irish in particular, took advantage of being classified as white in the American context. Irishmen took control of workplaces, unions, and politics, crucial steps in their upward mobility. It soon followed that middle-class status transformed them fully into Americans.

An abundance of books and articles dissecting the meanings of whiteness followed.[9] Whiteness studies hold white race, ordinarily invisible in the black/white dichotomy, up to the light. In them it appears as social, not biological, a powerful social construct letting whites think of themselves first and foremost as individuals. Although white people may exempt themselves from race, white privilege comes into view as a crucial facet of white race identity. At the same time, many other characteristics—class, region, gender, age, able-bodiedness, and sexual orientation—all affect the manifestation of this privilege.

Nowadays, whiteness studies analyze the porous nature of contemporary racial boundaries. In contrast to their nineteenth- and twentieth-century counterparts, multiracial people may now claim their own separate category.[10] In former times, however, one black ancestor, no matter

---

*After her stint as black, Grace Halsell passed as an Indian and later annoyed Zionists with her commentary on Israel.

how distant, could convey a permanent "taint" of blackness that made one a Negro, as in the case of Gustave de Beaumont's title character Marie. Race was central to identity, and people were assumed to remain permanently where they were born, especially if their races were stigmatized. In the words of Ralph Waldo Emerson, "Race is a controlling influence in the Jew, who, for two millenniums, under every climate, has preserved the same character and employments. Race in the negro is of appalling importance."[11] As we have seen, powerful men like Thomas Jefferson also bowed to the ideal of racial purity—he held that interracial sex would surely lead to degradation—even while contravening his view by having children in a stable, intimate relationship with one of his slaves.[12] Nowadays, only white supremacists and Nazis fetishize white racial purity.

Today the attractive qualities that Saxons-Anglo-Saxons-Nordics-whites were assumed to monopolize are also to be found elsewhere.* After a string of nonwhite Misses America, Jennifer Lopez and Beyoncé Knowles are celebrated as Hollywood beauties; Vijay Singh, Tiger Woods, and the Williams sisters, Venus and Serena, dominate elite sports; Robert Johnson (founder of BET network), Bill Cosby, and the financier Alphonse Fletcher Jr. have made millions; Oprah Winfrey is rich and famous. Colin Powell and Condoleezza Rice have been secretaries of state, and Alberto Gonzales attorney general. Even more to the point of uniting power and beauty, Barack Obama is president of the United States. First Lady Michelle Obama, whose skin color alone would have condemned her to ugliness in the twentieth century, figures as an icon of beauty and intelligence on the global stage. None of these individuals is white, but being white these days is not what it used to be.

Thus, it is sensible to conclude that *the* American is undergoing a fourth great enlargement. Although race may still seem overweening, without legal recognition it is less important than in the past. The dark of skin who also happen to be rich (say, people of South Asian, African American, and Hispanic background), and the light of skin (from any-

---

*Twenty-first-century holdouts could still cling to idealized notions of white-Anglo-Saxon-Protestantism, as in the case of the late Harvard political scientist Samuel P. Huntington in *Who Are We?: The Challenges to America's National Identity* (2004).

where) who are beautiful, are now well on the way to inclusion. Is this the end of race in America?

AT THE turn of the twenty-first century, it was starting to look that way. In 1997, the American Association of Physical Anthropologists urged the American government to phase out the use of race as a data category and to substitute ethnic categories instead.[13] Geneticists studying DNA—the constituent material of genes that issues instructions to our bodies in response to our surroundings—were also concluding that race as a biological category made no sense.

The habit of relating human heredity to the environment may be traced back to antiquity, but early nineteenth-century racial thinkers turned the notion around, deeming race a permanent marker for innate superiority or inferiority. Not until the 1850s did the influence of environment on heredity get rescued with Charles Darwin's *On the Origin of Species*. Darwin described a world much older than the biblical five thousand years, reasoning that heredity was not fixed, that generation after generation, living things change in response to their surroundings.[14] Race thinkers like Ripley selectively reinterpreted Darwinian evolution in the late nineteenth century, turning natural selection into a competition between unequal races. Similarly, eugenicists pitched in, reworking Gregor Mendel's discoveries on inheritance into a theory of racial unit traits (such as intelligence) in the early twentieth century, all in the service of racial hierarchy. In 1953 the field of molecular genetics emerged with the discovery by James D. Watson and Francis Crick of deoxyribonucleic acid (DNA), the molecule in chromosomes that carries our genes, the functional unit of heredity.* Genomes (all the genes in each cell of an organism) could be mapped as to function, first in simpler organisms like fruit flies, then in larger animals, and on to parts of the human genome. The closer to a complete human genome, the hotter

---

* Genes hold DNA and RNA (whose functions are only now being understood), the recipe for proteins that activate themselves in response to the environment. Not that the genome consists only of genes. Ninety-seven percent of the genome is a mixture of various sorts of DNA summed up as junk DNA whose purpose, if it has one, remains mysterious.

grew the competition to make it complete, and the more scholars sought to interpret its meaning.[15]

It was this science of molecular genetics that drove the longest nail into the theory of race. Even before the human genome mapping was complete, the American Association for the Advancement of Science (AAAS) concluded in 1995 that, in biological terms, race holds no scientific validity. Its only importance lay now in its role as a social category to strike down patterns of discrimination. Reporting on the AAAS meeting, major newspapers carried headlines proclaiming, "No Such Thing as Race, Genetic Studies Say."[16] Would this judgment hold once the entire human genome was parsed?

In June 2000, the race, then several years old, between the National Institutes of Health (governmental organizations) and Celera Genomics (a private company) was declared a tie by president Bill Clinton in the White House.* Some of the result triggered disappointment, even dismay: for example, humans turned out to have fewer genes than expected, some 40,000 genes on 100 trillion cells, rather a letdown for those expecting the more extravagant number of 100,000, as befitting such a smart species.[17] But, much more importantly, two facts shone clearly from this research: in the words of J. Craig Venter, then head of Celera Genomics, "Race is a social concept, not a scientific one. We all evolved in the last 100,000 years from the same small number of tribes that migrated out of Africa and colonized the world." Each person shares 99.99 percent of the genetic material of every other human being. In terms of variation, people from the same race can be more different than people from different races.[18] And in the genetic sense, all people—and all Americans—are African descended.

President Clinton closed his remarks in 2000 with an unequivocal

---

* Strictly speaking, the human genome that had been sequenced was not "the" genome of every human being, for despite a similarity of 99 percent of our genes from one person to another, each individual's genome is unique. The genome that Celera mapped was that of a particular individual, its founder, Craig Venter. Therefore "the" human genome that Celera owns is that of a particular white American man. Mapping a complete human genome now costs nearly $100,000, so few are likely to know themselves to this degree, and Venter's gene sequence will represent the normal for some time to come.

statement: "in genetic terms all human beings, regardless of race, are more than 99.9 percent the same. What that means is that modern science has confirmed what we first learned from ancient faiths. The most important fact of life on this earth is our common humanity." Press coverage amplified this news.

Subsequently, an intriguing discussion on race and genetics has been afoot among Jews. One side contends that Jews have nearly always seen themselves as a race, and that studies of Jewish DNA underscore the "tribal" nature of Jewish religion.[19] The other side warns about the chaos that could flow from focusing too tightly on the biological basis of Jewishness, for Jewish men and Jewish women do not share the same set of genes. While the Y chromosomes of Jewish men show a relatively high degree of similarity all over the world, they are particularly close to the configuration of Middle Easterners of any background. Jewish women's mitochondrial DNA, in contrast, shows much less similarity, leading to the conclusion that Jewish men often married non-Jewish women.[20] (It should be noted that other parts of the world also show genetic imbalances between the sexes. In Great Britain, for instance, Y chromosomes testify to the historical presence of male Vikings, while mitochondrial DNA remains more solidly Celtic, the pre-Roman genetic configuration of the islands as a whole.)[21] Treating Jewishness as something in the genes risks fissuring an already heterogeneous community.

The biological meaninglessness of classifying people according to race remained the scholarly consensus until about 2002. Then research came to light that sought to lump DNA patterns by population groups. This work produced a theory that DNA falls into five major groups—Africans, Europeans and Middle Easterners, East Asians, Melanesians, and American Indians—which happen to correspond more or less to those of Johann Friedrich Blumenbach and popular views.* (True to the disorderly history of race, a study in *Scientific American* in 2003 reported a four-way grouping.) The *New York Times* illustrated its story about this research with a long colored bar graph. Only in its last paragraph does the report

---

* According to Anne Fausto-Sterling, Neil Risch and his colleagues even use Blumenbach's term "Caucasian" for the European and Middle Eastern group.

explain that even though all people "share most of their genetic variability in common," the chart is based on "these genetic differences, not on the very much larger shared inheritance."[22] In short, the illustration is neither helpful nor accurate, in that it wildly exaggerates differences while omitting the overwhelming degree of similarity.[23]* True to racial thinking, differences were stressed and similarities played down. The idea of biological race was reemerging as genetic science.

This sort of reinterpretation seemed eerily familiar. Liberal social scientists and geneticists feared that some geneticists were once again searching for genetic causes underlying diseases like diabetes and cardiovascular disease that reflect racial disparities likely rooted in injuries of class and history. Lost in that speculation was the certainty that those diseases stem from a complex interplay between environment and the interaction of many genes, rather than the few genes governing superficial characteristics like skin color and hair texture.[24] Furthermore, rather than addressing poverty, social disarray, and unequal access to health care, genetics could reinforce the class and race status quo, thereby echoing the hereditarian gospel of early twentieth-century eugenics.[25]

Between 2002 and about 2005, this emphasis on racial genetic difference made some headway in medicine, where doctors and pharmaceutical companies pushed the idea of racialized populations and racialized medicine. They were talking about black people.[26] This was true even though the clearest cases of genetic diseases that occur only in particular populations, such as Tay-Sachs among people descended from European Jews, and hemochromatosis among Swedes, affect white people.[27]

Racial identity, interpreted as black, also presented an ideal marketing opportunity in 2004, when the NitroMed pharmaceutical company sought approval for the first racial drug, BiDil (a combination of isosorbide dinitrate and hydralazine hydrochloride), for treatment of heart disease. In fact, BiDil was an older, often ineffective drug repackaged for black consumption. Initially rejected by the Food and Drug Administration, it was approved in 2005 and is currently advertised for use on

---

*The methodologies used, the tracing of Alus and SNPs, do not explain whether Alus and SNPs play any active role in human behavior.

African Americans. As a combination of two drugs available generically, it pays off nicely for the company. BiDil does help some patients with heart disease, although it is currently being marketed only to one sector of society.[28]

ARGUMENTS OVER race in the human genome have subsided of late, leaving us with some intriguing data about personal appearance. Prevailing racial schemes now rest once again on concepts of skin color, hence "black" people and "white" people. But widely recognized is the fact that not only are "black" people actually various shades of brown and yellow but so too are "white" people, merely somewhat lighter and often with a lot more pink. As Blumenbach realized in the late eighteenth century, one group's skin color shades gradually into another's; there are no clearly demarcated lines. Some people who identify as "black" may have lighter-colored skin than others who identify as "white." Siblings with the same mother and father can display a range of skin colors. Race may be all about pigment, but what makes people's skin light or dark?

Skin color is a by-product of two kinds of melanin: red to yellow *pheomelanin* and dark brown to black *eumelanin* in reaction to sunlight.[29] And several genes interact to make people light or dark, reddish, brownish, or yellowish. Ancient scholars were wiser than they knew when they related skin color to climate. Today's biologists concur. Sunny climates do make people dark-skinned, and dark, cold climates make people light-skinned. How much of which sort of melanin people have in their skin—and to what degree it is expressed—depends entirely over time on exposure to the sun's ultraviolet (UV) radiation. Melanin both protects against excessive ultraviolet radiation and allows sufficient UV radiation to enter the body. Too much UV radiation causes skin cancer and can lead to death. Two vitamins, D and B3 (folate), play crucial roles.

Vitamin D and vitamin B3 also serve life's central activity of childbearing: insufficient folate impedes the growth of bone marrow, encourages neural tube defects, and disrupts the production of new cells, causing birth defects. UV radiation does not simply destroy, however; it also creates vitamin D, crucial for calcium absorption and bone growth. Not enough vitamin D from sunlight prevents the absorption of calcium, weakening the bones. In terms of reproduction, skin color manifests the balance between enough darkness for DNA synthesis and enough lightness for vitamin D absorption. As people have migrated around the world, their skin color has adjusted.

Our species originated in Africa some 1.2 million years ago, evolving from primates like chimpanzees. Chimpanzees, like most other animals, have light skin under dark hair. Shedding that thick coat of hair, humans quickly developed dark skin, and they stayed dark until leaving Africa for cloudier territory about 100,000 years ago, when residence in dark, wintry regions like northern Europe and northern Asia required another color change, this time from dark to light. Light-skinned Europeans and light-skinned Asians lost pigmentation through different genetic processes in Europe and Asia.

People can change color through natural selection fairly quickly, within a thousand years or so, or they can do it instantly by choosing a mate whose skin is a different color.* Those in polar regions, for instance, have turned darker again over time for protection against strong ultraviolet radiation. A paucity of melanin may cost us dearly as global warming exposes the earth to increased ultraviolet radiation.

In sum, humans change color in several ways, including seasonably and cosmetically. Those who are short on melanin are already taking steps to protect their offspring by using sunscreen and, perhaps unwittingly, by marrying darker-skinned people. Anyone in a mixed-race family knows of the impermanence of parental skin color, for the sex act immediately affects the very next generation. In addition, mutation of the SLC24A5 gene of human chromosome 15 can quickly and simply make skin more or less dark. Readers of this book will not live to see

---

*In an odd way, the weird theories of the mid-twentieth-century Nation of Islam (NOI) held a grain of truth within a nutty overall scheme. According to the NOI, a crazed black scientist had turned black people into whites through selective breeding as a punishment for wickedness. No such scientist existed, but whiteness out of blackness actually occurred over the course of thousands of years and residence in different climates.

global warming's massive affect on human skin color, but such transitions will surely occur if *Homo sapiens* is to persist.

Finally, then, what can be said about skin color and race? According to race thinking, race and color must agree—hence races designated according to color, as in "black," "white," "brown," "yellow," and "red." And race must be innate and permanent. Yet it has been obvious since the invention of racial science in the eighteenth century that skin color can change drastically from one generation to the next. All that is needed is sex between people of different colors, which has taken place as soon as people meet. Acknowledgment of the existence of people of "mixed race," as in the U.S. census, means acknowledgment of the impermanence of race.

WHERE ARE we now? Mapping the human genome elicited initial proclamations of human kindredness across the globe. Then race talk inscribed racial difference on our genes. That talk has not disappeared, but ideally we would realize that human beings' short history relates us all to one another. To speak in racial terms, incessant human migration has made us all multiracial.[30] Does this mean the human genome or civil rights or desegregation have ended the tyranny of race in America?

Almost certainly not. The fundamental black/white binary endures, even though the category of whiteness—or we might say more precisely, a category of nonblackness—effectively expands. As before, the black poor remain outside the concept of *the* American as an "alien race" of "degenerate families." A multicultural middle class may diversify the suburbs and college campuses, but the face of poor, segregated inner cities remains black.[31] For quite some time, many observers have held that money and interracial sex would solve the race problem, and, indeed, in some cases, they have. Nonetheless, poverty in a dark skin endures as the opposite of whiteness, driven by an age-old social yearning to characterize the poor as permanently other and inherently inferior.

ACKNOWLEDGMENTS

I have worked on this book too long and in too many places to craft adequate acknowledgments, but I know I owe thanks to many people and institutions and must make a sincere try. This project grew out of an invention of the 1990s: whiteness studies. While I learned a great deal from the work of historians in that field, overall, I missed a longer, broader view than I found in work focusing on the United States. I began to undertake my own adventure into whiteness studies in classes I taught at Princeton University. My first debts, therefore, relate to History 382, "Whiteness in Historical Perspective," and History 574, "Whiteness Studies," to my colleagues, who encouraged my thinking out loud, my students, whose curiosity led me on, and my graduate student preceptors, Crystal Feimster and Eric Yellin, who brought their own useful insights to bear.

When students mentioned their work in a class they abbreviated as "whiteness," it intrigued their families and friends as a topic of study at Princeton. Early on, students reported more interest at home in my racial background than in the material we were covering. But that preoccupation subsided. In more recent years, concerns about my race seem greatly to have faded, their place taken by open curiosity about the project. For this evolution, I thank the American people.

This project began in earnest in Germany, where my German-language teachers were Birgit Ölsanger and Renate Scherer. My scholarly colleagues in Europe—Lorraine Daston, Jeanette Demeestère, Ottmar Ette, Michael Hagner, Susanne Marchand, Renato Mazzolini,

Roberta Modugno, Nicolaas Rupke, and Patricia Springborg—offered illuminating discussion of the issues from European perspectives. In the United States I have benefited from conversations and correspondence with Hans Aarsleff, Priscilla Barnum, Ben Braude, David Brion Davis, David Cannadine, Hazel Carby, William Clark, Linda Colley, John Hope Franklin, David Freund, Gary Gerstle, Robert Gordon, Annette Gordon-Reed, Anthony Grafton, Lani Guinier, Matthew Guterl, Walter Johnson, Chin Jou, Michael Keevak, Mary Kelley, John Kenfield, Mary Lu Kirsty, Max Kortepeter, Stephen Kotkin, Bruce Levine, Bernard Lewis, Niamh Lynch, Rajiv Malhotra, Mark Mazower, Kerby Miller, Eduardo Pagan, Grace Palladino, Carl Rezak, David Roediger, Carl Schorske, Richard Slotkin, Thomas Sugrue, John Sweet, Andrew Szegedy-Maszak, and Eric Yellin. I owe special thanks to Angela Rosenthal, David Bindman, and Sarah Lewis for guidance in visual analysis and to Neil Baldwin for encouragement.

I have enjoyed presenting aspects of this project to colleagues at the Free University in Berlin, Wesleyan University, the Gilder Lehrman Center at Yale University, the NYU Biography Seminar, the Essex, New York, Public Library, Reed College, the University of Roma Tre, and in my own Princeton Department of History. I also had the pleasure of offering facets of this work as presidential addresses to the Southern Historical Association in 2007 and the Organization of American Historians in 2008, and I owe thanks to the editorial staffs of the *Journal of Southern History* and the *Journal of American History*.

This work has depended on literature, most especially on the collections and librarians in Princeton University's Firestone Library. People whose names I do not know have helped me immensely through interlibrary loan's "Article Direct" service. I do know the names of several in Firestone who have aided me: Elizabeth Bennett, Bobray J. Bordelon, Sharon Brown, Joel R. Burlingham, Mary George, Linda Oppenheim, AnnaLee Pauls, Sandy Rosenstock, Don Simon, and Don C. Skemer. Thank you. Working often outside Princeton and New Jersey, I also appreciate the useful resource of Google Books.

Princeton University has supported my scholarship for many years, especially through research funding from the Department of History and the Office of the Provost. Judy Hanson, Lynn Kratzer, and Pamela Long in the Department of History have kept me in touch with Princeton from Newark and beyond. My Princeton research assistants—Malinda Lindquist, Deborah Becher, and Jonathan Walton—kept me in research materials. In New York, many tasks have fallen to the assistants to Edwin Barber at W. W. Norton, most recently and heavily to Melanie Tortoroli. I also owe much gratitude to an omniscient copy editor, Otto Sonntag. My agent Charlotte Sheedy got this book off to its start, and my genius husband, Glenn Shafer, and my friend Thadious Davis have kept me going all these many years. Thank you. Thank you again.

I have dedicated this book to its two indispensables: my gentleman-scholar editor, Edwin Barber, and the resource at its foundation, Princeton University Library.

NOTES

INTRODUCTION

1 See, for instance, Ariela J. Gross, "Litigating Whiteness: Trials of Racial Determination in the Nineteenth-Century South," *Yale Law Review* 108, no. 1 (October 1998): 109–88, and Walter Johnson, "The Slave Trader, the White Slave, and the Politics of Racial Determination in the 1850s," *Journal of American History* 87, no. 1 (June 2000): 13–38.

2 See Martin Bernal, *Black Athena: The Afroasiatic Roots of Classical Civilization*, vol. 2, *The Fabrication of Ancient Greece, 1785–1985* (New Brunswick, NJ: Rutgers University Press, 1987), and "Race, Class, and Gender in the Formation of the Aryan Model of Greek Origins, *South Atlantic Quarterly* 94, no. 4 (Fall 1995): 786–1008, and Michele V. Ronnick, ed., *The Autobiography of William Sanders Scarborough: An American Journey from Slavery to Scholarship* (Detroit: Wayne State University Press, 2005), 175, 207, 243, 351.

CHAPTER 1: GREEKS AND SCYTHIANS

1 See Norman Davies, *Europe: A History* (New York: Oxford University Press, 1996), 7.

Nineteenth-century scholars sought an Aryan or Indo-European race of ancestors, even though cultural markers such as archaeological sites do not correlate reliably with languages or biological lineage. See Peter S. Wells, *Beyond Celts, Germans and Scythians* (London: Duckworth, 2001), Malcolm Chapman, *The Celts: The Construction of a Myth* (New York: St. Martin's Press, 1992), and J. P. Mallory, *In Search of the Indo-Europeans: Language, Archaeology and Myth* (London: Thames and Hudson, 1989).

2 In "Europa als Bewegung: Zur literarischen Konstruktion eines Faszinosum"

(unpublished paper, 2001), Ottmar Ette discusses the nowhereness of the idea of Europe. Like the idea of the Caucasus, that of Europe grows out of a vague borderland. See esp. 5, 15–17.

3 See Robert Bedrosian, "Eastern Asia Minor and the Caucasus in Ancient Mythologies," http://www.virtualscape.com/rbedrosian/mythint.htm.

4 Fritz F. Pleitgen, *Durch den wilden Kaukasus* (Cologne: Kiepenheuer & Witsch, 2000), 22–24, 26.

5 This discussion leans heavily on Wells, *Beyond Celts*, esp. 74–77, 104.

6 Hippocrates, *Airs, Waters, Places*, part 23, in *Hippocrates, with an English Translation by W. H. S. Jones*, vol. 1 (Cambridge: Harvard University Press, 1923), 24.

7 Tony Judt, "The Eastern Front, 2004," *New York Times*, 5 Dec. 2004; Davies, *Europe*, 53. See also Bryan Sykes, *The Seven Daughters of Eve* (New York: W. W. Norton, 2001).

8 See http://www.martinmchale.com/clan/celt.html.

9 See http://www.livius.org/he-hg/hecataeus/hecataeus.htm.

10 Pergamon and Altes Museum, Berlin, in http://www.livius.org/he-hg/herodotus/herodotus03.html.

11 "Herodotus," *Encyclopædia Britannica Online*, 21 May 2007, http://www.search.eb.com/eb/article-9040200.

12 See O. Kimball Armayor, "Did Herodotus Ever Go to the Black Sea?" *Harvard Studies in Classical Philology* 82 (1978): 57–62, Cheikh Anta Diop, *The African Origin of Civilization*, ed. and trans. Mercer Cook (Chicago: Lawrence Hill, 1974), 1:115 (n. 3), and Frank Martin, "The Egyptian Ethnicity Controversy and the Sociology of Knowledge," *Journal of Black Studies* 14, no. 3 (March 1984): 295–325. See also J. Harmatta, "Herodotus, Historian of the Cimmerians and the Scythians," Giuseppe Nenci, "L'Occidente 'barbarico,'" and discussion, in *Hérodote et les peuples non grecs*, ed. Olivier Reverdin and Bernard Grange, Entretiens sur l'antiquité classique, vol. 35 (Geneva: Vandœuvres, 1988), 115–30, 301–20. See also Michael Novak, *The Rise of the Unmeltable Ethnics: Politics and Culture in the Seventies* (New York: Macmillan, 1972), 96–97.

13 Herodotus, *Histories*, 4.75:239.

14 Francis R. B. Godolphin, "Herodotus; On the Scythians," *Metropolitan Museum of Art Bulletin*, n.s., 32, no. 5, From the Lands of the Scythians: Ancient Treasures from the Museums of the U.S.S.R., 3000 B.C.–100 B.C. (1973–74), 137. The quotes come from Herodotus, *Histories*, 4.64 and 4.65.

15 Herodotus, *Histories*, 4.67:236; 4.110–16:249–51.

16 Hippocrates, *Airs, Waters, Places*, part 24:135, 137.

17 Ibid.

18 Ibid., part 20:125.

19 Ibid., part 18:117, 119.

20 Ibid., parts 21–22:125, 127, 129.

21 Ibid., part 16:115; part 23:131, 133.

22 Ibid., part 16:115; part 23:131, 133.

23 Ibid., part 23:133.

24 D. C. Braund and G. R. Tsetskhladze, "The Export of Slaves from Colchis," *Classical Quarterly*, n.s., 39, no. 1 (1989): 114, 118–19; M. I. Finley, *Economy and Society in Ancient Greece* (New York: Viking Press, 1982), 169, 173; Orlando Patterson, *Slavery and Social Death: A Comparative Study* (Cambridge: Harvard University Press, 1982), 149–50.

25 British Broadcasting Corporation, "Ancient Greek Slavery and Its Relationship to Democracy," http://www.bbc.co.uk/dna/h2g2/A471467; Finley, *Economy and Society in Ancient Greece*, 167–73, 175.

26 M. I. Finley, "Was Greek Civilization Based on Slave Labour?" in *Slavery in Classical Antiquity: Views and Controversies* (Cambridge: Heffer, 1968), 150–52.

27 Herodotus, *Histories*, 4.1–4:215–18.

28 Ibid., 3.97:193.

29 Finley, "Was Greek Civilization Based on Slave Labour?" 146.

CHAPTER 2: ROMANS, CELTS, GAULS, AND GERMANI

1 Tacitus, *Germania*, ed. and trans. J. B. Rives (Oxford: Clarendon Press, 1999), 21.

2 *The Geography of Strabo*, Loeb Classical Library, 8 vols., Greek texts with facing English translation by H. L. Jones (Cambridge: Harvard University Press, 1917–32), book 4, chap. 4: 2, 238–39. Loeb edition on the web, http://penelope.uchicago.edu/Thayer/E/Roman/Texts/Strabo/home.html.

3 *The Geography of Strabo*, book 7, chap. 1 (Loeb vol. 3, p. 151), http://penelope.uchicago.edu/Thayer/E/Roman/Texts/Strabo/7A*.html.

4 For ancient Germans as noble savages, see Audrey Smedley, "Race," *Encyclopædia Britannica Online*, 5 Sept. 2007, http://www.search.eb.com/eb/article-234682. See also Bruce Baum, *The Rise and Fall of the Caucasian Race: A Political History of Racial Identity* (New York: New York University Press, 2006), 37.

5 For a broader explanation of Caesar's career and the place of the Gallic war within it, see Arnold Toynbee, "Caesar, Julius," *Encyclopædia Britannica Online*, 9 Sept. 2007, http://www.search.eb.com/eb/article-9737. On the sale of slaves and the role of Roman slave dealing, see Julius Caesar, *Seven*

Commentaries on the Gallic War, ed. and trans. Carolyn Hammond (Oxford: Oxford University Press, 1996), 52, 62, 227.

6 Caesar, *Gallic War,* xxvii, 3. Caesar's three-way division, nowadays familiar, was contested in its time.

7 Ibid., 181, 183, 193.

8 Ibid., 51, 57, 66, also 104, 116, 158, 186, 193, 236–37.

9 Ibid., 186.

10 Ibid., 29, 31. Of languages spoken in modern France, Breton (a Celtic language) seems more closely related to the Gallic language Caesar mentions than does French, a Latin language.

11 Ibid., 3, 131.

12 Ibid., 124, 129–31.

13 Ibid., 33.

14 Ibid., 95–96.

15 Pliny the Elder, *Natural History: A Selection,* trans. and ed. John F. Healy (Harmondsworth, UK: Penguin Books, 1991), 89.

16 Ibid., 42–43, 75, 376.

17 Ibid., 75–78, 105, 122.

18 Tacitus, *Germania,* 77–78.

19 Ibid., 83.

20 Ibid., 81–83, 86–87.

21 Ibid., 52–57, 62–63.

22 Ibid., 77.

23 Ibid., 85.

24 Ibid., 78.

25 Ibid., 77.

26 Caesar, *Gallic War,* 37, 95–96. See also Norman Davies, *Europe: A History* (New York: Oxford University Press, 1996), 53, 84, 214–18.

27 Peter John Heather, "Germany," *Encyclopædia Britannica Online,* http://www.search.eb.com/eb/article-58082; Rives, in Tacitus, *Germania,* 64–71.

28 *Oxford English Dictionary Online,* http://dictionary.oed.com/cgi/entry/5009 4001=3fquery_type=3dword&queryword=3dgerman&first=3d1&max_to _show=3d10&sort_type=3dalpha&result_place=3d2&search_id=3dBPKR -KKy4Nh-5252&hilite=3d50094001.

29 Davies, *Europe,* 222.

30 See Robert J. C. Young, *The Idea of English Ethnicity* (Malden, Mass.: Blackwell, 2008), 16–23, and Tom Shippey, "Tests of Temper," *TLS,* 17 October 2008, p. 12.

31 Edward James, "Ancient History: Anglo-Saxons," BBC.co.uk, http://www.bbc.co.uk/history/ancient/anglo_saxons/overview_anglo_saxons_01.shtml.

32 Tacitus, *Germania,* 214.

CHAPTER 3: WHITE SLAVERY

1 See Robert L. Paquette, "Enslavement, Methods of," in *Macmillan Encyclopedia of World Slavery*, vol. 1, ed. Paul Finkelman and Joseph C. Miller (New York: Macmillan Reference, 1998), 306, *Historical Encyclopedia of World Slavery*, ed. Junius P. Rodriguez (Santa Barbara, Calif.: ABC-CLIO, 1997), 368–69, and Junius P. Rodridguez, *Chronology of World Slavery* (Santa Barbara, Calif.: ABC-CLIO, 1999), 51–53.

2 James McKillop, "Patrick, Saint," in *A Dictionary of Celtic Mythology* (Oxford University Press, 1998), *Oxford Reference Online*, http://www.oxfordreference.com/views/ENTRY.html?subview=Main&entry=t70.e3369.

3 David Pelteret, "The Image of the Slave in Some Anglo-Saxon and Norse Sources," *Slavery and Abolition* 23, no. 2 (Aug. 2002): 76, 81–83.

4 Jenny Bourne Wahl, "Economics of Slavery," in *Macmillan Encyclopedia of World Slavery*, 1:271; Orlando Patterson, "Slavery," *Annual Review of Sociology* 3 (1977): 420.

5 The figures come from the *Domesday Book* of 1086, the Norman census of newly conquered Britain. See Robin Blackburn, "The Old World Background to European Colonial Slavery," in *The Worlds of Unfree Labor*, ed. Colin Palmer (Aldershot, UK: Ashgate, 1998), 90, originally published in *William and Mary Quarterly*, 3rd ser., S4, no. 1 (1997).

6 See David Turley, *Slavery* (Oxford: Blackwell, 2000): 142–43.

7 Robert Brennan, "The Rises and Declines of Serfdom in Medieval and Early Modern Europe," and Christopher Dyer, "Memories of Freedom: Attitudes towards Serfdom in England, 1200–1350," in *Serfdom and Slavery: Studies in Legal Bondage*, ed. M. L. Bush (London: Longman, 1996), 271, 277–79.

8 David Brion Davis, *Slavery and Human Progress* (New York: Oxford University Press, 1984), 54–55.

9 Alan Fisher, "Chattel Slavery in the Ottoman Empire," *Slavery and Abolition* 1, no. 1 (May 1980): 34–36; Iris Origo, "The Domestic Enemy: The Eastern Slaves in Tuscany in the Fourteenth and Fifteenth Centuries," *Speculum: A Journal of Mediaeval Studies* 30, no. 3 (July 1955): 312–24, 326–27, 337, 354.

10 See Linda Colley, *Captives* (New York: Pantheon, 2002), 47–52, 58, and Robert Davis, *Christian Slaves, Muslim Masters: White Slavery in the Mediterranean, the Barbary Coast, and Italy, 1500–1800* (Houndsmills, UK: Palgrave Macmillan, 2003), 3–6.

11 "Chapter II - Slavery and Escape" and "Chapter III - Wrecked on a Desert Island," The Project Gutenberg Etext of Robinson Crusoe, by Daniel Defoe, http://www.gutenberg.org/dirs/etext96/rbcru10.txt.

12 The phrase "vulnerable aliens" comes from M. I. Finley, quoted in Blackburn, "Old World Background to European Colonial Slavery," 111.

13 J. H. Galloway, *The Sugar Cane Industry: An Historical Geography from Its Origins to 1914* (Cambridge: Cambridge University Press, 1989), 11, 22–23; J. H. Galloway, "The Mediterranean Sugar Industry," *Geographical Review* 67, no. 2 (April 1977): 180–81, 189–90.

14 Sidney W. Mintz, *Sweetness and Power: The Place of Sugar in Modern History* (New York: Viking, 1985), 23–24, 28.

15 Blackburn, "Old World Background to European Colonial Slavery," 83–84, and Galloway, "Mediterranean Sugar Industry," 180–90.

16 See Davis, *Slavery and Human Progress*, 56.

17 Galloway, *Sugar Cane Industry*, 27, 31, 32, 42. Historians disagree on the degree to which Mediterranean slavery and Latin American–Caribbean slavery resembled each other. While Blackburn stresses the differences between the two slaveries, in scale permitted by plantation agriculture and capitalist processing and distribution and in ideology, Galloway and Mintz emphasize the similarities.

18 See Don Jordan and Michael Walsh, *White Cargo: The Forgotten History of Britain's White Slaves in America* (New York: New York University Press, 2008), 76–77.

19 Ibid., 84–85.

20 Ibid., 76, 171.

21 Ibid., 114–15.

22 *Historical Encyclopedia of Slavery*, 369.

23 See Edmund S. Morgan, *American Slavery, American Freedom: The Ordeal of Colonial Virginia* (New York: W. W. Norton, 1975), 236, A. Roger Ekirch, *Bound for America: The Transportation of British Convicts to the Colonies, 1718–1775* (Oxford: Clarendon Press, 1987), 125, and Grady McWhiney, *Cracker Culture: Celtic Ways in the Old South* (Tuscaloosa: University of Alabama Press, 1988), xiv.

24 Ekirch, *Bound for America*, 1, 26–27, 135, 139, 193; Gwenda Morgan and Peter Rushton, *Eighteenth Century Criminal Transportation: The Formation of the Criminal Atlantic* (Houndsmills, UK: Palgrave, 2004), 5, 7, 1; David W. Galenson, "Indentured Servitude," in *A Historical Guide to World Slavery*, ed. Seymour Drescher and Stanley L. Engerman (New York: Oxford University Press, 1998), 239.

25 See Michael A. Hoffman II, *They Were White and They Were Slaves: The Untold History of the Enslavement of Whites in Early America*, 4th ed. (Coeur d'Alene, Idaho: Independent History & Research Co., 1991), 6, 14, 39.

CHAPTER 4: WHITE SLAVERY AS BEAUTY IDEAL

1 François Bernier, "A New Division of the Earth," originally published anonymously in *Journal des Sçavans*, 24 April 1684, trans. T. Bendyshe, in *Memoirs Read before the Anthropological Society of London* 1 (1863–64): 360–64, in *The Idea of Race*, ed. Robert Bernasconi and Tommy L. Lott (Indianapolis: Hackett, 2000), 2–4.

2 This information comes from an audio recording of Dirk van der Cruysse speaking at the University of Paris IV (Sorbonne) on 13 Feb. 1999, available through the website of the Centre de Recherche sur la Littérature des Voyages, at http://www.crlv.org/outils/encyclopedie/afficher.php?encyclopedie_id=13. See also van der Cruysse, *Chardin le Persan* (Paris: Editions Fayard, 1998). The discussion of improving Persians' looks through intermarriage with Georgians and Circassians is at http://www.iranian.com/Travelers/June97/Chardin/index.shtml. See also Georgette Legée, "Johann Friedrich Blumenbach (1752–1840): La Naissance de l'anthropologie à l'epoque de la Révolution Française," in *Scientifiques et sociétés pendant la Révolution et l'Empire* (Paris: Editions du CTHS, 1990), 403.

3 *Journal du Voyage du Chevalier Chardin en Perse & aux Indes Orientales, par la Mer Noire & par la Colchide* (*The Travels of Sir John Chardin into Persia and the East Indies, 1673–1677*) (London: Moses Pitt, 1686), 78, 81–82. My translation.

4 Ibid., 70, 77, 80, 82.

5 Ibid., 105–6, 82–83.

6 Ibid., 105.

7 Ibid., 183, 204–5.

8 http://kaukasus.blogspot.com/2007/04/young-georgian-girl.htm and http://www.flickr.com/photos/24298774@N00/108738272, http://commons.wiki media.org/wiki/Image:Ossetiangirl1883.jpg, Corliss Lamont, *The Peoples of the Soviet Union* (New York: Harcourt, Brace, 1946), facing 79.

9 See Londa Schiebinger, *Nature's Body: Gender in the Making of Modern Science* (Boston: Beacon Press, 1993), 129–39, and "The Anatomy of Difference: Race and Sex in Eighteenth-Century Science," *Eighteenth-Century Studies* 23, no. 4 (Summer 1990): 401.

10 See Pierre H. Boulle, "François Bernier and the Origins of the Modern Concept of Race," in *The Color of Liberty: Histories of Race in France*, ed. Sue Peabody and Tyler Edward Stovall (Durham: Duke University Press, 2003), 11.

11 See Amjad Jaimoukha, *The Circassians: A Handbook* (Richmond, UK: Curzon, 2001), 16, 168–69.

12 *Oxford English Dictionary Online*, http/dictionary.oed.com/cgi/entry/0033 0118=3fsingle=3d1&query_type=3dword&queryword=3dodalisque&first=3 d1&max_to_show=3d10.

13 Immanuel Kant, *Observations on the Feeling of the Beautiful and Sublime* (1763), trans. John T. Goldthwait (Berkeley: University of California Press, 1960), 89.

14 Johann Gottfried von Herder, *Ideas for the Philosophy of History of Humanity* (1:256), quoted in Cedric Dover, "The Racial Philosophy of Johann Herder," *British Journal of Sociology* 3, no. 2 (June 1952): 127 (emphasis in original).

15 Edward Daniel Clarke, *Travels in Various Countries of Europe, Asia and Africa* (London: T. Cadell and W. Davies, 1810–23), 1:35–36.

16 Annette Gordon-Reed, *The Hemingses of Monticello: An American Family* (New York: W. W. Norton, 2008), 55–56, 120, 193, 162, 202, 536–39, 605.

17 See "Horrible Traffic in Circassian Women—Infanticide in Turkey," *New York Daily Times*, 6 Aug. 1856, http://chnm.gmu.edu/lostmuseum/lm/311/. See "Letter from P. T. Barnum to John Greenwood, 1864," http://chnm.gmu.edu/lostmuseum/lm/312. Barnum exhibited a woman purported to be a Circassian beauty and example of racial purity in 1865. This information comes from "The Lost Museum" website of American Social History Productions, Inc., George Mason University and the City University of New York. See also Sarah Lewis, "Effecting Incredulity: Comic Retraction as Racial Critique in the Circassian Beauty Spectacle," paper given at the 20th James A. Porter Colloquium on African American Art, Howard University, 18 April 2009.

18 *Classic Encyclopedia Online*, http://www.1911encyclopedia.org/Circassia.

19 See Joan DelPlato, *Multiple Wives, Multiple Pleasures: Representing the Harem, 1800–1875* (Madison, N.J.: Fairleigh Dickinson University Press, 2002), 22–25, 230–39, and Linda Nochlin, "The Imaginary Orient," in *The Politics of Vision: Essays on Nineteenth-Century Art and Society* (New York: Harper & Row, 1989), 33–59.

20 Stephen Railton and the University of Virginia, *Uncle Tom's Cabin and American Culture,* http://www.iath.virginia.edu/utc/sentimnt/grslvhp.html.

21 See Linda Nochlin, "The Imaginary Orient," *Art in America* 71, no. 5 (May 1983): 126.

22 See Reina Lewis, " 'Oriental' Femininity as Cultural Commodity: Authorship, Authority, and Authenticity," in *Edges of Empire: Orientalism and Visual Culture*, ed. Mary Roberts and Jocelyn Hackforth-Jones (Malden, Mass.: Blackwell, 2005), 95–120.

23 Orientalist scholarship has continued to explore the European gaze in art and literature and the ways its subjects have looked back. See, e.g., Reina Lewis, *Gendering Orientalism: Race, Femininity and Representation* (London:

Routledge, 1996), *Rethinking Orientalism: Women, Travel and the Ottoman Harem* (London: Tauris, 2004), and *Orientalism's Interlocutors: Painting, Architecture, Photography*, ed. J. Beaulieu and Mary Roberts (Durham: Duke University Press, 2002).

24 See Lewis " 'Oriental' Femininity," 100.

25 According to the website, it is dedicated to "the memories of the Circassian Genocide victims exiled from their land by Russian Empire." See http://www.circassianworld.com/About_Site.html.

CHAPTER 5: THE WHITE BEAUTY IDEAL AS SCIENCE

1 This discussion draws heavily on Alex Potts, *Flesh and the Ideal: Winckelmann and the Origins of Art History* (New Haven: Yale University Press, 1994). Also useful were Walter Pater, "Winckelmann," in *The Renaissance: Studies in Art and Poetry* (1873) (Oxford: Basil Blackwell, 1973), E. M. Butler, *The Tyranny of Greece over Germany: A Study of the Influence Exercised by Greek Art and Poetry over the Great German Writers of the Eighteenth, Nineteenth and Twentieth centuries* (New York: Macmillan, 1935), and Edouard Pommier, *Winckelmann, inventeur de l'histoire de l'art* (Paris: Gallimard, 2003). For a modern consideration of the hard, cold ideal body, see Leslie Heywood, *Dedication to Hunger: The Anorexic Aesthetic in Modern Culture* (Berkeley: University of California, 1996).

2 See Sander Gilman, *On Blackness without Blacks: Essays on the Image of the Black in Germany* (Boston: G. K. Hall, 1982), 26, Potts, *Flesh and the Ideal*, 160–61, and Steven Daniel deCaroli, "Go Hither and Look: Aesthetics, History and the Exemplary in Late Eighteenth-Century Philosophy" (Ph.D. diss., State University of New York at Binghamton, 2001), 248–316.

3 David Bindman, *Ape to Apollo: Aesthetics and the Idea of Race in the 18th Century* (Ithaca: Cornell University Press, 2002), 89–90.

4 See Pater, "Winckelmann," in *The Renaissance*, 191–92. See also Michael Bronski, "The Male Body in the Western Mind," *Harvard Gay & Lesbian Review* 5, no. 4: 28–30, and "Greek Revival: The Implications of Polychromy" and Thomas Noble Howe, "Greece, Ancient: Architectural Decoration, Colour," both *Grove Art Online*, http://www.groveart.com/shared/views/article.Html?section=art.034254.2.2.3.3. See also Miles Unger, "That Classic White Sculpture Once Had a Paint Job," *New York Times*, 14 Oct. 2007, Art 35, and Penelope Dimitriou, "The Polychromy of Greek Sculpture: To the Beginning of the Hellenistic Period," (Ph.D. diss., Columbia University, 1951), 1–15.

5 A. D. Potts, "Greek Sculpture and Roman Copies: Anton Raphael Mengs and

the Eighteenth Century," *Journal of the Warburg and Courtauld Institutes* 43 (1980): 150–51, Mark Stevens and Annalyn Swan, *de Kooning: An American Master* (New York: Knopf, 2004), 67, 102.

6 A history of the various controversial cleanings of the Parthenon sculptures appears in two versions by Ian Jenkins, *The 1930s Cleaning of the Parthenon Sculptures in the British Museum*, http://www.thebritishmuseum.ac.uk/parthenon/indes.html, and *Cleaning and Controversy: The Parthenon Sculptures 1811–1939*, British Museum Occasional Paper no. 146 (2001).

7 Potts, *Flesh and the Ideal*, 17; Pater, "Winckelmann," 185, 192; Butler, *Tyranny of Greece over Germany*, 28–34, 42–43.

8 E. M. Butler concluded that "the Germans have imitated the Greeks more slavishly; they have been obsessed by them more utterly, and they have assimilated them less than any other race. The extent of the Greek influence is incalculable throughout Europe; its intensity is at its highest in Germany." *Tyranny of Greece over Germany*, 6.

9 Johann Kaspar Lavater, *Essays on Physiognomy*, vol. 2, part 2, 362, 369.

10 Bindman, *Ape to Apollo*, 95, 118, 123.

11 Miriam Claude Meijer, *Race and Aesthetics in the Anthropology of Petrus Camper (1722–1789)* (Amsterdam: Rodopi, 1999), 97–115, Stephen Jay Gould, "Petrus Camper's Angle," *Natural History*, July 1987, pp. 12–18.

12 Charles White, *An Account of the Regular Gradation in Man, and in Different Animals and Vegetables; and from the Former to the Latter* (London, 1799), 134–35. See also Angela Rosenthal, "Visceral Culture: Blushing and the Legibility of Whiteness in Eighteenth-Century British Portraiture," *Art History* 27, no. 4 (Sept. 2004): 567–68, 572–74, 578.

CHAPTER 6: JOHANN FRIEDRICH BLUMENBACH NAMES WHITE PEOPLE "CAUCASIAN"

1 K. F. H. Marx, "Zum Andenken an Johann Friedrich Blumenbach," in *The Anthropological Treatises of Johann Friedrich Blumenbach ... With Memoirs of Him by Marx and Flourens and an Account of His Anthropological Museum by Professor R. Wagner, and the Inaugural Dissertation of John Hunter, M.D., on the Varieties of Man*, trans. Thomas Bendyshe (London: Longman, Green, Longman, Roberts, & Green, 1865), 26–27. See Lisbet Koerner, *Linnaeus: Nature and Nation* (Cambridge: Harvard University Press, 1999), 56; Tore Frängsmyr, "Introduction," in *Linnaeus: The Man and His Work*, ed. Tore Frängsmyr, rev. ed. (Canton: Mass.: Science History Publications, 1994 [originally published 1983]), ix; and Luigi Marino, *Praeceptores Germaniae: Göttingen 1770–1820* (Göttingen: Vandenhoeck & Ruprecht, 1995), 48–52, 74.

2 See Patricia Fara, *Sex, Botany and Empire: The Story of Carl Linnaeus and Joseph Banks* (Cambridge: Icon Books, 2003).

3 David M. Knight, *Science in the Romantic Era* (Aldershhot, UK: Ashgate Variorum, 1998), x; F. W. P. Dougherty, ed., *Commercivm Epistolicvm J. F. Blvmenbachii: Aus einem Briefwechsel des Klassischen Zeitalters der Naturgeschichte: Katalog zur Ausstellung im Foyer der Niedersächsischen Staats- und Universitätsbibliothek Göttingen 1. Juni–21. Juni 1984* (Göttingen: Göttingen University, 1984), 116.

4 Rudolph Wagner, "On the Anthropological Collection of the Physiological Institute of Göttingen" (Göttingen, 1856), in *Anthropological Treatises of Johann Friedrich Blumenbach*, 384.

5 Stefano Fabbri Bertoletti, "The Anthropological Theory of Johann Friedrich Blumenbach," in *Romanticism in Science: Science in Europe, 1790–1840*, ed. Stefano Poggi and Maurizio Bossi (Dordrecht: Kluwer Academic, 1994), 111–13.

6 *On the Natural Variety of Mankind*, 3rd ed. (1795), in *Anthropological Treatises of Johann Friedrich Blumenbach*, 227, 214.

7 *On the Natural Variety of Mankind*, 1st ed. (1775), in *Anthropological Treatises of Johann Friedrich Blumenbach*, 116–17.

8 See Comte de Buffon, *Histoire naturelle, géneralle et particulière, avec la description du Cabinet du Roy*, vol. 3, "Variétés dans l'Espèce Humaine," 373, 380, 384, http://www.buffon.cnrs.fr/ice/ice_book_detail.php?lang=fr&type=text&bdd=buffon&table=buffon_hn&bookId=3&typeofbookId=1&num=0.

9 *On the Natural Variety of Mankind*, 1st ed. (1775), 122.

10 Ibid,. 99–100. See also Michael Charles Carhart, "The Writing of Cultural History in Eighteenth-Century Germany" (Ph.D. Diss., Rutgers University, 1999), 38–39.

11 *On the Natural Variety of Mankind*, 3rd ed. (1795), 226–27.

12 Blumenbach also added the name "Mongolian" in the third edition. See Michael Keevak, *How East Asians Became Yellow* (Princeton: Princeton University Press, forthcoming).

13 *On the Natural Variety of Mankind*, 3rd ed. (1795), 209.

14 Ibid., 229, 264–65.

15 This is the language Johann Friedrich Blumenbach quotes in a footnote in the third edition (1795) of *On the Natural Variety of Mankind*. Chardin, vol. 1, p. 171, in Thomas Bendyshe, trans. and ed., *The Anthropological Treatises of Johann Friedrich Blumenbach* (London: Anthropological Society, 1865), 269.

16 Marx, "Zum Andenken an Johann Friedrich Blumenbach," 30 n. 1.

17 Dougherty, ed., *Commercivm Epistolicvm J. F. Blvmenbachii*, 76, 114–16, 148, 150, 171, and Helmut Rohlfing, ed., *"Ganz Vorzügliche und Unvergeßliche*

Verdienste"—Georg Thomas von Asch als Förderer der Universität Göttingen (Niedersächsiche Staats- und Universitätsbibliothek: Göttingen, 1998), 2–3; and Rolf Siemon, "Soemmerring, Forster und Goethe: 'Naturkundliche Begegnungen' in Göttingen und Kassel", http://www.sub.uni-goettingen.de/archiv/ausstell/1999/soemmerring.pdf.

18 For a thoughtful discussion of the position of the people of the Caucasus in the Russian context, see Bruce Baum, *The Rise and Fall of the Caucasian Race: A Political History of Racial Identity* (New York: New York University Press, 2006), chap. 7: " 'Where Caucasian Means Black': 'Race,' Nation, and the Chechen Wars," 192–233. Baum's book traces the history of the term "Caucasian" in racial, political, and geographic ideology.

19 F. W. P. Dougherty, the Canadian-born editor of Blumenbach's correspondence and papers in Göttingen, died in the mid-1990s, leaving the project incomplete and Blumenbach's personal life inaccessible.

20 The quoted phrase comes from Suzanne L. Marchand, *Down from Olympus: Archaeology and Philhellenism in Germany, 1750–1970* (Princeton: Princeton University Press, 1996), 193.

21 See Suzanne Zantop, *Colonial Fantasies: Conquest, Family, and Nation in Precolonial Germany, 1770–1870* (Durham: Duke University Press, 1997), 67–68.

22 See Luigi Marino, *Praeceptores Germaniae: Göttingen 1770–1820* (Göttingen: Vandenhoeck & Ruprecht, 1995), 112–16.

23 See Britta Rupp-Eisenreich, "Des choses occultes en histoire des sciences humaines: Le Destin de la 'Science Nouvelle' de Christoph Meiners," *L'Ethnographie* 2 (1983): 151. See also Frank W. P. Dougherty, "Christoph Meiners und Johann Friedrich Blumenbach im Streit um den Begriff der Menschenrasse," in *Die Natur des Menschen: Probleme der physischen Anthropologie und Rassenkunde (1750–1850)*, ed. Gunther Mann and Franz Dumont (Stuttgart: Fischer, 1990), 103–4, Marino, *Praeceptores Germaniae*, 111–14, and Suzanne Zantop, "The Beautiful, the Ugly, and the German: Race, Gender and Nationality in Eighteenth-Century Anthropological Discourse," in *Gender and Germanness: Cultural Productions of Nation*, ed. Patricia Herminghouse and Magda Mueller (Providence, R.I.: Berghahn Books, 1997), 23–26.

24 See Zantop, "The Beautiful, the Ugly, and the German," 28–29, and *Colonial Fantasies*, 87–90.

25 David Bindman, *Ape to Apollo: Aesthetics and the Idea of Race in the 18th Century* (Ithaca: Cornell University Press, 2002), 219–20.

26 Quotes in Zantop, "The Beautiful, the Ugly, and the German," 28–29. See also Rupp-Eisenreich, "Des choses occultes en histoire des sciences humaines,"

151, and Dougherty, "Christoph Meiners und Johann Friedrich Blumenbach," 103–4, Marino, *Praeceptores Germaniae*, 111–14.

27 Léon Poliakov, *The History of Anti-Semitism* (Philadelphia: University of Pennsylvania Press, 2003), 136; Baum, *Rise and Fall of the Caucasian Race*, 98.

CHAPTER 7: GERMAINE DE STAËL'S GERMAN LESSONS

1 J. Christopher Herold, one of her best-known biographers, entitled his book *Mistress to an Age*. See *Mistress to an Age: A Life of Madame de Staël* (Indianapolis: Bobbs-Merrill, 1958). Other useful de Staël biographies include Ghislain de Diesbach, *Madame de Staël* (Paris: Perrin, 1983), Maria Fairweather, *Madame de Staël* (New York: Carroll & Graf, 2005), and Francine du Plessix Gray, *Madame de Staël: The First Modern Woman* (New York: Atlas, 2008). De Staël's portraitist, the rococo artist Élisabeth-Louise Vigée-Lebrun (1755–1842), one of the foremost figure painters of her time, was known for her portraits of European aristocrats. One of two women admitted into the Académie Royale de Peinture et de Sculpture in 1783, she had to leave France during the revolution but returned during the reign of the first Emperor Napoleon.

2 Tess Lewis, "Madame de Staël: The Inveterate Idealist," *Hudson Review* 54, no. 3 (2001): 416–26.

3 The quote is from Emile Faguet in Jean de Pange, *Mme de Staël et la découverte de l'Allemagne* (Paris: Société Française d'Editions Littéraires et Techniques, 1929), 9.

4 Lydia Maria Child, *The Biographies of Madame de Staël and Madame Roland* (Boston: Carter and Hendee, 1832), 24.

5 In Helen B. Posgate, *Madame de Staël* (New York: Twayne, 1968), 19.

6 Child, *Biographies*, 90, 92.

7 Ibid., 1, 16.

8 Bonnie G. Smith, "History and Genius: The Narcotic, Erotic, and Baroque Life of Germaine de Staël," *French Historical Studies* 19, no. 4 (Fall 1996): 1061.

9 In Richmond Laurin Hawkins, *Madame de Staël and the United States* (Cambridge: Harvard University Press, 1930), 33–34, 72, 75.

10 Ibid., 9–11, 14, 27–28, 65.

11 Quoted ibid., 64.

12 Quoted ibid., 4.

13 De Staël, *De l'Allemagne* (Paris: Didot Frères, 1857), 9–10.

14 Ian Allan Henning maintains that "it is not possible to speak of Madame de Staël as a mediator between France and Germany without talking about

Charles de Villers." Kurt Kloocke, editor of the letters between Villers and de Staël, finds Villers's influence obvious, extending, perhaps, even to a measure of the inspiration of *De l'Allemagne*. See Henning, *L'Allemagne de Mme de Staël et la polémique romantique: Première fortune de l'ouvrage en France et en Allemagne (1814–1830)* (Paris: Ancienne Honoré Champion, 1929), 207, and Kloocke, ed., *Correspondance: Madame de Staël, Charles de Villers, Benjamin Constant* (Frankfurt am Main: Peter Lang, 1993), 3.

15 Ruth Ann Crowley, *Charles de Villers, Mediator and Comparatist* (Bern: Peter Lang, 1978), 17–19.

16 De Staël, *De l'Allemagne*, 85.

17 Emma Gertrude Jaeck, *Madame de Staël and the Spread of German Literature* (New York: Oxford University Press, 1915), 7.

18 Henning, *L'Allemagne de Mme de Staël*, 210.

19 Ibid., 211.

20 De Staël, *De l'Allemagne*, 128, 130.

21 Vivian Folkenflik, *Major Writings of Germaine de Staël* (New York: Columbia University Press, 1987), 183.

22 Henning, *L'Allemagne de Mme de Staël*, 240–43, 252–53.

23 Child, *Biographies*, 82.

24 Pange, *Mme de Staël*, 140–41.

CHAPTER 8: EARLY AMERICAN WHITE PEOPLE OBSERVED

1 Margo J. Anderson, *The American Census: A Social History* (New Haven: Yale University Press, 1988), 9, 12–14; Frederick G. Bohme, *200 Years of U.S. Census Taking: Population and Housing Questions, 1790–1990* (Washington, D.C.: Bureau of the Census, U.S. Department of Commerce, 1989), 1.

2 Alexander Keyssar, *The Right to Vote: The Contested History of Democracy in the United States* (New York: Basic Books, 2000), xxii–xxiii, 20–34, 52–76, 102, and Sean Wilentz, *The Rise of American Democracy: Jefferson to Lincoln* (New York: W. W. Norton, 2005), 27–28, 82–83, 17, 485. Keyssar and Wilentz both note historians' long neglect of the basic history of the right to vote, especially with regard to class. See also Wilentz, "On Class and Politics and Jacksonian America," *Reviews in American History* 10, no. 4 (Dec. 1982): 45–48, 59.

3 J. Hector St. John de Crèvecoeur, *Letters from an American Farmer and Sketches of Eighteenth-Century America* (originally published 1782) AS@ UVA Hypertexts, Letter 3, 54, http://xroads.virginia.edu/~HYPER/CREV/letter03.html. Postindustrial St. Johnsbury now figures as Vermont's capital of heroin addiction.

4 Ibid., 170. Letter 9, 223–25, 229, http://xroads.virginia.edu/~HYPER/CREV/letter09.html.

5 Thomas Jefferson, *Notes on the State of Virginia* (originally published 1787), AS@UVA Hypertexts, Query 18, http://xroads.virginia.edu/~HYPER/JEFFERSON/ch18.html.

6 Stanley R. Hauer, "Thomas Jefferson and the Anglo-Saxon Language," *PMLA* 98, no. 5 (Oct. 1983): 879, 881.

7 Thomas Jefferson, "A Summary View of the Rights of British America" (July 1774), in *The Papers of Thomas Jefferson*, ed. Julian P. Boyd et al. (Princeton: Princeton University Press, 1950–), 1:121–35, http://press-pubs.uchicago.edu/founders/documents/v1ch14s10.html.

8 Dumas Malone, *The Sage of Monticello: Jefferson and His Time*, vol. 6 (Boston: Little, Brown: 1981), 202–3.

9 John Adams to Abigail Adams, Philadelphia 14 Aug. 1776, in Charles Francis Adams, *Familiar Letters of John Adams and His Wife Abigail Adams, during the Revolution, with a Memoir of Mrs. Adams* (Boston: Houghton Mifflin, 1875), 210–11. See also Malone, *Sage of Monticello*, 6:202. For the other side of the seal, Jefferson suggested the children of Israel in the wilderness.

10 Thomas Jefferson, *Essay on the Anglo-Saxon Language*, in *The Writings of Thomas Jefferson*, ed. Andrew A. Lipscomb, vol. 18 (Washington, D.C.: Thomas Jefferson Memorial Association of the United States, 1904), 365–66.

11 Hauer, "Thomas Jefferson and the Anglo-Saxon Language," 883–86, 891.

12 Mark A. Noll, *Princeton and the Republic, 1768–1822: The Search for a Christian Enlightenment in the Era of Samuel Stanhope Smith* (Vancouver: Regent College, 2004), 68; Mark A. Noll, "The Irony of the Enlightenment for Presbyterians in the Early Republic," *Journal of the Early Republic* 5, no. 2 (Summer 1985): 166.

13 W. Frank Craven, from Alexander Leitch, *A Princeton Companion* (Princeton: Princeton University Press, 1978), http:://www/hsc/edu/pres/presidents/samuel_smith.html, and Hampden-Sydney College website: www.hsc.edu/hschistory/images/smith.jpg.

14 Winthrop D. Jordan, "Introduction," in Samuel Stanhope Smith, *An Essay on the Causes of the Variety of Complexion and Figure in the Human Species*, ed. Winthrop D. Jordan (Cambridge: Harvard University Press, 1965), xi–xxvi, William H. Hudnut III, "Samuel Stanhope Smith: Enlightened Conservative," *Journal of the History of Ideas* 17, no. 4 (Oct. 1956): 541–43.

15 Smith, *Essay on the Causes of the Variety*, 29, 40.

16 Mary Wollstonecraft, *Analytical Review*, vol. 2 (Dec. 1788): 432–39, 457–58, in *The Works of Mary Wollstonecraft*, ed. Janet Todd and Marilyn Butler (London: Pickering, 1990), 50–55, and Ramsay Notes from New York Public

Library, comp. Mary B. MacIntyre, New York, 1936 (New York Public Library APV/Ramsay: http://www.southern-style.com/Ramsay%20Family%20Notes .htm).

17 See Hudnut, "Samuel Stanhope Smith," 544–46.

18 Smith, *Essay on the Causes of the Variety*, 106, 157, 109.

19 Ibid., 47.

20 Ibid., 104.

21 Ibid., 43–44, 199; James Axtell, "The White Indians of Colonial America," *William and Mary Quarterly*, 3rd ser., 32, no. 1 (Jan. 1975): 57, 64.

22 Smith, *Essay on the Causes of the Variety*, 163.

23 For sustained analysis, see Mia Bay, *The White Image in the Black Mind: African-American Ideas about White People, 1830–1925* (New York: Oxford University Press, 2000).

24 *David Walker's Appeal to the Coloured Citizens of the World*, ed. Peter P. Hinks (University Park: Pennsylvania State University Press, 2002), xxxi–xxxii, 9–10, 19, 27, 58.

25 Bay, *White Image in the Black Mind*, 32–36.

26 *David Walker's Appeal*, 9, 33, 65.

27 Ibid., 12, 14.

28 Ibid., xv–xl.

29 Ibid., xli–xlii.

30 See Bay, *White Image in the Black Mind*, 46–50, and George R. Price and James Brewer Stewart, "The Roberts Case, the Easton Family, and the Dynamics of the Abolitionist Movement in Massachusetts, 1776–1870," *Massachusetts Historical Review* 4 (2002): *The History Cooperative*, 89–116.

31 George R. Price and James Brewer Stewart, eds., *To Heal the Scourge of Prejudice: The Life and Writings of Hosea Easton* (Amherst: University of Massachusetts Press, 1999), 71, 74, 80–81.

32 *Du système pénitentiaire aux Etats-Unis, et de son application en France; suivi d'un appendice sur les colonies pénales et de notes statistiques. Par MM. G. de Beaumont et A. de Tocqueville* (Paris: H. Fournier jeune, 1833)

33 Alexis de Tocqueville, *Democracy in America and Two Essays on America*, trans. Gerald E. Bevan, ed. Isaac Kramnick (New York: Penguin Classic, 2003), 479, 4.

34 Ibid., 440–41.

35 Ibid., 408, 426.

36 Ibid., 420.

37 Ibid., 412, 720, 742.

38 Ibid., 406–8.

39 See Margaret Kohn, "The Other America: Tocqueville and Beaumont on Race

and Slavery," *Polity* 35, no. 1 (Fall 2002): 170, esp. note 3, and Thomas Bender, "Introduction," *Democracy in America* (New York: Modern Library, 1981), xliii.

40 Gustave de Beaumont, *Marie, or Slavery in the United States* (1835), trans. Barbara Chapman (Baltimore: Johns Hopkins University Press, 1958), 5. See also Nell Irvin Painter, "Was Marie White?: The Trajectory of a Question in the United States," *Journal of Southern History* 74, no. 1 (Feb. 2008): 3–30.

41 Beaumont, *Marie*, 13, 15.

CHAPTER 9: THE FIRST ALIEN WAVE

1 See Kerby A. Miller, " 'Scotch-Irish' Myths and 'Irish' Identities in Eighteenth- and Nineteenth-Century America," in *New Perspectives on the Irish Diaspora*, ed. Charles Fanning (Carbondale: Southern Illinois University Press, 2000), 76–79, and Kerby A. Miller and Bruce D. Boling, "The New England and Federalist Origins of 'Scotch-Irish' Identity," in *Ulster and Scotland, 1600–2000: History, Language and Identity*, ed. William Kelly and John R. Young (Dublin: Four Courts, 2004), 105, 114–18.

2 *Catholic Encyclopedia*, http://www.newadvent.org/cathen/08677a.htm.

3 *Alexis de Tocqueville's Journey in Ireland: July–August, 1835*, ed. and trans. Emmet Larkin (Washington, D.C.: Catholic University of America Press, 1990), 2.

4 From Gustave de Beaumont, *Ireland: Social, Political and Religious* (1839), http://www.swan.ac.uk/history/teaching/teaching%20resources/An%20 Gorta%20Mor/travellers/beaumont.htm.

5 See David Nally, " 'Eternity's Commissioner': Thomas Carlyle, the Great Irish Famine and the Geopolitics of Travel," *Journal of Historical Geography* 32, no. 2 (April 2006): 313–35.

6 Thomas Carlyle, "The Present Time," http://cepa.newschool.edu/het/texts/ carlyle/latter1.htm.

7 Thomas Carlyle, *Occasional Discourse on the Nigger Question* (1853), http:// cepa.newschool.edu/het/texts/carlyle/odnqbk.htm.

8 See Peter Gray, *Victoria's Irish: Irishness and Britishness, 1837–1901* (2004), and Robert Knox, *The Races of Men: A Philosophical Enquiry into the Influence of Race over the Destinies of Nations* (1862) [this is the 2nd edition of *Races of Men: A Fragment*, published in 1850], in *Race: The Origins of an Idea, 1760–1850*, ed. Hannah Franziska Augstein (Bristol, UK: Thoemmes Press, 1996), 253.

9 Samuel F. B. Morse, *Imminent Dangers to the Free Institutions of the United*

States (1835), http://www.wwnorton.com/college/history/archive/resources/ documents/ch12_04.htm.

10 Ray Allen Billington, *The Protestant Crusade, 1800–1860: A Study of the Origins of American Nativism* (originally published 1938) (Chicago: Quadrangle, 1964), 122–27; Bruce Levine, "Conservatism, Nativism, and Slavery: Thomas R. Whitney and the Origins of the Know-Nothing Party," *Journal of American History* 88, no. 2 (Sept. 2001): 470.

11 *St. Joseph Messenger Online*: http://www.aquinas-multimedia.com/stjoseph/ knownothings.html.

12 Marie Anne Pagliarini, "The Pure American Woman and the Wicked Catholic Priest: An Analysis of Anti-Catholic Literature in Antebellum America," *Religion and American Culture* 9, no. 1 (Winter 1999): 99.

13 Billington, *Protestant Crusade*, 99–104, 107–8. Monk's confession first appeared serially in New York City's *Protestant Vindicator* in 1835. See Rebecca Sullivan, "A Wayward from the Wilderness: Maria Monk's *Awful Disclosures* and the Feminization of Lower Canada in the Nineteenth Century," *Essays on Canadian Writing* 62 (Fall 1997): 201–23.

14 See Susan M. Griffin, *Anti-Catholicism and Nineteenth-Century Fiction* (New York: Cambridge University Press, 2004).

15 Michael D. Pierson, " 'All Southern Society Is Assailed by the Foulest Charges': Charles Sumner's 'The Crime against Kansas' and the Escalation of Republican Anti-Slavery Rhetoric," *New England Quarterly* 68, no. 4 (Dec. 1995): 533, 537, 545.

16 Pagliarini, "The Pure American Woman," 97.

17 Campbell J. Gibson and Emily Lennon, "Historical Census Statistics on the Foreign-Born Population of the United States: 1850–1990," U.S. Bureau of the Census, Washington, D.C., Feb. 1999, Population Division Working Paper no. 29, http://www.census.gov/population/www/documentation/twps0029/ twps0029.html. Included among the immigrants were 1,135 Asians, 3,679 Italians, 13,317 Mexicans, and 147,711 Canadians. In 1850 the foreign-born population represented 9.7 percent of the total population. See also *Historical Statistics of the United States*, part 1, 1975: 106–7.

18 Kathleen Neils Conzen, "Germans," in *Harvard Encyclopedia of American Ethnic Groups*, ed. Stephan Thernstrom (Cambridge: Harvard University Press, 1980), 406–12; Library of Congress, European Reading Room, "The Germans in America," http://www.loc.gov/rr/european/imde/germchro .html. Rough estimates put German immigrants at one-third Catholic and the other two-thirds predominantly Lutheran and Reformed. Comparatively small in numbers were German Methodists, Baptists, Unitarians, Pietists, Jews, and Freethinkers. "The German Americans: An Ethnic Experience," http://www.ulib.iupui.edu/kade/adams/chap6.html.

19 In Sir Richard Steele, *Poetical Miscellanies, Consisting of Original Poems and Translations* (London, 1714), 201; *Oxford English Dictionary Online*.

20 Journal F No. I (1829?), pp. 113–14, in *The Journals and Miscellaneous Notebooks of Ralph Waldo Emerson*, (hereafter *JMNRWE*) vol. 12, *1835–1862*, ed. Linda Allardt (Cambridge: Harvard University Press, 1976), 152, and Journal GO (1952), p. 233, in *JMNRWE*, vol. 13, *1852–1855*, ed. Ralph H. Orth and Alfred R. Ferguson (Cambridge: Harvard University Press, 1977), 112.

21 Journal TU (1849), p. 171, in *JMNRWE*, vol. 11, *1848–1851*, ed. A. W. Plumstead, William H. Gilman, and Ruth H. Bennett (Cambridge: Harvard University Press, 1975), 148.

22 Journal GO (1852), p. 105, in *JMNRWE*, vol. 13, 77.

23 In Frank Shuffelton, *A Mixed Race: Ethnicity in Early America* (New York: Oxford University Press, 1993), 181.

24 Edward B. Rugemer, "The Southern Response to British Abolitionism: The Maturation of Proslavery Apologetics," *Journal of Southern History* 70, no. 2 (May 2004): 221.

25 For the electronic edition of *Cannibals All!*, go to *Documenting the American South*, University of North Carolina at Chapel Hill, http://docsouth.unc.edu/fitzhughcan/fitzcan.html#fitzix.

26 Douglass quoted in Patricia Ferreira, "'All but 'A Black Skin and Wooly Hair': Frederick Douglass's Witness of the Irish Famine," *American Studies International* 37, no. 2 (June 1999): 69–83.

27 O'Connell quoted in Gilbert Osofsky, "Abolitionists, Irish Immigrants, and the Dilemmas of Romantic Nationalism," *American Historical Review* 80, no. 4 (Oct. 1975): 892.

28 Ernest Renan, *Poetry of the Celtic Races, VI*, in Literary and Philosophical Essays, the Harvard Classics, 1909–14, http://www.bartleby.com/32/307.html.

29 Matthew Arnold, *On the Study of Celtic Literature. Complete Prose Works*, vol. 3, ed. R. H. Super (Ann Arbor, University of Michigan Press, 1960), 291–395.

30 Ray Allen Billington, "The Know-Nothing Uproar," *American Heritage* 10, no. 2 (Feb. 1952): 61; Billington, *Protestant Crusade*, 220–31.

31 Tyler Anbinder, "Ulysses S. Grant, Nativist," *Civil War History: A Journal of the Middle Period* 43, no. 2 (June 1997): 130.

32 Dale T. Knobel, "Beyond 'America for Americans': Inside the Movement Culture of Antebellum Nativism," in *Immigrant America: European Ethnicity in the United States* (New York: Garland, 1994), 10; Michael F. Holt, "The Politics of Impatience: The Origins of Know Nothingism," *Journal of American History* 60, no. 2 (Sept. 1973): 313.

33 Knobel, "Beyond 'America for Americans,' " 11.

34 *Catholic Encyclopedia,* http://www.newadvent.org/cathen/08677a.htm.

35 Stephen E. Maizlish, "The Meaning of Nativism and the Crisis of the Union: The Know-Nothing Movement in the Antebellum North," in *Essays on American Antebellum Politics, 1840–1860,* ed. Stephen E. Maizlish and John J. Kushma (College Station: University of Texas at Arlington, [1982]), 166.

36 Maizlish, "Meaning of Nativism," 187.

37 Gregg Cantrell, "Sam Houston and the Know-Nothings: A Reappraisal," *Southwestern Historical Quarterly* 96, no. 3 (Jan. 1993): 326–43; Anbinder, "Ulysses S. Grant, Nativist," 119–41. Both Cantrell and Anbinder note that biographers of Houston and Grant mute or ignore their subjects' nativist enthusiasms.

38 Cantrell, "Sam Houston," 330; Anbinder, "Ulysses S. Grant, Nativist," 123.

39 Congressman William Russell Smith, 15 Jan. 1855, in Jeff Frederick, "Unintended Consequences: The Rise and Fall of the Know-Nothing Party in Alabama," *Alabama Review,* Jan. 2002, p. 3.

CHAPTER 10: THE EDUCATION OF RALPH WALDO EMERSON

1 Robert C. Gordon, *Emerson and the Light of India: An Intellectual History* (New Delhi: National Book Trust, 2007), 21–23, and Ralph Waldo Emerson, *Lectures and Biographical Sketches,* 371–404, http://emersoncentral.com/mary_moody_emerson.htm.

2 Philip Nicoloff, "Historical Introduction," in *Complete Works of Ralph Waldo Emerson,* vol. 5, *English Traits* (hereafter *CWRWE,* vol. 5, *English Traits*) (Cambridge: Harvard University Press, 1994), xiv.

3 John Bernard Beer, "Coleridge, Samuel Taylor," *Encyclopædia Britannica Online,* 24 Oct. 2005, http://www.search.eb.com/eb/article-1409.

4 See Phyllis Cole, *Mary Moody Emerson and the Origins of Transcendentalism: A Family History* (New York: Oxford University Press, 1998), 5, 164, 170, 180, 242, 307.

5 Kenneth Marc Harris, *Carlyle and Emerson: Their Long Debate* (Cambridge: Harvard University Press, 1978), 10, 11, 56.

6 Simon Heffer, *Moral Desperado: A Life of Thomas Carlyle* (London: Weidenfeld and Nicolson, 1995), 48, 52, 66.

7 Ibid., 129.

8 The articles by Carlyle that Emerson admired were "Jean Paul Friedrich Richter," *Edinburgh Review,* 1827; "State of German Literature," ibid., 1828; "Goethe's Helena," *Foreign Review,* 1828; "Goethe," ibid., 1828; "Life of Heyne," ibid., 1828; "Novalis," ibid., 1829; "Signs of the Times," *Edinburgh*

Review, 1829; "John Paul Friedrich Richter Again," *Foreign Review*, 1830; "Schiller," *Fraser's Magazine*, 1831; "The Nibelungen Lied," *Westminster Review*, 1831; "German Literature of the Fourteenth and Fifteenth Centuries," *Foreign Quarterly Review*, 1831; "Taylor's Historic Survey of German Poetry," *Edinburgh Review*, 1831; "Characteristics," ibid., 1831. These essays and reviews directly preceded Carlyle's writing *Sartor Resartus* and indicate his immersion in German literature. See Henry Larkin, *Carlyle and the Open Secret of His Life* (originally published 1886) (New York: Haskell House, 1970), 13. Larkin served as Carlyle's research assistant and general factotum during the last ten years of Carlyle's life.

9 Lawrence Buell, *Emerson* (Cambridge: Harvard University Press, 2003), 15.

10 See Frederick Wahr, *Emerson and Goethe* (Ann Arbor: George Wahr, 1915), 79.

11 *CWRWE*, vol. 5, *English Traits*, 9–12; Robert E. Burkholder, "Notes," ibid., 356.

12 Larkin, *Carlyle*, 59.

13 Wahr, *Emerson and Goethe*, 22.

14 Fred Kaplan, *Thomas Carlyle: A Biography* (Ithaca: Cornell University Press, 1983), 232–33, 369; Townsend Scudder, *The Lonely Wayfaring Man: Emerson and Some Englishmen* (London: Oxford University Press, 1936), 29, 34–37.

15 Quote from 1849 in Harris, *Carlyle and Emerson*, 27.

16 Scudder, *Lonely Wayfaring Man*, 139. Ruskin quoted in Buell, *Emerson*, 328.

17 Matthew Guinn, "Emerson's Southern Critics, 1838–1862," *Resources for American Literary Study* 25, no. 2 (1999): 174–91, 186.

18 Phyllis Cole, "Stanton, Fuller, and the Grammar of Romanticism," *New England Quarterly* 73, no. 4 (Dec. 2000): 556.

19 Jefferson quoted in Buell, *Emerson*, 370.

20 Nicoloff, "Historical Introduction," xxi; L. P. Curtin Jr., *Anglo-Saxons and Celts: A Study of Anti-Irish Prejudice in Victorian England* (Bridgeport, Conn.: Conference on British Studies at the University of Bridgeport, 1968), 76.

21 Joan von Mehren, *Minerva and the Muse: A Life of Margaret Fuller* (Amherst, University of Massachusetts Press, 1994), 236.

22 Historians have taken note of the resemblances between Carlyle's German nationalism and that of twentieth-century German National Socialists. See J. Salwyn Schapiro, "Thomas Carlyle, Prophet of Fascism," *Journal of Modern History* 17, no. 2 (June 1945): 97–115.

23 Heffer, *Moral Desperado*, 52.

24 Quoted ibid., 165–67.

25 Quoted ibid., 197.

26 "Permanent Traits of the English National Genius," in *The Early Lectures of Ralph Waldo Emerson*, ed. Stephen E. Whicher and Robert E. Spiller, vol. 1 (Cambridge: Harvard University Press, 1959), 241.

27 *Early Lectures of Ralph Waldo Emerson*, 233, 234–35; CWRWE, vol. 5, *English Traits*, 54.

28 CWRWE, vol. 5, *English Traits*, 71.

29 Carlyle to Emerson, London, 12 Aug., 1834, The Project Gutenberg EBook of The Correspondence of Thomas Carlyle and Ralph Waldo Emerson, 1834–1872, vol. 1, http://www.gutenberg.org/dirs/1/3/5/8/13583/13583.txt; Harris, *Carlyle and Emerson*, 138.

30 Quoted in Kaplan, *Thomas Carlyle*, 249.

31 Carlyle to Emerson, Annan, Scotland, 18 Aug., 1841, http://www.gutenberg.org/dirs/1/3/5/8/13583/13583.txt.

32 Quoted in Harris, *Carlyle and Emerson*, 147–48. See also Phyllis Cole, "Emerson, England, and Fate," in *Emerson—Prophecy, Metamorphosis, and Influence: Selected Papers from the English Institute*, ed. David Levin (New York: Columbia University Press, 1975), 83–105.

33 Carlyle to Emerson, London, 24 June 1833, http://www.gutenberg.org/dirs/1/3/5/8/13583/13583.txt.

34 Quotes in Scudder, *Lonely Wayfaring Man*, 153, 169.

35 CWRWE, vol. 5, *English Traits*, 170.

CHAPTER 11: *ENGLISH TRAITS*

1 Philip Nicoloff, "Historical Introduction," in *The Collected Works of Ralph Waldo Emerson*, vol. 5, *English Traits* (hereafter CWRWE, vol. 5, *English Traits*) (Cambridge: Harvard University Press, 1994), xiii–xiv, notes Emerson's playfulness and wit that convey the author's "thorough delight in his subject." Wallace E. Williams calls *English Traits* Emerson's "wittiest book" in "Historical Introduction," CWRWE, vol. 4, *Representative Men: Seven Lectures* (Cambridge: Harvard University Press, 1987), xlix. See also Nell Irvin Painter, "Ralph Waldo Emerson's Saxons," *Journal of American History* 95, no. 4 (March 2009): 977–85.

2 *The Early Lectures of Ralph Waldo Emerson*, ed. Stephen E. Whicher and Robert E. Spiller (Cambridge: Harvard University Press, 1959), 234–41, 248.

3 Nicoloff, "Historical Introduction," xlviii–xlix, liii. The Princeton University library holds five editions of *English Traits*, from 1856, 1857, 1869, 1916, and 1966, in addition to versions that are part of collected works.

4 Journal entry for 30 Sept. 1856, in *The Journals of Charlotte Forten Grimké*,

ed. Brenda Stevenson (New York: Oxford University Press, 1988), 164, 191–92.

5 See Elisa Tamarkin, "Black Anglophilia: or, The Sociability of Antislavery," *American Literary History* 14, no. 3 (Fall 2002): 447, 452, 455.

6 Several historians have thoughtfully analyzed the race-gender anxieties of white American men. The classic work is Richard Slotkin's *Regeneration through Violence: The Mythology of the American Frontier, 1600–1860* (Middletown, Conn.: Wesleyan University Press, 1973). C. Anthony Rotundo terms the idealization of primal virility the "masculine primitive" and notes a sense of the "perils of civilization." Often these historians concentrate on crises at the turn of the twentieth century; however, Emerson, the great voice of American thought, expressed such notions in the antebellum era in phrases that carried over into the lexicon of late nineteenth-century Americans. For Emerson, the prime race in question was "Saxon," as opposed to Celtic. By the mid-twentieth century, historians took to replacing "Saxon" or "Anglo-Saxon" with "white," to sharpen the opposition to nonwhite and as though all three designations meant the same thing. But the black/white opposition suiting later generations of historians did not always conform to the meaning of those writing earlier. See E. Anthony Rotundo, *American Manhood: Transformations in Masculinity from the Revolution to the Modern Era* (New York: Basic Books, 1993), Gail Bederman, *Manliness and Civilization: A Cultural History of Gender and Race in the United States, 1880–1917* (Chicago: University of Chicago Press, 1995), Michael S. Kimmel, *Manhood in America: A Cultural History* (New York: Free Press, 1996), and John Pettegrew, *Brutes in Suits: Male Sensibility in America, 1890–1920* (Baltimore: Johns Hopkins University Press, 2007).

7 "Permanent Traits of the English National Genius," in *Early Lectures of Ralph Waldo Emerson*, 241. Michael S. Kimmel quotes a late nineteenth-century American calling for "a saving touch of old fashioned barbarism." See "Consuming Manhood: The Feminization of American Culture and the Recreation of the Male Body, 1832–1920," *Michigan Quarterly Review* 3, no. 1 (Winter 1994): 7–10, 13–16, 29.

8 *CWRWE*, vol. 5, *English Traits*, 23, 155.

9 Gildas, *The Ruin of Britain* (ca. 540), quoted in Bryan Sykes, *Saxons, Vikings, and Celts: The Genetic Roots of Britain and Ireland* (New York: W. W. Norton, 2006), 256–57.

10 *CWRWE*, vol. 5, *English Traits*, 23.

11 Emerson, "Permanent Traits of the English National Genius," 242.

12 *CWRWE*, vol. 5, *English Traits*, 33. For the comparison of people to fruit trees, see *CWRWE*, vol. 4, *Representative Men* (1987), 56; *Journals and*

NOTES TO PAGES 169–76

Miscellaneous Notebooks of Ralph Waldo Emerson (hereafter *Journals*), vol. 11, *1848–1851*, ed. A. W. Plumstead, William H. Gilman, and Ruth H. Bennett (Cambridge: Harvard University Press, 1975), 8, 42, 131, 142, 152, 283, 357; *Journals*, vol. 10, *1847–1848*, ed. Merton M. Sealts Jr. (Cambridge: Harvard University Press, 1973), 5, 91, 99–100. See also Horace S. Kallen, *Culture and Democracy in the United States: Studies in the Group Psychology of the American Peoples* (New York: Boni and Liveright, 1924), 329.

13 *CWRWE*, vol. 5, *English Traits*, 32, 154.

14 Ibid., 36.

15 Ibid., 2.

16 In *Journals*, vol. 10, 221. On Greenough see F. O. Matthiessen, *American Renaissance: Art and Expression in the Age of Emerson and Whitman* (1941, 1968), 140, 148, quoted in Robert D. Richardson Jr., *Emerson: The Mind on Fire: A Biography* (Berkeley: University of California Press, 1995), 539. See also "Horatio Greenough," Smithsonian American Art Museum online, http://americanart.si.edu/search/artist_bio.cfm?ID=1935.

17 *CWRWE*, vol. 5, *English Traits*, 34.

18 Ibid., 18.

19 Ibid., 35.

20 Ibid., 169.

21 Robert Knox, *The Races of Men: A Philosophical Enquiry into the Influence of Race over the Destinies of Nations* (1862) [this is the 2nd edition of *Races of Men: A Fragment*, published in 1850.] See also Hannah Franziska Augstein, ed., *Race: The Origins of an Idea, 1760–1850* (Bristol, UK: Thoemmes Press, 1996), 246.

22 *CWRWE*, vol. 5, *English Traits*, 118–19.

23 In *Journals*, vol. 13, *1852–1855*, ed. Ralph H. Orth and Alfred R. Ferguson (Cambridge: Harvard University Press, 1977), 83, 128–29.

24 Ibid., 39.

25 Ibid., 398.

26 *CWRWE*, vol. 2, *Essays: First Series* (Cambridge: Harvard University Press, 1979), 33, 43. Journal AZ (1849), p. 20, in *Journals*, vol. 11, 192.

27 *Journals*, vol. 13, *1852–1855*, 115–16, 248.

28 *CWRWE*, vol. 5, *English Traits*, 171.

29 See http://www.fordham.edu/halsall/source/magnacarta.html and "Magna Carta," *Encyclopædia Britannica Online*, http://www.search.eb.com/eb/article-9050003.

30 See Hugh A. MacDougall, *Racial Myth in English History: Trojans, Teutons, and Anglo-Saxons* (Hanover: University Press of New England, 1982), 26–37, 56–62, 81–86, 91–92.

31 James A. Secord, "Behind the Veil: Robert Chambers and *Vestiges*," in *History, Humanity and Evolution*, ed. James Moore (Cambridge: Cambridge University Press, 1989), 178, 182, 185–86. See also James A. Secord, *Victorian Sensation* (Chicago: University of Chicago Press, 2000).

32 Editor's note, "Robert Chambers, *Vestiges of the Natural History of Creation* (New York, 1845), in Emerson's library," in *Journals*, vol. 9, *1843–1847*, ed. Ralph H. Orth and Alfred R. Ferguson (Cambridge: Harvard University Press, 1971), 64, 211.

33 Robert Chambers, *Vestiges of the Natural History of Creation* (1st ed., 1844), ed. James Secord (Chicago: University of Chicago Press, 1994), 306, from the Unofficial Stephen Jay Gould Archive online, http://www.stephenjaygould.org/library/vestiges/chapter16.html.

34 Chambers, *Vestiges of the Natural History of Creation*, chap. 16; Milton Millhauser, *Just before Darwin: Robert Chambers and* Vestiges (Middletown, Conn.: Wesleyan University Press, 1959), 33, 118, 128, 147.

35 Millhauser, *Just before Darwin*, 5, 8–9, 22–28, 31–34.

36 Nicoloff, "Historical Introduction," xxii, xxvi.

37 Millhauser, *Just before Darwin*, 32.

38 See Richardson, *Emerson*, 518. Also xxii–xxvi in *CWRWE*, vol. 5, *English Traits*, and Journal CO (1851), p. 81: "And Knox's law of races, that nature loves not hybrids, & extinguishes them. That the race colony detached from the race deteriorates to the crab." Note, "See Robert Knox, M.D., *The Races of Men: A Fragment* (Philadelphia, 1850), pp. 52, 86, 107, 317," in *Journals*, vol. 11, *1848–1851*, 392.

39 Knox, *Races of Men* (1850), 6.

40 Knox, *Races of Men* (1862), in Augstein, ed., *Race*, 248. For the controversy over Knox's actual scientific influence, see Peter Mandler, "The Problem with Cultural History," *Cultural and Social History* (2005): 101–2.

41 See Athena S. Leoussi, "Pheidias and 'L'Esprit Moderne': The Study of Human Anatomy in Nineteenth-Century English and French Art Education," *European Review of History* 7, no. 2 (Autumn 2000): 16–188.

42 Knox, *Races of Men* (1850), 7, quoted in Cora Kaplan, "White, Black and Green: Racialising Irishness in Victorian England," in Peter Gray, ed., *Victoria's Ireland?: Irishness and Britishness, 1837–1901* (Dublin: Four Courts Press, 2004), 51. Knox, a southern Scot like Carlyle, also wrote in terms of "we Saxons."

43 Emerson, *CWRWE*, vol. 5, *English Traits*, 28.

44 Ibid., 29.

45 Ibid., 32, 86, 91. With a somewhat different meaning from my own, Cornel West cites Emerson's "double consciousness." West notes that, for Emerson,

historical circumstances cannot be understood apart from race. See West, *The American Evasion of Philosophy: A Genealogy of Pragmatism* (Madison: University of Wisconsin Press, 1989), 34, 39.

CHAPTER 12: EMERSON IN THE HISTORY OF AMERICAN WHITE PEOPLE

1 Sophia Peabody (later the wife of Nathaniel Hawthorne) wrote her intellectual sister about Emerson in 1838, before he had gained his greatest prominence. Quote from Robert D. Richardson Jr., *Emerson: The Mind on Fire: A Biography* (Berkeley: University of California Press, 1995), 524; see also 522–23.

2 Theodore Parker quoted in 1850 in Neil Baldwin, *The American Revelation: Ten Ideals That Shaped Our Country from the Puritans to the Cold War* (New York: St. Martin's Press, 2005), 61.

3 See, e.g., Joel Porte, *Representative Man: Ralph Waldo Emerson in His Time* (originally published 1979) (New York: Columbia University Press, 1988), 1, 8, 19.

4 *The Collected Works of Ralph Waldo Emerson*, vol. 5, *English Traits* (hereafter *CWRWE*, vol. 5, *English Traits*) (Cambridge: Harvard University Press, 1994), 24.

5 An example of Emerson's depiction of black people as a piteous race of permanent enslavement appears in one of Emerson's clearest antislavery statements: *An Address delivered in the court-house in Concord, Massachussetts, on 1st August, 1884: on the anniversary of the emancipation of the negroes in the British West Indies* (Boston: J. Munroe, 1844).

6 Journal V, pp. 62–63, in *The Journals and Miscellaneous Notebooks of Ralph Waldo Emerson* (hereafter *Journals*), vol. 9, *1843–1847*, ed. Ralph H. Orth and Alfred R. Ferguson (Cambridge: Harvard University Press, 1971), 125.

7 *Journals*, vol. 11, *1848–1851*, ed. A. W. Plumstead, William H. Gilman, and Ruth H. Bennett (Cambridge: Harvard University Press, 1975), xv. Emerson's comments on the Fugitive Slave Act of 1850 take up pp. 343–65 of vol. 11 of *Journals*.

8 Journal CO, p. 59, in *Journals*, vol. 11, 385.

9 Journal DO, p. 188, and Journal VS, p. 280, in *Journals*, vol. 13, *1852–1855*, 54, 198.

10 *Journals*, vol. 9, *1843–1847*, 233.

11 Journal Y (1845), pp. 119–20, *Journals*, vol. 9, *1843–1847*, 299–300.

12 *Journals*, vol. 14, *1854–1861*, ed. Susan Sutton Smith and Harrison Hayford (Cambridge: Harvard University Press, 1978), 171.

13 Journal AB (1847), pp. 105–7, and Journal GH (1847), p. 3, *Journals*, vol. 10,

1847–1848, ed. Merton M. Sealts Jr. (Cambridge: Harvard University Press, 1973), 44–45, 131.

14 Philip L. Nicoloff finds Emerson's instances of racial thought "almost countless." See *Emerson on Race and History: An Examination of* English Traits (New York: Columbia University Press, 1961), 120. Lawrence Buell, *Emerson* (Cambridge: Harvard University Press, 2003), 248, adds that Emerson "never ceased to harbor racist views of Anglo-Saxon superiority."

15 For a thoughtful analysis of "Fate" in *The Conduct of Life*, see Eduardo Cadava, "The Guano of History," in *Of Mourning and Politics* (Cambridge: Harvard University Press, forthcoming), and Eduardo Cadava, *Emerson and the Climates of History* (Stanford: Stanford University Press, 1997). Cadava's and my use of "Fate" differs from that of Phyllis Cole from a generation ago in "Emerson, England, and Fate," in *Emerson: Prophecy, Metamorphosis, and Influence: Selected Papers from the English Institute* (New York: Columbia University Press, 1975), 83–105.

16 Journal CO, 1851, pp. 28–29, in *Journals*, vol. 11, *1848–1851*: 376.

CHAPTER 13: THE AMERICAN SCHOOL OF ANTHROPOLOGY

1 Henry S. Patterson, "Memoir of the Life and Scientific Labors of Samuel George Morton," in *Types of Mankind, or Ethnological Researches, Based upon the Ancient Monuments, Paintings, Sculptures, and Crania of Races, and upon Their Natural, Geographical, Philological, and Biblical History: Illustrated by Selections from the Inedited Papers of Samuel George Morton, M.D. (Late President of the Academy of Natural Sciences at Philadelphia) and by Additional Contributions from Prof. L. Agassiz, LL.D.; W. Usher, M.DD; and Prof. H. S. Patterson, M.D. by N. C. Nott, M.D., and Geo. R. Gliddon* (Philadelphia: J. B. Lippincott, 1857), xxx.

2 Paul A. Erikson, "Morton, Samuel George (1799–1851)," in *History of Physical Anthropology*, vol. 1, ed. Frank Spencer (New York: Garland, 1997), 65–66.

3 Samuel George Morton, *Crania Ægyptiaca, or Observations on Egyptian Ethnography, Derived from Anatomy, History and the Monuments* (Philadelphia: John Penington, 1844), 3–4, 46.

4 Ibid., 65–66; Patterson, "Memoir of Samuel George Morton," xxxvii, xlii.

5 Quoted in Karen E. Fields, "Witchcraft and Racecraft: Invisible Ontology in Its Sensible Manifestations," in *Witchcraft Dialogues: Anthropological and Philosophical Exchanges*, ed. George Clement Bond and Diane M. Ciekawy

(Athens: Ohio University Center for International Studies, 2001), 304; Max Weber, "The Religion of Non-Privileged Strata," in *Economy and Society*, ed. Geunther Roth and Claus Wittich (Berkeley: University of California Press, 1978), 490–91.

6 See the controversy as related in *Bulletins de la Société d'Anthropologie de Paris* (1861): 176, 184–88, 259, 274. The notes to this discussion cite Morton, Nott, Gliddon, and Morton's biographer J. Aitken Meigs.

7 See Reginald Horsman, *Josiah Nott of Mobile: Southerner, Physician, and Racial Theorist* (Baton Rouge: Louisiana State University Press, 1987), 113–18.

8 Ibid., 206.

9 Arthur de Gobineau, *The Inequality of Human Races*, trans. Adrian Collins, preface by George L. Mosse (New York: Howard Fertig, 1999), xii. See also Stephen Jay Gould, "Ghosts of Bell Curves Past," *Natural History* 104, no. 2 (Feb. 1995): 12–19.

10 "Jones, Sir William," *Encyclopædia Britannica Online*. 1 Oct. 2007, http://www.search.eb.com/eb/article-9043950.

11 Tocqueville to Gobineau, Saint-Cyr, 20 Dec. 1853, in Alexis de Tocqueville, *"The European Revolution" and Correspondence with Gobineau*, ed. and trans. John Lukacs (Westport, Conn.: Greenwood Press, 1959), 231–33. See also Tocqueville to Gobineau, Paris, 15 May 1852, ibid., 221–23.

12 Robert J. C. Young, *Colonial Desire: Hybridity in Theory, Culture and Race* (London: Routledge, 1995), 130–35. On Henry Hotze, see Robert E. Bonner, "Slavery, Confederate Diplomacy, and the Racialist Mission of Henry Hotze," *Civil War History* 51, no. 3 (2005): 288–311. See also Horsman, *Josiah Nott*, 205–9.

13 Jean Boissel, *Gobineau: Biographie: Mythes et réalité* (Paris: Berg International, 1993), 129–30.

14 See esp. Arthur de Gobineau, *Essai sur l'inégalité des races humaines*, in *Œuvres*, vol. 1, ed. Jean Gaulmer and Jean Boissel (Paris: Gallimard, 1983), 243, 275, 285–86, 344, 773, 922, 923, 978.

15 The Cornell University Library's electronic texts: http://cdl.library.cornell.edu/cgi-bin/moa/pageviewer?frames=1&cite=http%3A%2F%2Fcdl.library.cornell.edu%2Fcgi-bin%2Fmoa%2Fsgml%2Fmoa-idx%3Fnotisid%3DABK9283-0007%26byte%3D145175765&coll=moa&view=50&root=%2Fmoa%2Fputn%2Fputn0007%2F&tif=00007.TIF&pagenum=102.

16 In *American Journal of the Medical Sciences* 6 (1843): 252–56.

17 J. C. Nott, "Postscriptum," *Types of Mankind*, xiii.

18 Paul A. Erickson, "American School of Anthropology," in *History of Physical Anthropology*, vol. 2, ed. Frank Spencer (New York: Garland, 1997), 690.

CHAPTER 14: THE SECOND ENLARGEMENT OF AMERICAN WHITENESS

1 Geoffrey C. Ward, *The Civil War: An Illustrated History* (New York: Alfred A. Knopf, 1990), 50; Ella Lonn, *Foreigners in the Union Army and Navy* (Baton Rouge: Louisiana State University Press, 1951), 146–47, 659–61, 666–74.

2 David W. Blight, *Race and Reunion: The Civil War in American Memory* (Cambridge: Harvard University Press, 2001), 75–76, terms Decoration Day "America's first multiracial, multiethnic commemoration."

3 Ibid., 74–75, 276.

4 See Erika Lee, "American Gatekeeping: Race and Immigration Law in the Twentieth Century," in *Not Just Black and White: Historical and Contemporary Perspectives on Immigration, Race, and Ethnicity in the United States,* ed. Nancy Foner and George M. Fredrickson (New York: Russell Sage Foundation, 2004), 124.

5 Two foundational texts of whiteness studies examine this process. See David R. Roediger, *The Wages of Whiteness: Race and the Making of the American Working Class* (London: Verso, 1991 and 1999), and Noel Ignatiev, *How the Irish Became White* (New York: Routledge, 1995).

6 "Fate," in *Conduct of Life, CWRWE,* vol. 6 (Cambridge: Harvard University Press, 2003), 9.

7 Journal CO, 1851, pp. 102–3, in *Journals and Miscellaneous Notebooks of Ralph Waldo Emerson,* vol. 11, *1848–1851,* ed. A. W. Plumstead, William H. Gilman, and Ruth H. Bennett (Cambridge: Harvard University Press, 1975), 397–98.

8 Henry Cabot Lodge, *A Short History of the English Colonies in America* (New York: Harper & Brothers, 1881), 66, 72, 73.

9 Henry Cabot Lodge, "The Distribution of Ability in the United States," *Century Magazine* 42, n.s. 20 (Sept. 1891): 688–89; Dumas Malone, "The Geography of American Achievement," *Atlantic* 154, no. 6 (Dec. 1934): 669–80; John Hammond Moore, "William Cabell Bruce, Henry Cabot Lodge, and the Distribution of Ability in the United States," *Virginia Magazine of History and Biography* 86, no. 3 (July 1978): 355–61.

10 Lodge, "Distribution of Ability," 693–94.

11 James Phinney Munroe, *A Life of Francis Amasa Walker* (New York: Henry Holt, 1923), 5.

12 Francis Amasa Walker, "Immigration and Degradation," *Forum* 2 (1891): 418–19, 420, 421, 425–26.

13 Francis A. Walker, "Restriction of Immigration," *Atlantic Monthly* 77, no. 464 (June 1896): 829.

CHAPTER 15: WILLIAM Z. RIPLEY AND
THE RACES OF EUROPE

1 Arthur Mann, "Gompers and the Irony of Racism," *Antioch Review* 13, no. 2 (June 1953): 212, incorrectly ascribes the phrase to the longtime head of the American Federation of Labor, Samuel Gompers. While Gompers (himself an immigrant from England of Jewish background) undeniably made racist comments regarding immigrants from southern and eastern Europe, the quoted phrase comes from a column by the woman suffragist Lydia Kingsmill Commander, "Evil Effects of Immigration," *American Federationist* (Oct. 1905): 749.

2 "When Ripley Speaks, Wall Street Heeds," by H.I.B., *New York Times*, 26 Sept. 1926, SM7; William Z. Ripley, "Race Progress and Immigration," *Annals of the American Academy of Political and Social Science* 34, no. 1 (July 1909): 130.

3 "When Ripley Speaks, Wall Street Heeds."

4 William Z. Ripley, *The Races of Europe: A Sociological Study* (New York: D. Appleton, 1899), ix.

5 See Michael Dietler, " 'Our Ancestors the Gauls': Archaeology, Ethnic Nationalism, and the Manipulation of Celtic Identity in Modern Europe" (originally published 1994), in *American Anthropology, 1971–1995: Papers from the* American Anthropologist, ed. Regna Darnell (Arlington, Va: American Anthropological Association, 2002): 732, 738.

6 Ripley, *Races of Europe*, 37.

7 Ibid., 332.

8 C. Loring Brace terms *The Races of Europe* "gobbledygook . . . a classic illustration of the antiscience stance of Romanticism." See *"Race" Is a Four-Letter Word: The Genesis of the Concept* (New York: Oxford University Press, 2005), 171.

9 Charles W. Chesnutt, "What Is a White Man?" *Independent*, 30 May 1889, pp. 693–94.

10 Ripley, *Races of Europe*, following p. 208.

11 Ibid., facing p. 394.

12 Ibid., 394–95.

13 Ibid., 318.

14 Review by W.L. of "The Races of Europe," *New York Times*, 27 Aug. 1899, IM 10–11.

15 Otis Tufton Mason, "The Races of Europe: A Sociological Study," *American Anthropologist*, n.s. 1, no. 4 (Oct. 1899): 770–73. Mason belonged to the anthropology faculty of the University of North Carolina at Chapel Hill and regularly reviewed books for the *American Anthropologist.*

16 Ripley to Edward Robert Anderson Seligman, Boston, 27 Nov. 1901, Butler Rare Book and Manuscript Library, Columbia University.

17 "Future Americans Will Be Swarthy. Prof. Ripley Thinks Race Intermixture May Reproduce Remote Ancestral Type. TO INUNDATE ANGLO-SAXON. His Burden, Though Physically Thus Engulfed, Will Be to Bear Torch of Civilization," *New York Times*, 29 Nov. 1908, p. 7.

18 William Z. Ripley, "The European Population of the United States," *Journal of the Royal Anthropological Institute of Great Britain and Ireland* 38 (July 1908): 224–25, 234, 239–40.

19 Ripley to Edward Robert Anderson Seligman, Cambridge, Mass., 21 Nov. 1901, Butler Rare Book and Manuscript Library, Columbia University.

20 Arthur Schlesinger Jr., "The 'Hundred Days' of F.D.R.," *New York Times Book Review*, 10 April 1983, http://www.nytimes.com/books/00/11/26/specials/schlesinger-hundred.html.

21 Ida S. Ripley died in 1966. See *New York Times*, 19 March 1966, p. 29.

CHAPTER 16: FRANZ BOAS, DISSENTER

1 Claudia Roth Pierpont, "The Measure of America: How a Rebel Anthropologist Waged War on Racism," *New Yorker*, 8 March 2004, p. 52.

2 See George W. Stocking Jr., *Race, Culture, and Evolution: Essays in the History of Anthropology* (Chicago: University of Chicago Press, 1968, 1982), 167.

3 Douglas Cole, *Franz Boas: The Early Years, 1858–1906* (Seattle: University of Washington Press, 1999), 60.

4 Quoted ibid., 72.

5 Ibid., 132, 136.

6 Lee D. Baker, *From Savage to Negro: Anthropology and the Construction of Race, 1896–1954* (Berkeley: University of California Press, 1998), 103.

7 Boas to President Nicholas Murray Butler, New York, 15 Nov. 1902, in *A Franz Boas Reader: The Shaping of American Anthropology, 1883–1911*, ed. George W. Stocking Jr. (Chicago: University of Chicago Press, 1974 and 1982), 290; Stocking, *Race, Culture, and Evolution*, 166; Cole, *Franz Boas*, 220, 284. See also Vernon J. Williams Jr., *Rethinking Race: Franz Boas and His Contemporaries* (Lexington: University Press of Kentucky, 1996), 9–12.

8 In *Franz Boas Reader*, 242.

9 "The Outlook for the American Negro," in *Franz Boas Reader*, 310–11, 314–15.

10 Ibid., 310–11, 314–15.

11 In Leonard B. Glick, "Types Distinct from Our Own: Franz Boas on Jewish

Identity and Assimilation," in *American Anthropology, 1971–1995: Papers from the* American Anthropologist (Lincoln: University of Nebraska Press, 2002), 356–58, 360–61.

12 In Glick, "Types Distinct from Our Own," 341.

13 Gompers went so far as to charge that Chinese men love to "prey upon Americans girls" and "do not care how old the boys are." See Arthur Mann, "Gompers and the Irony of Racism," *Antioch Review* 13, No. 2 (June 1953): 208–9.

14 George M. Fredrickson, "Prejudice and Discrimination, History of," in *Harvard Encyclopedia of American Ethnic Groups*, ed. Stephan Thernstrom (Cambridge: Harvard University Press, 1980), 836–37, 843–45; John Higham, *Strangers in the Land: Patterns of American Nativism, 1860–1925* (New Brunswick: Rutgers University Press, 1955), 46–48, 69.

15 Higham, *Strangers in the Land*, 26–27, 92–93.

16 Williams, *Rethinking Race*, 23–24. Williams terms anthropologists' response to Boas "almost hysterical."

17 In Thomas F. Gossett, *Race: The History of an Idea in America* (Dallas: Southern Methodist University Press, 1963), 307.

18 Franz Boas, *"The Races of Europe"* (review), *Science*, n.s. 10, no. 244 (1 Sept. 1899): 292–96.

19 See Allan Chase, *The Legacy of Malthus: The Social Costs of the New Scientific Racism* (New York: Alfred A. Knopf, 1977), 96, and Cole, *Franz Boas*, 268.

20 Stocking, *Race, Culture, and Evolution*, 174–77.

21 Franz Boas, *Changes in Bodily Form of Descendants of Immigrants* (reprinted from the *Reports of the United States Immigration Commission*) (New York: Columbia University Press, 1912), 33, 59. See also Corey S. Sparks and Richard L. Jantz, "Changing Times, Changing Faces: Franz Boas's Immigrant Study in Modern Perspectives," *American Anthropologist* 105, no. 2 (June 2003): 333–37.

22 U.S. Immigration Commission, *Brief Statement of the Conclusions and Recommendations of the Immigration Commission, with Views of the Minority* (Washington, D.C.: Government Printing Office, 1910), 12–13, 35–36.

23 Baker, *From Savage to Negro*, 107.

24 See John Bodnar, *The Transplanted: A History of Immigrants in Urban America* (Bloomington: Indiana University Press, 1985), 86–89, 102–11, 123–28.

25 Humbert S. Nelli, "Italians," and Arthur A. Goren, "Jews," in *Harvard Encyclopedia of American Ethnic Groups*, 554, 585–86; "Jews Who Have Served in the United States House of Representatives," Jewish Virtual Library of the American-Israeli Cooperative Enterprise, http://www.jewishvirtuallibrary.org/jsource/US-Israel/housejews.html.

26 A full examination of newly cosmopolitan urban culture appears in Ann Douglas, *Terrible Honesty: Mongrel Manhattan in the 1920s* (New York: Farrar, Straus and Giroux, 1995).

27 Williams, *Rethinking Race*, 6, 16–17.

28 For an extended discussion of *The Melting Pot*, see Werner Sollors, *Beyond Ethnicity: Consent and Descent in American Culture* (New York: Oxford University Press, 1986), 66–99, and David Biale, "The Melting Pot and Beyond: Jews and the Politics of American Identity," in *Insider/Outsider: American Jews and Multiculturalism*, ed. David Biale, Michael Galchinsky, and Susan Heschel (Berkeley: University of California Press, 1998), 17–33. See also Todd M. Endelman, "Benjamin Disraeli and the Myth of Sephardi Superiority," *Jewish History* 10, no. 2 (Sept. 1996): 22, 25, 28, 30–32.

29 Online version at V Dare.com, http://www.vdare.com/fulford/melting_pot_play.htm.

CHAPTER 17: ROOSEVELT, ROSS, AND RACE SUICIDE

1 Thomas G. Dyer, *Theodore Roosevelt and the Idea of Race* (Baton Rouge: Louisiana State University Press, 1980), 2–3. See also Horace M. Kallen, *Culture and Democracy in the United States: Studies in the Group Psychology of the American People* (New York: Boni and Liveright, 1924), 129.

2 *The Naval War of 1812* (New York: Putnam's Sons, 1882); *Thomas Hart Benton* (Boston: Houghton Mifflin, 1887); *Gouverneur Morris* (New York: Houghton Mifflin, 1888); *The Winning of the West*, 4 vols. (New York: Putnam's Sons, 1889–96).

3 Quoted in Dyer, *Theodore Roosevelt*, 51–52, 66.

4 Neil Baldwin, *Henry Ford and the Jews: The Mass Production of Hate* (New York: Public Affairs, 2001), 33–34.

5 In Dyer, *Theodore Roosevelt*, 53, and Edward N. Saveth, *American Historians and European Immigrants, 1875–1925* (New York: Columbia University Press, 1948), 18–25, 51–52, 62.

6 Saveth, *American Historians*, 35, n. 11, 41, 59.

7 Quoted in Dyer, *Theodore Roosevelt*, 53, and Saveth, *American Historians*, 139.

8 Quoted in Dyer, *Theodore Roosevelt*, 144–45.

9 Quoted ibid., 152.

10 Edward A. Ross, "race suicide," in "The Causes of Racial Superiority," *Annals of the American Academy of Political and Social Science* 18 (1901): 67–89. See also Daniel T. Rodgers, *Atlantic Crossings: Social Politics in a Progressive Age* (Cambridge: Harvard University Press, 1998).

11 Howard W. Odum, *American Sociology: The Story of Sociology in the United*

States through 1950 (New York: Longmans, Green, 1951), 98–102, http://spartan.ac.brocku.ca/~lward/Odum/BiographicalSketches/Ross.html.

12 Ross, "Causes of Race Superiority," 68, 70, 73, 75, 83, 85.

13 Ibid., 75, 79, 84–86.

14 Edward Alsworth Ross, "The Value Rank of the American People," *Independent* 57 (Nov. 1904): 1061.

15 Ross, "Causes of Race Superiority," 89; Ross, "The Value Rank of the American People," 1063.

16 Ross, "Causes of Race Superiority," 74, 80.

17 In Jonathan Peter Spiro, "Patrician Racist: The Evolution of Madison Grant" (Ph.D. diss., University of California at Berkeley, 2000), 265. See also Jonathan Peter Spiro, *Defending the Master Race: Conservation, Eugenics, and the Legacy of Madison Grant* (Burlington: University of Vermont Press, 2008).

18 See David R. Roediger, *The Wages of Whiteness: Race and the Making of the American Working Class* (London: Verso, 1991 and 1999), for a detailed account of the role of labor organization in race formation. See *Journal of American Ethnic History* 16, no. 3 (Spring 1997): 6, 16–18, 31, and Patrick J. Blessing, "Irish," Humbert S. Nelli, "Italians," and Arthur A. Goren, "Jews," in *Harvard Encyclopedia of American Ethnic Groups*, ed. Stephan Thernstrom (Cambridge: Harvard University Press, 1980), 538, 553, 582, 585.

19 Rudolph J. Vecoli, " 'Free Country': The American Republic Viewed by the Italian Left, 1880–1920," in *In the Shadow of the Statue of Liberty: Immigrants, Workers, and Citizens in the American Republic, 1880–1920*, ed. Marianne Debouzy (Urbana: University of Illinois Press, 1992), 34; Salvatore Salerno, "*I Delitti della Razza Bianco* (Crimes of the White Race): Italian Anarchists' Racial Discourse as Crime," in *Are Italians White? How Race Is Made in America*, ed. Jennifer Guglielmo and Salvatore Salerno (New York: Routledge, 2003), 112, 120

CHAPTER 18. THE DISCOVERY OF DEGENERATE FAMILIES

1 See Philip R. Reilly, *The Surgical Solution: A History of Involuntary Sterilization in the United States* (Baltimore: Johns Hopkins University Press, 1991), 9–10, and Nicole Hahn Rafter, *White Trash: The Eugenic Family Studies, 1877–1919* (Boston: Northeastern University Press, 1988), 1–17.

2 The first description included a notice of Dugdale's "noble lineage—his family having come into England with the Conqueror." The second description comes

NOTES TO PAGES 257–64

from Arthur H. Estabrook, *The Jukes in 1915* (Washington, D.C.: Carnegie Institution, 1916), v–vii. The New York Prison Association, founded in 1844, changed its name to the Correctional Association of New York in 1961.

3 Cesare Lombroso, *L'uomo delinquente* (1876); Martino Beltrani-Scalia, *La riforma penitenziaria in Italia* (1879).

4 Richard L. Dugdale, *"The Jukes": A Study in Crime, Pauperism, Disease and Heredity, also Further Studies of Criminals*, 5th ed. (New York: G. P. Putnam's Sons, 1895), 70.

5 Ibid., 13 (emphasis in original).

6 Ibid., 18–26, 31, 38.

7 Ibid., 60–61.

8 Nicole H. Rafter, "Claims-Making and Socio-Cultural Context in the First U.S. Eugenics Campaign," *Social Problems* 38, no. 1 (Feb. 1992): 17, 20–22, and Joan Waugh, *Unsentimental Reformer: The Life of Josephine Shaw Lowell* (Cambridge: Harvard University Press, 1997), 3–11.

9 Reilly, *Surgical Solution*, 12–13.

10 See Christine Rosen, *Preaching Eugenics: Religious Leaders and the American Eugenics Movement* (Oxford: Oxford University Press, 2004), 27–29, and Genevieve C. Weeks, *Oscar Carleton McCulloch, 1843–1891: Preacher and Practitioner of Applied Christianity* (Indianapolis: Indiana Historical Society, 1976).

11 *Eugenics, Genetics and the Family* 1 (1923): 398–99, http://www.eugenics archive.org/eugenics/image_header.pl?id=1489. See also William Alexander Percy, *Lanterns on the Levee: Recollections of a Planter's Son* (originally published 1941) (Baton Rouge: Louisiana State University Press, 1973), 19–20.

12 Oscar C. McCulloch, *The Tribe of Ishmael: A Study in Social Degradation*, 4th ed. (originally published 1888) (Indianapolis: Charity Organization Society, 1891), 3, 5, 7.

13 See Don Jordan and Michael Walsh, *White Cargo: The Forgotten History of Britain's White Slaves in America* (New York: New York University Press, 2008), 87–90, 128–31, esp. 130.

14 See Michael A. Hoffman II, *They Were White and They Were Slaves: The Untold History of the Enslavement of Whites in Early America*, 4th ed. (Coeur d'Alene, Idaho: Independent History & Research Co., 1991), 99–100.

15 A loyalist refugee from Georgia, Stokes wrote in 1783. A. Roger Ekirch, *Bound for America: The Transportation of British Convicts to the Colonies, 1718–1775* (Oxford: Clarendon Press, 1987), 193.

16 Theodore Roosevelt, *The Winning of the West* (originally published 1889) (New York: G. P. Putnam's Sons, 1917), 105–6.

17 See Mai M. Ngai, "The Architecture of Race in American Immigration Law:

A Reexamination of the Immigration Act of 1924," *Journal of American History* 86, no. 1 (June 1999): 74–75, and Rosen, *Preaching Eugenics*, 27.

18 [Alice McCulloch, ed.], *The Open Door. Sermons and Prayers by Oscar C. McCulloch, Minister of Plymouth Congregational Church, Indianapolis, Indiana* (Indianapolis: Press of Wm. B. Burford, 1892), xx. See also Weeks, *Oscar Carleton McCulloch*, and Nathaniel Deutsch, *Inventing America's "Worst" Family: Eugenics, Islam, and the Fall and Rise of the Tribe of Ishmael* (Berkeley: University of California Press, 2009).

19 David Starr Jordan, *The Heredity of Richard Roe: A Discussion of the Principles of Eugenics* (Boston: American Unitarian Association, 1911), 100, 121.

CHAPTER 19: FROM DEGENERATE FAMILIES TO STERILIZATION

1 Lelia Zenderland, *Measuring Minds: Henry Herbert Goddard and the Origins of American Intelligence Testing* (Cambridge: Cambridge University Press, 1998 and 2001), 16, 28, 41–42, 54–57, 338, and Philip R. Reilly, *The Surgical Solution: A History of Involuntary Sterilization in the United States* (Baltimore: Johns Hopkins University Press, 1991), 20.

2 Allan Chase, *The Legacy of Malthus: The Social Costs of the New Scientific Racism* (New York: Alfred A. Knopf, 1977), 114.

3 Ibid., 118–19.

4 Ibid., 144–45. On Galton see also Stephen Jay Gould, *The Mismeasure of Man*, rev ed. (New York: W. W. Norton, 1996), 105–13.

5 Daniel J. Kevles, *In the Name of Eugenics: Genetics and the Uses of Human Heredity*, 2nd ed. (Cambridge: Harvard University Press, 1995), 7–9, 12.

6 Francis Galton, *Memories of My Life* (London: Methuen, 1908), at http://galton.org/books/memories/chapter-XXI.html.

7 In Chase, *Legacy of Malthus*, 101–2.

8 In C. Loring Brace, *"Race" Is a Four-Letter Word: The Genesis of the Concept* (New York: Oxford University Press, 2005), 180 (emphasis in original).

9 For a longer explanation, see Gould, *Mismeasure of Man*, 191–93.

10 Kevles, *In the Name of Eugenics*, 48–49.

11 Ibid., 47.

12 Zenderland, *Measuring Minds*, 153–55, 175.

13 Ibid., 154, 169–70.

14 In Chase, *Legacy of Malthus*, 151. See also John Lisle, "The Kallikak Family, A Study of Feeble-Mindedness by Henry Herbert Goddard," *Journal of the*

American Institute of Criminal Law and Criminology 4, no. 3 (Sept. 1913): 471.

15 In Chase, *Legacy of Malthus*, 148–50.

16 The statement figured in the 1907 presidential address of Amos Butler to the National Conference of Charities and Corrections. See Allison C. Carey, "Gender and Compulsory Sterilization Programs in America: 1907–1950," *Journal of Historical Sociology* 11, no. 1 (March 1998): 81.

17 In Reilly, *Surgical Solution*, 46.

18 Zenderland, *Measuring Minds*, 149–50, 189, 227.

19 In Reilly, *Surgical Solution*, 86. In *Segregation's Science: Eugenics and Society in Virginia* (Charlottesville: University of Virginia Press, 2008), 8–13, 25–33, 98–104, Gregory Michael Dorr points to Virginians' enduring fascination with "blood" as a motor of human destiny, beginning with Thomas Jefferson's *Notes on the State of Virginia* and extending through the 1967 U.S. Supreme Court decision *Loving v. Virginia* striking down anti-miscegenation laws.

20 Paul Lombardo, "Eugenic Sterilization Laws," Image Archive on the American Eugenics Movement, Dolan DNA Learning Center, Cold Spring Harbor Laboratory, http://www.eugenicsarchive.org/html/eugenics/essay 8text.html.

21 Harry H. Laughlin, director in charge of the Eugenics Record Office of the Department of Genetics of the Carnegie Institute of Washington, D.C., in Stephen Jay Gould, "Carrie Buck's Daughter," *Natural History* 111, no. 6 (July–Aug. 2002): 12 (originally published July 1984).

22 In Gould, "Carrie Buck's Daughter."

23 Carey, "Gender and Compulsory Sterilization Programs," 74.

24 Chase, *Legacy of Malthus*, 126, 135; Zenderland, *Measuring Minds*, 324.

25 Paul A. Lombardo, "Facing Carrie Buck," *Hastings Center Report*, 1 March 2003, 15.

CHAPTER 20: INTELLIGENCE TESTING OF NEW IMMIGRANTS

1 Robert M. Yerkes, "Testing the Human Mind," *Atlantic Monthly* 131 (March 1923): 359, 364–65, 370. The Boasian anthropologist Robert Lowie of the University of California at Berkeley took Yerkes to task for interpreting national groups in racial terms, as Yerkes does on pp. 364–65 of his *Atlantic Monthly* article. See Robert Lowie, "Psychology, Anthropology, and Race," *American Anthropologist*, n.s. 25, no. 3 (July–Sept. 1923): 299.

2 Carl C. Brigham, *A Study of American Intelligence* (Princeton: Princeton University Press, 1923), 13. Stephen Jay Gould discusses the Army IQ tests at length, noting the high frequency of zeros on the tests, indicating that soldiers had simply not answered the questions. Such results should have alerted testers to the tests' unsuitability. Gould, *The Mismeasure of Man*, rev. ed. (New York: W. W. Norton, 1996), 230–33. Truman Lee Kelley had reached a similar conclusion in *Interpretation of Educational Measurement* (Yonkers-on-Hudson, N.Y.: World, 1927).

3 Brigham, *Study of American Intelligence*, 48.

4 Quoted in Leila Zenderland, *Measuring Minds: Henry Herbert Goddard and the Origins of American Intelligence Testing* (Cambridge: Cambridge University Press, 1998 and 2001), 264.

5 Henry H. Goddard, "Mental Tests and the Immigrant," *Journal of Delinquency* 1, no. 5 (Sept. 1917): 224.

6 Zenderland, *Measuring Minds*, 266, 273.

7 Goddard, "Mental Tests and the Immigrant," 243, 252, 266. In this essay Goddard recognizes that mental handicap can be the result of heredity ("morons beget morons") or of deprivation. He also concedes that so-called morons may have their place as drudges. See pp. 269, 270. These qualifications disappeared in the xenophobic 1920s discussion of immigration restriction.

8 Donald A. Dewsbury, "Robert M. Yerkes: A Psychobiologist with a Plan," in *Portraits of Pioneers in Psychology*, ed. Gregory A. Kimble, C. Alan Boneau, and Michael Wertheimer, vol. 2 (Washington, D.C.: American Psychological Association, 1966), 92, 87–88.

9 Daniel J. Kevles, "Testing the Army's Intelligence: Psychologists and the Military in World War I," *Journal of American History* 55, no. 3 (Dec. 1968): 565.

10 Wade Pickren, "Robert Yerkes, Calvin Stone, and the Beginning of Programmatic Sex Research by Psychologists, 1921–1930," *American Journal of Psychology* 110, no. 4 (Winter 1997): 608.

11 Daniel J. Kevles, *In the Name of Eugenics: Genetics and the Uses of Human Heredity*, 2nd ed. (Cambridge: Harvard University Press, 1995): 80.

12 Ibid., 80–81.

13 Zenderland, *Measuring Minds*, 293, 297.

14 Yerkes, "Testing the Human Mind," 359, 364, 370.

15 Quoted in Gould, *Mismeasure of Man*, 224–25n. Gould explains the ways military reluctance affected the tests' administration and reduced the reliability of the results. For a fuller explanation of the Army's response, see Kevles, "Testing the Army's Intelligence," 571–80.

16 The report, entitled *Psychological Examining in the United States Army*, was published in 1921.

17 David Owen, "Inventing the SAT," *Alicia Patterson Foundation Reporter* 8, no. 1, 1985, http://www.aliciapatterson.org/APF0801/Owen/Owen.html.

18 Matthew T. Downey, *Carl Campbell Brigham: Scientist and Educator* (Princeton: Educational Testing Service, 1961), 5–7.

19 Ibid., 26.

20 Brigham, *Study of American Intelligence*, vii.

21 Ibid., 124.

22 Ibid., 146.

23 Ibid., vi, 159. See also Jonathan Peter Spiro, "Patrician Racist: The Evolution of Madison Grant" (Ph.D. diss., University of California at Berkeley, 2000), 428, 437.

24 Georges Vacher de Lapouge, *L'Aryen: Son rôle social* (Paris: A. Fontemoing, 1899), 345.

25 U.S. Senate, 61st Cong., 3rd sess., Reports of the Immigration Commission, *Dictionary of Races or Peoples* (Washington, D.C.: Government Printing Office, 1911), 5.

26 Brigham, *Study of American Intelligence*, 100, 101, 107, 110–11.

CHAPTER 21: THE GREAT UNREST

1 See "Lost Laughter," *Time.com*, 26 Oct. 1936, http://www.time.com/time/magazine/article/0,9171,788569-1,00.html, Roger Penn Cuff, "The American Editorial Cartoon: A Critical Historical Sketch," *Journal of Educational Sociology* 19, no. 2 (Oct. 1945): 93, 95, and S. K. Stevens, "Of Men and Many Things," *Pennsylvania History* 14 (Jan. 1947): 55.

2 Richard A. Easterlin, "Immigration: Social Characteristics," in *Harvard Encyclopedia of American Ethnic Groups*, ed. Stephan Thernstrom (Cambridge: Harvard University Press, 1980), 482.

3 The material that follows comes from Nell Irvin Painter, *Standing at Armageddon: The United States, 1877–1919*, rev. ed. (New York: W. W. Norton, 2008), 261–63, 293–390.

4 Tony Michels, *A Fire in Their Hearts: Yiddish Socialists in New York* (Cambridge: Harvard University Press, 2005), 3.

5 William Preston, *Aliens and Dissenters: Federal Suppression of Radicals, 1903–1933*, 2nd ed. (Urbana: University of Illinois Press, 1994), 99.

6 W. E. B. Du Bois from *Darkwater: Voices from Within the Veil* (1920) in *W. E. B. Du Bois: A Reader*, ed. David Levering Lewis (New York: Henry Holt, 1995), 458.

7 Ray Roun cartoon, *Saturday Evening Post*, 12 Feb. 1921, p. 21. This cartoon illustrates Kenneth L. Roberts's "Plain Remarks on Immigration for Plain Americans."

8 Painter, *Standing at Armageddon*, 362–65, 368–70.

9 Ibid., 372–73.

10 Jan Cohn, *Creating America: George Horace Lorimer and the* Saturday Evening Post (Pittsburgh: University of Pittsburgh Press, 1989), 103, 130–31.

11 Howard C. Hill, "The Americanization Movement," *American Journal of Sociology* 24, no. 6 (May 1919): 630.

12 See Neil Baldwin, *Henry Ford and the Jews: The Mass Production of Hate* (New York: Public Affairs, 2001), 38–42. The graduation ceremony description is on 42.

CHAPTER 22: THE MELTING POT A FAILURE?

1 Jonathan Peter Spiro, "Patrician Racist: The Evolution of Madison Grant" (Ph.D. diss., University of California at Berkeley, 2000), 498. See also Jonathan Peter Spiro, *Defending the Master Race: Conservation, Eugenics, and the Legacy of Madison Grant* (Burlington: University of Vermont Press, 2008).

2 See Jan Cohn, *Creating America: George Horace Lorimer and the* Saturday Evening Post (Pittsburgh: University of Pittsburgh Press, 1989), 10, 28–29, 166, and "Lorimer, George Horace" (2007), in *Encyclopedia Britannica Online*, http://searchj.eb.com/eb/article-9048978. See also Frederick Allen, "Star-Spangled Bigot," *American Heritage*, Nov.–Dec. 1989, pp. 63–64.

3 John T. Frederick, "Kenneth Roberts," *English Journal* 30, no. 6 (June 1941): 436–37, 438.

4 Jack Bales, *Kenneth Roberts* (New York: Twayne, 1993), 11.

5 "Angry Man's Romance," cover story, *Time*, 25 Nov. 1940, http://www.time.com/time/magazine/article/0,9171,884165,00.html.

6 Jack Bales, *Kenneth Roberts: The Man and His Works* (Metuchen, N.J.: Scarecrow Press, 1989), viii.

7 Ibid., xvi; Edgar Allen Beem, *Downeast Magazine*, Aug. 1997, in "Kenneth Lewis Roberts," http://www.waterborolibrary.org/maineaut/r.htm. Roberts, like many other writers obsessed by race, died childless.

8 Bales, *Kenneth Roberts* (1989), 23–24.

9 Kenneth L. Roberts, "Plain Remarks on Immigration for Plain Americans," *Saturday Evening Post*, 12 Feb. 1921, pp. 21, 22, 44; Roberts, *Why Europe Leaves Home* (Indianapolis: Bobbs-Merrill, 1922), 21–22, 96, 104, 113–14.

10 Roberts, *Why Europe Leaves Home*, 20–22, 54, 230–32, 271.

11 Ibid., 15, 37, 41, 76–78.

12 E. A. Ross, *The Old World in the New: The Significance of Past and Present Immigration to the American People* (New York: Century, 1914), 150–51, 256, 285–89 (emphasis in original).

13 Ibid., 289–90.

14 Roberts, *Why Europe Leaves Home,* 48, 50; Bales, Kenneth Roberts (1989), 17.

15 See, e.g., *New York Times,* 31 May 1937, p. 15.

16 Spiro, "Patrician Racist," viii, 6–22, 209, 225–26.

17 Madison Grant, *The Passing of the Great Race, or The Racial Basis of European History,* 4th ed. (New York: Charles Scribner's Sons, 1921), xxxiii. Grant's title page listed his scholarly bona fides: Chairman, New York Zoological Society, Trustee, National Museum of National History, Councilor, National Geographic Society. Grant's editor at Scribner's was Maxwell Perkins, the legendary editor of F. Scott Fitzgerald, Ernest Hemingway, and Thomas Wolfe. In 1926 Scribner's published Hemingway's novella quoting Grant's work in the title: *The Torrents of Spring: A Romantic Novel in Honor of the Passing of a Great Race.* See Spiro, "Patrician Racist," 334–35.

18 Madison Grant, "Discussion of Article on Democracy and Heredity," *Journal of Heredity* 10, no. 4 (April 1919): 165.

19 Spiro, "Patrician Racist," 325.

20 Grant, *Passing of the Great Race* (1921), 54.

21 Ibid., 13, 16, 18–19, 27–29.

22 Ibid., 39.

23 Franz Boas, "Inventing a Great Race," *New Republic,* 13 Jan. 1917, pp. 305–7.

24 Spiro, "Patrician Racist," 355, 358, 363.

25 Grant, *Passing of the Great Race* (1921), 215, 229–30.

26 Ibid., 217–19.

27 "An Appeal for Coöperation toward Lasting Peace" (1916), in David Starr Jordan, *The Days of a Man: Being Memories of a Naturalist, Teacher and Minor Prophet of Democracy,* vol. 2, *1900–1921* (Yonkers-on-Hudson, N.Y.: World Book, 1922), 688.

CHAPTER 23: ANTHROPOSOCIOLOGY: THE SCIENCE OF ALIEN RACES

1 F. Scott Fitzgerald, *The Great Gatsby,* Ruth Prigozy, ed. (New York, Oxford University Press: 1998), 14.

2 Benoit Massin, "L'Anthropologie raciale comme fondement de la science politique: Vacher de Lapouge et l'échec de l' "anthroposociologie" en France (1886–1936)," in *Les Politiques de l'anthropologie: Discours et pratiques en*

France (1860–1940), ed. Claude Blanckaert (Paris: L'Harmattan, 2001), 296. See also George Mosse, *Toward the Final Solution: A History of European Racism* (New York: H. Fertig, 1978).

3 However, Jacques Barzun says Gobineau's *Essai* was immediately read "by at least a score of notables": Renan, Taine, Nietzsche, Wagner, Quatrefages, Schopenhauer, and others, all of whom already embraced racial determinism. Barzun misses the Nott translation. See Barzun, *Race: A Study in Superstition*, rev. ed. (New York: Harper & Row, 1965), (originally published in 1937 as *Race: A Study in Modern Superstition*), x, 61, 200–218.

4 Georges Vacher de Lapouge, "L'Anthropologie et la science politique," *Revue d'Anthropologie* (1887): 150–51, in Jonathan Peter Spiro, "Patrician Racist: The Evolution of Madison Grant" (Ph.D. diss., University of California at Berkeley, 2000), 290.

5 For a history of such notions, see Jacques Barzun, *The French Race: Theories of Its Origin and Their Social and Political Implications prior to the Revolution* (New York: Columbia University Press, 1932). See also Anthony M. Ludovici, "Dr. Oscar Levy," *New English Weekly* 30 (1946–47): 49–50, and "A Book to Stir Up Prejudice," *New York Times Review of Books*, 28 July 1906, BR 472.

6 Spiro, "Patrician Racist," 287.

7 Ibid., 493.

8 Pierre-André Taguieff, *La Couleur et le sang: Doctrines racistes à la française*, new ed. (Paris: Mille et une Nuits, 2002), 239, 272. Lapouge's books were *Les Sélections sociales* (1896), *L'Aryen: Son rôle social* (1899), and *Race et milieu social: Essais d'anthroposociologie* (1909).

9 Mike Hawkins, *Social Darwinism in European and American Thought, 1860–1945* (Cambridge: Cambridge University Press, 1997), 117.

10 Massin, "L'Anthropologie raciale," 302; Jennifer Michael Hecht, *The End of the Soul: Scientific Modernity, Atheism, and Anthropology in France* (New York: Columbia University Press, 2003), 168, 172, 193. See also Hecht, "Vacher de Lapouge and the Rise of Nazi Science," *Journal of the History of Ideas* 61, no. 2 (April 2000): 285–304.

11 Taguieff, *La Couleur et le sang*, 270–71; Massin, "L'Anthropologie raciale," 283, 305, 290.

12 Taguieff, *La Couleur et le sang*, 288–93; Massin, "L'Anthropologie raciale," 274.

13 Georges Vacher de Lapouge, *L'Aryen: Son rôle social* (Paris: A. Fontemoing, 1899), 483.

14 Ibid., 464–83.

15 Spiro, "Patrician Racist," 283–84, 365–66.

16 Lapouge, *L'Aryen*, 345.

17 Madison Grant, *Passing of the Great Race, or The Racial Basis of European History*, 4th ed. (New York: Charles Scribner's Sons, 1921), 231–32.

18 Ibid., 184–85.

19 Russell A. Kazal, *Becoming Old Stock: The Paradox of German-American Identity* (Princeton: Princeton University Press, 2004), 4–6, 151–92.

20 Kathleen Neils Conzen, "Germans," in *Harvard Encyclopedia of American Ethnic Groups*, ed. Stephan Thernstrom (Cambridge: Harvard University Press, 1980), 410, 422–23.

21 J. B. Moore, review of *The French Revolution in San Domingo*, by T. Lothrop Stoddard, in *Political Science Quarterly* 31, no. 1 (March 1916): 179–80.

22 Matthew Pratt Guterl, *The Color of Race in America, 1900–1940* (Cambridge: Harvard University Press, 2001), 51–52; Spiro, "Patrician Racist," 439–42.

23 Lothrop Stoddard, *The Revolt against Civilization: The Menace of the Under Man* (New York: Charles Scribner's Sons, 1922), 56, 63.

24 Ibid., 10 (emphasis in original).

25 Ibid., 245, 248, 252, 254, 262–63.

26 Ibid., 23–25, 63–64, 69, 71–72, 94–96, 113, 151–52, 163, 210 (emphasis in original).

27 Ibid., 63, 71, 72.

28 The *Post* editorials appeared in April and May 1921. See Jan Cohn, *Creating America: George Horace Lorimer and the* Saturday Evening Post (Pittsburgh: University of Pittsburgh Press, 1989), 135–36, 155.

29 William McDougall, *Is America Safe for Democracy?* (New York: Charles Scribner's Sons, 1921), appendix V, 209.

30 Elazar Barkan, *The Retreat of Scientific Racism: Changing Concepts of Race in Britain and the United States between the World Wars* (Cambridge: Cambridge University Press, 1992), 190–203.

31 Jack Bales, *Kenneth Roberts: The Man and His Works* (Metuchen, N.J.: Scarecrow Press, 1989), 19.

32 Spiro, "Patrician Racist," 448.

33 Cohn, *Creating America*, 195–96.

34 Richard Slotkin, *Lost Battalions: The Great War and the Crisis of American Nationality* (New York: Henry Holt, 2005), 459.

35 Richard V. Oulahan, "Tense Feeling on Ku Klux," *New York Times*, 29 June 1924, pp. 1, 7. See also *New York Times*, 23 June 1924, p. 1.

36 "Deeper Causes," editorial, *New York Times*, 5 July 1924, p. 12.

37 Calvin Coolidge, "Whose Country Is This?" *Good Housekeeping*, Feb. 1921, pp. 13, 14, 109.

38 Neil Baldwin, *Henry Ford and the Jews: The Mass Production of Hate* (New York: Public Affairs, 2001), 45–47.

39 Ibid., 25.

40 On the peace ship, see Nell Irvin Painter, *Standing at Armageddon: The United States, 1877–1919*, rev. ed. (New York: W. W. Norton, 2008), 308–9.

41 Baldwin, *Henry Ford and the Jews*, 98, 263–65, 306. W. J. Cameron went on to publish his own Anglo-Israelite paper after the closing of the *Dearborn Independent*.

42 Baldwin, *Henry Ford and the Jews*, 309.

43 Ibid., 82–83, 97, 144, 201.

CHAPTER 24: REFUTING RACIAL SCIENCE

1 Walter Lippmann, "A Future for the Tests" *New Republic* 33 (29 Nov. 1922): 10.

2 Franz Samelson, "From 'Race Psychology' to 'Studies in Prejudice': Some Observations on the Thematic Reversal in Social Psychology," *Journal of the History of the Behavioral Sciences* 14 (1978): 273.

3 Daniel J. Kevles, "Annals of Eugenics: A Secular Faith—III," *New Yorker*, 22 Oct. 1984, pp. 100–101, 107–8; Elazar Barkan, *The Retreat of Scientific Racism: Changing Concepts of Race in Britain and the United States between the World Wars* (Cambridge: Cambridge University Press, 1992), 209.

4 Vincent P. Franklin, "Black Social Scientists and the Mental Testing Movement, 1920–1940," in *Black Psychology*, ed. Reginald L. Jones, 3rd ed. (Berkeley, Calif.: Cobb & Henry, 1991), 207.

5 Bond in the *Crisis* 28 (1924), quoted in John P. Jackson Jr., " 'Racially Stuffed Shirts and Other Enemies of Mankind': Horace Mann Bond's Parody of Segregationist Psychology in the 1950s," in *Defining Difference: Race and Racism in the History of Psychology*, ed. Andres S. Winston (Washington, D.C.: American Psychological Association, 2004), 264–65. See also Franklin, "Black Social Scientists," 205–7. Franklin also discusses the theory that black intelligence is related to the amount of "white blood" in the black individual. Supposedly the whiter the Negro, the smarter. Otto Klineberg disproved this assertion in his 1935 *Negro Intelligence and Selective Migration*.

6 Kevles, "Annals of Eugenics," 107.

7 Samelson, "From 'Race Psychology' to 'Studies in Prejudice,' " 268–71.

8 Robert E. Park, "Human Migration and the Marginal Man," *American Journal of Sociology* 33, no. 6 (May 1928): 887–90, 892–93.

9 Edward Alsworth Ross, *Seventy Years of It: An Autobiography* (New York: D. Appleton-Century, 1936), 276. Emphasis in original.

10 Lelia Zenderland, *Measuring Minds: Henry Herbert Goddard and the Origins of American Intelligence Testing* (Cambridge: Cambridge University Press,

1998, 2001), 324–26; *Human Intelligence: Historical Influences, Current Controversies, Teaching Resources*, Indiana University, http://www.indiana .edu/%7Eintell/kallikak.shtml

11 Franz Boas, *Anthropology and Modern Life* (originally published 1932), with a new introduction and afterword by Herbert S. Lewis (New Brunswick, N.J.: Transaction Publishers, 2004), 273, 282–83.

12 Barkan, *Retreat of Scientific Racism*, 94.

13 Otto Klineberg, "Reflections of an International Psychologist of Canadian Origin," *International Social Science Journal* 25, nos. 1–2 (1973): 40–41. See also Wayne H. Holtzman and Roger W. Russell, "Otto Klineberg: A Pioneering International Psychologist," *International Journal of Psychology* 27, no. 5 (Oct. 1992): 346–65.

14 See Otto Klineberg, *A Study of Psychological Differences between 'Racial' and National Groups in Europe*, Archives of Psychology, no. 132 (New York, 1931).

15 Klineberg, "Reflections," 41–42.

16 Carl C. Brigham, "Intelligence Tests of Immigrant Groups," *Psychological Review* 37, no. 2 (March 1930): 164, 165.

17 Judith Schachter Modell, *Ruth Benedict: Patterns of a Life* (Philadelphia: University of Pennsylvania Press, 1983), 23–26, 56; Margaret M. Caffrey, *Ruth Benedict: Stranger in This Land* (Austin: University of Texas Press, 1989), 17, 21–22, 40–41.

18 Caffrey, *Ruth Benedict*, 64.

19 Modell, *Ruth Benedict*, 64–67.

20 Ibid., 84; Caffrey, *Ruth Benedict*, 75–81; Margaret Mead, *Ruth Benedict* (New York: Columbia University Press, 1974), 8. Mead's book includes photographs and excerpts from Benedict's journals and letters.

21 Caffrey, *Ruth Benedict*, 93–98; Virginia Heyer Young, *Ruth Benedict: Beyond Relativity, Beyond Pattern* (Lincoln: University of Nebraska Press, 2005), 7–8.

22 Lois W. Banner, *Intertwined Lives: Margaret Mead, Ruth Benedict, and Their Circle* (New York: Alfred A. Knopf, 2003), 411.

23 This is the subject of Banner, *Intertwined Lives*.

24 Margaret Mead, *An Anthropologist at Work: Writings of Ruth Benedict* (Boston: Houghton Mifflin, 1959), and *Ruth Benedict*.

25 Mead, *Ruth Benedict*, 2.

26 Mary Catherine Bateson, "Foreword," in Ruth Benedict, *Patterns of Culture* (originally published 1934) (Boston: Houghton Mifflin, 1989), ix.

27 Margaret Mead, *Blackberry Winter: My Earlier Years* (originally published 1972) (New York: Kodansha International, 1995), 130–31.

28 Louise Lamphere, "Unofficial Histories: A Vision of Anthropology from the Margins," *American Anthropologist* 106, no. 1 (March 2004): 134.

29 Caffrey, *Ruth Benedict*, 122, 160–61, 187. See also Banner, *Intertwined Lives*, 202.

30 Benedict, *Patterns of Culture*, 11, 15, 78–79, 233–37.

31 Caffrey, *Ruth Benedict*, 278, 284–85.

32 Ruth Benedict, *Race: Science and Politics* (New York: Modern Age Books, 1940), v–vi.

33 Benedict, *Race* (1940), 9, 12–17.

34 Ibid., 3, 119–27.

35 Ibid., 6, 30–31, 37.

36 Ruth Benedict, *Race: Science and Politics*, rev. ed. (New York: Viking Press, 1943), v.

37 Benedict, *Race* (1940), vii; (1943), xi–xii; (1945), xi.

38 Jacques Barzun, *Race: A Study in Superstition*, rev. ed. (New York: Harper & Row, 1965); M. F. Ashley Montague, *Man's Most Dangerous Myth: The Fallacy of Race*, 3rd ed. (New York, Harper & Brothers, 1952), 1. See also Karen E. Fields, "Witchcraft and Racecraft: Invisible Ontology in Its Sensible Manifestations," in *Witchcraft Dialogues: Anthropological and Philosophical Exchanges*, ed. George Clement Bond and Diane M. Ciekawy (Athens: Ohio University Center for International Studies, 2001), 283–315.

39 United Nations Educational, Scientific and Cultural Organization, *The Race Concept: Results of an Inquiry* (Paris: United Nations, 1952), 7–8.

40 Ruth Benedict and Gene Weltfish, *Races of Mankind* (1943), in *Race: Science and Politics*, rev. ed. (1943), 176.

41 Ibid., 176–77.

42 Ibid., 182–83.

43 Carleton S. Coon, *Adventures and Discoveries: The Autobiography of Carleton S. Coon* (Englewood Cliffs, N.J.: Prentice-Hall, 1981), 129.

44 Ibid., 131, 137–38.

45 Samelson, "From 'Race Psychology' to 'Studies in Prejudice,' " 268, 272–73.

46 Mead, *Ruth Benedict*, 53.

CHAPTER 25: A NEW WHITE RACE POLITICS

1 Neil Baldwin, *Henry Ford and the Jews: The Mass Production of Hate* (New York: Public Affairs, 2001), 108–20.

2 Ibid., 148–51.

3 In *Anthology of American Literature*, 4th ed., vol. 2, ed. George McMichael, Frederick Crews, J. C. Levenson, Leo Marx, and David E. Smith (New York: Macmillan, 1989), 1351–52.

4 Donald W. Rogers, "Introduction—The Right to Vote in American History," in *Voting and the Spirit of American Democracy: Essays on the History of Voting Rights in America*, ed. Donald W. Rogers (Urbana: University of Illinois Press, 1990), 11–12; Paul Kleppner, *Who Voted?: The Dynamics of Electoral Turnout, 1870–1980* (New York: Praeger, 1982), 20–62.

5 Kristi Andersen, *The Creation of a Democratic Majority, 1928–1936* (Chicago: University of Chicago Press, 1979), 38–40, 42, 51, 87–88, 90; Kleppner, *Who Voted?*, 68–70.

6 Louis Adamic, *Laughing in the Jungle: The Autobiography of an Immigrant in America* (New York: Harper & Brothers, 1932), 105.

7 Allan J. Lichtman, *Prejudice and the Old Politics: The Presidential Election of 1928* (Chapel Hill: University of North Carolina Press, 1979), 5–6, 200–201, 231, 233. Lichtman takes issue with Samuel Lubell's designation of 1928 as a critical election. For Lichtman, Smith brought out urban voters, but the election did not signal a new era in U.S. politics (pp. 94–95, 122).

8 According to Michael Denning, Americans born between 1904 and 1923 constituted a huge working-class generation, "the most working-class cohort in American history," with the highest number of people ever identifying themselves as workers. Denning, *The Cultural Front: The Laboring of American Culture in the Twentieth Century* (London: Verso, 1997), 8–9.

9 Andersen, *Creation of a Democratic Majority*, 112–13, 93.

10 See Nancy Weiss, *Farewell to the Party of Lincoln: Black Politics in the Age of FDR* (Princeton: Princeton University Press, 1983), 209–39.

11 Baldwin, *Henry Ford and the Jews*, 294, 297.

12 David M. Kennedy, *Freedom from Fear: The American People in Depression and War, 1929–1945* (New York: Oxford University Press, 1999) 216, 230–31.

13 Alan Brinkley, *Voices of Protest: Huey Long, Father Coughlin, and the Great Depression* (New York: Alfred A. Knopf, 1982), 82–121. Coughlin was especially influential in 1934–35.

14 David Nasaw, *The Chief: The Life and Work of William Randolph Hearst* (Boston: Houghton Mifflin, 2000), 488–90, 494–98.

15 *Reader's Digest*, Nov. 1939, pp. 62–67.

16 Baldwin, *Henry Ford and the Jews*, 281–88.

17 Horace M. Kallen, "Democracy versus the Melting-Pot," *Nation*, 18 Feb. 1915, pp. 190–94, and 25 Feb. 1915, pp. 217–20, and *Culture and Democracy in the United States: Studies in the Group Psychology of the American Peoples* (New York: Boni and Liveright, 1924). See also Sidney Ratner, "Horace M. Kallen and Cultural Pluralism," *Modern Judaism* 4, no. 2 (May 1984), 185.

18 Kallen, "Democracy versus the Melting-Pot," 192.

19 Ibid., 194.

20 Ibid., 220. Werner Sollors summed up Kallen's vision as "Once a trombone, always a trombone!" in *Beyond Ethnicity: Consent and Descent in American Culture* (New York: Oxford University Press, 1986), 185.

21 Randolph Bourne, "Trans-National America," *Atlantic Monthly* 118 (July 1916): 93; John Dewey, "The Principle of Nationality," *Menorah Journal* 3, no. 3 (Oct. 1917): 206, 208.

22 Adamic, *Laughing in the Jungle*, 67–70, 98, 101–2, 109.

23 Ibid., 262–65; Louis Adamic, *My America, 1928–1938* (New York: Harper & Brothers, 1938), 48; Dale E. Peterson, "The American Adamic: Immigrant Bard of Diversity," *Massachusetts Review* 44, nos. 1–2 (Spring–Summer 2003): 235.

24 Adamic, *My America*, 135, 191.

25 Ibid., 188.

26 Louis Adamic, "Thirty Million New Americans," *Harper's Magazine* 169 (Nov. 1934): 684, 694.

27 Immigrants as dung in Adamic, *Laughing in the Jungle*, 18–20, 104, 254, 292–93, 298, 320; the quote appears on 104. Adamic never lost sight of the tremendous toll of industrial accidents on immigrants' bodies and lives. Workplace accidents also appear as a routine part in the work of Pietro di Donato. The opening scene of his *Christ in Concrete*, a 1937 novel of Italian immigrant bricklayers, describes a deadly industrial accident. *Christ in Concrete* succeeded wildly on its initial publication, then largely disappeared from the canon of immigrant literature. Thomas J. Ferraro, in *Feeling Italian: The Art of Ethnicity in America* (New York: New York University Press, 2005), 52–60.

28 Adamic, "Thirty Million New Americans," 684, 687, 694.

29 Barbara Diane Savage, *Broadcasting Freedom: Radio, War, and the Politics of Race, 1938–1948* (Chapel Hill: University of North Carolina Press, 1999), 22–24. See also the "Inventory of the Rachel Davis DuBois Papers, 1920–1993" in the Friends Historical Library of Swarthmore College, http://www.swarthmore.edu/Library/friends/ead/5035dubo.xml#bioghist.

30 Savage, *Broadcasting Freedom*, 24–26, 291.

31 Ibid., 61; Kennedy, *Freedom from Fear*, 761.

CHAPTER 26: THE THIRD ENLARGEMENT OF AMERICAN WHITENESS

1 Gary Gerstle, *American Crucible: Race and Nation in the Twentieth Century* (Princeton: Princeton University Press, 2001), 188, 196, 203–4.

2 James N. Gregory, "The Southern Diaspora and the Urban Dispossessed:

Demonstrating the Census Public Use Microdata Samples," *Journal of American History* 82, no. 1 (June 1995): 112, 117; Gerstle, *American Crucible*, 35, 196.

3 Norman Mailer, *The Naked and the Dead* (New York: Rinehart, 1948), 18–20, 63–67, 156–64, 222–35.

4 Thomas A. Guglielmo, "Fighting for Caucasian Rights: Mexicans, Mexican Americans, and the Transnational Struggle for Civil Rights in World War II Texas," *Journal of American History* 92, no. 4 (March 2006): 1215–16. After 1945, Native American Indians were included with Caucasians (1232).

5 Joseph Heller, *Now and Then: From Coney Island to Here* (New York: Alfred A. Knopf, 1998), 152–53.

6 Ira Katznelson, *When Affirmative Action Was White: An Untold History of Racial Inequality in Twentieth-Century America* (New York: W. W. Norton, 2005), 101–2. See also John M. Kinder, "The Good War's 'Raw Chunks': Norman Mailer's *The Naked and the Dead* and James Gould Cozzen's *Guard of Honor*," *Midwest Quarterly* 46, no. 2 (Winter 2005): 106, 187–202.

7 David M. Kennedy, *Freedom from Fear: The American People in Depression and War, 1929–1945* (New York: Oxford University Press, 1999), 760.

8 "Lindbergh Sees a 'Plot' for War," *New York Times*, 12 Sept. 1941, p. 2; "The Un-American Way," ibid., 26 Sept. 1941, p. 22. See also "Lindbergh Is Accused of Inciting Hate," ibid., 14 Sept. 1941, p. 25.

9 Quoted in Gerstle, *American Crucible*, 173–74. See also 153, 170–75. Jonathan J. Cavallero, "Frank Capra's 1920s Immigrant Trilogy: Immigration, Assimilation, and the American Dream," *MELUS* 29, no. 2 (Summer 2004): 27–53, reminds readers that Capra's three films of the 1920s treat the American immigrant experience and criticize the materialism at the core of the American dream.

10 Gerstle, *American Crucible*, 166, 172.

11 Louis Adamic, *A Nation of Nations* (New York: Harper & Brothers, 1945), 7.

12 In Gary Gerstle, "The Working Class Goes to War," in *The War in American Culture: Society and Consciousness during World War II*, ed. Lewis A. Erenberg and Susan E. Hirsch (Chicago: University of Chicago Press, 1996), 118. Cynthia Skove Nevels, *Lynching to Belong: Claiming Whiteness Through Racial Violence* (College Station: Texas A&M University Press, 2008), 1, 6–7, 36, 154–160, makes a similar point.

13 David R. Roediger, ed., *Black on White: Black Writers on What It Means to Be White* (New York: Schocken, 1998), 19. In 1965 the noted African American theologian Howard Thurman contended, "The immigrant who comes to this country seeking a new home soon realizes . . . [that the] sooner he accepts the dominant mood, the sooner will he be accepted, not as a foreigner but as a white American. . . . That he may have been the victim of racial, religious, or

political persecution in his homeland does not matter. The general tendency is for him to make his place in the new world secure by ingratiating himself to the white community as a *white* man in good standing." Thurman, *The Luminous Darkness: A Personal Interpretation of the Anatomy of Segregation and the Ground of Hope* (New York: Harper & Row, 1965), 36.

14 Michael Novak, *The Rise of the Unmeltable Ethnics: Politics and Culture in the Seventies* (New York: Macmillan, 1972), 106–7.

15 Karen Brodkin, *How Jews Became White Folks and What That Says about Race in America* (New Brunswick: Rutgers University Press, 1998), 10–11, 17.

16 Heller, *Now and Then*, 167.

17 Ibid., 167–68.

18 Richard D. Alba, *Italian Americans: Into the Twilight of Ethnicity* (Englewood Cliffs, N.J.: Prentice-Hall, 1985), 75, 83–84.

19 See Rudolph M. Susel, "Slovenes," in *Harvard Encyclopedia of American Ethnic Groups*, ed. Stephan Thernstrom (Cambridge: Harvard University Press, 1980), 941.

20 Theda Skocpol, "The G.I. Bill and U.S. Social Policy, Past and Future," *Social Philosophy and Policy* 14 (Summer 1997): 96–97.

21 Kenneth T. Jackson, *Crabgrass Frontier: The Suburbanization of the United States* (New York: Oxford University Press, 1985), 206.

22 Katznelson, *When Affirmative Action Was White*, 112–15.

23 See David Kushner, *Levittown: Two Families, One Tycoon, and the Fight for Civil Rights in America's Legendary Suburb* (New York: Walker, 2009). See also Tom Vanderbilt, "Alien Nations," *Bookforum* 15, no. 5 (Feb.–March 2009): 14.

24 The American Experience, "Miss America," http://www.pbs.org/wgbh/amex/missamerica/peopleevents/e_inclusion.htm.

25 Michelle Mart, "The 'Christianization' of Israel and Jews in 1950s America," *Religion and American Culture: A Journal of Interpretation* 14, no. 1 (2004): 116–25.

26 Robert Zussman, "Review: Still Lonely after All These Years," *Sociological Forum* 16, no. 1 (March 2001): 157–58.

27 Carol A. O'Connor, "Sorting Out the Suburbs: Patterns of Land Use, Class, and Culture," *American Quarterly* 37, no. 3 (1985): 383.

28 Lizabeth Cohen, *A Consumers' Republic: The Politics of Mass Consumption in Postwar America* (New York: Alfred A. Knopf, 2004), 122–23.

29 Louise DeSalvo, *Crazy in the Kitchen: Food, Feuds, and Forgiveness in an Italian American Family* (New York: Bloomsbury, 2004), 9–13.

30 Cohen, *Consumers' Republic*, 152–53.

31 Thomas A. Guglielmo, " 'No Color Barrier' Italians, Race, and Power in the

United States," in *Are Italians White? How Race Is Made in America*, ed. Jennifer Guglielmo and Salvatore Salerno (New York: Routledge, 2003), 29.

32 Jonathan Rieder, *Canarsie: The Jews and Italians of Brooklyn against Liberalism* (Cambridge: Harvard University Press, 1985), 27–28.

33 See Douglas S. Massey and Nancy A. Denton, *American Apartheid: Segregation and the Making of the Underclass* (Cambridge: Harvard University Press, 1993). Whereas the role of government was glaringly obvious and unpleasant in the creation and maintenance of public housing for the urban poor, e.g., Chicago's depressing Robert Taylor projects, the crucial federal role in financing suburbanization was hidden, allowing home buyers to believe they had acquired their homes purely through their own virtuous, hard work. See David Freund, "Marketing the Free Market: State Intervention and the Politics of Prosperity in Metropolitan America," in *The New Suburban History*, ed. Kevin M. Kruse and Thomas J. Sugrue (Chicago: University of Chicago Press, 2005), 11–32, Thomas J. Sugrue, *Sweet Land of Liberty: The Forgotten Struggle for Civil Rights in the North* (New York: Random House, 2008), 201–7, and Thomas J. Sugrue, "The New American Dream: Renting," *Wall Street Journal*, 14–15 Aug. 2009, W1–2.

34 James Loewen, *Sundown Towns: A Hidden Dimension of American Racism?* (New York: New Press, 2005), 6–17.

35 Katznelson, *When Affirmative Action Was White*, 114–15; Cohen, *Consumers' Republic*, 167–72.

36 Herbert J. Gans's pioneering study, *The Levittowners: Ways of Life and Politics in a New Suburban Community* (New York: Pantheon Books, 1967), notes racial restriction only in passing, and not until p. 185.

37 Restrictive covenants can be used for a variety of ends, from stipulating lot size to regulating where owners can cut down trees. However, the restrictive covenants in question here deal with race. When the Roosevelt administration created the FHA in 1934, its manual to sellers included a model racially restrictive covenant on the ground that "if a neighborhood is to retain stability, it is necessary that properties shall continue to be occupied by the same social and racial classes." After the U.S. Supreme Court outlawed the enforcement of racially restrictive covenants in *Shelley v. Kraemer* (1948), the FHA and the VA continued to practice segregation, but not in writing. Their lending did not open suburban housing to African Americans until the 1970s. See http://www.developmentleadership.net/current/worksheet.htm.

38 Kenneth T. Jackson, "Race, Ethnicity, and Real Estate Appraisal: The Home Owners Loan Corporation and the Federal Housing Administration," *Journal of Urban History* 6 (1980): 433. On racial segregation in the mid-twentieth-century North, see Sugrue, *Sweet Land of Liberty*.

CHAPTER 27: BLACK NATIONALISM AND WHITE ETHNICS

1 Bruce Perry, *Malcolm: The Life of a Man Who Changed Black America* (Barrytown, N.Y.: Station Hill Press, 1991), 2–3, 113–17, 139–41, 161–62.

2 *Autobiography of Malcolm X as Told to Alex Haley* (New York: Ballantine Books, 1965), 404. See also Thulani Davis and Howard Chapnick, *Malcolm X: The Great Photographs* (New York: Stewart Tabori and Chang, 1993).

3 Perry, *Malcolm*, 115–16; Nell Irvin Painter, *Creating Black Americans: African-American History and Its Meanings* (New York: Oxford University Press, 2006), 254.

4 Perry, *Malcolm*: 181. See also Nell Irvin Painter, "Malcolm X across the Genres," *American Historical Review* 98, no. 2 (April 1993): 396–404.

5 Perry, *Malcolm*, 175–76.

6 Michael Novak, *The Rise of the Unmeltable Ethnics: Politics and Culture in the Seventies* (New York: Macmillan, 1972), 71–77.

7 James Baldwin, *The Price of the Ticket: Collected Nonfiction, 1948–1985* (New York: St. Martin's Press, 1985), xiv, xviv, xx, 431–32.

8 Margaret Mead and James Baldwin, *A Rap on Race* (Philadelphia: Lippincott, 1971), and Kai T. Erikson, *In Search of Common Ground: Conversations with Erik H. Erikson and Huey P. Newton* (New York: W. W. Norton, 1973).

9 Michael Omi and Howard Winant, *Racial Formation in the United States from the 1960s to the 1990s*, 2nd ed. (New York: Routledge, 1994), 99.

10 See Mary Waters, *Ethnic Options: Choosing Identities in America* (Berkeley: University of California Press, 1990), 90–93, and Micaela de Leonardo, "Racial Fairy Tales," *Nation* 253, no. 20 (9 Dec. 1991): 752–54. Herbert Gans coined the phrase "symbolic ethnicity" in "Symbolic Ethnicity: The Future of Ethnic Groups and Cultures in America," *Ethnic and Racial Studies* 2 (Jan. 1979): 1–20.

11 Pierre L. van den Berghe, *Race and Ethnicity: Essays in Comparative Sociology* (New York: Basic Books, 1970), 10. Van den Berghe explains, "What makes a society multiracial is not the presence of physical differences between groups, but the attribution of social significance to such physical differences as may exist."

12 See Richard Alba, *Ethnic Identity: The Transformation of White America* (New Haven: Yale University Press, 1990), and Waters, *Ethnic Options*.

13 Novak, *Rise of the Unmeltable Ethnics*, 135, 166–67, 198.

14 Ibid., 67, 71, 77.

15 Dan T. Carter, *The Politics of Rage: George Wallace, the Origins of the New Conservatism, and the Transformation of American Politics* (New York: Simon and Schuster, 1995), 137–38, 146–51.

16 Michael Novak, "Novak: The Rise of Unmeltable Ethnics, Part I," 30 Aug. 2006, http://www.firstthings.com/onthesquare/?p=450.

17 James Traub, "Nathan Glazer Changes His Mind, Again," *New York Times*, 28 June 1998.

18 Nathan Glazer and Daniel P. Moynihan, *Beyond the Melting Pot: The Negroes, Puerto Ricans, Jews, Italians, and Irish of New York City*, 2nd ed. (New York: MIT Press, 1970), 16–17.

19 Alejandro Portes, "The Melting Pot That Did Happen," *International Migration Review* 34, no. 1 (Spring 2000): 243–44.

20 Glazer and Moynihan, *Beyond the Melting Pot*: lxii–lxvi, lxviii, lxxiv (quote on lxxxiii, emphasis added). Michael Novak quoted this insult in *Rise of the Unmeltable Ethnics*, 93.

21 Glazer and Moynihan, *Beyond the Melting Pot*, xvi.

CHAPTER 28: THE FOURTH ENLARGEMENT OF AMERICAN WHITENESS

1 Victoria Hattam, "Ethnicity and the Boundaries of Race: Rereading Directive 15," *Daedalus* 134, no. 1 (Winter 2005): 61–62, 67.

2 *Measuring America: The Decennial Census from 1790 to 2000*, U.S. Department of Commerce, U.S. Census Bureau (Washington, D.C.: Government Printing Office, 2002), 100, and Jennifer L. Hochschild, "Looking Ahead: Racial Trends in the United States," *Daedalus* 134, no. 1 (Winter 2005): 71.

3 Hochschild, "Looking Ahead," 76.

4 Richard D. Alba, *Ethnic Identity: The Transformation of White America* (New Haven: Yale University Press, 1990), 9–12.

5 Lillian Smith, *Killers of the Dream*, rev. ed. (New York: W. W. Norton, 1978), 36–37, 84, 90–94, 123–24, 163–65.

6 John Howard Griffin, *Black like Me* (Boston: Houghton Mifflin, 1961); Robert Bonazzi, *Man in the Mirror: John Howard Griffin and the Story of Black like Me* (Maryknoll, N.Y.: Orbis Books: 1997), 54–92.

7 Grace Halsell, *Soul Sister: The Journal of a White Woman Who Turned Herself Black and Went to Live and Work in Harlem and Mississippi* (New York: World Publishing, 1969), and Grace Halsell, *In Their Shoes* (Forth Worth: Texas Christian University Press, 1996), 123–68.

8 See Troy Duster, "The 'Morphing' Properties of Whiteness," in *Making and Unmaking of Whiteness*, ed. Birgit Brander Rasmussen, Eric Klineberg, Irene J. Nexica, and Matt Wray (Durham: Duke University Press, 2001), 129.

9 David R. Roediger, *The Wages of Whiteness: Race and the Making of the American Working Class* (London: Verso, 1991), and *How Race Survived U.S. History: From the American Revolution to the Present* (New York: Verso, 2008). See also Kimberlé Crenshaw et al., eds., *Critical Race Theory: The Key Writings That Formed the Movement* (New York: New Press, 1995), Richard Delgado, ed., *Critical Race Theory: The Cutting Edge* (Philadelphia: Temple University Press, 1995), Richard Delgado and Jean Stefancic, eds., *Critical White Studies: Looking behind the Mirror* (Philadelphia: Temple University Press, 1997), and Ian F. Haney Lopez, *White by Law: The Legal Construction of Race* (New York: New York University Press, 1996), provide useful introductions. See also Theodore W. Allen, *The Invention of the White Race, Volume 1: Racial Oppression and Social Control* (London: Verso, 1994) and *Volume 2: The Origin of Racial Oppression in Anglo-America* (London: Verso, 1997).

10 Rasmussen et al. eds., *Making and Unmaking of Whiteness*, 7. To confuse matters further, sociologists have discovered that multiracial people change their identities according to context. Other people's perceptions influence how their identity gets phrased.

11 See chapter 11. The quote comes from *The Collected Works of Ralph Waldo Emerson*, vol. 5, *English Traits*, ed. Philip Nicoloff (Cambridge: Harvard University Press, 1994), 26.

12 See Annette Gordon-Reed, *The Hemingses of Monticello: An American Family* (New York: W.W. Norton, 2008), 536–39.

13 Editorial, *Nature Genetics* 24, no. 2 (Feb. 2000): no pagination.

14 Joseph L. Graves Jr., *The Emperor's New Clothes: Biological Theories of Race at the Millennium* (New Brunswick: Rutgers University Press, 2001), 155–56.

15 William S. Klug and Michael R. Cummings, *Concepts of Genetics*, 6th ed. (Upper Saddle River, N.J.: Prentice Hall, 2000), 5–7, 17–18, and Matt Ridley, *Genome: The Autobiography of a Species in 23 Chapters* (New York: HarperCollins, 2000), 123–24.

16 The newspaper stories ran on 21 Feb. 1995. See Graves, *Emperor's New Clothes*, 155–56.

17 Ridley, *Genome*, 247, and Arthur L. Caplan, "His Genes, Our Genome," *New York Times*, 3 May 2002, p. A23.

18 Natalie Angier, "Skin Deep," *New York Times*, 5 Feb. 2001, pp. 14–15.

19 This is the view of the journalist Jon Entine, a fellow (like Michael Novak) of the American Enterprise Institute and author of *Taboo: Why Black Athletes Dominate Sports and Why We are Afraid to Talk about It* (2000) and *Abraham's Children: Race, Identity, and the DNA of the Chosen People* (2007).

20 Hillel Halkin, "Jews and Their DNA," *Commentary*, Sept. 2008, pp. 37–43,

and reader letters from *Commentary*, Dec. 2008, unpaginated. Halkin is a columnist for the *New York Sun* and frequent *Commentary* contributor.

21 Bryan Sykes, *Saxons, Vikings, and Celts: The Genetic Roots of Britain and Ireland* (New York: W. W. Norton, 2006), 279–87.

22 Nicholas Wade, "The Palette of Humankind," *New York Times*, 24 Dec. 2002, p. F3. See also Anne Fausto-Sterling, "Refashioning Race: DNA and the Politics of Health Care," *differences* 15, no. 3 (2004): 10.

23 Michael Bamshad and Steve E. Olson, "Does Race Exist?" *Scientific American*, Dec. 2003, pp. 78–85.

24 Fausto-Sterling, "Refashioning Race," 30. See also a report from the National Human Genome Center of the Howard University College of Medicine: Charmaine D. M. Royal and Georgia M. Dunston, "Changing the Paradigm from 'Race' to Human Genome Variation," *Nature Genetics Online*, 26 Oct. 2004.

25 Lehrman, "Reality of Race," 33. See Troy Duster, *Backdoor to Eugenics* (New York: Routledge, 1990).

26 See Sally Satel, "I Am a Racially Profiling Doctor," *New York Times*, 5 May 2002, p. 56.

27 Fausto-Sterling, "Refashioning Race," 17–18. It is often assumed that sickle-cell anemia occurs only among African-descended people, which is not the case. The sickling trait evolved in malarial regions, and people descended from such places, e.g., Italy and Greece, are also susceptible to sickle-cell anemia.

28 Michael J. Bamshad and Steve E. Olson, "Does Race Exist?" *Scientific American.com* 10 Nov. 2003. Bamshad and Olson conclude, "If races are defined as genetically discrete groups, no. But researchers can use some genetic information to group individuals into clusters with medical relevance." Also Troy Duster, "Race and Reification in Science," *Science* 307, no. 5712 (18 Feb. 2005): 1050–51. See also *Wikipedia*, "Isosorbide dinitrate/hydralazine," http://en.wikipedia.org/wiki/Isosorbide_dinitrate/hydralazine, and BiDil's website, headlined, "Prescription Drug for African Americans with Heart Disease," and showing an Asian American M.D. and an African American patient, http://www.bidil.com/.

29 The material in this section comes from several sources: Nina G. Jablonski and George Chaplin, "The Evolution of Human Skin Coloration," *Journal of Human Evolution* 39 (2000): 57–106, and "Skin Deep," *Scientific American*, Oct. 2002, pp. 74–82; and R. L. Lamason, V. A. Canfield, and K. C. Cheng, "SLC24A5, a Putative Cation Exchanger, Affects Pigmentation in Zebrafish and Humans," *Science* 310 (Dec. 16, 2006): 1782–86. See also Rick Weiss, "Scientists Find a DNA Change That Accounts For White Skin," *Washington Post*, 16 Dec. 2005, p. A01, *ScientificAmerican.com*, 16 Dec. 2005, Christen Brownlee, *Science News Online*, week of 17 Dec. 2005 (vol. 168, no. 25), and *Wikipedia*: http://en.wikipedia.org/wiki/Human_skin_color.

30 Aravinda Chakravarti, "Kinship: Race Relations," *Nature* 457 (22 Jan. 2009): no pagination.

31 Consider Newark, New Jersey, a place supposedly characterized by "ruin, a town known only for murder, blight, and feckless negritude . . . a state of spiritual and moral zombiehood . . . angry Zulus . . . a Mugabe manqué . . . the Heart of Newark Darkness." Scott Rabb, "The Battle of Newark," *Esquire,* July 2008, pp. 66–73, 116–17.

ILLUSTRATION CREDITS

Chapter 1, figure 1. Courtesy of Maps.com.

Chapter 4, figure 1. http://kaukasus.blogspot.com/2007/04/young-georgian-girl .html, 29 April 2007, and http://www.flickr.com/photos/24298774@N00/ 108738272.

Chapter 4, figure 2. http://commons.wikimedia.org/wiki/Image:Ossetian_girl _1883.jpg.

Chapter 4, figure 3. Courtesy Sovfoto, Inc.

Chapter 4, figure 4. Courtesy Bowdoin College Museum of Art, Brunswick, Maine. Gift of the Homer Family.

Chapter 4, figure 5. Courtesy Réunion des Musées Nationaux / Art Resource, N.Y., Louvre, Paris, France.

Chapter 4, figure 6. Courtesy Réunion des Musées Nationaux / Art Resource, N.Y., Louvre, Paris, France.

Chapter 4, figure 7. Gift of William Wilson Corcoran. Corcoran Gallery of Art, Washington, D.C.

Chapter 4, figure 8. Courtesy Sterling and Francine Clark Art Institute, Williamstown, Massachusetts.

Chapter 4, figure 9. Copyright © 2009 Succession H. Matisse/Artists Rights Society (ARS), New York. Musée d'Art Moderne, Centre Georges Pompidou, Paris, France.

Chapter 4, figure 10. "Book Cover" from Orientalism by Edward Said. Copyright © 1978 by Edward Said. Used by permission of Vintage Books, a division of Random House, Inc.

Chapter 4, figure 11. Courtesy Thomas Zummer.

Chapter 5, figure 1. Courtesy the Metropolitan Museum of Art/Art Resource, N.Y.

Chapter 5, figure 2. Alinari/Art Resource, N.Y.

Chapter 5, figure 3. Courtesy Princeton University Archives. Department of Rare Books and Special Collections. Princeton University Library.

Chapter 5, figure 4. Reproduced by permission of the Huntington Library, San Marino, California.

Chapter 6, figure 1. Courtesy Niedersächsische Staats- und Universitätsbibliothek, Gottingen, Germany.

Chapter 6, figure 4. Courtesy Sovfoto, Inc.

Chapter 6, figure 5. Courtesy Niedersächsische Staats- und Universitätsbibliothek, Göttingen, Germany.

Chapter 6, figure 7. Courtesy Gleimhaus Literaturmuseum, Halberstadt, Germany.

Chapter 7, figure 1. Bildarchiv Preussicher Kulturbesitz/Art Resource, N.Y.

Chapter 8, figure 1. Courtesy Princeton University Archives, Department of Rare Books and Special Collections, Princeton University Library.

Chapter 8, figure 2. Courtesy Princeton University Archives, Department of Rare Books and Special Collections, Princeton University Library.

Chapter 8, figure 3. Courtesy Art Resource. Photo: Réunion des Musées Nationaux/Art Resource, N.Y.

Chapter 8, figure 4. Courtesy of the Yale University Library.

Chapter 10, figure 1. Courtesy Concord Free Public Library.

Chapter 10, figure 2. Courtesy of George Eastman House, International Museum of Photography and Film.

Chapter 14, figure 2. Courtesy MIT Museum.

Chapter 15, figure 9. Courtesy *New York Times* archives.

Chapter 16, figure 1. Courtesy American Philosophical Society.

Chapter 17, figure 2. Courtesy Wisconsin Historical Society, WHS Image ID 63842.

Chapter 18, figure 2. Courtesy American Philosophical Society.

Chapter 18, figure 3. Courtesy Stanford University Archives.

Chapter 19, figure 1. Courtesy Arthur Estabrook Papers, M. E. Grenander Department of Special Collections and Archives, University of Albany Libraries (SUNY Albany).

Chapter 22, figure 1. Courtesy *Time* magazine.

Chapter 22, figure 2. Courtesy Picture History.

Chapter 22, figure 3. Photograph © 2010 Museum of Fine Arts, Boston.

Chapter 22, figure 4. Photograph © 2010 Museum of Fine Arts, Boston.

Chapter 24, figure 1. Courtesy Special Collections, Vassar College Library.

Chapter 24, figure 2. Map from "The Races of Mankind," copyright 1943 by The Public Affairs Committee, Inc., from *Race: Science and Politics*, by Ruth

Benedict. Used by permission of Viking Penguin, a division of Penguin Group (USA), Inc.

Chapter 25, figure 1. Courtesy Princeton University Archives, Department of Rare Books and Special Collections. Princeton University Library.

Chapter 25, figure 2. Courtesy Immigration History Research Center, University of Minnesota.

Chapter 26, figure 1. Courtesy Picture History.

Chapter 27, figure 1. Malcom X at a Harlem civil rights rally © Bettman/CORBIS.

Chapter 28, figure 1. *Measuring America: The Decennial Censuses from 1790 to 2000*. (US Department of Commerce, US Census Bureau, Washington, D.C.: Government Printing Office), 2002: 100.

INDEX

Page numbers in *italics* refer to illustrations.

Senate, U.S., 299
Seneca Falls, N.Y., 137
"sentimentalism," 291, 307
Sephardic Jews, 243
Service Bureau for Intercultural Education, 355
Servicemen's Readjustment Act (1944), 366
Seven Years' War, 68, 108
sex trade, white slavery and, 14, 15n, 43, 46–58, 84
sexual potency, immigrants and, 209–10, 211, 225
sexual practices:
    of Amazons, 11
    of Britons, 23
    of Germani, 22, 28–29
    of Scythians, 11
Seymour, Horatio, 203
Shakespeare, William, 39
Shaler, Nathaniel Southgate, 199–200, 245, 308
Sharp, Granville, 176
Shaw, George Bernard, 316n
Sherman Anti-Trust Act (1890), 235
Short, William, 51n
Short History of the English Colonies in America, A (Lodge), 207–8
Siberia, 5
Sicilians, 218, 237, 238
Sicily, 5, 37
Simon, Theodore, 272, 278
Sinatra, Frank, 368
Sinclair, Upton, 352
Singh, Vijay, 389
Sitting Bull, 20
Sixth International Birth Control Conference (1925), 314
skin color, 4
    of African Americans, 50–51, 54, 130, 220
    climate as determinant of, 114–16, 117, 394
    global warming and, 395–96
    as meaningless concept in antiquity, 1
    race as defined by, ix, 42, 79–80, 118, 130, 132, 185, 198, 217, 223, 308, 396
    in racial hierarchies, 180

in racial taxonomies, 75–76, 86, 337, 338, 339, 394
savagery linked to, 117–18
variation in, 338, 339, 394–96
see also blackness; pigmentation; whiteness
skull measurement, 65–67, 68, 69, 75, 81, 82, 87, 191–93, 194, 197, 200, 236, 252, 253
see also cephalic index; head shape
Slave Market (Gérôme), 54, 55
"slave names," 374n
slaves, slavery:
    abolition of, 57–58
    in ancient Greece, 12–15
    in ancient Rome, 16–17, 18, 34
    blackness linked to, ix, xi, 42, 56, 273
    blacks as, 40, 41, 42, 53, 54
    in Britain, 36, 37–38, 57–58
    in British colonies, 174
    Carlyle on, 158
    children as, 13, 14, 15, 18, 36, 40–41, 46, 56, 194n, 263
    Crèvecoeur on, 109–10
    as divided between laborers and sex slaves, 43
    Emerson's opposition to, 157–58, 163, 185, 186, 187, 188, 190
    eunuchs as, 11, 36–37, 53
    indentured servitude and, 40–42, 174, 194n
    Jefferson on, 110
    labor and, 43
    literature of, 34
    persistence of, 57n
    race as basis of, xi, 34, 43, 51, 87, 113, 185, 190
    serfdom as form of, 36
    stereotypes of, 35
    Tocqueville on, 126–27
    of white races, *see* white slavery
    women as, 13, 18, 36
    see also white slavery, women in
slaves, slavery, in U.S., 50–51, 54, 98, 132, 156, 173, 189, 377
    abolitionists and, 58, 119, 121, 143, 158, 163, 166, 174, 177, 190, 198
    as damaging to white southerners, 109, 110, 126–28, 130, 186, 208

Know-Nothings and, 150
race theory as justification for, 190,
194, 198, 201, 217
see also slaves, slavery
slave trade:
Atlantic, 38, 40, 42, 58, 66
in Black Sea region, 4, 12–15, 33, 39,
43, 46, 58
demographic mixing and, xi
in Eastern Europe, ix
in Italy, 36–37
in Mediterranean, 35, 38–40
in Middle Ages, 32–33, 34–37
sugar trade and, 38–40
by Vikings, 34–36
warfare and, 13
Slavs, 30, 198, 220, 253, 287
ancestors of, 4
as U.S. immigrants, 206, 225, 233, 234,
293, 352, 354, 356–57, 366, 378
SLC24A5 gene, 395
Slovaks, 378, 379
Slovenians, 352
Smith, Alfred E., 324–25, 344, 347
Smith, Lillian, 387
Smith, Samuel Stanhope, 113–18, *114,*
121, 179, 191*n,* 237
Snake Charmer, The (Gérôme), 57
social Darwinism, 314
Socialist Party, U.S., 294, 346
socialist realism, 370
socialists, socialism, 295, 296, 298, 300
sterilization opposed by, 276
social sciences, 72
Social Security Administration, 348
*Social Systems of American Ethnic
Groups, The* (Warner and Srole),
210*n*
Society for Ethical Culture, 242
Somerset, James, 176–77
Somerset decision (1772), 175, 176–77
Sorrows of Young Werther, The (Goethe),
102
Soul Sister (Halsell), 388
Southard, Elmer Ernest, 282
South Asians, 79
South Carolina, 234, 277
Southern Christian Leadership Council,
355*n*

Southern Literary Messenger, 157*n*
Southern Pacific Railroad, 293
South Ossetia, 4, 72
Soviet Union, 15*n*
Spain, 180, 220
Spanish-American War (1898), 235, 246
Spanish Civil War, 341
Spargo, John, 343
Sparks, Corey S., 240*n*
Spartacus, 13, 17
slave revolt led by, 16–17
Spectateur du Nord, 99
spice trade, 39
Srole, Leo, 210*n*
Staël, Germaine Necker de, 90, 91–103,
92, 159
Goethe admired by, 91, 101–2,
154–55
literary career of, 95–96, 98–103, 152,
153, 154–55, 156
outspokenness of, 94, 95, 102
on race, 99–100
Stalin, Joseph, 84*n*
Standard Oil Company, 293
Stanford, Mrs. Leland, 251*n*
Stanford-Binet intelligence tests, 276
Stanton, Elizabeth Cady, 158
States' Rights Party, 373*n*
statistics, 269
stature:
as heritable trait, 281
as racial trait, 214, 221, 238, 252, 307,
340
Stavropol Kray, 72
Stephenson, David, 345
sterilization, 273–77, 281
Stewart, Maria, 121
"stock," use of term, 167
Stoddard, Lothrop, 305, 311, 318–20, *318,*
319, 320, 321, 323–24, 345
Stowe, Harriet Beecher, 51, 135, 158
Strabo, 17–18, 21
Strong, Josiah, 247–48
Study of American Intelligence, A
(Brigham), 285–90, *287, 288,* 305,
330–31
Sturleson, Snorro, 168*n*
Styria, Austria, 6
suburbia, 366–67, 369–70